Praise for *O Say C‹*

"Encyclopedic.... [I]mmensely interesti.ɡ ⸻ ⸻.

—Peter Sagal, *New York Times Book Review*

"A thoughtful and elegant history of America's national anthem."

—*Economist* (UK)

"A fascinating history of America's national anthem that examines the origins of the song and the many ways it has been used."

—Glenn C. Altschuler, *Minneapolis Star Tribune*

"A captivating chronicle of America's song.... [Mark] Clague provides a rich, keyhole history of Key and the anthem's creation, clearing up many misconceptions along the way.... *O Say Can You Hear?* is a deeply felt and meticulously researched study that all Americans should read and linger over."

—Peggy Kurkowski, *Washington Independent Review of Books*

"[Mark Clague's] book matches rigorous scholarship with clear, engaging writing on a wide range of anthem-related questions"

—Colin Woodard, *Washington Post*

"Musicologist Clague debuts with a sparkling study of America's national anthem.... Stuffed with colorful character sketches, intriguing historical arcana, and memorable musical insights, this pitch-perfect history hits all the right notes."

—*Publishers Weekly*, starred review

"In contemporary culture wars, where everything gets reduced to partisan politics, Clague's thoughtful and comprehensive history will resonate."

—*Booklist*, starred review

O Say Can You Hear?

O Say Can You Hear?

A Cultural Biography of
The Star-Spangled Banner

MARK CLAGUE

W. W. NORTON & COMPANY
Celebrating a Century of Independent Publishing

For information about permission to reproduce selections from this book, write to
Permissions, W. W. Norton & Company, Inc., 500 Fifth Avenue, New York, NY 10110

For information about special discounts for bulk purchases,
please contact W. W. Norton Special Sales at
specialsales@wwnorton.com or 800-233-4830

Manufacturing by Lakeside Book Company
Book design by Chris Welch
Production manager: Lauren Abbate

Library of Congress Cataloging-in-Publication Data

Names: Clague, Mark, 1966– author.
Title: O say can you hear? : a cultural biography of
"The Star-spangled banner" / Mark Clague.
Description: First edition. | New York : W. W. Norton & Company,
Inc., 2022. | Includes bibliographical references and index.
Identifiers: LCCN 2022008993 | ISBN 9780393651386 (cloth) |
ISBN 9780393651393 (epub)
Subjects: LCSH: Star-spangled banner (Song) | Patriotic
music—United States—History and criticism.
Classification: LCC ML3561.S8 C46 2022 | DDC 782.42/15990973—dc23
LC record available at https://lccn.loc.gov/2022008993

ISBN 978-1-324-06447-3 pbk.

W. W. Norton & Company, Inc., 500 Fifth Avenue, New York, N.Y. 10110
www.wwnorton.com

W. W. Norton & Company Ltd., 15 Carlisle Street, London W1D 3BS

1 2 3 4 5 6 7 8 9 0

To Rich, who set an example of what a scholar should be.

To my parents, Allan and Rosemary, who planted the seeds of my love of U.S. history.

To Laura, who believed in me.

Contents

Prologue

On March 15, 1889, hurricane winds struck Samoa's Apia Harbor in the South Pacific, catching two anchored American warships by surprise. The *USS Vandalia* fought the storm valiantly but eventually crashed onto a reef, took on water, and sank. Decks awash in the rocky shallows, her masts somehow remained above the pounding waves, supporting dozens of survivors clinging to life in the rigging while the storm continued to rage.

Also disabled but still floating, the larger *USS Trenton* was adrift nearby. With no working engines, the flagship was powerless to help. As night fell, the storm miraculously began pushing the *Trenton* toward the *Vandalia*. When the *Trenton*'s brass band struck up *The Star-Spangled Banner*, "men who had exhausted every means, during the whole of that awful day, of rendering some assistance to their comrades now seemed inspired to greater efforts."

As the *Trenton* approached the reef, its inspired crew maneuvered alongside her submerged sister. Its survivors jumped onto the *Trenton*'s deck, only moments before the *Vandalia*'s main mast collapsed. A line was thrown to the remaining sailors clinging to life on the *Vandalia*'s still-standing foremast. They too escaped to safety.

ON OCTOBER 20, 1968, more than one hundred demonstrators marched from Nebraska's Creighton University to downtown Omaha, singing *We Shall Overcome* and carrying signs denouncing the Vietnam War. A group of pro-war youth soon confronted them, throwing eggs, epithets, and water balloons, while demanding that officers monitoring the protest break up the rally. When the peaceful protest was allowed to continue, the frustrated pro-war force began singing *The Star-Spangled Banner*, vowing to drown out their adversaries in song. Instead, anti-war activists joined the collective chorus, singing enthusiastically along with their opponents. The pacifists' leader then suggested that both sides share a single bullhorn and give alternating speeches to argue their competing views. A police sergeant later remarked, "I think that was great—letting both sides speak. That's an example of democracy in action."

ON JUNE 11, 2013, in San Antonio, eleven-year-old Sebastien De La Cruz approached center court holding a wireless microphone. He wore traditional Mexican mariachi dress—a formal *traje de charro* with a vest, bolero jacket, necktie, and chaps. An announcer introduced the San Antonio native as "*El charro de oro*—the boy with the golden voice." Game three of the National Basketball Association championship finals between the San Antonio Spurs and the Miami Heat was set to begin as soon as the boy, who had risen to national fame as a competitor on the television show *America's Got Talent*, sang *The Star-Spangled Banner*.

De La Cruz approached the performance with a carefully rehearsed professional focus. His full, strong voice soon elicited cheers from the crowd. He hit the anthem's high notes on the words "glare" and "air" with power and intensity. The crowd approved. A television close-up showed him pointing to the U.S. flag, held proudly by a military color guard nearby, to

Sebastien De La Cruz as "Super Mariachi Boy" by LALO ALCARAZ.

emphasize "that our flag was still there." Cheers continued for his bluesy ornaments on the word "wave," seeming to illustrate the motion of America's flag billowing in the breeze. In the song's final phrase, he shifted to falsetto for the word "free" and flipped up a fourth—a virtuoso gesture usually reserved for operatic sopranos, not young men. His performance was a triumph. On the final word "brave," the singer pumped his fist in the air, and the crowd roared.

On the social media app Twitter, however, dozens of American viewers reacted negatively to the image of a boy in mariachi dress singing the U.S. anthem: "Why is a foreigner singing the national anthem," one asked, and then answered, "I realize it's in San Antonio but that still ain't Mexico." Another protested, "Who let this illegal alien sing our national anthem?" while still another opined, "Is this the American National Anthem or the Mexican Hat Dance? Get this lil kid out of here." None of these comments concerned the quality of De La Cruz's performance. They responded only to his appearance—reinforced by his name and costume—as violating the boundaries of a narrowly conceived American identity. Civil rights activists connected the online storm to "wider anger aimed at Latinos and immigrants, and over immigration reform legislation in Congress."

As the controversy burned through the next day in repostings, blogs, and news reports, others tweeted support for De La Cruz: "Why are ppl so upset over a Hispanic singing the national anthem. He's probably got more roots in here than most 'Americans,'" a typical comment ran. The Chicano political cartoonist Lalo Alcaraz drew a heroic caricature of the singer as Superman to register his support. "Super Mariachi Boy" stands proud and sings. His diamond-shaped crest and its emblematic initial S invokes both Superman and Sebastien. De La Cruz is thereby claimed as the iconic American patriot—the personification of youthful strength, clean-cut innocence, and moral determination. Like his namesake, Super Mariachi Boy strives to serve the nation, not with super strength but with his powerful voice. For Chávez Foundation chairman Jaime Martinez, the controversy showed that the nation still had a long way to go to fully understand that *The Star-Spangled Banner* "doesn't just belong to white people, it belongs to all of us."

THESE THREE ANTHEM moments illustrate some of the many roles that *The Star-Spangled Banner* plays in American life. In Apia Harbor, the song inspired heroism, putting into action its proclamation that the United States was "the home of the brave." At the Vietnam War protest, the lyric, sung initially as a weapon, was transformed into a harmonious ritual of community when the anti-war protesters joined in singing. By doing so, they disabled the implicit critique that to protest is necessarily to be disloyal or un-American.

With the De La Cruz controversy, the anthem struck a more contemporary but no less sour note. Online debate made an implicit social dissonance around multiculturalism explicit and audible. As a result, the meaning and reach of the term "American" was itself debated. One firm answer came from the NBA for game four two nights later. In a rare move, the league invited De La Cruz to perform the anthem again. The singer's personal grace and firm resolve enabled him to reclaim and proclaim a proud American identity.

What is it about *The Star-Spangled Banner* that makes these symbolic negotiations possible? Who wrote the words and why? Is it a poem or a lyric and does it matter? What does it even mean? Where did the music come from, and why is the melody so difficult to sing? How did it become the national anthem, and why is it performed at seemingly every American sporting event? Is the anthem political? Should it be? And what about the song today? Is it essentially racist? How does the lyric intersect with current discussions of race, gender, and ethnicity in the United States? Can *The Star-Spangled Banner* still serve to unify the nation at all?

This book leverages history to answer these questions and more. It is based on more than a decade of research that began when I first showed my students a video of Jimi Hendrix performing *The Star-Spangled Banner* at Woodstock in 1969. My goal was to inspire a discussion about patriotism and protest. As I hoped, my students had questions. But their questions sent me on my own journey of discovery. As I learned more and more about the song, I began to understand that the simple story I had learned as a child was just the beginning of a much more fascinating tale. The legend I was taught about Francis Scott Key and his anthem contained almost as much fantasy as fact. Even more interesting was what happened after the song's creation: how war transformed its meaning, how Americans wrote hundreds of alternative lyrics to the same melody, and how musicians reimagined the music to tell other stories. Key's song was not one thing but many, and these many anthems had something important to say about what it meant to be American.

I invite you to be as fascinated by *The Star-Spangled Banner* as I have been. The chapters herein are organized in a rough chronological order to emphasize the historical development of the lyric and music over time. While the details are powerful, you may choose to read the text in any order. Each chapter is organized around a theme with its own narrative arc and conclusions. The chapters build upon one another, certainly, but they can also be read independently, as a guidebook to the anthem's political import and cultural impact. Readers interested in military history, for example, may wish to jump to Chapter 4, "The *Banner* at War." For others, current debates about the word "slave" in Key's lyric may make Chapter 8, "The Anthem and Black Lives," especially urgent. Feel free to visit the places you wish to explore in whatever order you like.

O Say Can You Hear? is the tale of a song Americans have long been arguing about and that they will continue to argue about. In fact, my research shows, such arguments reside at the core of the song's traditional social function: to bring passion, energy, and conflicting opinions to the urgent issues of the day. The research explored here reveals that *The Star-Spangled Banner* is a powerful tool of democracy. Because a song must be sung, it is less a thing than an activity. The anthem is thus not a static icon but a patriotic act—a way Americans have long expressed personal devotion to the nation in order to inspire and recruit support, sometimes for a particular viewpoint or political party and sometimes in an attempt to unify the nation to confront an existential threat or national crisis.

Several themes rise to the fore in the pages that follow. One is that *The Star-Spangled Banner* has always been political. Another is that the song became the anthem not by law but through use and custom. Most significant is how the story of *The Star-Spangled Banner* reshapes our understanding of American patriotism itself.

In the early nineteenth century—in the days when the United States was first struggling to realize the ideals of its founding documents in day-to-day practice—patriotism was a cacophonous and contested space in which love of country was embraced, manipulated, and redefined by every faction. *The Star-Spangled Banner* was a powerful force in this rhetorical melee. But its patriotism was neither blind nor sacred. Patriotism was instead a social tool—an emotional appeal to call out the militia to the common defense, to get voters to show up at the polls, and to celebrate moments of triumph. The melody accompanied debate, praised allies, assigned blame, and asserted new ideas about what America could and should be. Patriotism was a way to advance the American experiment, and in this regard, song was special. Song used not only words but music—the magic of emotion—to recruit passion in service of nation.

The Star-Spangled Banner embodies what one observer of American democracy, the French political theorist Alexis de Tocqueville, called a "patriotism of reflection." Tocqueville analyzed patriotism—what he refers to as the "Public Spirit in the United States"—as a continuum between a "patriotism of instinct" and a "patriotism of reflection." He defined instinctual patriotism as a "natural fondness" for one's birthplace and a "taste for . . . ancestral traditions." Instinctual patriots were those (such as his French compatriots) who ceded the responsibility of governing to the state, often a king. It was patriotic devotion to another. The United States, instead, was characterized by a "patriotism of all."

Tocqueville asserted that at its best, patriotism is a tool of a thriving democracy. It is a thoughtful form of civic participation. A productive patriotic attachment, he theorized, is based on granting political rights to "all members of the community." It is not instinctual but learned through the responsibility of mutual governance. It is a "thinking patriotism of republican citizens," one "perhaps less generous and less ardent, but more fruitful and more lasting." It is nurtured by the "spread of knowledge," by "laws," and "by the exercise of civil rights" that entwine the interests of the individual with the community and thus offers benefits to both. For Tocqueville, a reflective patriotism was an engaged and personal commitment to community, one that could inspire and sustain democracy. Social scientists today use the term "constructive patriotism" for Tocqueville's notion.

To explore the use of *The Star-Spangled Banner* in the history of American life is to discover a constructive patriotism in the song's multiple forms and ever-changing messages, its many alternative lyrics and musical interpretations. Each version, arrangement, and performance sends a message. The symbolic value of *The Star-Spangled Banner* is thus located not solely in representations of unity but also in the day-to-day particulars of how people make use of the song. It is an engine of community. While its long history adds weight to its symbolic effect, its position as anthem is not guaranteed. Such a song accrues meaning and merit through use, only then becoming the anthem. As this book will show, the defining events in the song's symbolic history have been celebrations, elections, protests, and wars, especially the Civil War. It was the war between the states to end slavery that forged Key's song as the sonic symbol of union and thus the nation's anthem.

Often unnoticed and ignored is the fact that the first verse of Francis Scott Key's famous lyric—the verse that Americans sing—ends in a question mark.

> O! say does that Star-Spangled Banner yet wave,
> O'er the land of the free and the home of the brave?

On one level, Key's question refers literally to a flag above Baltimore's Fort McHenry in 1814. Yet today, every time Key's song is sung, those who join in its ritual have the opportunity to renew this question. They can join in the search for a more perfect response to the nation's fundamental questions, answers grounded in a clear-eyed view of the past that build upon the nation's espoused ideals to respond to the unique challenges of the present. Throughout American history, *The Star-Spangled Banner* has asked and in turn helped to answer this fundamental question: what does it mean to be American?

Additional resources of interest to readers of *O Say Can You Hear?*— including recordings, new research findings about *The Star-Spangled Banner*, and a database of American Anacreontic lyrics—can be found at starspangledmusic.org.

O Say Can You Hear?

Chapter 1

American Dreams

Francis Scott Key and the Writing of *The Star-Spangled Banner*

> The national air of a people must come from some great event in
> the life of the Nation perhaps some crisis. It must be spontaneous; it
> must appeal to national pride and the national sentiment, and then,
> when it does that the country takes it up and clings to it as jealously
> as it does to its other traditions.
>
> —*John Philip Sousa (1889)*

Song as History
August 6, 1834, Frederick, Maryland

In the U.S. elections of 1834, the balance of power in Congress was up for grabs, and the tide was turning against President Andrew Jackson. Francis Scott Key was in Frederick, Maryland, a short distance from his boyhood home and the town in which he had opened his first law office more than three decades earlier. He was attending a political jubilee and barbecue hosted by fellow Jacksonian Democrats. It was at such celebrations, parades, and dinners with their continual toasts, songs, and speechifying that the work of the new American democracy was done. Some four hundred friends and supporters had come to honor Key's brother-in-law, Roger B. Taney, who was returning to Maryland to practice law following a tumultuous nine months as U.S. secretary of the Treasury.

The sun was bright and hot that afternoon. Taney offered two lengthy political speeches, expressing full support for President Jackson and his

Bank War against the "money aristocracy." Key was no less a Jackson man. But having to support a large household and cover the debt for his parents' estate kept him focused on his profitable legal career—he could not afford to run for public office. Still, after thirty years of work in and around federal politics, he had become a political insider nevertheless. He had argued dozens of cases before the Supreme Court and become acquainted with a succession of the nation's revolutionary and political leaders—President Jackson, of course, as well as former presidents James Madison, James Monroe, and John Quincy Adams, Chief Justice John Marshall, Senator Henry Clay, and even the Revolutionary War hero the Marquis de Lafayette. For the charismatic Key, a few were foes but most of them were friends.

Key had fallen under General Jackson's populist spell about seven years earlier. Becoming a Jacksonian had been an ideological leap for the onetime Federalist, but Key had done so with enthusiasm. He even became a periodic member of the president's infamous "kitchen cabinet" of unofficial advisers. Just the year before, the president had rewarded Key for his loyalty and service, appointing him district attorney for Washington, D.C. Indeed, things were going well for Key. A few days before, he had turned fifty-five. His legal practice was thriving. He tithed to his church and gave generously to his charities. He and his wife, Polly, had brought eleven children into the world. In terms of social influence and material comfort, Key had come a long way since moving his law practice from Frederick to the Federal City in 1805.

At the barbecue, someone shouted yet another toast: To "Francis Scott Key—a friend of the administration and an incorruptible patriot; worthy of being honored, wherever genius is admired or liberty cherished, as the author of *The Star-Spangled Banner.*" Key stood up. Confident in his skills at extemporizing, he discarded his scripted political remarks and instead spoke on a subject he had never addressed in public and never would again—his famous song.

You have been pleased to declare your approbation of my song. Praise to a poet could not be otherwise than acceptable; but it is peculiarly gratifying to me, to know that, in obeying the impulse of my own feelings, I have awakened yours. The song, I know, came from the heart, and if it has made its way to the hearts of men, whose devotion to their country and the great cause of Freedom I know so well, I could not pretend to be insensible to such a compliment.

Key then spoke about how he had created the "song" (as he calls it) in 1814, after witnessing firsthand the British bombardment at the heart of the Battle of Baltimore. Other than these few spoken comments, which were recorded by a newspaper correspondent, Key never secured these memories in print. Even this account is abbreviated, as the facts about the battle were unimportant. Many in his audience remembered the War of 1812 firsthand. Key's oratory was thus short on detail but long on patriotic grandiloquence.

You have recalled to my recollection the circumstances under which I was impelled to this effort. I saw the flag of my country waving over a city—the strength and pride of my native State—a city devoted to plunder and desolation [sic] by its assailants. I witnessed the preparation for its assaults, and I saw the array of its enemies as they advanced to the attack. I heard the sound of battle; the noise of the conflict fell upon my listening ear, and told me that "the brave and the free" had met the invaders.

Then did I remember that Maryland had called her sons to the defense of that flag. . . . Then did I remember that there were gathered around that banner, among its defenders, men who had heard and answered the call of their country—from these mountain sides, from this beautiful valley, and from this fair city of my native county; and though I walked upon a deck surrounded by a hostile fleet, detained as a prisoner, yet was my step firm, and my heart strong. . . .

Through the clouds of war, the stars of that banner still shone in my view, and I saw the discomfited host of its assailants driven back in ignominy to their ships. Then, in that hour of deliverance and joyful triumph, the heart spoke; and "Does not such a country, and such defenders of their country, deserve a song?" was its question.

With it came an inspiration not to be resisted; and even though it had been a hanging matter to make a song, I must have written it. Let the praise, then, (if any be due), be given not to me, who only did what I could not help doing; not to the writer, but to the inspirers of the song. . . .

I will therefore propose as a toast—[to] the real authors of the song, "The Defenders of *The Star-Spangled Banner*: What they would not strike to a foe, they will never sell to traitors."

Over more than two centuries of patriotic performance, parody, and protest, *The Star-Spangled Banner* has become ever more deeply ingrained in the American experience, more emotionally resonant, more authoritative, and more controversial than its lyricist could have ever imagined. That it is still sung at all would have amazed Key. In his America, political songs were topical newspaper ballads, short-lived lyrics written to well-known tunes about current issues and events. They were an almost daily invention. Yet Key's song became the nation's one and only anthem, a singular, enduring lyric that invokes unity through ritual and repetition. That *The Star-Spangled Banner* continues to spark conversation and controversy, however, proves that its original power for construction remains. It is a tool for building community. It is both a living historical practice and an ongoing act of citizenship.

Francis Scott Key's fame today rests solely on his having written *The Star-Spangled Banner*. In his day, however, the socially connected lawyer was respected for his legal acumen, admired for his religious devotion, and celebrated for his oratorical eloquence. In 1814, not long before writing his lyric, he gave his first prominent public address outside the courtroom— a speech for the Washington Society of Alexandria. Key, who likely met George Washington in person when he was eleven years old, used the first president's Farewell Address of 1798 as his focus. He reiterated Washington's warnings against partisanship and emphasized the general's admonitions to embrace religious devotion. Key's words spoke directly to the nation's ongoing partisan divide between Federalists, like himself, who opposed the War

DEFENCE OF FORT M'HENRY.

The annexed song was composed under the following circumstances—
A gentleman had left Baltimore, in a flag of truce for the purpose of get-
ting released from the British fleet, a friend of his who had been captured
at Marlborough.—He went as far as the mouth of the Patuxent, and was
not permitted to return lest the intended attack on Baltimore should be
disclosed. He was therefore brought up the Bay to the mouth of the Patapsco, where the flag vessel was kept under the guns of a frigate, and
he was compelled to witness the bombardment of Fort M'Henry, which
the Admiral had boasted that he would carry in a few hours, and
that the city must fall. He watched the flag at the Fort through the
whole day with an anxiety that can be better felt than described, until
the night prevented him from seeing it. In the night he watched the Bomb
Shells, and at early dawn his eye was again greeted by the proudly waving
flag of his country.

Tune—Anacreon in Heaven.

O! say can you see by the dawn's early light,
  What so proudly we hailed at the twilight's last gleaming,
Whose broad stripes and bright stars through the perilous fight,
  O'er the ramparts we watch'd, were so gallantly streaming?
And the Rockets' red glare, the Bombs bursting in air,
Gave proof through the night that our Flag was still there;
  O! say does that star-spangled Banner yet wave,
  O'er the Land of the free, and the home of the brave?

On the shore dimly seen through the mists of the deep,
  Where the foe's haughty host in dread silence reposes,
What is that which the breeze, o'er the towering steep,
  As it fitfully blows, half conceals, half discloses?
Now it catches the gleam of the morning's first beam,
In full glory reflected now shines in the stream,
  'Tis the star spangled banner, O! long may it wave
  O'er the land of the free and the home of the brave.

And where is that band who so vauntingly swore
  That the havoc of war and the battle's confusion,
A home and a country, shall leave us no more?
  Their blood has washed out their foul footsteps pollution.
No refuge could save the hireling and slave,
From the terror of flight or the gloom of the grave,
  And the star-spangled banner in triumph doth wave,
  O'er the Land of the Free, and the Home of the Brave.

O! thus be it ever when freemen shall stand,
  Between their lov'd home, and the war's desolation,
Blest with vict'ry and peace, may the Heav'n rescued land,
  Praise the Power that hath made and preserv'd us a nation!
Then conquer we must, when our cause it is just,
And this be our motto—" In God is our Trust ;"
  And the star-spangled Banner in triumph shall wave,
  O'er the Land of the Free, and the Home of the Brave.

Defence of Fort McHenry, the first imprint of Francis Scott Key's lyric,
likely September 17, 1814. Key is not named as author, but the tune,
Anacreon in Heaven, to which the words are to be sung, is identified.
As a result, while Key's words have the look of a poem, they were from
the start a song lyric inseparable from a specific melody.

of 1812 with Britain, and the Democratic-Republicans who had declared it.
His speech was soon published.

Francis Scott Key was born in Frederick County, Maryland, on August 1,
1779. The future Georgetown lawyer was a descendant of English immigrants to the New World. On his father's side, his great-great-grandfather
Philip Key had arrived in Maryland in 1719 or early 1720. His mother's

ancestors included Henry Charlton, who arrived in Virginia even earlier in 1623. Key received a classical education at St. John's College in Maryland's capital city, Annapolis, from 1789 to '96 and then followed family tradition by making law his profession. His father, John Ross Key (1754–1821), was a country lawyer, gentleman farmer, and judge, who at age sixteen inherited the family plantation and married Key's mother, Anne, five years later. That same year his father answered the call to support the American Revolution, joining the Western Maryland Rifles as a second lieutenant in 1775. In 1778 he became justice of the peace in Frederick, Maryland, and the next year his son, Francis Scott, was born. Yorktown in 1781 was John Ross Key's third and final stint in the revolutionary militia. He was soon promoted to captain and led the Frederick Light Dragoons, which joined with the Continental Army in the siege that ended the war.

Key's uncle, Philip Barton Key (1757–1815), was also a lawyer, but in many ways the opposite of Francis's father. Uncle Philip fought on the British side of the American Revolution as a captain in the Maryland Loyalists Battalion. Immediately after the war, he wisely escaped to London, where he studied law. Returning to the United States in 1785, Philip moved to Annapolis and apprenticed with future Supreme Court justice Gabriel Duvall, establishing a thriving legal practice in Maryland's capital city in 1790. While the young Francis served his primary legal apprenticeship with Annapolis judge Jeremiah Townley Chase, he presumably picked up some nuances of English law from his uncle. Uncle Philip soon became one of Annapolis's leading citizens, winning a seat in the Maryland House of Delegates in 1794 and becoming the town's mayor in 1797. In 1801 President John Adams appointed him chief judge of the Fourth Circuit, and he soon moved his thriving practice to the nation's capital. In 1806 he renounced his British pension and ran successfully for a seat in Congress as a Federalist, serving three consecutive terms. Both father and uncle would have a profound influence on Francis. He would name one of his six sons John Ross (1809–37) and another Philip Barton (1818–59).

Although Francis Scott Key opposed the War of 1812, seeing his homeland attacked and looted by the British convinced him to join the Georgetown militia. He cannot be called a soldier. Key served in an artillery unit for two short stints of about two weeks each, first as a gunner's mate in July 1813 and then as a quartermaster the following June. Yet his heritage, upbringing, and especially his professional life in Washington placed him at the heart of America's experiment in democratic governance. The story of how he came to write his country's signature song has much to say about what song meant in early America and what it can mean today.

The Rescue of Dr. William Beanes
September 1–17, 1814, Baltimore Harbor to Chesapeake Bay and Back

On the morning of September 5, 1814, Key set sail from Baltimore Harbor, heading down the Patapsco River through to the Chesapeake Bay in search of the British fleet. He was on a mission to negotiate the release of Dr. William Beanes (1749–1828), a sixty-five-year-old American physician and surgeon who had been taken into British custody after the burning of Washington. The prisoner and Key were obliquely connected. Beanes was the family doctor of Key's sister-in-law Maria Lloyd West. Her husband, Richard, had convinced Key to pursue the mission. Dr. Beanes had even once cared briefly for Key himself, when the lawyer fell ill during his circuit court travels.

Key left Baltimore aboard an American ship whose name is lost to history. Her owner and captain, John Ferguson, led a nine-man crew. The ship had been hired by John Stuart Skinner (1788–1851), the U.S. agent for the exchange of prisoners. As a diplomatic cartel, it carried no weapons and displayed a flag of truce to guarantee safe passage as part of its mission to parley with the enemy. Before leaving Washington, Key had gathered a batch of letters written by British prisoners in U.S. custody. More to the point, he carried a letter from U.S. General John Mason to British Major General Robert Ross, demanding Beanes's release.

Mason's letter made explicit that the arrest and imprisonment of the doctor, who was "unarmed and entirely of non-combatant character," represented a "departure from the known usages of civilized warfare." Beanes was being treated as a common criminal and threatened with transfer to Canada to stand trial for treason. The risk to the doctor was real and urgent. As a noncombatant, he did not enjoy the conventional protections of a military prisoner of war. The U.S. government also had little room to maneuver on his behalf. Paying ransom to release a civilian would set a dangerous precedent, endangering the liberty of all nonmilitary bystanders by making their capture profitable. The United States could not risk turning every American into a potential spoil of war. The Beanes affair was atypical and had to remain so. His imprisonment spoke to something more personal—some insult or offense of honor.

On August 28, following the decisive British triumph at Washington, Beanes and other local citizens in Maryland arrested four British soldiers who were working their way back to the coast to rejoin their fleet. They were jailed. Shortly after midnight that evening, "50 or 60" British cavalry galloped to Beanes's estate in Upper Marlboro. They arrested Beanes and two others, and threatened to burn the nearby town to ashes if their fellow soldiers were not released by noon the next day. When the jailed British soldiers were offered in exchange for the Americans, the British released the other Americans held as barter, but not the doctor. Beanes was transferred to the HMS *Tonnant*, the flagship of Vice Admiral George Cockburn, and held captive.

Key was an astute choice for the mission to rescue Beanes. He was skilled, loyal, and available. He was also expendable. He was not an elected official or a military leader, yet as a Georgetown resident and son of a revolutionary soldier, he was trusted by U.S. officials. Simultaneously, he was connected by blood to an uncle who had served in the British military. Key could draw on the details of English law, and if an appeal to religion were needed, the pious Key was a lifelong member of the Episcopal Church, a derivative of the Church of England and the church of the British king. Key thus had a deep well of resources with which to negotiate Beanes's release.

Skinner too was a strong and experienced advocate. He had served as the U.S. agent of prisoners since the beginning of the war and was already personally acquainted with Cockburn and other British commanders. John Quincy Adams later described him as one who combined the "ruffian, patriot and philanthropist." Skinner was both in charge of the mission and annoyed to have been ordered to take a civilian along. For him, Key was a burden. The Americans reached the British fleet at the "mouth of the Potomac" on September 7. Their various letters had been delivered in advance. At 2:10 p.m. the *Tonnant* anchored and brought Key and Skinner aboard. When Key spoke of their mission to free Beanes, "his application was received so coldly, that he feared it would fail." The Americans were then invited to a late afternoon meal with Admirals Alexander Cochrane and Edward Codrington, as well as General Ross. With wine "in free circulation," Skinner recalled that Codrington had insulted the honor of U.S. Commodore David Porter, blaming him for mistreating a British prisoner accused of insolence. The negotiation was not off to an auspicious start.

Ross was convinced that Beanes was guilty of treason against the British Crown and refused to release him. It seems that as British forces first approached Washington, they had commandeered Beanes's home for their headquarters. Beanes, probably hoping to prevent the British from ransacking his property, had welcomed the British with open arms under a flag of truce. The British had thus recognized him as a loyalist and paid him for his food, drink, and supplies. Beanes was indeed a staunch Federalist who opposed the war against Britian, yet despite his Scottish brogue accent, he was a third-generation American who had served the Continental Army as a young surgeon during the Revolution. Beanes's ruse worked spectacularly, but his subsequent arrests of British soldiers had revealed his deceit.

In the end, Ross agreed to discharge Beanes, but not because of the Americans' protests or arguments. British animosity toward the doctor's betrayal never faded. Instead, the letters Key had collected from wounded British infantry praising their American caregivers provided the general with a face-saving excuse to release Beanes without pardoning his betrayal. Precisely how the negotiation succeeded is lost between two brief and competing accounts, one by Skinner and the other by Taney. Both were written many years after the events described. Skinner reported that Beanes's release was agreed to privately between himself and Ross. Taney placed Key in the center of the action. Regardless, the

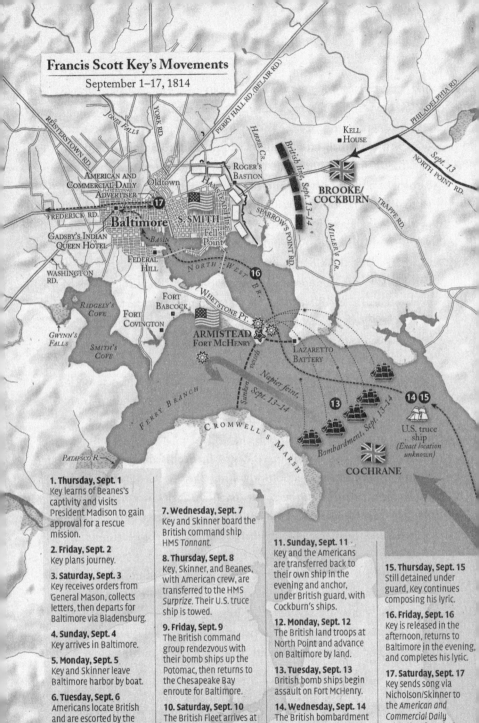

Francis Scott Key's Movements
September 1–17, 1814

REISTERSTOWN RD.
JONES FALLS
YORK RD.
PERRY HALL RD. (BELAIR RD.)
HARRIS CR.
British line, Sept. 13
KELL HOUSE
PHILADELPHIA RD.
Sept. 13
NORTH POINT RD.

AMERICAN AND COMMERCIAL DAILY ADVERTISER
Oldtown
ROGER'S BASTION
HAMPSTEAD HILL
BROOKE/ COCKBURN
TRAPPE RD.
FREDERICK RD.
17
Baltimore
S. SMITH
SPARROW'S POINT RD.
MILLER'S CR.

GADSBY'S INDIAN QUEEN HOTEL
Basin
Fell's Point
WASHINGTON RD.
FEDERAL HILL
NORTH WEST BR.
WHETSTONE PT.
16

RIDGELY'S COVE
FORT BABCOCK
GWYNN'S FALLS
FORT COVINGTON
ARMISTEAD Fort McHenry
LAZARETTO BATTERY

SMITH'S COVE
FERRY BRANCH
Napier feint, Sept. 13–14
Sunken vessels
Sept. 13–14
14 **15**
U.S. truce ship (Exact location unknown)

PATAPSCO R.
CROMWELL'S MARSH
13
Bombardment, Sept. 13–14
COCHRANE

1. Thursday, Sept. 1
Key learns of Beanes's captivity and visits President Madison to gain approval for a rescue mission.

2. Friday, Sept. 2
Key plans journey.

3. Saturday, Sept. 3
Key receives orders from General Mason, collects letters, then departs for Baltimore via Bladensburg.

4. Sunday, Sept. 4
Key arrives in Baltimore.

5. Monday, Sept. 5
Key and Skinner leave Baltimore harbor by boat.

6. Tuesday, Sept. 6
Americans locate British and are escorted by the HMS *Royal Oak* to command ship.

7. Wednesday, Sept. 7
Key and Skinner board the British command ship HMS *Tonnant*.

8. Thursday, Sept. 8
Key, Skinner, and Beanes, with American crew, are transferred to the HMS *Surprize*. Their U.S. truce ship is towed.

9. Friday, Sept. 9
The British command group rendezvous with their bomb ships up the Potomac, then returns to the Chesapeake Bay enroute for Baltimore.

10. Saturday, Sept. 10
The British Fleet arrives at the mouth of the Patapsco River in the evening.

11. Sunday, Sept. 11
Key and the Americans are transferred back to their own ship in the evening and anchor, under British guard, with Cockburn's ships.

12. Monday, Sept. 12
The British land troops at North Point and advance on Baltimore by land.

13. Tuesday, Sept. 13
British bomb ships begin assault on Fort McHenry.

14. Wednesday, Sept. 14
The British bombardment ceases and Key sees Fort McHenry's storm flag.

15. Thursday, Sept. 15
Still detained under guard, Key continues composing his lyric.

16. Friday, Sept. 16
Key is released in the afternoon, returns to Baltimore in the evening, and completes his lyric.

17. Saturday, Sept. 17
Key sends song via Nicholson/Skinner to the *American and Commercial Daily Advertiser* for printing and leaves for Frederick.

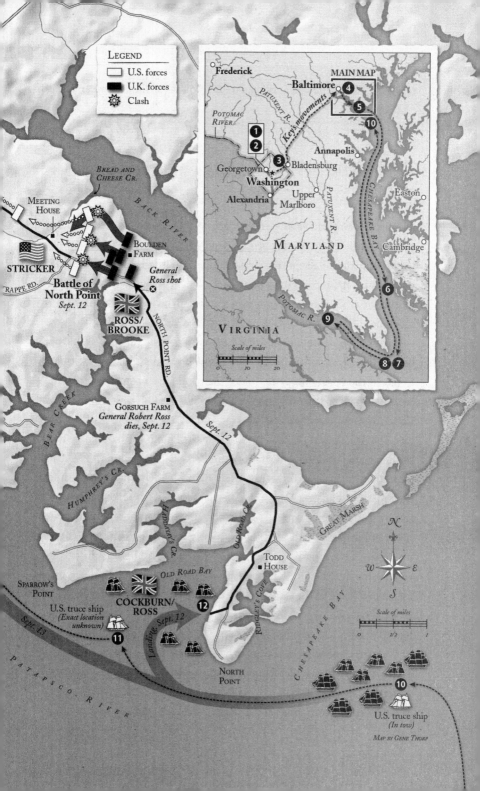

LEGEND

U.S. forces

U.K. forces

Clash

Bread and Cheese Cr.

MEETING HOUSE

STRICKER

BACK RIVER

BOULDEN FARM

General Ross shot ⊗

Battle of North Point *Sept. 12*

"RAPPE RD."

ROSS/ BROOKE

NORTH POINT RD.

BEAR CREEK

HUMPHREY'S CR.

GORSUCH FARM *General Robert Ross dies, Sept. 12*

Sept. 12

HIPKIN'S CR.

OLD ROAD CR.

GREAT MARSH

TODD HOUSE

RIDGELY'S COVE

OLD ROAD BAY

SPARROW'S POINT

U.S. truce ship *(Exact location unknown)* **11**

COCKBURN/ ROSS

Landing, Sept. 12

Sept. 13

12

PATAPSCO RIVER

NORTH POINT

CHESAPEAKE BAY

N / W E / S

Scale of miles 0   1/2   1

10

U.S. truce ship *(In tow)*

MAIN MAP

Frederick

POTOMAC RIVER

PATUXENT R.

Key's movements

Baltimore **4**

5

10

1 **2**

3

Georgetown

Washington

Bladensburg

Annapolis

Alexandria

Upper Marlboro

PATUXENT R.

CHESAPEAKE BAY

Easton

M A R Y L A N D

Cambridge

Potomac R.

9

6

V I R G I N I A

Scale of miles 0   10   20

8 **7**

Map by Gene Thorp

result was the same—Beanes was free. Yet none of the Americans were truly at liberty.

The Battle of Baltimore
September 7–14, Baltimore

On the morning of September 7—the very day Beanes's release would be secured—British plans changed. Instead of departing the Chesapeake, they would make Baltimore their next target. Unusually high tides, British intelligence, and reports from Baltimore's own newspapers expressing dismay at the city's poor readiness for an attack all conspired to shift British thinking.

Early on the eighth, Key and Skinner were informed that they would not be permitted to leave the British fleet. Instead the Americans were transferred to the frigate *Surprize,* under the command of the admiral's son Sir Thomas Cochrane. It would be their residence for the next four days. Royal Marines took charge of the Americans' truce ship and placed her in tow. The British fleet then headed back up the Potomac to reconnect with the bomb ships it needed to attack Baltimore. All told, Britain would bring more than fifty ships to the battle, although the delay needed to gather their forces would give American defenders precious time to prepare.

Key was no doubt anxious about the attack. Baltimore was home to many of his friends and professional colleagues. His wife's sister Rebecca lived there. Exacerbating his worry, Key had overheard British officers discussing the destruction they planned for the city. "The admiral had intimated his fears that the town must be burned: and I was sure that, if taken, it would have been given up to plunder," Key wrote later, adding with particular exasperation that the town "was filled with women & children."

Washington had been a primarily symbolic target. Only three weeks before, the British had desecrated its federal buildings with fire, exposing America's patriotic hubris and insulting its pride. However, Washington's population had been largely spared of suffering. Baltimore would be different, and for Britain's sailors, this difference was not only strategic but personal.

Baltimore had long been in British sights for revenge. The third-largest city in the United States and an active port and shipbuilding center, its quick "Baltimore Clippers" had taken the U.S. government's War of 1812 authorization of piracy as a mandate. Since war had been declared, Baltimore privateers had commandeered some five hundred British merchant ships with cargo valued in the millions of dollars. Most notorious was the fourteen-gun schooner *Chasseur*. In the summer of 1814, as the British fleet harassed the Chesapeake, the "Pride of Baltimore" had captured or sunk seventeen British vessels off the coast of England and Ireland. The Royal Navy thus sought retribution. Moreover, Baltimore's docks would provide valuable spoils. If there was any town that the British would like to burn to ashes, it was Baltimore.

Admiral Cockburn had advocated that the British attack the "hornet's nest" of Baltimore immediately after the burning of Washington, using an undefended land route to get there. General Ross, however, had chosen to reunite with their ships. Despite the delay, Cockburn would still convince his comrades to make a bold attack. British ships would enter Baltimore Harbor and, as their cannons scattered the volunteer militia defending the city from behind, a land assault by British marines would take the city. The only thing standing in their way was the star-shaped Fort McHenry and its American troops, guarding the entrance to Baltimore Harbor.

Key held out hope, but he could not dismiss British confidence as bravado. British military professionalism had easily routed a more numerous but inexperienced American militia at the Battle of Bladensburg. This defeat had led immediately to the burning of Washington later that same afternoon. Key had witnessed this embarrassment firsthand. His home and family threatened, he had volunteered as an aide to General Walter Smith, commander of the First Columbian Brigade. Key did not fight, but had ferried messages among U.S. military leaders coordinating Washington's defense. He spent the few brief hours of the battle itself alongside his Georgetown artillery unit. Despite America's superior numbers and tactical position, the poorly managed defense crumbled. Georgetown's artillery held its ground, retreating from the battlefield only upon direct orders, some men howling in anger and others weeping at the defeat. Cockburn and Ross soon walked into Washington unopposed. They looted the White House, dined at President Madison's table, then burned the building to the ground, along with the Treasury, the Navy Yard, and the Capitol Building. Key had argued cases before the bar of the Capitol's Supreme Court chambers, now reduced to ashes.

Baltimoreans, for their part, had been preparing for the attack since August 24, when they saw smoke rising over the District of Columbia, just thirty-eight miles away. The city's defenders comprised some seventeen thousand riflemen, artillerymen, and cavalry of the Maryland Militia's Third Division, augmented by Baltimore residents, including free and enslaved Black men. An order taking effect on September 5 required "all free people of color" to assist in the construction of defensive works, promising pay of fifty cents a day and "a soldier's rations." Major General Samuel Smith organized the city's defenses. He was uncompromising in his preparations—"forts, redoubts and entrenchments are thrown up all around the town and the place has nothing to fear," a fellow officer would write.

Major George Armistead, who had been in charge of McHenry since June 1813, anticipated the attack as well. He knew the redcoats were coming and had requested "a flag so large that the British will have no difficulty in seeing it from a distance." The resulting thirty-by-forty-two-foot garrison flag would be the largest flag used in the War of 1812. The proud ensign was created in 1813 by local flagmaker Mary Pickersgill, working alongside assistants including her thirteen-year-old daughter, Caroline, her nieces, Eliza and Margaret Young, and the thirteen-year-old African American indentured apprentice Grace Wisher. They completed the huge flag in about seven weeks and delivered it, along with a smaller storm flag measuring seventeen by twenty-five feet for use in bad weather. The flags featured fifteen stars and fifteen stripes—the era's official design.

As days passed and no British attack came, Baltimoreans began to relax. That changed at dusk on Saturday, September 10, when lookouts saw the first distant ships coming up the Chesapeake. Major Armistead was informed that a British flotilla had been spotted at the mouth of the Patapsco, "with every indication of an attempt on the City of Baltimore." To save the city, the Americans would have to hold Fort McHenry.

Back with the British fleet, Admiral Cochrane informed Skinner that he and his American compatriots would be released only after the battle was completed. As Skinner remembered, "Dining every day with the Admiral and a large party of army and navy officers, . . . objects and plans were freely spoken of." The British could not risk the Americans revealing these plans to the city's defenders. However, the British expected Baltimore, like Washington, to fall quickly and thus the Americans' detention would be brief. Skinner demanded they at least be returned to their own ship.

Skinner's request was honored Sunday evening, but the Americans were joined by a redcoat guard. Their ship dropped anchor at the "mouth of the Patapsco," likely somewhere below Sparrows Point near Old Road Bay, a good eight miles from Fort McHenry. They were held under the "guns of a frigate." The precise location is uncertain, but from here, using a spyglass, the Americans would track the battle's movements. Skinner suggested that the truce ship raise its own red, white, and blue flag, echoing the fort's gesture of defiance.

What inspired Admiral Cockburn's bold confidence in challenging McHenry was the recent arrival of the *HMS Terror*. Commissioned in June 1813, it was the newest and most advanced weapon of its kind. The bomb vessel combined sail and steam power, was 201 feet long, and weighed a massive 325 tons. A decade of technical advances in rigging, mast placement, ordnance, and structural design meant that such Vesuvius-class ships marked a new era in seaborne weaponry. The ships were named for what in 1814 was still an active Italian volcano. Vesuvius had erupted six times in the eighteenth century, and as recently as 1794. Most famously, it rained destruction upon the ancient city of Pompeii in A.D. 79. These ships were intended to do the same to British land targets. The Royal Navy had requisitioned the *Terror* two years prior, specifically "to annoy the coast of America."

Vesuvius ships were heavily reinforced to withstand the powerful recoil of their massive ten- and thirteen-inch mortars. The guns hurled explosive-filled bombs of up to 220 pounds as far as two and a half miles. Baltimore's *Niles Weekly Register* would report that with every bomb fired at the fort, the ships "were forced two feet into the water by the force . . . straining every part from stem to stern." The amount of gunpowder and shot needed to operate them called for a separate support vessel to carry the weight and reduce the chance of accidental explosion. On August 9 and 10, in what would be a prelude to Baltimore, the *Terror* had hurled some 170 bombs at the shipbuilding town of Stonington, Connecticut. Stonington withstood the attack, but Americans quickly learned to fear the *Terror.* The ship's name alone was meant to induce local leaders to surrender without a single mortar fired, as happened in Alexandria, Virginia, immediately after the capture of Washington.

McHenry, however, would not surrender without a fight. The fort was manned by a thousand soldiers, primarily the U.S. Army's Third Artillery. Supporting these professional troops were three companies of Maryland Militia, including McHenry's Baltimore Fencibles, a volunteer artillery company of eighty men founded and led by Judge Joseph Hopper Nicholson. The judge's wife, Rebecca, was the elder sister of Key's wife, Polly. A staunch supporter of the war, Judge Nicholson recognized that after Napoleon's April 1814 defeat in Continental Europe, Britain's seasoned troops would be redeployed to America. The real battles of America's War of 1812 would now be fought. In a letter to the U.S. Navy secretary, Nicholson wrote, "We should have to fight hereafter not for 'free trade and sailors rights,' not for conquest of the Canadas, but for our national existence."

Starting at three a.m. on Monday, September 12, Ross and Cockburn began landing some 4,700 men at North Point, just ten miles from the city. Their forces included Colonial Marines, Black men who had escaped slavery in the United States and volunteered to fight against their former masters. They were fierce fighters and valuable to the British cause.

U.S. General Samuel Smith had correctly anticipated the land assault from North Point up the Patapsco Neck and had deployed 3,200 men to block the redcoats' approach. General Ross, however, had no respect for

America's raw, largely untrained defenders. He was overheard that morning saying that he could not care less "if it rained militia." Ross and Cockburn, with a small advance party, worked their way toward the city; the rest of the British infantry would catch up later. They paused to take a hearty breakfast at a local farmhouse. While there, Ross interviewed three captured U.S. soldiers who claimed that twenty thousand defended the city. Ross reportedly laughed when he realized that Baltimore's defenders were militiamen. Soon he and his guard were on the move again, their red coats standing out prominently among the trees. Shots rang out, but nobody was hit. Moments later three concealed American sharpshooters opened fire, striking Ross in the right shoulder. The musket ball passed into his lung. The wound was fatal.

To British regulars, Ross had seemed invincible. Twice since arriving in America, the horse he was riding had been shot from underneath him, yet the general had escaped unscathed. Now his death was a devastating blow. The British won this initial skirmish, but the cost would prove too high. As a British chaplain reported, "there was not amongst us one man who did not feel that the victory had been purchased at a terrible price,—it had cost the life of our General, and in so doing, had crippled all our resources."

Back on the Patapsco River, Americans hoped the Royal Navy's big ships would be grounded in its shallow waters. The Royal Navy's skill and determination in navigating the shoals discouraged the Americans, and British ships advanced toward Fort McHenry. As a result, the American gun barges that were guarding the narrow passage leading to Baltimore Harbor soon received desperate orders to gather ballasted boats and sink them across the channel between McHenry and the three-gun Lazaretto Battery. The scuttled vessels, stretched along with a chain across the passage, were intended to prevent British ships from running at full speed past the fort's guns.

On the morning of Tuesday, September 13, five British bomb ships—*Aetna* (built in 1803), *Meteor* (1803), *Devastation* (1804), *Volcano* (1804), and *Terror* (1813)—were positioned in a semicircle about two miles from Fort McHenry. The bomb ships were supported by another dozen ships, among them the *Erebus*, which added another terrifying and unique British weapon to the mix: Congreve rockets.

In basic appearance, the rockets, invented by William Congreve, looked much like today's toy Fourth of July bottle rockets, but at a scale for vengeance. The heavy shipborne versions weighed either one hundred or three hundred pounds. What they lacked in accuracy, they made up for in noise and flame. Their screaming, unpredictable trajectories terrified inexperienced troops and townspeople. A smaller field version had been used with particular effectiveness at the Battle of Bladensburg, chasing America's militia from the field and inspiring what some commentators had called the "Bladensburg Races." By contrast, the ship-based rockets of the *Erebus* were enormous—measuring twenty-five to twenty-seven feet long and tipped with explosive charges encased in metal. They could set a town aflame.

By six-thirty a.m. the bomb ships had begun their assault. *Volcano* fired first, testing its range. Admiral Cochrane boasted that McHenry would not resist for more than two hours.

Where was Key's American truce ship during the battle? Neither Taney's account nor Skinner's mentions it, but at some point that day, it may have moved closer to the battle. A contemporary sketch shows what appears to be an American boat attached to the British attack squadron. A possible location is near the mouth of Bear Creek, about four miles from the fort. Cochrane may even have ordered the Americans to be brought alongside the British ships in hope that after the fort's defeat, they could help negotiate its surrender. Wherever he was, Key watched the shelling throughout the day, reassured by the continuing presence of McHenry's proud flag.

British cannons maintained a relentless hail on the fort. "Four or five bombs were frequently in the air at a time," reported the *Register*, often "making a double explosion." The rockets flew wildly, but the high-arching trajectories of the mortar shells, packed with twenty pounds of explosives, easily carried over the fort's walls, yet the stone, brick, and earth of Fort McHenry proved remarkably resilient. Fortunately for the Americans as well, the bombs' wooden fuses were unreliable. While timed to explode directly over the fort, many failed to detonate. A driving rain that fell for much of the day and night may have increased the bombs' rate of failure. One bomb burst through the roof of McHenry's powder magazine. If it had detonated, some three hundred barrels of powder stacked three tiers high would have burst the fort's walls from within. Miraculously, the bomb failed to explode. Suddenly aware of the risk, Armistead had the powder moved outside the fort's rear wall to reduce the danger.

At about three p.m., the British ships, likely thinking that their attack by now had compromised McHenry's ability to respond, moved closer to the fort in hopes of improving their aim and effectiveness. But now that they were finally in range of the American guns, they were vulnerable. The fort launched a furious counterattack. The skirmish lasted for some thirty minutes. "The balls now flew like hail stones," the *Register* reported, "and the Britons . . . hoisted their sails and were off in a moment." Having moved out of range of McHenry's batteries, the bomb ships resumed their monotonous firestorm. McHenry, however, had done damage. It had hit the *Volcano* five times, and the *Devastation* was taking on water.

As darkness fell on Fort McHenry, Pickersgill's giant banner became soaked in the heavy rain. Its weight might well have snapped the fort's ninety-foot wooden flagpole, so the defenders replaced it with the smaller storm flag.

Back aboard the truce ship, Beanes, who had lost his eyeglasses, asked Key repeatedly if the flag was still there. Flashes of lightning or the rockets' own glare may have illuminated the smaller flag momentarily, but proof that the Americans held firm was offered mainly by the continuing noise of the bombardment. Silence would have been the concern. If the shelling ceased, it could mean that the British had taken the fort. As long as the battle's cacophony rang, Key knew the British assault remained unsuccessful.

At about one a.m., nine British barges laden with Royal Marines slipped quietly past the darkened fort. A blue British signal flare informed British ground forces at the gates of the city that a diversion was under way. Unable to defeat McHenry and thus get British cannons into Baltimore Harbor, Cochrane instead hoped to pull the American militia away from the city. The sound of British oars on the water, however, alerted nearby Fort Babcock to the deception. The American defenders opened fire as did the battery at Fort

Covington, awakening further support from McHenry and the city battery as well. The British feint proved no more successful than the bombardment itself.

Unknown to Cochrane, it was also unnecessary. The Royal Army had already decided to forgo its attack. By three a.m. the British regulars were marching back to North Point. Many were frustrated, others relieved. "It was the universal belief throughout our little army, that had General Ross survived, Baltimore would have been in our possession," wrote one soldier.

By Dawn's Early Light by Edward Percy Moran (c. 1912). This painting imaginatively reconstructs the moment that inspired Key's song. But Key, who would have needed a spyglass to see the flag, is shown too near Fort McHenry and on a British ship, rather than on the unarmed American truce vessel from which he witnessed the bombardment.

The British bombardment continued until about four a.m. Logs from the *Volcano* reveal that in the twenty-two hours since dawn on September 13, this one ship alone had fired 278 bombs. Armistead's report to the U.S. Army estimated that the British launched 1,500 to 1,800 shells that day, an average of more than one each minute.

Key, Beanes, and Skinner maintained their vigil into the morning hours of the fourteenth. Before dawn, the guns fell silent, which must have sparked their greatest fears. As Taney reported the tale, Key and Skinner

> paced the deck for the residue of the night in painful suspense, watching with intense anxiety for the return of day; . . . as soon as it dawned, and before it was light enough to see objects at a distance, their glasses were turned to the fort, uncertain whether they should see there the stars and stripes, or the flag of the enemy. At length the light came, and they saw that "our flag was still there."

Most accounts of Key's star-spangled creativity suggest a resulting flash of poetic inspiration, that Key's vision of the flag precipitated a rush of patriotic fervor in poetry. The reality was more prosaic. Skinner, Beanes, and Key remained under British guard for three more days, "until the fleet was ready to set sail." Key thus had at least sixty hours in which to write his song, imagining new words to fit a melody he already knew well. It was a time of confusion and uncertainty. American troops remained on alert, perplexed by the redcoats' unexplained withdrawal from the city's doorstep. Maryland's militiamen were weary; they had not slept for two days. General Smith wisely refrained from mounting a counterattack.

The British were in no rush to depart, or to clarify their intentions. The fleet was now safely out of range of American guns. British troops gradually returned to their ships. Their professional officers filed reports, taking stock of munitions used and equipment lost or damaged. British casualties were counted, the wounded given medical care, and each of the fifty ships was inspected, repaired, and made ready. The British spent two and a half days preparing to set sail. Theirs was no hasty retreat.

During the delay, Skinner went about his duties, writing dispatches and reports and continuing to liaise with the British, as was his role. Admiral Cochrane told him of General Ross's death and credited the blockade of sunken ships across the channel with having turned the battle.

Key, in contrast, had nothing but time on his hands. His mission was long complete. Beanes was free. At about nine a.m. on the day the bombardment ended, McHenry's American defenders raised their proud garrison flag, replacing the storm flag that Key would have seen at dawn. "At this time our morning gun was fired," wrote Private Isaac Munroe, "the flag hoisted, Yankee Doodle played, and we all appeared in full view of a formidable and mortified enemy." But the battle was not necessarily over, and in any event Key and his companions had little reliable information, except what Skinner was able to glean from the British. General Smith himself was still uncertain if the British retreat was a ruse, and he was just learning that Ross had been killed. Only gradually did the Americans come to understand that the British had given up on taking Baltimore. Taney's report that *The Star-Spangled Banner* was written "in the fervor of the moment, when he saw the enemy hastily retreating to their ships," takes on a different meaning against the reality of the slow British withdrawal. Key's "moment" lasted for the better part of three days.

Key, Beanes, and Skinner finally returned to Baltimore Harbor at dusk on Friday, September 16. Their vessel had been at sea for twelve days. Reporters peppered the trio with questions. Skinner estimated that the British had lost "between 5 and 6 hundred men." Beanes reported that the enemy was "much disappointed in not being able to carry Baltimore." A reporter for Philadelphia's *Political and Commercial Register* interviewed Key, filing his account the next day.

> *Baltimore, 17th Sept. 1814*
>
> *The enemy have not moved since my last. Mr. Key of this place arrived yesterday evening in a flag, which was sent down before the attack and detained until yesterday. He states that the officers of the enemy spoke of going to Poplar Island to repair some of their vessels,*

*and from thence to proceed to Halifax. But he believed this to be far
from their intention.*

Some forty-two years later Taney recalled that in creating *The Star-
Spangled Banner,* Key "had written some lines, or brief notes that would aid
him in calling them to mind, upon the back of a letter which he happened
to have in his pocket . . . he finished it in the boat on his way to the shore,
and wrote it out as it now stands, at the hotel, on the night he reached Baltimore." Key's polished handwritten copy survives and has been on display at the Maryland Historical Society since 1956. Yet Taney's tale needs
qualification. Aboard an American diplomatic vessel, Key had access to
ample writing supplies. If Key had required fresh paper to work out multiple drafts, it was close at hand. More likely, he simply preferred to work
out the lyric in his head. Memorization was a skill he prized. He would, for
example, never give his children handwritten copies of his famous lyric, as
he did for a few friends. His children were expected to memorize it.

That the British detained Key, Beanes, and Skinner for the better part
of three days seems excessive. It may have been functional, as Skinner
continued to liaise with the British command, but for Key and Beanes, it
must have been frustrating. For Beanes, it was one final insult. It was also
a message to America that although Baltimore still stood, British power
in the Chesapeake remained unchallenged. For Key's lyric, this extended
period of gestation may have been critical. Key later described its writing
as difficult—as a "hanging matter"—and not something that fell easily into
place. The ironic result is that British pride and military procedure may
have produced a delay that was essential to the creation of one of America's
most enduring patriotic statements.

Deciphering Key's Song

Key's lyric was published as a broadside ballad or newspaper ballad—a set
of words to be sung to a well-known popular tune as a commentary on the
day's issues and events. Sometimes credited with spreading the news when

literacy was not universal, such lyrics were but crude carriers of facts. Instead, newspaper ballads conveyed the emotions of the era's happenings. Before photography, audio recording, and video, and certainly before the tweets and emojis of social media, topical poetry paired with melody expressed the feelings behind the news, the tears of tragedy, the joys of triumph. The art of newspaper song helped readers experience and process the emotional significance of historic events.

Newspaper ballads were common, everyday acts during the first century of U.S. history. Educated men and women who had the leisure to dabble in songwriting contributed these lyrics to the political discourse of the era. Newspapers received many such submissions and editors selected only the most compelling examples for publication. Politically engaged readers knew to look for them. They appeared regularly in sections titled "Native Genius," "Apollo's Fount," "The Parterre," or "Poet's Corner." Especially artful, clever, or provocative lyrics went viral. They were reprinted from one paper to the next, from one town to its neighbor, and so on.

Appearing under the title *Defence of Fort McHenry,* Key's song was printed in at least thirty-seven newspapers, riding and reinforcing a wave of patriotic optimism inspired by Baltimore's success. Papers from Vermont to Mississippi, representing both major political parties, reprinted Key's lyric. No other song of the era became so broadly popular so fast. Its first newspaper imprint, in the *Baltimore Patriot* on September 20, noted that Key's "beautiful and animating effusion . . . has already been extensively circulated." This was no accident. One of McHenry's thousand defenders, Private Severn Teackle, reported in a letter that "we have a song composed by Mr. Key of G. Town, which was presented to every individual in the fort in a separate sheet." It is likely that Judge Nicholson, working with Key, commissioned and distributed these first handbill prints, guaranteeing wide awareness. The prints were both tokens from a grateful city and patriotic propaganda, strategically shared (see page 5).

Key's song offers a compact and fervent account of his personal experience of the Battle of Baltimore. Skinner called it "a versified and almost literal transcript of our expressed hopes and apprehensions, through that ever-memorable period of anxiety to all, but never of despair." Its first verse tells of the bombardment of Fort McHenry, the second of viewing the flag. The darker third verse focuses on the simultaneous attack on the city by land, while the fourth offers a vision of peace, hope, and national promise. As a whole, the lyric traces a volatile emotional journey, from fear and uncertainty through relief and pride, to anger and determination, to pious gratitude and prayer, and finally to patriotic devotion.

The text as reproduced here is taken from the first edition handbill print created soon after the Battle of Baltimore. Key, anxious to get back to his family following the battle, nevertheless remained in town long enough to carry copies of this edition with him, and thus it seems likely that he approved its final form.

VERSE 1

O! say can you see by the dawn's early light,
    What so proudly we hailed at the twilight's last gleaming,
Whose broad stripes and bright stars through the perilous fight,
    O'er the ramparts we watch'd, were so gallantly streaming?
And the Rockets' red glare, the Bombs bursting in air,
Gave proof through the night that our Flag was still there;
        O! say does that star-spangled Banner yet wave,
        O'er the Land of the free, and the home of the brave?

The opening verse paints a dramatic picture of the bombardment of Fort McHenry and the heroic defiance of its defenders. The U.S. flag, flying proudly over the fort, serves as a poetic symbol of their stalwart devotion and courage. They remained at their posts under relentless attack by British bomb ships, the era's most fearsome naval weapons. As twilight turns to night, the lyric's narrator can no longer see the flag. Key himself is this anonymous narrating witness, anxious for Baltimore and for his nation.

British rockets and bombs burst into the night and painted the sky red. The terror of the bombardment is felt in Key's expressive choice of words,

The first sheet music edition of Key's song, 1814, arranged by
Thomas Carr of Baltimore. This edition was also the first to use the title
The Star Spangled Banner and to add the sharp to the fourth scale degree of the
melody, shown here in measures six and ten. Note too the absence of the
three opening pick-up notes characteristic of the melody today.

mainly those he selects for the melody's highest pitches. Usually discussed
as making Key's song hard to sing, these notes—more than an octave and
a half above the melody's lowest pitch—are vital musically because they
signal the point of greatest dramatic tension in each verse. The apex of the
dramatic arch is sounded to the words "rockets' red glare." Britain's Con-

greve missiles, designed to strike fear in the enemy, represent the emotional height of American anxiety. Yet the explosions are also strangely reassuring, as each blast confirms that the battle continues—and thus that the fort has not yet fallen into enemy hands. While Key's first verse is sung today as if it were the complete song, it is instead intentionally incomplete. The opening verse ends with a question mark, asking—is America's flag still there, is Baltimore safe, is the nation still independent and free?

Verse 2
On the shore dimly seen through the mists of the deep,
 Where the foe's haughty host in dread silence reposes,
What is that which the breeze, o'er the towering steep,
 As it fitfully blows, half conceals, half discloses?
Now it catches the gleam of the morning's first beam,
In full glory reflected now shines in the stream,
 'Tis the star-spangled banner, O! long may it wave
O'er the land of the free and the home of the brave.

The patriotic auditor now sees through the eyes of the lyric's narrator. The second verse shares his struggle as dawn breaks to see which flag flies above McHenry. Is it the American Stars and Stripes or the British Union Jack? As Key looks to the fort on shore, across the water, and through the morning mists and maybe the battle's lingering smoke, he knows British ships lurk unseen, their guns silent. They have stopped firing— is it because British soldiers now occupy the fort or because they have called off a failed attack? The flag, hanging limp against its pole, withholds its identity. Over the steep embankments of the fort, a fitful breeze attempts to lift the flag, promising to reveal its design. Finally, wind and sun catch the flag at once, and the Star-Spangled Banner is declared, gloriously reflected on the water in Key's spyglass. The question posed in the chorus of the opening verse has now been answered, transformed into a statement of patriotic pride, relief, joy, and hope—long may the nation's ensign wave. The melody's emotional apex is no less dramatic here. Its high notes mark the moment when the song's narrator catches sight of America's flag.

Verse 3

And where is that band who so vauntingly swore
That the havoc of war and the battle's confusion,
A home and a country, shall leave us no more?
Their blood has washed out their foul footsteps' pollution.
No refuge could save the hireling and slave,
From the terror of flight or the gloom of the grave,
And the star-spangled banner in triumph doth wave,
O'er the Land of the Free, and the Home of the Brave.

The third verse is bloody, retaliatory, and vexed. It uses the word "slave." As much about the land assault as the naval bombardment, the lyric conveys Key's disgust at the enemy's ruthless plans to loot Baltimore and to burn to the ground a city housing women and children. Its opening question mocks the enemy's failed threats, while the subsequent line declares crassly that the enemy's very footsteps are now cleansed away by their own blood. The melody's high point is again telling. It reverses the equation of fear. During the bombardment, Baltimore was afraid, but now that America's flag still flies, it is the enemy that is in hasty retreat and that suffers without refuge. Only the grave can release it from the relentless pursuit of Baltimore's defenders. Key insults the enemy as a mere "hireling and slave."* His murderous language is striking and in one sense the most typical feature of the lyric as a memorial battle ode.

Key's bloodstained lyric speaks to his bitter anger. He had formerly idolized and idealized the British, making his disillusionment all the more painful. Himself of proud British ancestry, Key was a moderate, pro-British Federalist who had opposed the War of 1812. For him, the English

---

* The racial implications of the phrase "hireling and slave" are discussed in Chapter 8.

had been a model of civility and honor—personally, professionally, and politically. But the British burning of America's capital, the callous imprisonment of Beanes, and threats to pillage Baltimore had punctured Key's admiration. It was the boorish behavior of the royal military's leaders that most shocked him. "Never was a man more disappointed in his expectations than I have been as to the character of the British officers," Key wrote not long after returning to shore. "With some exceptions, they appeared to be illiberal, ignorant and vulgar, and seem filled with the spirit of malignity against every thing American." His banner lyric waves in mocking triumph.

VERSE 4

O! thus be it ever when freemen shall stand,
    Between their lov'd home, and the war's desolation,
Blest with vict'ry and peace, may the Heav'n rescued land,
    Praise the Power that hath made and preserv'd us a nation!
Then conquer we must, when our cause it is just,
And this be our motto—"In God is our Trust;"
        And the star-spangled Banner in triumph shall wave,
        O'er the Land of the Free, and the Home of the Brave.

Key's final verse opens with a proclamation and prayer that Americans, when in just defense of their homeland, would be forever blessed with victory and peace. He implores the "Heav'n-rescued land" to turn to God in gratitude, admonishing his fellow Americans to become more devout in appreciation of their very preservation. The emotional apex of the final verse gives voice to his proposed motto of piety ("In God is our Trust") and invokes the figure of the reluctant militiaman, someone like Key himself, leery of war but willing to fight in just defense of home and country. The language of the final repeating chorus is again adjusted, as it has been for each of the previous verses, to trace the emotional development of the story. The closing question posed in the first verse is now supplanted by a final declaration of triumph.

In each chorus, that is, in the final two lines of each verse, the melodic shape of the lyric again plays a role, musically, emotionally, and rhetorically. The word "free" (in "Land of the Free") is set to the same pinnacle pitch—the note that marks the high point of "red glare" in verse one. The return to this pitch creates an artful close to the melody, as the concluding phrase retraces the melodic journey of the previous seven lines. By setting the word "free" to this final climactic pitch, Key also reinforces the fundamental achievement of America's Revolution (breaking from the British king) and the founding ideal of the nation (liberty). The chorus thus provides a cathartic close to the lyric's depiction of the British attack in each verse, and offers a democratic exclamation point to the song's patriotic message.

The myths surrounding Key's writing of The Star-Spangled Banner—that it was written in a flash of revelation when Key was held prisoner on a British ship with only a scrap of paper at hand—serve to enhance the story by amplifying Key's heroism and the lyric's patriotic credentials. They also hide its political intent. The brevity and simplicity of Key's inspiration obscure any other motive or design. This illusion is enhanced by the absence of the name of its author—a known Federalist—in early prints and reprints, as well as by Key's later claims that the true author of his lyric was not him but the heroism of Baltimore's defenders. For the historian, however, claims to be apolitical are among the certain signs that politics is at play. For Key, such claims reveal a hope to transcend partisan division to foment a unifying nationalism. Composed over days not hours, his lyrical argument was surgically constructed to achieve its effect.

Among the literary devices that reveal Key's political intent is his use of pronouns. His language recruits both singer and auditor into the construct of nation. The most important word of the lyric may well be the opening "you." It brings the auditor into the story and into dialogue with the lyric, asking a question—"O! say, can YOU see?" It thus initiates a personal relationship to the lyric's patriotic proposals. This "you" is immediately incorporated into the proud "we" of the lyric's second line, a "we" that recalls the unifying symbol of the nation's flag and the "we" that watches over the ramparts to give witness to the battle's drama. Soon the "what" we hailed similarly becomes "our" flag. By verse three, "we" is transformed into "us," now under threat from the British. In the final verse, God has "preserved us a nation," and unifying plural pronouns and possessives flood the lyric's emotional climax: "we must," "our cause," "our motto," "our Trust." Rather than a passive account of the battle, Key's song offers a story of political manipulation and construction—it does not simply observe a nation triumphant but works to build one, assembling individuals into a unified whole.

Key paints a picture of a united, pious, and powerful nation. Yet in 1814 none of these propositions were true, least of all to Key's way of thinking. Both before and after he wrote his lyric, he railed against the partisan division between anti-war Federalists and pro-war Democrats. In his 1814 address honoring George Washington, he had also admonished his listeners to be more pious. And Key knew firsthand that America's military had been unable to protect the nation's capital. The city had been taken by the British in only a few hours, and its gleaming white buildings burned.

Most telling, Key's call for unity was itself political. While British aggression had tempered his own pacifist stance, northern Federalists continued to criticize the war with Britain. He considered such opposition while the nation was under attack to be a betrayal. It put personal economic interests ahead of country. His call for unity was thus an implicit critique of anyone who sustained the nation's partisan divide. Yet Key's abstract language avoids assigning blame, which would have sown further division. The lyricist instead uses patriotism in celebration of victory as a solution to partisanship, even as his notion of patriotism is built upon the foundation of his own Federalist views.

Key's fourth verse offers the poet-lawyer's summary argument and calls for a shift in national sentiment. A deeply religious man, fearful of God's chastening wrath, Key saw the burning of Washington as divine punishment and the comparative escape of Baltimore as providential. Key feared for Baltimore, not only because of British military superiority but because he believed the war to be immoral and unjustified. Baltimore, as a stronghold of the Democratic-Republican Party, had been particularly enthusiastic about the declaration of war in 1812. In early October 1814, Key wrote to his friend and fellow anti-war activist John Randolph about the anxieties he experienced during the battle.

> Sometimes, when I remembered that it was there [Baltimore] the declaration of this abominable war was received with public rejoicings, I could not feel a hope that they would escape, and again when I thought of the many faithful, whose piety lessens that lump of wickedness I could hardly feel a fear.

For Key, Baltimore's survival was a signal of God's "forbearance, long-suffering and tender mercy." God had answered Americans' prayers, truly rescued the United States, and the nation must now put its trust in God. "I hope I shall never cease to feel the warmest gratitude when I think of His most merciful deliverance," Key wrote to Randolph. For Key, Baltimore's survival was a sign of redemption, an indication that America's sins had been forgiven. It was a time to unify.

Key's lyric has been criticized as having limited aesthetic value. Its wording can be viewed as archaic or too difficult to remember as patriotic song. But these qualities were not so much faults at the time of its invention. *Analectic Magazine,* an American monthly that offered extracts of the era's best writing alongside literary criticism, republished *Defence of Fort McHenry* in its November 1814 issue. Its compilers noted that the verses had been published in many newspapers, but that "their merit entitles them to preservation in some more permanent form than the columns of a daily paper."

This reprinting offered a meaningful literary endorsement of Key's song. In July the same magazine had featured a lengthy unsigned review, potentially written by editor Washington Irving himself, of a volume of American patriotic poetry by Edwin Holland. The review found the book burdened by "portentous" language and lacking originality and thus emblematic of the poor state of American patriotic poetry as a whole. "Our national songs," the critic observed, "are full of ridiculous exaggeration, and frothy rant, and commonplace bloated up into fustian." To date, despite "thousands of pens . . . drawn forth in every part of the union," the reviewer concluded, no American poet had managed to produce a patriotic song of "sterling merit." Yet, by publishing Key's lyric just four months later, the magazine suggested that the pen of Francis Scott Key had finally crafted that long-hoped-for song of "poetical independence."

On December 24, 1814, the Treaty of Ghent ended the War of 1812. Its terms restored all territories to their pre-war status. The nation's borders had not changed, yet the United States had been transformed. The most lasting result of the war may have been the construction of American national pride itself. Uncle Sam had been born, both literally and figuratively. On display at the National Museum of American History since 1964, Mary Pickersgill's giant Fort McHenry garrison flag became the nation's sacred relic. And Francis Scott Key's *The Star-Spangled Banner*—unlike a literary mountain of competing but forgotten American broadside lyrics, hundreds written to the very same tune—has survived and thrived.

Chapter 2

Origins of a Melody

The Music of *The Star-Spangled Banner*

Our national anthem is about as patriotic as "The Stein Song," as
singable as *Die Walküre,* and as American as "God Save the Queen."

—*Charles Braun (1965)*

The Power of Music

So often overshadowed by complaints ("it's too hard to sing") or dismissed as trivial ("it's a bawdy old drinking song"), the music of
The Star-Spangled Banner is actually a potent source of the song's
expressive range and social power. The tune can open a flood of tears as in
1963, when it was intoned on a church organ to conclude the requiem funeral
mass of President John F. Kennedy. It can also be joyful and celebratory,
uniting the nation in collective pride when American athletes—say, the 1980
"miracle on ice" men's hockey team, or Simone Biles, the most decorated U.S.
gymnast in history—stand atop the medal podium to receive Olympic gold.

By any measure, the tune is remarkable. As one of the longest-surviv-
ing, actively performed melodies in Western culture, it has thrived across
four centuries and thus keeps company with Beethoven's *Ode to Joy* and
France's *La Marseillaise.* It is immediately recognizable after just three
notes. Its emblematic arpeggiated descent—"O-o say"—calls an assembly
to attention, outlines the tune's martial import, and articulates its own
harmonic foundations.

The lowest note of *The Star-Spangled Banner* melody functions as what musicians call the tonic. The root of the melody's home key, it serves as the song's base and springboard. At its midpoint, the tune makes a surprising but vital upward leap. Rising to unusual heights, it demands exclamatory energy from its singer. "And the rockets' red glare" conveys threat, tension, anxiety, and challenge, but also power, commitment, and fearlessness. The word "glare," sung to the tune's highest sustained pitch, has vexed many a would-be performer. Yet to sound this note true and in tune is to signal the melody's extraordinary ambition, not only to symbolize heroism but in a sense to be heroic. This challenge overcome, the melody marches forward in a final concluding phrase with a dramatic return to its highest pitch and a firm, resolute closing cadence.

The melody's precise origin was long shrouded in mystery and controversy. It was borrowed whole from a song known variously in early America as *To Anacreon in Heaven, Anacreon in Heaven, To Anacreon,* or simply *Anacreon.* It was composed by the Englishman John Stafford Smith in about 1773 as the club anthem for a music fraternity in London known as the Anacreontic Society and published under the title *The Anacreontic Song.* Francis Scott Key thus did not write the music of his famous song; instead he crafted a new lyric to fit what in his day was a typical tune for political parody. In his lifetime, Key wrote four songs and nine hymns in this manner, always crafting new lyrics to an established musical model. It is thus a seemingly small but significant error to say that Key wrote a "poem," even though his lyric often appears in print as a set of words without music. Key instead wrote a song, imagining his words as already alloyed with the emotional power of a specific and particularly dynamic melody.

The Anacreontic Society and Composer John Stafford Smith

London's Anacreontic Society was founded in 1766 as part of a vibrant English social club scene that continues to the present day. It was one of many musical clubs, the most august and influential of which was the

Nobleman and Gentleman's Catch Club (founded in 1761). In the City of London, where domestic space was and remains at a premium, such clubs provided both the physical and the social space necessary for personal and professional networks to grow. These clubs were also a powerful political force, signaling that a broad social transformation had begun, one leading away from the royal court and toward a public culture and a constitutional monarchy.

Anacreontic Society members included nobles with seats in the House of Lords and members of the rising class of businessmen and professionals, what was described as a diverse mix of "peers, commoners, aldermen, gentlemen, proctors, actors, and polite tradesmen." Annual dues of one gold guinea, later increased to three, put membership out of reach for the working classes, including professional musicians. Yet as music making was the club's featured attraction, it was in everyone's interest to pretend otherwise. The city's best instrumentalists and vocalists were admitted free as honorary members.

Music making was the activity and passion that brought these society members together. The Catch Club's mission focused on history and legacy: the singing of old English madrigals to recover an already mythic British past while nurturing new compositions through its competitions. But the Anacreontic Society imbibed contemporary musical delights—concertizing, singing, sociality, and fun—very much in the present. The club's namesake was the Greek poet Anacreon (c.582–c.485 B.C.), reflecting the European Enlightenment's fascination with classical antiquity. One of the nine lyric poets of ancient Greece, Anacreon had been popular both in his hometown of Teos and later in his adopted city of Athens. His statue was featured on the Acropolis.

Anacreon's poetry, especially as it was known to the eighteenth century, came from the *Anacreontea*, a medieval collection including verse not just by the Greek master but also by imitators. Dating from the first century B.C. to sixth century A.D., its poems are thought to include contributions from some fifty-nine poets. Questions of attribution and authorship later ravaged Anacreon's literary reputation, but in Renaissance and early modern Europe, his verse was wildly popular. First published in Paris in 1554, the *Anacreontea* spread across the continent, to Madrid and Rome in the south and to London and Edinburgh in the north. Reprints and translations were common, as only Homer was then better known among ancient Greek writers. Thus, in eighteenth-century England, to name a social club in Anacreon's honor was to be both culturally sophisticated and trendy.

Anacreon's lyrics should be thought of as songs—all Greek poetry was sung to musical accompaniment. Apart from a few hymns for military heroes, the subject matter of Anacreontic verse was the rich pleasures of daily life: love, wine, youth, beauty, and revelry, often expressed through allegorical figures such as Venus, Bacchus, and Cupid. The name Anacreon was thus synonymous with bacchanalian abandon and gave the club an undoubtedly deserved reputation for alcohol consumption. Such a mixture of music and sociability would certainly have attracted club members, but a balancing principle of the *Anacreontea* is moderation. The sensual is celebrated, but at a distance; drunkenness was boorish, and sex indiscreet. Frivolity and farce were likely the club's most typical social infractions.

Every year beginning in November, when the club's wealthier members returned to London from their country mansions, and running until April, when the spring season began, an Anacreontic Society meeting was held every other Wednesday, for a series of twelve. After the year's opening business meeting of dinner and singing, subsequent gatherings began at seven p.m. with a concert of instrumental music that lasted until about 9:45 p.m. Continental repertoire, often by Mozart or Haydn, was performed likely without rehearsal by a mix of top-flight professional instrumentalists and amateur players. Formal programs were not printed, but regular newspaper accounts reported that symphonic works would typically begin and end the program, with concertos, chamber works (often string quartets), duets, solo sonatas, and the occasional vocal solo between. The best professional players were featured in the chamber works and solos. At the height of the club's popularity in the 1780s, tickets were issued and up to four hundred people might attend. Members were exclusively male, although a 1787 renovation to the concert room added a shielded upper gallery to which women were admitted.

Following the concert, members, musicians, and guests adjourned to an adjacent room for a cold supper, returning not long afterward to the concert's grand ballroom to sing. Women were to have departed by this time. The concert seating was replaced with benches and tables set with alcoholic punch, wine, and shrub (a rum-based cocktail). The club's president sat in the middle of a raised dais flanked on either side by professional vocal performers, including a mix of skilled church musicians and singer-actors from London's West End theaters. Repertoire featured part songs, solos, and duets in the English glee tradition, composed primarily by English musicians. Formal toasts might occur between songs.

Song selections were drawn from popular catches, canons, and glees, and their performances required musical sophistication and training. Attendees joined in the repeated choruses, but they could be criticized if their limited musical skills detracted from the aesthetic beauty of the singing. Enthusiastic applause awarded the best performers, and quiet attention was required, if only to appreciate the repertory's detailed lyrical humor. Nonmusical relief was offered by comic monologues or "imitations" of leading actors, sometimes offered by the club's amateurs, as well as "salt box solos, and miniature puppet shews; in short every thing that mirth can suggest."

The formal meeting ended at midnight or one a.m., when the club president left the chair and most attendees departed. Decorum soon dissolved, and more vivacious members might remain until two or even four a.m. One rather prim musical professional noted, "The president having left the chair, . . . the proceedings were very disgraceful to the society; as the greatest levity, and vulgar obscenity, generally prevailed." That on some occasions members reportedly headed home at daybreak contributed to the club's reputation for drunkenness.

Two songs were repeated at every Anacreontic meeting. *Non nobis Domine* (Not unto us, O Lord) was sung after each meal. Then as today, this beautiful canonic setting of the Latin thanksgiving grace was often misattributed to the sixteenth-century English Renaissance composer William Byrd. Its performance was among the society's musical gems. As one observer noted, "all the principal vocal performers in England, sacred and theatrical, are honorary members of the Society, *Non nobis Domine* cannot be sung better; nor indeed so well elsewhere." When the company next moved from the dining room back to the concert space, members were called to order by a ritualized performance of the club's constitutional air, *The Anacreontic Song*. One of the club's presidents, Edward Mulso, reportedly was capable of singing the song himself, but the anthem was more typically sung by a professional vocalist. Its chorus, however, was repeated in harmony by the general membership, giving voice to a reinforcing ritual of unity and camaraderie. This solo call and affirming group response would become vital to the melody's future use in American politics.

The Anacreontic Song was written in 1773 or a bit before and reflects the society's increasing popularity. First gathering in a small public house, the Anacreontic Society moved through a sequence of larger quarters. Its earliest gatherings were less formal affairs, likely without the rigid three-part structure dividing concert, meal, and singing. After relocating to the larger London coffeehouse on Ludgate Hill, paid membership expanded to twenty-five, with each member allowed to bring a guest. The creation of a club anthem during this period of growth celebrated and amplified the club's success. It served not only to unite the membership in song but echoed across London as a powerful advertisement and recruitment tool, signaling the club's dual mission of harmony and fun.

Published about five years later, an early sheet music imprint of *The Anacreontic Song* lacks several vital historical details. The page indicates no year of publication, no date when either the music or the text was written, and most surprising, no composer's name. Published between 1778 and 1781, the imprint credits only the lyricist Ralph Tomlinson (1744–78), an attorney who served the society as an early leader. That he is identified as the "late president" suggests that the edition may have been a tribute following his death. The publisher is also identified. Longman and Broderip was primarily a piano manufacturer and was one of the Anacreontic

The earliest known sheet music edition of *The Anacreontic Song*, c. 1778.

Society's commercial members. By joining the society, music businesses connected with bourgeois music lovers and thus potential customers.

Remarkably, the melody's composer—John Stafford Smith (1750–1836)—was not conclusively identified until 1977, when the discovery of a diary entry by an Anacreontic Society keyboardist resolved a long-standing musicological debate. Precisely how Stafford Smith came to write the music is so far lost to history, but as a regular performer at Anacreontic Society meetings and a rising star in London's musical scene, he was a shrewd if obvious choice.

John Stafford Smith (1750–1836), composer of
The Anacreontic Song, at about age seventy.

Stafford Smith, still in his early twenties, was already an award-winning
composer when he undertook the task of setting Ralph Tomlinson's lyrics
to music. Born on March 30, 1750, the son of organist Martin Smith had
been raised for an illustrious musical career. His earliest position was as a
boy chorister in Gloucester Cathedral, where his father worked. Located
about one hundred miles west of London, the cathedral features an ornate
gothic tower, and as the burial place of King Edward II, it falls only a bit
shy of Westminster Abbey and St. Paul's Cathedral in architectural splendor. By 1761 the eleven-year-old was living in London as a chorister of the
Chapel Royal, the ecclesiastical entourage of George III and his court. John
was a pupil of William Boyce, the Chapel Royal's senior composer and
organist. Martin Smith had thus accomplished every parent's dream, setting his child on a path to certain success. His talented musical son was in
the nation's cultural capital, living and learning among its most powerful
and socially connected church musicians. A notable career lay before him.

By 1772, when Stafford Smith would have been commissioned to compose the Anacreontic Society's club anthem, his songs were being featured at the more established and prestigious Catch Club. Two of his original compositions were published in its annual collection of musical highlights. The next edition reveals that the young composer had won two of the Catch Club's prestigious gold prize medals, awarded to the year's best examples of the peculiarly English a cappella men's vocal genres favored by its members: canon, catch, and glee.

Canons are short contrapuntal compositions, usually featuring two or three voices, based on the technique of musical imitation, in which a melody is sounded and repeated in layers to create a rich harmonic tapestry. Pachelbel's accompanied canon is the most famous today, but the grace *Non nobis Domine,* mentioned before, represents the more typical vocal genre preferred by London's clubs. Catches, also known as rounds, were the canon's secular comic cousins. *Frère Jacques* and *Row, Row, Row Your Boat* are contemporary examples. Another type of multipart vocal composition was the glee. Here composers created extended, four- and five-part hymnlike settings of serious texts in contrasting sections. Each verse was accompanied by new music. Subjects could be sacred or secular—communal, idyllic, philosophical, or dramatic. Glees often featured musical imitation and word painting in which melodic gestures bring the meaning of words to life. A well-known contemporary example is the word "low" in Garth Brooks's anthem *Friends in Low Places.* The country star sings the word "low" on a pitch near the bottom of his vocal range, emphasizing the literal meaning of the lyric.

In 1773 Stafford Smith won the canon prize for *O Remember* and the catch prize for *On Sally Salisbury.* Over the next four years, he would win five more times, including four times for glees—the most sophisticated category. Each prize medal was minted from ten guineas' worth of gold, enough money to sustain a middle-class lifestyle for several months. Thus, by recruiting Stafford Smith as both performer and composer, the Anacreontic Society gained access to one of the city's most successful and ambitious young musicians. While the Anacreontics did not award prizes, *The Anacreontic Song* was a winner—it would be among the era's most popular songs and certainly its most enduring.

The Anacreontic Song

In six verses, *The Anacreontic Song* tells the imaginary tale of the club's founding in the guise of classical mythology. It describes the poet Anacreon's patronage, the jealousy of the god Jove, the defense of the club by Apollo and Momus, and finally Jove's blessing of its future success. The song's artful synthesis of words and music both describes and enacts the club's dual mission of providing musical and social delight. Stafford Smith's music is shaped by its content—story, text, and social function. The music aspires both to artistry and to optimism. It is intentionally difficult to sing, an appropriately impressive showpiece for the club's musical ambitions. It is buoyant, athletic, brash, and carefree. The lyric flows smoothly in even, rapid-fire rhythms, as the dotted militaristic rhythms of *The Star-Spangled Banner* we know today had yet to appear. The same music accompanies each verse. It is neither a canon, nor a catch, nor a glee, but combines aspects of each in its repetition, humor, and sophistication. Stylistically, Stafford Smith's music looks back rather than forward, evoking something akin to a strophic folk song and thus suggesting that the club's origins lie in a timeless legendary past.

Tomlinson's words do not mirror Anacreon's poetic models, instead they seem characteristically English. Their eight-line stanzas and rolling triple meter (technically, anapestic tetrameter) are typical, but their rhyme scheme—with a distinctive added internal rhyme in line five—appears unique. The form's wordy patter is especially effective for storytelling, an advantage Tomlinson used to narrate his elaborate, pseudo-classical saga.

The first verse calls on Anacreon to serve as the club's patron saint. The ancient poet responds affirmatively, lending his name and inspiration to the "sons of harmony" and instructing them to "intwine [sic] the myrtle of Venus and Bacchus's vine"—that is, to combine sociality and conviviality. The lyric also offers insight into the club's unique artistic interests. The poet's blessing invokes "voice, fiddle, and flute," a combination of vocal and instrumental music that distinguishes the Anacreontics both from the Catch Club's exclusive focus on singing and from London's other purely instrumental concert societies.

In verse two, "old Thunder"—the king of the gods, known as Jupiter or Jove in Roman mythology—has heard of Anacreon's endorsement and worries that the club's infectious revelries will seduce and distract the gods themselves. Already the club members are off to Rowley's, a London coffeehouse, to begin their celebration of music and mirth.

1. To ANACREON in Heav'n, where he sat in full glee,
    A few sons of harmony sent a Petition,
    That he their inspirer and patron would be;
    When this answer arriv'd from the jolly old Grecian—
        Voice, Fiddle, and Flute,
        No longer be mute;
    I'll lend ye my Name and inspire ye to boot:
    And, besides, I'll instruct ye like me, to intwine
    The myrtle of Venus with Bacchus's vine.

2. The news through Olympus immediately flew;
    When old Thunder pretended to give himself airs—
    If these mortals are suffer'd their scheme to pursue,
    The devil a goddess will stay above stairs.
        Hark! already they cry,
        In transports of joy,
    A fig for Parnassus! to Rowley's we'll fly
    And there, my good fellows, we'll learn to intwine
    The myrtle of Venus with Bacchus's vine.

3. The yellow-hair'd god, and his nine fusty maids,
   To the hill of old Lud will incontinent flee,
   Idalia will boast but of tenantless shades,
   And the biforked hill a mere desart [sic] will be
   My thunder, no fear on't,
   Shall soon do its errand,
   And, dam'me! I'll swinge the ringleaders, I warrant.
   I'll trim the young dogs, for thus daring to twine
   The myrtle of Venus with Bacchus's vine.

4. Apollo rose up; and said, Pr'ythee ne'er quarrel,
   Good King of the Gods, with my vot'ries below:
   Your thunder is useless—then, shewing his laurel,
   Cry'd, "Sic evitabile fulmen, you know!
   Then over each head
   My Laurels I'll spread;
   So my sons from your crackers no mischief shall dread,
   Whilst snug in their club-room, they jovially twine
   The myrtle of Venus with Bacchus's vine.

5. Next Momus got up, with his risible phiz,
   And swore with Apollo he'd cheerfully join—
   The full tide of harmony still shall be his,
   But the song, and the catch, & the laugh shall be mine:
   Then, Jove, be not jealous
   Of these honest fellows.
   Cry'd Jove, We relent, since the truth you now tell us;
   And swear, by Old Styx, that they long shall intwine
   The myrtle of Venus with Bacchus's vine.

6. Ye sons of Anacreon, then, join hand in hand;
   Preserve unanimity, friendship, and love!

'Tis your's to support what's so happily plann'd;
You've the sanction of gods, and the fiat of Jove.
    While thus we agree,
    Our toast let it be.
May our club flourish happy, united, and free!
And long may the sons of Anacreon intwine
The myrtle of Venus with Bacchus's vine.

Original version of the lyric to The Anacreontic Song (c. 1773).

Jove's anxieties continue in verse three as he imagines that the sun god, "yellow-hair'd" Apollo, along with his nine muses that inspire all creativity, will abandon their sacred duties to join the clubmen on London's Ludgate Hill. The home of the goddess Venus—Idalia—may similarly become a vacant land of loveless spirits. Finally, he fears that the "biforked hill" of Mount Olympus itself will be abandoned. To prevent such catastrophes, Jove vows to storm the club, sending his bolts of lightning to disperse its soirée. He will execute its leaders, promising to "swinge" them in a hangman's noose.

Apollo, the god of music, rises to the club's defense in verse four. He sanctions the Anacreontics as his artful worshippers and vows to shield them from Jove's "crackers" with a canopy of evergreen laurels, representing both his praise and protection. In verse five, Momus, the spirit of criticism and the personification of satire and mockery, likewise endorses the club. He proclaims the society above reproach, granting to Apollo the beauty of their harmony while claiming their humor for himself. Jove relents and swears his unbreakable oath on the underworld's River Styx that the club shall thrive.

The final verse is set in the present. It calls upon the society's members to join hands in unity, friendship, and love. They vow to support the club's musical alloy of camaraderie and fellowship in the service of joy, community, and freedom. As in each prior verse, the final two lines are repeated by the members as a chorus in four-part harmony, both empha-

A late eighteenth-century illustration of the Anacreontic lyric. A smiling Momus (center) presents "The Humble Petition of the Members of the Anacreontic" to Jove (second from left, holding a lightning bolt) with Juno. Behind Momus, Apollo, wearing a crown of laurel and holding a lyre, flirts with a warrior goddess, possibly Minerva. A book of music lies on the clouds. At the far left, the messenger god Mercury (the patron of poetry) holds his caduceus and looks toward Venus, accompanied by a cupid figure in the foreground. The sons of Anacreon observe the scene from behind. A cherub flies above and holds a parchment that reads "Anacreontic Society." Neither Bacchus nor Anacreon is depicted.

sizing their musical skill and reiterating their patron's proviso to combine music and mirth. This repeating tagline, invoking Venus and Bacchus, underscores the club's purpose of fun and friendship. It has also misled some commentators who imagine orgiastic meetings of sexual indulgence marinated in alcohol.

Certainly, the eighteenth-century English social club scene was well lubricated by wine and other spirits. The London coffeehouse indeed served coffee, but it was better known for its Dorchester beer, Welsh ale, and a signature punch made from three different recipes, with arrack spirits, Jamaica rum, or French brandy. Although both boiling and fermenting made water safe to drink in this era, drinking coffee or tea was likely frowned upon at Anacreontic gatherings. Catch Club members who drank coffee or tea were asked to remove themselves and their "unnatural mixtures" to a distant table to avoid offending their compatriots. The reference to Venus here is also potentially confusing: it is less sexual than social. While some London clubs admitted women or were even for women solely, Anacreontic Society events were for the "sons of Anacreon." While the women's gallery may have created enticing erotic tensions for some, there's little evidence that women interacted with male members during society meetings, and thus lustful heterosexual pursuit, at least, was not on the agenda.

Through club life, elite men forged a network of economic and political allies; wine may have nurtured joviality and counteracted performance anxieties, but the expression of their friendship was to make music together. That the sheet music imprint of *The Anacreontic Song* identifies their meeting place as a "tavern" undoubtedly fueled the song's twentieth-century reputation as a drinking song. But the Crown and Anchor was not a stereotypical English pub. It was an upscale restaurant and event space with a "great room" that could host an orchestral concert attended by hundreds of listeners. The highest quality of music making was all but a feature of the Crown and Anchor. Its concert room had long hosted London's Academy of Ancient Music, from its founding in 1726 until 1784. Other music clubs that called the "tavern" home included the Madrigal Society, the Glee Club, the Abbey Glee Club, and the Society of Musicians. Known today as "The Proms," an early version of London's annual Promenade Concerts took place there in the 1730s and '40s.

Verse six of the lyric does offer a toast to the club's prosperity. Clubmen may well have dropped their joined hands to raise a glass to the society's future—punctuating a musical ritual of social bonding with alcohol. In this sense, the song can be seen as a drinking song. But the purpose of the song was to facilitate unity and devotion. "It's a club song, not a pub song," explained the American baritone Thomas Hampson. The verse charges members with the responsibility to support and perpetuate the club and to preserve the unity ritualized in the linking of hands across the membership. The toast is thus less an excuse to imbibe than a celebratory promise.

Stafford Smith's setting is strophic—that is, the same music accompanies each verse. A through-composed glee would have been more fashionable in London and more typical of the composer's style, but it would have been less effective as an anthem. Four melodic gestures carry the tune through four pairs of lines within the eight-line form of each verse. While its first two phrases use a single repeated melody, the third reaches dramatically into the vocalist's upper range. These high notes deliver immediate intensity to the indented lines of Tomlinson's text. The final phrase offers a strong concluding statement. Overall, the melody traverses an emotional arc that moves through repeated struggle, then climax, and finally to resolution. This narrative structure supports the storytelling trajectory of each verse with a triumphant dramatic shape. Both text and music demand a brisk, up-tempo rendition that celebrates the Anacreontic Society as a whole, while giving its members a boost of energy to launch the final portion of their meetings, a session of song that might last two hours or more.

The Anacreontic Society's role as a bridge between private and public music making is signaled by frequent reviews of the club's meetings in daily newspapers, such as London's *Gazetteer, Public Advertiser,* and *Times.* These commentaries might include a list of the works played in the instrumental concert or mentions of particularly effective or poor performances. Reports about renditions of the club's anthem either praise the performer who brought the song to life or critique a disrespectful or too comic rendition. Such reviews reveal three things: first, that the song was so well known among the public as to merit regular attention in the press; second, that a dramatized performance tradition of *The Anacreontic Song* existed in which the performer did not just sing but acted out the lyric; and finally, that there was a fundamental tension within the club between those who desired a decorous, organized, and music-focused evening and those for whom fun should prevail over artistry.

On November 16, 1787, for example, a *Times* reviewer praised the bass Thomas Sedgwick, with qualification:

> When the company returned from supper, Mr. Sedgwick sung the Anacreontic song. He sung it well; but (and that is an unlucky word) we would, with due deference, advise him to stick close to his author, and not attempt to excite an impulse which was never intended.

In this instance, one of the professionals who most frequently performed the club's anthem acted out the text in ways that overshadowed his singing. This reviewer attended Anacreontic meetings with music foremost in mind. A similar music-focused review of October 1788 praised the evening as "the most respectable we ever remember, . . . conducted with great order and good management."

Sedgwick's performances, celebrated in other reviews, made use of the virtuosic opportunities provided by Stafford Smith's musical setting— some of the same musical challenges that bedevil singers of *The Star-Spangled Banner* today. However, the melody was written not for the entire membership to sing but rather as a showpiece for a single professional singer to display the club's artistic accomplishments through individual talent and skill. The song's difficulty was thus among its virtues, not a flaw. It was composed to enable the exceptional singer to impress. Its wide melodic range from lowest to highest pitches highlighted the soloist's vocal talent and training, while its six verses required heroic endurance. Smith's setting is thus designed expressly for a skilled soloist. It was never intended for thousands of fans gathered at an American stadium.

That Stafford Smith's song became popular outside the club's meetings is due primarily to the society's professional singer-actors. A dramatized rendition of the club anthem could be featured as a stage encore or as part of a skit in London's commercial theaters. The actor Charles Bannister (1738–1804) may well have inaugurated such public notoriety as a feature of his benefit concerts. In the seventeenth and eighteenth centuries, prominent performers throughout Europe typically staged benefits to raise funds for their personal support. Anacreontic Society connections provided useful access to wealthy supporters who had the means to patronize such benefits. The first public notice of *The Anacreontic Song* in the London *Times* appears in the first year of the paper's existence—in an advertisement for an April 1785 benefit at the Theatre-Royal in the Covent Garden district. That it is mentioned in an advertisement at all reveals that the song was already a public attraction. For this event, Charles Bannister sang the "celebrated Anacreontic Song" in support of his son John Bannister (1760–1836), an actor whose career would eventually eclipse that of his father. The club anthem was presented as part of a "musical prelude" titled *The Sons of Anacreon,* in effect a dramatization of an Anacreontic Society meeting.

Such benefit performances continued on a seemingly annual basis and always featured *The Anacreontic Song.* Especially if acted to a comic extreme, the song was apparently a sensational delight that offered an intriguing window into the lifestyle of the city's elites. In 1788 the Royalty Theatre featured "A Musical Entertainment, called SOCIAL HARMONY, Or, the Sons of Anacreon," featuring "by particular desire, for this Night only, The Anacreontic Song, . . . By Mr. Sedgwick." Even after the Anacreontic Society disbanded in 1793, the song continued to draw crowds. A 1798 advertisement announced a benefit at the Theatre-Royal for two other prominent singer-actors who had been honorary members—William Barrymore and the previously mentioned Thomas Sedgwick. The program featured a drama entitled "The Anacreontic Society Revived," with Sedgwick in the role of club president performing the society's "celebrated song." Thus, a nostalgic reenactment became a variety show vehicle, featuring a succession of popular tunes to help leading performers and raise money for their support.* *The Anacreontic Song* became wildly popular as a result.

---

* Such dramatizations would be repeated in the United States, introducing *The Anacreontic Song* to American audiences; see Chapter 3.

The Revolutionary Politics of a Club Song

London's eighteenth-century social clubs responded to and accelerated a social transformation—from monarchy to democracy—that would take place over some three centuries in Britain. Whereas in the seventeenth century, social life centered on the royal court, by the nineteenth century the public sphere dominated cultural and political activity. While commoners and tradesmen participated in social clubs, the Sons of Anacreon did not necessarily embrace all social classes. Members were drawn from the comfortable financial class. Yet Anacreontic meetings were also structured in ways to enable broader participation, especially in comparison to more exclusive clubs. While Catch Club meetings began in the late afternoon, Anacreontic meetings began in the evening, after a professional, merchant, banker, or tradesmen could have completed a day's work. Guests and honorary members further expanded the club's social reach.

The founding documents of the Anacreontic Society have yet to resurface, but one rule of club harmony is clear: no politics. A *Times* account of 1788 attacks the actor Charles Dignum, who had "put the whole [meeting] into confusion" by singing a parody of the song the "*Plough Boy,* charging a late Chief Justice with the murder of Nuncomar." A "general hiss followed" from the politically "mixt company," and the "member was called on to give his reasons for taking a liberty contrary to the general rule of the Anacreontic Society." The quick intervention of the president, who called a glee, "restored harmony to the Sons of Anacreon" and navigated the company through the violation of etiquette.

Dignum's song seems to have referred to the first judicial hanging in India under British rule in 1775, but the controversy was apparently still sufficiently bitter as to strike a false chord thirteen years later. This moment of political division, however, underscores the club's unified nationalism as revealed by a song that did not engender controversy. The sheet music imprint of *On the Death of General Wolfe* celebrates Sedgwick's performance of the song at the Anacreontic Society. The text glorifies the patriotic sacrifice of James Wolfe, the British general who died from wounds at the Battle of Quebec in 1759. This brief but pivotal skirmish with the French helped decide the French and Indian War and secured Canada for the British. Overt nationalism was thus not considered divisive among the Sons of Anacreon.

Anacreontic members were far from revolutionaries yet shared a new spirit of self-determination. Tomlinson's lyric can thus be viewed as an allegory of British politics. Club members incite and overcome the wrath of Jupiter—the king of the gods and, by analogy, the king of England. Apollo and other gods may represent the club's noble members who offer legitimacy and protection to its proceedings, while the club's activities are celebrated for their artistry (by Apollo) or dismissed as inoffensive humor and innocent play (by Momus). But such social play is never innocent. The network of interpersonal alliances created by the club stood outside the king's purview and was in this sense subversive.

Such social stagecraft also helps explain a subtle shift in Tomlinson's lyric. While it invokes a Greek patron (the poet Anacreon) and a specifically Greek mythological setting (Mount Olympus and the River Styx), the gods who animate the story are referred to by their Roman names—Venus, not Aphrodite; Bacchus, not Dionysus; Jove, not Zeus. Apollo's name had no specifically Roman version, but the god shouts down Jove in Latin (not Greek), crying out "*Sic evitabile fulmen*" (lightning is avoidable). Such Roman references over Greek are politically significant.

In eighteenth-century Enlightenment Europe, political theory was dominated by the ideals of the Roman Republic. This adoration of Rome was, however, inherently unstable. It celebrated an era of state military power and an emperor's benevolent rule, while introducing notions of public power. A republic was incongruent with monarchy, the form of heritable divine authority that dominated France and England during this period. Tomlinson's text similarly rises out of this Enlightenment milieu. Its Roman gods are recast as symbols of heroic character and individuality.

Venus represents passion, sociality, and prosperity; Bacchus, born of a mortal mother, is something of an outsider in the Olympian pantheon. He is the god of wine and of wild abandon, who challenges authority. The personification of satire and mockery, Momus—more a literary figure than a mythological one—offers a similar check to power. Tomlinson represents him as a symbol of mirth, yet in Enlightenment thought, he was seen as a source of satire. The Dutch humanist Erasmus even saw Momus as a champion of criticizing authority.

Humor seemingly defuses social tension in *The Anacreontic Song* with a toast and a laugh. The club's rule was to avoid politics, yet its very existence spoke to the dawn of a new political age that would disrupt not only the monarchy but eventually the British Empire. That *The Anacreontic Song* would cross the Atlantic to fuel the early political passions of Americans is thus not surprising. The new and old worlds shared this same cultural heritage, and Anacreon was known in the colonies as well as in England. The *Virginia Gazette* published Anacreon's ode "On Women," celebrating beauty, in 1770, while the *Independent Gazetteer* in Philadelphia printed "On the Rose" in 1787. The first American Anacreontic parody sung to Stafford Smith's melody seems to have been a lyric by Francis Hopkinson, a signer of the Declaration of Independence, who in 1790 penned three alternative verses in the Anacreontic vein using its distinct rhyme scheme to create a drinking song variant, now with Bacchus as the disruptive hero fighting off the jealousies of the gods Apollo and Neptune. It remained unpublished until 1951.

A small step further enables American colonists to see the celebration of Republican Rome in *The Anacreontic Song* as a cause for revolution. As the historian Gordon S. Wood notes, "The late eighteenth century in the Atlantic world might be better called 'the age of the republican revolution.' For it was republicanism and republican principles, not democracy, that brought down the ancient monarchies." The model for these political shifts was republican Rome. The eighteenth-century fascination with antiquity—reinforced and celebrated by works of art including *The Anacreontic Song*—helped build a foundation for revolutionary political change. It is thus not surprising that the final verse of the club's anthem

The Bicentennial Monument to John Stafford Smith in Gloucester
Cathedral, 100 miles west of London, England (pictured 2016).

concludes with the hopeful proclamation "may our Club flourish happy,
united, and free!" Such values echo the unalienable rights of the American revolutionaries—"Life, Liberty, and the pursuit of Happiness." Written just before America's Declaration of Independence, the lyric resonated
and was reprinted in full in the United States.

John Stafford Smith died on September 21, 1836, and was buried at the parish church of St. Luke, Chelsea, an Anglican church in London consecrated in 1824. The church still stands today, but its surrounding cemetery has been converted into a city park and school playground bustling with children. Stafford Smith's grave is lost, his headstone possibly among the fencelike rows of all-but-anonymous monuments worn smooth by the elements and relocated in an arch surrounding the chapel. No marker recognizes his final resting place.

He is not forgotten, however, at Gloucester Cathedral, where two flags—the Union Jack and the Star-Spangled Banner—fly above a plaque that honors the contributions of the city's native son. Here the composer's achievements are recontextualized for the twentieth century. Great Britain and the United States of America are again united—as allies in wars that saw the restoration of British pride and the rise of its former colony as a world power. The plaque reads:

> In memory of John Stafford Smith 1750–1836 who was born in this city son of Martin Smith organist of the Cathedral 1743–1782, was a composer of distinction, a well-known musical antiquary, and organist of the Chapel Royal London. He will long be remembered as composer of the tune of the National Anthem of the United States of America.

The paired flags were added in 1977, in celebration of the bicentennial of the United States, by the Rotary Clubs of Gloucester and New York City. They represent a rare moment when patriotic sentiment expresses not national pride but international friendship. In ways both large and small, the club anthem created by Ralph Tomlinson and John Stafford Smith more than fulfilled its promise—it not only helped build a new nation, but it also joined two nations hand in hand.

Chapter 3

Banner Ballads

The Many Lyrics of *The Star-Spangled Banner*

One good song is worth a dozen addresses or proclamations.

—*Joel Barlow (1780)*

When the Warrior Returns
February 16, 1804, Tripoli Harbor

On February 16, 1804, a squad of U.S. Navy volunteers under the command of Stephen Decatur, Jr., set sail in the aptly named *Intrepid*. They were on a remarkable mission—to retake the captured frigate *USS Philadelphia*, held by enemy hands. The *Philadelphia* and its sixteen thirty-two-pound cannons had been an intimidating enforcer of the U.S. blockade of Tripoli's port during the Tripolitan War (1801–5), America's first declared military conflict. In pursuit of an enemy runner some four months earlier, the *Philadelphia* had been lured onto an uncharted reef and run aground. Desperate efforts to free her had failed, and she was soon captured and her crew imprisoned. It was a bitter embarrassment to the U.S. Navy and American honor. Commodore Edward Preble promised to rescue the ship or burn it.

Sailing slowly into Tripoli Harbor under the dim light of a crescent moon, the *Intrepid* was in actuality the captured Tripolitan ketch *Mastico* in disguise. The American ship was pretending to be a British merchantman, heavily laden with cargo, that had lost her anchors in a recent storm. As night fell, the *Intrepid* arrived within hailing distance of the *Philadelphia*. An armed boarding party hid below decks, while a small crew—disguised as Maltese sailors and including five Sicilian volunteers who spoke Arabic—remained on deck. They requested permission to tie up to the *Philadelphia* for the night. Permission was granted, but something gave the ruse away. An enemy guard suddenly yelled, *"Americanos!"*

With swords ablaze, the Americans leaped aboard the captured *Philadelphia* and quickly overwhelmed the Tripolitans. Twenty corsairs were killed, while the rest jumped overboard. Only one American was wounded. Finding the ship disabled and knowing they would soon be under attack from the port's guns, the Americans set the *Philadelphia* ablaze. She soon lit up the night sky, broke free of her moorings, and exploded on the beach. Her destruction was a symbolic blow to Tripoli. For the Americans, the ship had been lost, but the daring raid had created something new and unexpected: the nation's earliest naval heroes, most notably, the soon-to-be-promoted-to-captain Stephen Decatur, Jr.

In late 1805, Decatur, along with Charles Stewart and other officers, returned to the U.S. capital. Georgetown citizens reserved McLaughlin's Tavern to host a dinner in their honor. The festivities began at four p.m. on December 6, with General John Thomson Mason presiding. As was the custom in Federal America, more than two dozen toasts were offered. The first was to "Our Country—may it remain the residence of Liberty, of Hospitality, and of Patriotism." Toasts to the president, to Congress, and to the secretary of the navy followed. A glass raised to Commodore Preble served as the signal for a new song. Its five verses had been written specifically for the occasion and were sung "in superior stile" to the novel accompaniment of two clarinets. The lyric celebrated the navy's newest heroes:

1. When the Warrior returns from the battle afar
   To the Home and the Country he nobly defended,
   Oh! warm be the welcome to gladden his ear,
   And loud be the joy that his perils are ended!
   In the full tide of song, let his fame roll along

To the feast-flowing board let us gratefully throng.
Where mixt with the olive the laurel shall wave,
And form a bright wreath for the brow of the brave.

Following the lead of the solo singer, the whole company joined to repeat the chorus:

Where mixt with the olive the laurel shall wave,
And form a bright wreath for the brow of the brave.

Among these choristers was the lyric's author, Francis Scott Key, who had just moved to the capital in hopes of establishing a legal practice at the heart of the still-new federal government. The song thus not only praised the dinner's heroic guests but introduced the young lawyer to his future clients as an eloquent patriot.

Key composed *When the Warrior Returns* using the era's standard technique of fitting new words to an already popular melody—in this case, *Anacreon in Heaven*. Despite its English origins, Key would have known the tune as the propulsive musical vehicle of rousing Fourth of July songs and other specifically American lyrics. He would use the same melody almost nine years later to compose *The Star-Spangled Banner*.

2. COLUMBIANS! a band of your brothers behold!
    Who claim their reward of thy hearts' warm emotion,
    When your cause, when thy honor urg'd onward the bold,
    In vain frown'd the desert—in vain rag'd the ocean.
    To a far distant shore—to the battle's wild roar,
    They rush'd, thy fair fame and thy rights to secure,
    Then, mixt with the olive, the laurel shall wave,
    And form a bright wreath for the brow of the brave.

3. In the conflict resistless, each toil they endur'd
    Till their foes fled dismay'd from the war's desolation;

And pale beam'd the Crescent, its splendor obscur'd
By the light of *the star-spangled flag* of our nation,
   Where each flaming star gleam'd a meteor of war,
   And the turban'd heads bow'd to the terrible glare,
     Then mixt with the olive the laurel shall wave,
     And form a bright wreath for the brow of the brave.

4. Our fathers, who stand on the summit of fame,
   Shall exultingly hear, of their sons, the proud story,
   How their young bosoms glow'd with the patriot flame,
   How they fought, how they fell, in the blaze of their glory,
     How triumphant they rode o'er the wandering flood,
     And stain'd the blue waters with infidel blood;
     How mixt with the olive the laurel did wave,
     And form a bright wreath for the brows of the brave.

5. Then welcome the warrior return'd from afar,
   To the home and the country he so nobly defended,
   Let the thanks due to valor now gladden his ear,
   And loud be the joy that his perils are ended;
     In the full tide of song, let his fame roll along,
     To the feast-flowing board let us gratefully throng,
     Where mixt with the olive the laurel shall wave,
     And form a bright wreath for the brow of the brave.

The remaining verses of Francis Scott Key's *When the Warrior Returns* (1805).

Words had long been Key's gift and power. His schoolboy poetry had won him Polly as his wife, his courtroom orations could sway a jury, and his lyrics could inspire a crowd. *When the Warrior Returns* was an immediate success, especially impressive as it was his first known effort in song. No fewer than fifteen newspapers from Maine to Charleston reprinted his verses. More remarkably, these papers included both Federalist and Dem-ocratic-Republican imprints.

Key's song asserted Federalist priorities—a strong navy and the strong central government necessary to support it—but his lyrical style did not rely on partisan bluster. Rather than shout, Key offered a series of evoc-ative patriotic vignettes. His approach was literary rather than topical. He did not include the names of the honorees, for example, but spoke in abstractions inspired by their deeds. "It is a native production," wrote one editor praising the lyric, "which the pride of a Philenia or Menander would not blush to own." The *New-York Evening Post* cheered Key's song as one that "would not discredit the pen of a Payne," referring to Robert Treat Paine, Jr., then America's leading poet for occasional song and ded-icatory odes.

When the Warrior Returns tells us something about Key, about the tune, and about the era's fascination with political song. It affirms that Key knew the Anacreontic melody well before writing *The Star-Spangled Banner.* It shows that he associated the tune with American military heroism. It also proves that Key wrote song lyrics to a specific melody and not a poem. Among the most egregious myths told about *The Star-Spangled Banner* is the oft-repeated tale that someone other than Key matched text to tune. Some credit Joseph Nicholson with the insight and claim that he directed the lyric's first imprint to indicate "Tune: Ana-creon in Heaven."

Another legend credits the pairing to the actor and musician Ferdinand Durang, who was stationed with a militia near Baltimore not long after Key's lyric was written. Some fifty-seven years after the events described, a militia mate told the widely read *Harper's Magazine* that Durang, having been given a barely legible handwritten copy of Key's text, rifled through a "volume of flute music" and "whistled snatches of tune after tune," exclaiming "Boys, I've hit it" when he discovered *Anacreon in Heaven.* This story could well be true, but it implies a falsehood. Durang did not "discover" a tune that fit Key's words, as the story suggests; rather, he sim-ply located the sheet music to the melody around which Key had built the lyric from its inception. With the sheet music at hand, Durang was able to perform it.

It would be difficult to overemphasize just how typical it was, in Key's era, to compose new lyrics to popular tunes. Thousands of such lyrics were published in daily newspapers, as single song sheets, and in book collections known as songsters. These were the viral memes, tweets, and TikToks of early America. Today we think of songs differently. Since its invention in 1877, audio recording has carried songs from place to place in complete and unique performances. In Key's day, however, recording did not exist. Songs could be shared as sheet music, but engraving music notation required expensive, skilled, and time-consuming labor. In contrast, movable type to print just their words was cheap and ubiquitous.

So in Federal America, songs traveled as printed sets of lyrics, sung to a limited repertory of a few dozen well-known tunes. For political songs, the melodies of *Anacreon in Heaven* and *Yankee Doodle* were the musical vehicles most commonly used. In fact, more than 130 sets of American lyrics had been written to the tune of *Anacreon* before Key created the only one that is still remembered. Thus, when Key asked "O say can you see?," he was not starting a conversation or political debate, but joining one that had begun some three decades earlier.

When a new song lyric was printed, its melody was often, but not always, explicitly identified. If the tune's name was absent, part of the reader's delight in it was to puzzle out which melody matched its rhythm and rhyme. Anacreontic lyrics were particularly distinctive. Their wordy stanzas allowed for detailed commentary, while their literary sheen tended toward more serious, even flamboyant poetry. In contrast, the short pithy lines of *Yankee Doodle* tended toward biting humor, insults, and mockery. Both tunes were upbeat. Their brisk tempos energized an audience, while compressing their message into a brief, more practical time frame. As a result, patriotic lyricists might contribute seven, nine, eleven, or even fourteen stanzas for a partisan dinner or Fourth of July celebration. The repeating choruses of both songs urged the audience to participate, recruiting enthusiasm and consolidating support.

Broadside lyrics were necessarily composed to a literary model. A template was especially helpful in writing lyrics based on *The Anacreontic Song*, as its tricky poetic conventions feature a distinctive internal rhyme that frustrated more than one of the era's poets. One did not accidentally write a poem fulfilling the eccentricities of the Anacreontic form with its eight-line, nine-rhyme, triple-meter stanzas. Known technically as anapestic tetrameter, its four sets of one stressed and two unstressed syllables populating each of eight lines was common enough in English verse. The extra rhyme, however, was unique. The fifth line of each stanza is divided into two rhyming halves, such that the end rhymes of lines five and six are complemented by an additional internal rhyme. Not all lyricists recognized this distinctive quirk, but it is characteristic of the form. Key, for example, always honored this detail. In *The Star-Spangled Banner*, the triple rhyme is heard in verse one as the lyric "And the rockets' red *glare*, the bombs bursting in *air*, / Gave proof through the night that our flag was still *there.*" In *Warrior Returns*, Key's triple rhymes are often oblique or slanted—that is, their sounds are similar rather than identical—but nevertheless they follow the Anacreontic form—too closely, in fact, for their author to have created them without direct knowledge of the original lyric or one of its close derivatives.

The Anacreontic model most likely known to Key was *Adams and Liberty* (1798). It was by far the most popular and frequently printed Anacreontic broadside in the United States prior to *The Star-Spangled Banner*. It boasted no fewer than six different sheet music editions. Any of them would have provided the necessary material for Key's realization of *Warrior Returns* at the Georgetown dinner, both the lyrical model and the musical notation needed for its accompanying clarinets. Another intriguing potential source is *The Baltimore Musical Miscellany*, a two-volume set published in 1804–5. Its namesake city was only about forty miles from Key's Georgetown home, and Key visited frequently on business. The book included both the original lyric of *The Anacreontic Song* and the melody's musical notation. It also contained three additional sets of lyrics written to the tune: *Adams and Liberty*, the jovial English parody *New Bibo*, and the first American printing of a rare lyric first published in Edinburgh in 1792. Titled *The Social Club*, this lyric includes the signal adjectival phrase "star-spangled" that Key would later make famous, coining its use in reference to the U.S. flag.

In *Warrior Returns*, Key used flag imagery to represent each combatant. Instead of bombs bursting in air, Key imagined each "flaming star" of America's ensign as a "meteor of war" (that is, as a cannonball). He further invoked themes—home (verse one) and just cause (verse two)—as well as specific words that he would use again nine years later: "band," "war's desolation," "home and country," "blood," "perils," and "glare." Most tellingly, Key featured the same rhyme ("wave" and "brave") for the concluding chorus of both songs. The likely explanation for these many similarities is that in 1814, when Key composed *The Star-Spangled Banner* while at anchor in the Patapsco River, he recalled his own *When the Warrior Returns* as his model.

The Anacreontic Song Comes to America
January 9, 1793, Philadelphia

The Anacreontic Song was introduced to the United States by a procession of English singer-actors affiliated with the Old American Company (1752–1805), one of the first professional theater troupes in America. Today's equivalent would be a set of touring Broadway musical theater performers. As early as January 9, 1793, in Philadelphia's Southwark Theatre, the song was performed as the grand finale to a variety set of solo and part songs described as "a catch club" and dramatized under the title *Liberty Hall! or, the Anacreontic Society*. The skit offered a comic parody of elite English life. Singing the solo that evening was a singer-actor identified, as was typical of the era, as only "Mr. Chambers." The whole company returned to the stage for the finale in the role of Anacreontic Society members, singing along for the concluding chorus of each verse. Several in the cast that evening would play ongoing parts in spreading the vivacious new melody up and down the eastern seaboard.

Chambers might well have learned both song and skit in London, where he had appeared at the Royalty Theatre in 1787 and 1788 and at the more illustrious Haymarket in 1789. The Anacreontic Society was then approaching the height of its popularity, and both the song and a similar skit were performed in London. The American premiere that evening in Philadelphia, however, was a one-time affair, a benefit for two other actors recently arrived from England—Mr. West and Mr. Prigmore. Contracted actors typically would be guaranteed at least one such benefit each year from which they would receive all ticket revenue as bonus pay.

When the Old American Company appeared in New York five months later, it again presented a song set, but now under the title *The Catch Club.* This time the benefit was specifically for Mr. West, who sang the solo for *The Anacreontic Song.* As before, the company presented the song as the finale of a boozy comedy performed by an all-male cast singing a mixture of songs—sentimental, comic, and convivial. This repertory included the lament for lost love *From Night to Morn I Take My Glass,* the humorous catches *'Twas You Sir* (that kiss'd the pretty girl) and *Here Lies Poor Tommy Day,* the rousing trio *Here's a Health to All Good Lasses,* and the hedonist anthem *With My Jug in One Hand and My Pipe in the Other.* That *The Anacreontic Song* was introduced to America as part of a drunken theatrical farce may be responsible for its reputation as a drinking song.

Transforming an Anacreontic meeting into a comic skit not only made for good entertainment, it was a pragmatic recital vehicle for professional performers. By any name, the spoof was a variety show of solo and part songs. The skit's specific repertory was flexible, and thus it could feature the signature songs of any participating actor. It needed minimal rehearsal and could include any number of performers. Its overall length also could be adjusted to create a full evening's entertainment or to offer just a short interlude. Finally, *The Anacreontic Song* served as a rousing theatrical climax. It brought the whole company back on stage for a gala number and bow. Just as important, it brought the audience to its feet, invited them to sing along, and created a joyful finale that left patrons hungry for more.

The Fount.

For the COLUMBIAN CENTINEL.

MR. RUSSELL,

S'IL vou plait, you may amuse your poetico-politico readers with the following. The elegance of the *original* all acknowledge ; and though the *Parody* may fail in that quality, it excels it in being TRUE. 'Tis *true*, 'tis a pity ; and pity if it 'tis true.   CANTAB.

Parody :

Of the excellent Song, "TO ANACREON IN HEA-VEN."

TO G***T in *New-York*, where he reigns in full glee,
Some *Anti*'s have lately prefer'd their petition,
That he their *Inspirer* and *Champion* would be ;
When this answer arriv'd from this Chief of Sedition.
   Of JAY, WILCOCKS, and KING,
     Let us make the world ring,
I'll lend you my PASCAL, (so fit for the string,)
And besides I'll instruct you how you may convey,
All COLUMBIA's *Glory* and *Freedom* away.

The news through *Columbia* immediately flew,
PACIFICUS rose, and thus vented his cares :
" If these traitors are suffer'd their schemes to pursue,
" Like *France* we shall soon be a nation of bears :
   " Hark ! already they cry,
     " In transports of joy,
" Away to G***T let us instantly fly—
" And this Chief will assist us, that we may convey,
" All COLUMBIA's *Glory* and *Freedom* away.

"*Wealth*, *Commerce* and *Peace*, which each passing gale courts,
" From *America* then, will instantly go,
" Our shores then will boast of but tenantless ports,
" And cities all streaming with bloodshed will flow."
   " But *Congress*, no fear on't,
     " Will soon do their errand,
"And smartly will swinge the proud *Envoy*, I warrant,
" And lash those assassins, who'd wish to convey
" All COLUMBIA's *Glory* and *Freedom* away.

Then FREEDOM rose up, with her cap and her spear,
" And swore, by *Columbia* she ever would stand,
" That her sons should receive not a insult nor sneer,
" While her laws should drive *Anarchy* out of the land :
   "Then while transports resound,
     " And *Discord*'s fast bound,
" And American brows are with laurels hung round,
" We, free and united, our laws will obey—
" And drive from COLUMBIA, the *Faction* away."

" No, (JUSTICE cry'd out) no, your plan you must alter,
" Nor sully your hands with these reptiles so low;
" Leave *Antis* to me, (then producing a halter)
" Cry'd, *sic evitabile restis*, you know ;
   "Then make use of the string,
     " For these *Antis*' shall swing,
"So must all, who disgrace on their country wou'd bring,
" And when they're dispatch'd you triumphant my say,
" *Peace*, *Liberty*, *Laws* and *Good Order*,—huzza !"

Ye COLUMBIANS so faithful then join heart and hand,
Be steadfast, nor fear the dark Jacobin's rod ;
'Tis yours to preserve what your Fathers have plan'd,
You've the sanction of FREEDOM, and fiat of GOD.
   While thus we agree,
     Our toast let it be,
May our country be happy, united and free.—
And long may the sons of COLUMBIA defend—
Her Rulers and Laws, 'till with time they shall end.

A typical early American newspaper ballad—*To Genêt in New-York*. This 1793 lyric mocks the efforts of French ambassador Edmond-Charles Genêt to secure U.S. military aid for France in its war against Britain. His diplomacy ran counter to President George Washington's official policy of neutrality and thus is attacked in this parody song written by a pro-British American lyricist. It is the second known American lyric published to fit the tune of *The Anacreontic Song*. Such lyrics offered commentary on the day's social and political events, using music to add emotion to public debate. Compelling examples went viral and were reprinted from one town newspaper to the next.

This was a winning formula. Such dramatizations in turn fueled the popularity of the melody in America.

Just over a month after its New York City premiere, the melody received its first published American parody—a July 1793 lyric titled *For the Commemoration of the Glorious Fourteenth of July*. The new song celebrated the anniversary of Bastille Day and the French revolutionaries who had stormed the Parisian fortress and political prison in 1789. Its five verses were signed "Julia" and appeared in New York's *Weekly Museum,* the same newspaper that had announced Mr. West's benefit performance six weeks earlier. Surprisingly, the melody's English origin seems not to have discouraged its use for a pro-French song.

American politics of the era were defined by pro-British or pro-French sympathies. Federalists, led by John Adams, favored Britain; Democratic-Republicans, led by Thomas Jefferson, supported France and, by 1793, its ruthless Jacobin faction. In December, Boston's Federalists penned a musical response to "Julia" using the same melody. The lyric, titled *To Genêt in New-York,* borrowed from the English original to mock French ambassador, Edmond-Charles Genêt. The ambassador had earned George Washington's ire by raising military aid for France despite a U.S. policy of neutrality. This song demonstrates that from the outset, each of America's competing political factions claimed the rousing tune as their own. The melody spoke to supporters of both parties.

The following year the Anacreontic Society's club model was itself transplanted to the United States. An evening of "catches and glees" was announced for February 1, 1794, under the auspices of the Charleston Anacreontic Society. This South Carolina club appears to have been the first, but was not the last, American organization to imitate the London original. The most vibrant American offshoot was New York's Columbian Anacreontic Society. Over its eight-year existence beginning in 1795, it became a locus of musical excellence in the city's cultural life, featuring biweekly singings and presenting a popular annual concert.

New York's Anacreontics organized quickly, hosting their first meeting in late February at the city's fashionable Tontine Coffee House and

The singer-actor John Hodgkinson
(1766–1805), pictured in an engraving by Cornelius Tiebout, published
in 1800. A member of the Old
American Company, Hodgkinson
played an active role in populariz-
ing both *The Anacreontic Song* and
its melodic twin *Adams and Liberty*
in Federalist America.

adopting a set of "regulations" two months later. Just two weeks after that,
the "brothers" presented their first concert for "about two hundred and
fifty Ladies and Gentlemen of their acquaintance." The *Daily Advertiser*
remarked, "we do not recollect to have ever witnessed an entertainment
more respectably and genteelly attended; or which passed off with more
harmony and satisfaction." Although billed as "amateurs," the Columbians featured musical professionals, including skilled instrumentalists and
even alumni from the Old American Company. The actor John Hodgkinson, who had played the role for the Old Americans, now served as the
actual president of a real Anacreontic society.

On one level, the Columbians' first public performance simply translated *The Catch Club* drama into an actual club meeting. Composer Benjamin Carr accompanied singers on the keyboard, while other singers had
the backing of a small professional orchestra of violins, wind instruments,
and "a great drum." George Edward Saliment played flute, and the composer and violinist James Hewitt led the ensemble as concertmaster. But

the concert differed significantly both from its London model and from the Old American Company's farcical re-creations. Women were allowed in the audience and were featured on stage. Maybe as a result, the performance embraced a decorous tone, presenting a more auspicious image for the society's organizers—New York's bourgeois, mercantile elite—and their female companions.

The concert balanced entertainment with artistic seriousness. It began with "The Passions," an ode to the kaleidoscopic emotions of music by the English poet William Collins (1721–59). Hodgkinson's recitation was illustrated by the orchestra with music by the English composer Thomas Arne. Hodgkinson then sang an "affectingly delightful" rendition of the soldier's ballad *Tom Tackle*, while as president "his dignified stile in the chair" was reportedly "perfectly characteristic of the honest, cheerful old bard who gives his name to this pleasing society." Hodgkinson's wife, Frances Brett, sang the maiden's lament *My Plaint in No-one Pity Moves*. Other songs included *The Soldier Tired*, a lullaby; *Shakespeare's Madrigal*—likely "Sigh No More Ladies," from *Much Ado about Nothing; Old Thomas Day, Around the High Oak,* and *The Pretty Brunette*. There were no drinking songs and no political songs. A newspaper correspondent praised the evening:

> Not a false chord was struck, nor one harsh note to be heard through all the sublime pieces of music that were selected for the night. A night which offered the richest feast to the heart of every amateur—a night honored by the presence of nearly two hundred of the "fairest of the fair," whose approving smiles gave the highest relish to the entertainment, and formed a grand assemblage, of elegance, innocence, beauty, and harmony, at once so dazzling to the imagination, that words would convey but a faint idea of the divine scene.

Without doubt, the evening's highlight was the closing song. *The Anacreontic Song* was sung solo by Hodgkinson, and as required by Anacreontic ritual, the Columbians echoed the repeating chorus of each verse. For the final verse, all stood and, as directed by the lyric, "joined hand in hand to support unanimity, freedom and love." The same critic waxed rhapsodic at the effect: "Those who had come with intent to remain spectators were involuntarily impelled into the vortex of harmony that enveloped the room—all became daughters and sons of the 'jolly old Grecian'; it was one family, happiness beamed in every countenance." Both song and society had triumphed. Six weeks later Hodgkinson's repeated *The Anacreontic Song* in New York for the ticket-buying public as part of an encore theatrical presentation of *The Catch Club*.

From these beginnings, the Anacreontic melody grew ever more popular in early America. The complete original lyrics of *The Anacreontic Song* were published on the heels of these early performances in collections known as songsters. The first to include the text was *The Syren*, published in 1793 in New York, where the song had been introduced that year. Other printings followed in Philadelphia (1795, 1796, and 1797), Worcester and Wilmington (1797), and Baltimore (1799). More than a dozen additional books published before 1800 contain at least one American parody lyric set to the tune, and many dozens more appeared in the first ten years of the new century. Later Anacreontic societies were formed in Philadelphia, New York, and Baltimore, and the benefit skits, under titles such as *The Catch Club* and *The Sons of Anacreon*, continued for at least twenty more years.

The Political Thunder of *Adams and Liberty*
May 31, 1798, Boston

In early 1798 American patriotism was ascendant, spurred by the young nation's first, although undeclared, military conflict—the so-called Quasi War with France. Many Americans feared a possible French invasion and rallied to the country's defense with nationalist bombast. The poet Thomas Paine, who later changed his name to Robert Treat Paine, Jr., in part to avoid confusion with the more famous revolutionary pamphleteer of *Common Sense* (1776), used the opportunity of writing an anniversary ode for the Massachusetts Charitable Fire Society to create an ardent, if pompous, patriotic song. Written to the Anacreontic tune, *Adams and Liberty* itself caught fire. An overtly Federalist anthem, the song spread rapidly among the party faithful. No fewer than seventeen different newspapers reprinted the lyric within two months of its premiere.

Boston's Fire Society was incorporated in 1794 to provide financial relief to the many who suffered from this characteristic and devastating danger in early American cities. Its constitution required it to host an annual fundraising event. Each year, after a full membership meeting, the society's leaders would sponsor a formal public address, accompanied by music, prayers, poetry, and song, much of it commissioned for the occasion. The goal was to inspire the attendees' charitable generosity. For their first annual meeting, Paine wrote a song titled *Rise, Columbia*. He wrote them another anniversary song in 1796 and was commissioned to compose a song for 1798 as well. Reportedly, he was paid $750 for this third effort. It was an extraordinary sum for the era, akin to $15,000 in 2020 dollars. Even so, this fee represented just the beginning of the poet's financial aspirations for his new musical project.

The explosive popularity of *Adams and Liberty* benefited from an adroit publicity campaign tied to the business efforts of America's nascent publishing industry. Federal copyright protections had been enacted only a few years before, with the Copyright Act of 1790. Authors and publishers could finally hope to turn words into profit. Paine leveraged the Fire Society benefit as a high-profile launch, using newspapers as a marketing tool to spur commercial sales. As newspaper reprintings produced no income, Paine instead issued his song as sheet music. It was a savvy business decision, as printed music sold for premium prices. Six different music publishers in Boston and New York issued editions. New York's featured a portrait of President Adams, making it a patriotic keepsake.

The use of a foreign tune to animate the lyric also offered Paine and his publishers a financial advantage. Early American copyright protection did not extend across international borders, so the lyricist who used the Anacreontic tune not only leveraged its growing popularity but took advantage of a copyright loophole to avoid dividing the song's income with a composer. Had Paine commissioned original music from an American, he would have needed to pay a royalty. Nevertheless, dashes of fresh musical creativity helped popularize Paine's song. Its sheet music arrangement includes an inventive animated bass line and a decorative descant. Unknown to previous editions of *The Anacreontic Song*, these musical infusions added sonic delight to Paine's song that propelled both singer and listener through its rather long text.

Paine likely encountered the Anacreontic melody a year earlier, in Boston's Federal Street Theatre. In 1797 Susanna Rowson, a pioneering author, actress, and future educator, wrote and produced a patriotic evening of music, theater, song, and dance titled *The Birthday; or Rural Fete* in honor of President George Washington's sixty-fifth anniversary. It included a new birthday song written to the tune of *Anacreon* that, mimicking the mythological language of the English original, found Minerva advocating on behalf of the Goddess Columbia to inspire a prophecy of Washington's military and political leadership. Performed in the show by Rowson's more vocally skilled husband, it was immediately reprinted. Paine later bought five copies.

Paine's own song premiered the following year on May 31, 1798, although a newspaper item announcing the title ran five days earlier. "Mr. Thomas Paine has composed a song, called 'Adams and Liberty,'" Boston's *Columbian Centinel* proclaimed, "which we can say, for energy of sentiment, and ardency of patriotism, will stand unrivalled in our language." The paper predicted that once it was published, "it will be sung on every public occasion, where patriotism is the order of the day." Seemingly on cue, another city paper soon announced, "To-morrow morning will be published, . . . and sold at all the Book-stores, The Boston Patriotic Song, called ADAMS and LIBERTY."

On the day of the premiere, Fire Society members processed to Stone Chapel (now King's Chapel) for "prayers and lessons." Following the annual oration, a Dr. Fay performed *Adams and Liberty* "in a style of excellence that made joy beam from every countenance, and the house resound with the loudest plaudits." Its nine verses made the new song even longer than the London original. Remarkably, Paine's lyric said nothing about the Fire Society or its mission. Instead, it offered a litany of Federalist positions, dripping with patriotic fervor. It called upon the "sons of Columbia" to protect the rights which America's revolutionary sires had won. It praised the new nation's commercial prowess and demanded that naval cannons defend its "free charter of trade." Verse three, likely referring to the Reign of Terror's many executions, described France as an enemy "recumbent in blood."

Paine also made clever use of two meanings of the word "Constitution." On one level it referred to the nation's 1789 governing document and its protections of freedom, while on another it referred to a new 1797 warship (the *Constitution,* later known as *Old Ironsides*) and the protections it offered from French attack. Paine's closing steeled the nation to repulse a possible French invasion and placed George Washington, whom Federalists hoped to call back to military service, as the guard at "Freedom's temple." The song concludes by professing loyalty to the nation and its Federalist President John Adams:

9. Let Fame to the world sound America's voice;
     No intrigues can her sons from their government sever;
   Her pride is her Adams; Her laws are his choice,
     And shall flourish, till Liberty slumbers forever.
          Then unite heart and hand,
          Like Leonidas' band,
     And swear to the God of the ocean and land;
                    CHORUS
   That ne'er shall the sons of Columbia be slaves,
   While the earth bears a plant, or the sea rolls its waves.

The final two lines of each verse comprise the traditional Anacreontic chorus, sung once by the soloist and then echoed by the crowd. Paine's insistence that the sons of Columbia resist European domination was thus reinforced eighteen times. Its evocation of "slaves" referred here not to actual Black American slaves held captive as labor, but rather to America's white male citizens who refused to be subject to a king (see Chapter 8).

The newspaper's prophecy of Paine's musical success soon rang true. *Adams and Liberty* immediately appeared as part of other patriotic celebrations, such as the anniversary festival of the Ancient and Honorable Artillery Company of Massachusetts. The English-born actress Catherine Graupner became the first woman known to have sung the Anacreontic melody in America when she performed *Adams and Liberty* at the Washington Hall Theatre in Salem. It was soon performed in New York and Philadelphia as well. The actor John Hodgkinson sang *Adams and Liberty* at Harvard's 1798 commencement dinner. The song was even being performed by the general public. On August 11, as a carriage carrying President Adams passed over Trenton Bridge in Massachusetts, a choir assisted by townspeople performed what a local paper called "the classic song of *Adams and Liberty*." In less than three months, Paine's song had gone from being literally unknown to a "classic."

While in Federalist areas *Adams and Liberty* was a popular rallying cry, the nation's Democratic-Republicans regarded it as nothing less than a weapon to intimidate, shame, and silence. In early America, singing could function as a form of violence. Political song could drown out opposition, both literally and socially. During that year's Independence Day celebrations in Portland, Maine, for example, a community event became a vehicle of Federalist demagoguery. A local paper observed that the "voice of discord was not heard" that day, "all was harmony, hilarity, and joy." But after *Adams and Liberty* was sung, "nothing Frenchified was admitted." Democratic-Republicans were vilified. A toast to the U.S. Army praised its aggressive response not only to foreign "invasion" but to domestic "insurrection." When an attendee shouted "ETERNAL DEATH and OBLIVION to JACOBINISM!" the newspaper explained that "a thunder of applause shook the hall for minutes" afterward. In such an atmosphere, discord was not so much harmonized as suppressed.

A Democratic-Republican critic decried the effectiveness of such partisan toasts and their tuneful rancor. "No less delusive than the orations are the toasts," complained the economic populist and Jefferson supporter Abraham Bishop. "It is well known," he continued, "that if you set up any thing and pray for it, and preach for it, and toast it, the thing becomes of consequence.... Federalists rise; make the air ring, cannons make your speeches, and if any growling Jacobin should damp the general joy by speaking..., blow him in the air."

Yet song could also inspire debate and protest. In June 1798 four Federalist bills—what would soon be known as the Alien and Sedition Acts—were being debated in Congress. Seeking to quash Democratic-Republican support for the French, these notorious laws restricted citizenship, provided for the deportation of noncitizens, and limited freedom of speech and of the press. Arguing against the proposed laws, a writer in Boston's *Independent Chronicle* penned a satirical letter citing Paine's lyric as an example of speech that might soon become illegal. He directed an ironic question to the paper's editor: "I wish Mr. Printer to be informed how I am to manage the matter" of singing Paine's lyric "after the Sedition Bill passes, as I should be loath" in singing the song "to be taken up as a propagator of seditious or unconstitutional principles." He worried that any "body of men ... *combining* in a *vocal* manner" and "declaring sentiments hostile to the United States" might be engaging in sedition. "I only wish to steer right," he deadpanned, "and not when I am singing a song, to be in danger of being arrested." The paper's editor offered no response, but on July 14 President Adams did. He signed the Alien and Sedition Acts into law.

Paine's song sparked an explosion of *Anacreontic* creativity by poets of both parties. Federalist imitations appeared first. Published on July 18, a bit more than a month after Paine's lyric premiered, the song *Our Country's Efficiency* was even more thunderous in praise of Adams and in its call to suppress opposing voices. Its eleventh and final verse reads:

INTRIGUE and SEDITION shall ne'er cut the *band*
That encircles our GOVERNMENT, LAWS, FAITH AND UNION!

We'll support ev'ry CLAIM *on the ocean and land,*
　And with WISDOM *and* JUSTICE *e'er be in communion!*
　　Then let this be our cry—
　　That "DIVIDED *we die!*
　"And, UNITED *we fear not a foe 'neath the sky!"*
AND NE'ER SHALL COLUMBIA BE ROBB'D OF A RIGHT,
While the sun rules the day, or the moon rules the night!

The use of italics here suggests that the entire assembly (including the audience) was to join in singing and thus amplified much of the lyric's impassioned concluding verse.

That October another bombastic Federalist lyric was written to the Anacreontic melody in honor of President Adams's birthday. In 1799 five additional pro-Federalist lyrics would appear to the same tune—*The Times, American Independence, Washington and Adams, Columbia's Boast,* and *Columbia Exult!* Instead of naming *The Anacreontic Song* as the melody to which they were to be sung, they cited *Adams and Liberty* as their model. One pro-Federalist editor praised these national poets as a kind of literary militia:

> The Poets of our country are, almost without an exception, Patri-
> ots. In rousing the American people to a sense of their danger from
> foreign intrigue and internal faction, they have been in the advance
> guard. That they are not wearied in well doing, almost every pub-
> lic celebration gives abundant evidence—The tuneful bard of New
> Hampshire on the last anniversary of the President's natal day, pro-
> duced a song which would not suffer in those ranks where "Adams
> and Liberty" should be the commander.

Adams and Liberty and its offshoots also reveal that American politi-
cians campaigned in local and national elections even in the era before direct presidential suffrage. In the presidential contest of 1800, both par-

ties nominated a ticket. Adams and Charles Pinckney represented the Federalists; Jefferson and Aaron Burr ran for the Democratic-Republicans. A Boston newspaper supporting independent electors not beholden to party complained about the din of Anacreontic songs supporting the Federalists.

FOR a few Elections back, there have been a number of *noisy individuals* on Faneuil-Hall stairs, crying out *Washington and Adams.* They made it a fort of *watch-word* on every electioneering occasion. We can hardly choose a Constable, but what we hear *Washington and Adams.* These *Stair-Way Orators* are so tutored by *their masters,* that their several parts are all previously allotted them. The full sounding base, tenor, and treble, afford the most melodious concert to the throng while ascending to the Hall . . . politely accosting him with *Adams and Liberty.*

Instead the writer hoped, "let each Candidate stand on his own merit, detached from *Washington and Adams.*"

Not to be outdone, Jefferson's supporters created a rival campaign song that rehabilitated the Federalist tune. It began,

AWAKE, ye Columbians, from slumber arise!
Your foes loudly threaten to humble your nation;
Once more by your valor (which reached to the skies)
Strike death to each despot who aims at invasion.
The charter you hold
May it never be sold,
Nor your country be conquer'd nor barter'd for gold;
Then join in the prayer, and heaven implore
That your country be happy till "time be no more."

The lyric argued that Adams was the one that "Europe enslaves" and dismissed Britain's navy as to simply "laugh at their threats."

The Anacreontic melody's wide social range is remarkable. Despite its British pedigree and Federalist popularity, the tune never became the sole possession of one party. When Jefferson became president, the song *Jefferson & Liberty* was sung in celebration. When Jefferson allowed the Alien and Sedition Acts to expire, another Anacreontic lyric proclaimed that "we can now speak and print without fear." Federalists tended their electoral wounds with the same tune, singing *The Yeomen of Hampshire,* while yet another Anacreontic lyric called for national unity across party lines. Two years later even the American consul to Britain salved political wounds to the tune by singing a song in celebration of Jefferson's election at a dinner in London, the city of the melody's birth.

The Anacreontic melody thus gave voice to competing political ideas and emotions on both sides of America's initial partisan battles. While at times a vehicle for debate, the melody more often recruited partisan support and denounced the opposition. For America's musical patriots, partisan and not, *Anacreon in Heaven* had become an American tune. On one hand, this was unremarkable. The United States was a former British colony, influenced through and through by English culture. The melody was thus part of America's heritage, and such British influence was common in music. America's first revolutionary song—*The Liberty Song* (1768)—was written to the tune of *Heart of Oak,* which was the march of the Royal Navy. *Yankee Doodle* likewise began its American life as a British song insulting American colonists; it was soon co-opted as a raucous anthem of American pride. The Anacreontic melody's American history similarly reveals the power of cultural transformation, as by 1798 it had become definitively American.

The most common Anacreontic parodies are songs for Independence Day, the first U.S. holiday. Even the young Walt Whitman wrote one such lyric. On July 4, 1776, the Second Continental Congress approved the text of the Declaration of Independence; the first anniversary was celebrated the very next year in 1777. Even before *Adams and Liberty* appeared, the Anacreontic melody propelled Fourth of July effusions, beginning in 1795 with *The Anniversary of American Independence.* Composed for a dinner in Paris hosted by the future U.S. president James Monroe, who was then American minister at Paris, the song further demonstrates the melody's chameleon-like ability to cross national boundaries. This lyric was sung to an English melody to celebrate America's revolution in order to inspire French political change and thus "diffuse the same joy to the whole human race!"

Anacreon and the War of 1812

War between Britain and France continued to define U.S. politics in the early 1800s, and the Anacreontic melody served as an additional vehicle of debate. During his two presidential terms (1801–9), Thomas Jefferson sought to avoid war. His initial strategy was economic sanction. Financial warfare was experimental, but it was also more likely to damage Jefferson's Federalist opponents than his own supporters. In April 1806 he signed the Non-Importation Act to prevent certain British goods from entering the country and thus pressure Britain to respect U.S. sovereignty. One Anacreontic balladeer argued the opposite in the song *Verses to My Country*: that American economic opportunity rather than protectionism would recruit foreign allies and preserve the nation.

The following year Jefferson signed the more restrictive Embargo Act, demanding that both Britain and France respect American trade. It too failed, deeply damaging the domestic economy and exposing American military weakness. To support Jefferson's strategy, however, an Anacreontic lyric touted the embargo as a means to avoid war, at least until the U.S. Navy could be rebuilt and thus made strong enough to protect the nation's shipping. Its final verse concluded:

From the deep we withdraw till the tempest be past,
Till our flag can protect each American cargo,
While British ambition's dominion shall last,
Let us join heart and hand to support the EMBARGO,
    For EMBARGO and peace
    Will promote our increase;

Then embargo'd we'll live, till injustice shall cease;
    For ne'er till old ocean, retires from his bed,
    Will Columbians by Europe's proud tyrants be led.

When the United States declared war on Britain in June 1812, Anacreontic parodies were deployed to rally the nation. The war's first engage-
ment—the Battle of Queenston Heights, in Ontario—inspired one such
song, even though New York's militia failed to secure a foothold in Canada. Several Anacreontic recruiting songs called on men to join the militia.
One chorus rang out—"Then unite, all ye sons of Columbia, unite, / Your
country now calls you, prepare for the fight." A subsequent lyric blamed
the war on both Britain and France, thus appeasing domestic party divisions in its call. Another urged "Arouse! one and all; hear the patriot call,
'United we stand, and divided we fall.'" Anti-war lyrics also appeared. One
Massachusetts lyric asked, "Shall the record of Washington's virtues sub-
lime, / That rescued from Tyranny's thralldom our Nation, / By discord
be torn from the volume of time, / and doom'd like our Peace, to a vile
immolation?"

As the war progressed, Anacreontic lyrics traced America's fate in
seemingly every battle. *Rights of America* celebrated the sea victories of
the *USS Constitution*, the *Wasp*, and Decatur's defeat of *HMS Macedonian*.
That August the *Baltimore Patriot*—the paper that one year later would be
first to publish Key's lyric—printed an Anacreontic lyric to boost U.S. military resolve. As Fort McHenry prepared to defend Baltimore, the song—
spoofing the London original—rallied local patriots in proud defiance.

Since now fairly engaged in this glorious cause,
    Let's face, as brave freemen, Britannia's thunder;
Defending our trade, and all national laws,
    We'll dash the hard chains of our brethren asunder.
            Voice, fiddle, and flute,
            No longer be mute,
    We've refus'd thus to crouch, and have conquered to boot.

And ne'er shall a true son of Freedom again
See his flag or his brother abus'd on the main.

At least twenty additional Anacreontic lyrics addressing the War of 1812 would appear before Key penned his famous one: *American Blues, Columbia Victorious, Decatur's Victory, Ye Tars of Columbia,* and *Haughty England,* among them. The attack on Baltimore itself would be memorialized in several broadsides, not only Key's but one to the tune of *Yankee Doodle,* titled *The Battle of Baltimore,* and even an additional Anacreontic lyric titled *The Battle of North Point.* No fewer than eleven other War of 1812 songs would be written to the Anacreontic melody after Key's famous lyric was published. They include *The Victory at New Orleans, Freedom of the Seas, Peace and Honour,* and *On the Restoration of Peace.* Key's *Warrior Returns* was even resurrected for the cause, appearing in at least four newspapers in 1813–14. The War of 1812 thus inspired a vigorous lyrical conversation, and *Anacreon in Heaven* was its primary musical vehicle, giving voice to more than three dozen songs. When Key picked the same tune to celebrate the *Defence of Fort McHenry,* he simply made the obvious choice.

IN ITS MAY 1814 issue, Philadelphia's *Port-Folio* magazine published what might be the first call in American history to compose a national anthem. It observed that "national songs" inspire among the people "a glowing and permanent love of country" and in the warrior "an enthusiastic passion for glory and an invincible resolution in the hour of battle." It offered a fifty-dollar prize for the "best national song" with a text adapted to "some popular tune now in vogue" or, better yet, to "a new bold, and striking national air." No partisan submissions would be accepted, nor would texts that addressed foreign nations.

As the magazine hoped to print the new song for Independence Day, submissions were due by June 15. Given only a few weeks to work, only twelve competitors submitted songs, and none used newly composed music. Eight were eliminated immediately, but among four finalists, one stood out as superior—a lyric titled *The Birth-Day of Freedom,* to be sung to the Anacreontic tune. The first of its nine verses reads:

> ALL hail to the BIRTH of the happiest LAND,
>   That the Sun in his journey is proud to awaken;
> Here—ENERGY—ENTERPRISE—KNOWLEDGE command,
>   By OBSTACLE hearten'd—by DANGER unshaken.
>   VIRTUE, VALOUR unite,
>   Prop the PILLAR OF MIGHT,
>   Rear'd by HIM, who surmounts it an ANGEL OF LIGHT!
>   CHORUS
>   Oh! proud beat our *Hearts,* and our *Valour* swells high,
>   On the BIRTH-DAY OF FREEDOM—the FOURTH OF JULY!

In the end, the magazine concluded that while the top submission had "great merit," it lacked the "qualities essential to a permanent national song." Ironically, *The Star-Spangled Banner* would appear just three months after the contest closed.

The *Port-Folio* competition was the first of dozens of attempts to compose, commission, or inspire an anthem for the United States. The universal result had been disappointment. Most often no song was declared the winner. At the beginning of the Civil War in 1861, the prize offered was $500 for a fully original song and $250 for a winning lyric to a pre-existing melody. No winner was named. In 1892 Antonín Dvořák, recruited as the director of New York's National Conservatory, created a work he described as the "future American anthem" by improvising an original tune to fit the words of *My Country 'Tis of Thee.* In 1919 George Gershwin—not yet the nationally famed composer of *Fascinating Rhythm* and *Rhapsody in Blue*— entered a Hearst Newspapers competition to write a national anthem. His Sousa-inspired march tune *O Land of Mine, America* fell short of the $2,000 grand prize, but was awarded one of ten honorable mentions and

$100. Reader votes gave the grand prize to the song *My Country* by Herman T. Koerner, but it was soon forgotten.

Several other songs were seriously considered as the national anthem: *Hail Columbia, My Country 'Tis o' Thee,* and *America the Beautiful,* as well as *The Star-Spangled Banner.* But none of them were composed for a competition or were even intended as the national anthem. Rather, each song captured the public's sentiment at a critical moment in the nation's history.

Officially, the signature of President Herbert Hoover on a bill passed by the House and the Senate made *The Star-Spangled Banner* the U.S. national anthem on March 3, 1931. The bill, however, simply recognized a status that Key's song had long enjoyed in civic ritual.

Anthems are not made. They become, through an unpredictable process of community construction. They are not affirmed by law but are ingrained in cultural memory through use and repetition over the course of decades. For *The Star-Spangled Banner,* the use that has repeatedly galvanized and deepened its role as a symbol of the nation has been war.

Chapter 4

The *Banner* at War

A Song Sanctified

> Every rendition of *The Star-Spangled Banner,* or sight of the flag,
> should stir our national pride, and inspire us to be better Americans.
>
> —*Admiral Harry W. Hill (1954)*

Victory and Sacrifice
July 3, 1898, Santiago, Cuba

The magazine's cover image had been drawn from a photograph. It showed a U.S. naval band performing atop the mammoth thirteen-inch gun turret of the *USS Oregon,* one of the navy's first modern battleships. Titled "The Star-Spangled Banner," the *Harper's Weekly* cover celebrated the unprecedented U.S. victory at the Battle of Santiago de Cuba on July 3, 1898. An American squadron had sunk all six Spanish ships—four armored cruisers and two destroyers. While 1,889 enemy sailors were taken prisoner, American seamen had suffered only two casualties. Spain sued for peace.

As America's international ambitions grew, Key's song gave voice to a growing patriotic fervor, catalyzed by the explosion of the *USS Maine* in Havana Harbor in February and fueled by yellow journalism. The ship's sinking sparked the Spanish-American War. "Remember the Maine," the papers shouted. Key's lyric was soon reprinted widely in versions of one, three, four, and five verses. Some dropped Key's bloody third verse, while

The band of the battleship *Oregon* performs *The Star-Spangled Banner*,
Santiago, Cuba, July 3, 1898.

others appended a Civil War–era addition by Oliver Wendell Holmes, Sr.
That the American victory was so swift and decisive amplified the patriotic
wave. The war had lasted only ten weeks. "Never in the history of this country," wrote one observer, "has the Fourth of July been so universally celebrated as it was this year. . . . *The Star Spangled Banner* was the song of the
day. It was whistled in the streets, played at the opera and sung at home."

The sacrifice of life in service of country is the most sacred of patriotic expressions. Born of battle, Key's song recites a tale of heroism to
inspire future acts of bravery and devotion. Its lyrical celebration is further

enhanced by the melody's musical vigor—its propulsive rhythm, strong harmonies, and towering melodic range. The anthem thus serves as a rallying cry at times of military conflict. It prepares the nation for war and gathers recruits for service. It calls the nation to unite against a common foe and gives troops courage as they march into harm's way. In times of war, patriotism becomes a sword. In fact, The Star-Spangled Banner's effectiveness as a war cry is one reason it is difficult to replace as the anthem. During times of global peace and domestic pain, America the Beautiful may seem more appropriate as the nation's signature song. In times of war, however, this hymn fades away; its evocation of majestic mountains and fruited plains inspires neither confidence nor sacrifice. Instead, in times of threat and uncertainty, the people of the United States, placing their trust in a muscular military, turn to The Star-Spangled Banner. War has cemented the bond between song and flag, music and nation.

Both banners—flag and song—were first carried together into battle in 1846. The Mexican-American War, fought to annex disputed Mexican lands, rationalized that aim with the tenets of Manifest Destiny and used Key's song as a tool to rally support. The U.S. Army occupied foreign soil in part to goad Mexico into an attack that would justify war. A propagandistic letter, credited to an American soldier serving on the Rio Grande, described the conflict's opening shots:

> Dear Friends—the ball opened yesterday morning from the Mexican line. They fired the first shots at reveille, and . . . their mortars . . . kept the atmosphere in continual confusion. . . . But notwithstanding the "Star Spangled Banner" still waves over the "land of the free and home of the brave."

Reprinted in papers throughout the United States, the missive echoed Key's lyric to inspire support for the just-declared war. Politicians paraphrased Key's song further to argue for increased military spending. Speaking to the House that same month, a Missouri representative quoted the lyric to conclude his emphatic request for an army budget increase: "I

believe war is just; and may this be our motto—'In God is our Trust'; and
'May the star spangled banner long wave, O'er the land of the free and the
home of the brave.'"

An Anacreontic lyric entitled *The Texas War Cry*—but now citing *The
Star-Spangled Banner* as its melodic model—shouted "Up Texians, 'rouse
hill and dale with your cry." It intertwined lyrical appeals for an independent Republic of Texas with the musical signature of the United States. Its
chorus echoed the familiar melody to deliver a determined promise.

For the bright star of Texas shall never grow dim,
While her soil boasts a son to raise rifle or limb.

Other lyrics set to the *Banner* melody celebrated the war's volunteers
as well as the mythical inspiration of frontiersman Davy Crockett, who
had perished at the Alamo in 1836. One even argued for unity in a nation
already deeply divided into North and South by the question of slavery.
The States of the Union! (1847) suggested that Americans rise as one against
Mexico, ignoring the raving "Northern fanatics" (abolitionists) as well as
the rash "chivalric Southerner" (secessionists), fourteen years before the
Civil War began.

Forging an Anthem—The Civil War

The Civil War marks an inflection point in the history and symbolism
of *The Star-Spangled Banner*. On July 4, 1861, all thirty-four stars on the
American flag were retained, despite the Confederate secession, making
it the visual manifestation of Union. Key's poetic choice five decades earlier to use the same ensign as his lyric's central image had woven flag and
song into a single symbolic alloy. As the flag's sonic equivalent, Key's song
became the auditory symbol of Union, a role it had played at least since
1832, when it accompanied toasts to "The Union" during the South Carolina nullification crisis. But Key's lyric assumed an ever deeper symbolic
importance in the Civil War. Its invocation of the "land of the free" took

on new meaning. As a result, the war's blood sacrifice not only ended slavery and saved the Union but also consecrated both flag and song as sacred symbols of nation.

As war loomed, the song's popularity increased dramatically. A January 1861 rally at National Hall in Philadelphia, for example, affirmed support for the Union. The city's *Daily Evening Bulletin* reported that while the band played many patriotic songs, *The Star-Spangled Banner* was "the greatest favorite, and the people seemed never to tire listening to and applauding it." When a soprano costumed as the Goddess Columbia sang it at a concert in Louisville, Kentucky, "every verse was re-echoed back amidst a torrent of applause." Key's complete lyric was reprinted in hundreds of Northern newspapers in the 1850s and '60s, helping to build unity as war approached and hold it together after war was declared.

Even before the war's first shots were fired at Fort Sumter, *The Star-Spangled Banner* was firmly positioned in American cultural life alongside *Hail Columbia* as one of the nation's two primary patriotic anthems. As Northern patriotic sentiment soared after South Carolina's secession, Key's song grew in prominence. On February 4, 1861, when Rossini's opera *The Barber of Seville* was presented at the Brooklyn Academy of Music, the American soprano Isabella Hinckley sang two new pro-Union verses to *The Star-Spangled Banner* as a substitution aria in Rosina's lesson scene. As she began the first chorus, someone in the audience handed her a cloth flag, and the audience rose to its feet in rapturous applause. Her lyric concluded with the chorus "'Tis the star spangled banner that floats o'er the wave, / Oh, God, give them courage that banner to save." An encore was demanded, so she sang the first verse of Key's original. "It was awful stuff," wrote a Confederate sympathizer in the audience.

Some two weeks later the same opera company performed Verdi's novelty *Un Ballo in Maschera* in Manhattan. The curtain rose to reveal the entire cast in a half circle, then Hinckley stepped forward and sang the first verse of *The Star-Spangled Banner*. As the vocal corps echoed the chorus, a huge American flag fell open from atop the stage. "The effect was electric," wrote a newspaper critic. The audience sprang to its collective feet with cheers that made "the gilded rafters ring." The motivation for this patriotic display was soon made clear. President-elect Abraham Lincoln, visiting New York on the way from Springfield to his inauguration, was attending the evening's performance.

The martial strains of *The Star-Spangled Banner* rallied support for the Union cause, recruited volunteers, saluted Union troops, and galvanized the determination of soldiers headed into the field. Unionists used both song and flag as tools. "Flag-raising was the order of the day, and the *Star-Spangled Banner* was heard in every gathering," wrote one observer. Now mass-produced rather than hand-sewn, American flags were displayed in homes and businesses throughout the North and in border states that remained loyal. A loyalist newspaper in Richmond, Virginia, even attempted to keep the Union's flag above its offices. That effort lasted only a single day.

Both Maryland and Virginia bordered the nation's capital, and both were slave states. Virginia seceded, while Maryland remained but was bitterly divided. The state's historic relationship to Key's song played a role in the debate. One Maryland paper reprinted Key's lyric on its front page under the headline "An Old Song for a New Occasion" and claimed that "anti-secession spirit is vastly in the ascendant." A writer to the *Baltimore Sun* observed "a large preponderance of sincere Union sentiment" and concluded with the hope that Marylanders would stand fast by the old flag "'whose broad stripes and bright stars' still wave over the immortal fort," referring to nearby Fort McHenry. However, another Marylander vehemently disagreed, contributing "A Parody" of Key's song to the papers.

> Oh! say, can you see, through the gloom of the night,
>   The flag we once hailed, with its meteor-light gleaming?
> Now robbed of its glory and shorn of its light,
>   In the hands of a Despot, so hatefully streaming.
> 'Mid oppression's red glare, and freemen's despair.
> Its stars are all dim—our flag is not there!
> No more does the Star-Spangled Banner now wave

O'er the Land of the Free and the Home of the Brave.

Later verses revealed no irony in calling the South the land of freedom, while asserting that the North was the land of the "tyrant and slave," casting Lincoln as a despot and the Unionists who followed his command as his enslaved vassals.

Among the Civil War's first shots were those fired on April 19, 1861, when the Union's Sixth Massachusetts Regiment was attacked by Confederate sympathizers as it marched through Baltimore on its way to Washington's defense. Four Yankees and a dozen Rebels died in the skirmish, inspiring the Confederate anthem *Maryland, My Maryland*. The new lyric was sung to the tune of *Lauriger Horatius*, still remembered today as the German Christmas song *O Tannenbaum*. The state was held under tight Union control throughout the war. Many Marylanders, including members of Key's own family, fled south to join the Confederate Army.

Upon arriving in D.C., the Sixth Massachusetts joined other companies in taking an oath of allegiance to the Union. A letter from one soldier recounted that just as they returned to their emergency quarters in the Senate chambers of the Capitol, "all of us sung the chorus of the Star-Spangled Banner, and seven hundred men re-echoed in the capitol the soul-stirring lines: 'The star-spangled banner, O long may it wave, O'er the land of the free and the home of the brave.'" "You should have heard," the writer exclaimed, "how those hollow arches, partitions and halls rung out with the refrain which the 'Infantry' has taken for its rallying cry."

Confederate Variations

One who deeply resented that Key's song had become the emblem of abolition and Union was the lyricist's daughter Ellen Lloyd Key Blunt. Living in France while pursuing a career in the theater, Blunt wrote the pro-Confederate poem *The Southern Cross*, dedicated to "His Excellency President Davis." Calling on Confederate men to "stand for our Southern rights!," it decries that Northerners are "singing our song of triumph" and "waving our flag." The younger Key echoes signal words from her father's lyric, lamenting that his song has been broken like "the heart strings of the Nation's harmony" and concludes that, "Sadly, it floateth from us, Sighing o'er land and wave, 'Till mute on the lips of the Poet, It sleeps in his Southern grave." Although *The Star-Spangled Banner*'s author had been dead for some nineteen years, many recruited his memory for the Confederate cause. An immediate concern of the Confederacy was to authorize a flag to carry into battle. Some claimed that the new Confederate nation was the true America and thus the rightful heir to its spangled symbols. A correspondent to a Confederate newspaper admitted, "I never could learn to get entirely over a certain moisture of the eyelids that always comes to me when listening to the sweet and stately melody of the Star-Spangled Banner." The paper's editors agreed—"these tunes and anthems of right belong to the South . . . we should cherish and perpetuate them, instead of throwing them back into the possession of those who have causelessly and wantonly become our enemies, . . . let us claim them as our own legitimate property. They are a proud portion of our birthright."

When the Confederacy's Provisional Congress met in February 1861 to draft a constitution, Mississippi delegate Walker Brooke proposed a resolution to design a flag "as similar as possible to the flag of the United States." To support his proposal, he argued that *The Star-Spangled Banner* used a melody "of Irish extraction" with words written "by a Southern man on board of a British man of war, which was employed in bombarding a Southern fort." While the details of his argument were incorrect, his sentiment was clear. However, a South Carolina delegate objected strenuously, saying that the "stars and stripes have always appeared to me to be the emblem of a hostile and tyrannical government." The resolution was soon withdrawn.

Confederate newspaper editors agreed that the Union's flag and song were now forbidden. No wartime printings of Key's lyric have surfaced in North or South Carolina, Virginia, Georgia, or Florida. Nostalgia for the old flag, however, would create practical problems on the battlefield. The Confederacy soon adopted an official flag—the Stars and Bars. It used the same colors and basic design as the Stars and Stripes and was thus easily confused in the heat of battle, causing Confederate troops to fire on their compatriots. The Confederacy switched flag designs several times during the course of the war in a never fully realized search for a viable alternative.

Southern poets added a confusing lyrical voice to the Confederacy's quest for a new flag, celebrating its new visual designs with words written to the *Banner* melody. While *The Flag of the South* praised the growing ranks of seceding states, two different lyrics titled *The Stars and Bars* expressed a mixture of contempt for the previous, now enemy banner and praise for the South's new flag. One asked, "O say does that Rag-Strangled Banner still wave, / O'er the land of the thief and the home of the slave?" The other concluded with a chorus that introduced Confederates to their new ensign by paraphrasing Key's earlier words—"For the bright stars and broad bars in triumph now wave, / O'er the land of the free and the home of the brave." Yet another alternative lyric to the same tune, titled *The Starry-Barred Banner,* rather awkwardly described the translation of symbols from one flag to the other.

> O, who ever knew so majestic a view
>   As yon flag now presents, that the pure breeze is kissing,
> It resembles, 'tis true, the old "Red, White and Blue,"
>   But its stars are more bright, while the stripes are all missing;
> Still the *stars* are all there—those that seem to be gone
>   Were but false *Northern lights,* which all patriots disown,
> While the *bars* take the place of the "gridiron prongs"—
> Since each *stripe* to the Yankees so rightly belongs.

Another *Banner* parody titled *The Southern Cross* was published too early to be about the square Confederate Battle flag of the same name. Its words were later set to distinctive new music. One extraordinary Southern *Banner* variant intones a rare loyalist voice sounding far below the Mason-Dixon Line. Written in 1863 by a "lady in Austin" for a group of Texans who had gone into hiding to evade "forced service in arms against their country," the lyric proclaims the loyalists will never be "slaves of a traitor."

Other Confederate lyricists used the *Banner* melody to mock the Northern enemy. *The President's Chair* called on Southern men to defend Jefferson Davis, the Confederacy's new president, from the "black northern hordes now infesting our borders." An additional *Banner* variant praised Confederate General Stonewall Jackson, while yet another celebrated the "Banner of States Rights." Most powerfully, *The Flag of Secession* opened by declaring, "Oh, say can't you see by the dawn's early light, / What you yesterday held to be so vaunting and dreaming," and concluded by celebrating the South as "the land of the freed and the home of the brave." Remarkably, a loyalist poet in Baltimore heard this secessionist song and penned a mocking lyrical reply:

> Oh, yes, I have seen by the early dawn's light,
>   What your minions have hailed as the flag of secession,
> Bass rebeldom's glory—a pitiless sight—
>   Defiantly waves o'er the Union's possession;
>   With Davis, your tool,
>   In a fantastical school,
> You'll pillage and burn or the country you'll rule,
> Then "the flag of secession" in darkness will wave
> O'er the downfall of Freedom, and Liberty's grave.

By 1862, however, Confederates had largely given up on Key's song and its melody. They began singing *Farewell to the Star Spangled Banner*, a new song with new words to a new tune.

Union Reinforcements

In the North, both flag and song thrived. Union poets created more than two dozen alternative and additional sets of lyrics, to be sung to the *Banner* tune. Many early variants seem calculated to inflame passions and thus galvanize volunteers. Recruiting was a perpetual need, and the nation's spangled symbols, along with financial bonuses, were effective enlistment tools. One lyric, *The Flag of Fort Sumter,* leveraged outrage over the Confederate seizure of the federal fort that began the war. Its final verse called for volunteers to fight "Till the foes of our Union are vanquished forever!"

Another Northern recruiting song, written to the *Banner* tune, celebrated the sacrifice of Colonel Elmer Ellsworth, who was shot at point-blank range on May 24, 1861, becoming the first Union officer killed in the war. A dashing leader whose admiration for French-Algerian Zouave troops had brought their training methods and baggy uniforms to the Union cause, Ellsworth had personally removed a Confederate flag—one large enough to be seen from the White House—from atop an Alexandria, Virginia, inn. Moments later the pro-Southern innkeeper killed him as he descended from the roof. His death became national news, and the rallying cry "Remember Ellsworth" would inspire Union troops in the years to come. Each verse of his memorial lyric concluded with an unlikely but clever rhyme—"While a heart-throb shall beat in the 'Land of the Brave,' / Your war cry be Ellsworth, the gallant Zouave."

Despite this flurry of parodies, Key's original lyric continued to dominate the Union's symbolic soundscape. One Union soldier remarked in a letter home that the "great danger threatening our country . . . cements us all together as one man, ready to . . . sacrifice our lives, . . . for the integrity of our glorious old stars and stripes. We don't sing anything but national songs, and the harmonious strains of the 'Star Spangled Banner,' and good old 'America' may constantly be heard swelling up from the various company quarters." The brass band of a Black fraternal organization even serenaded the White House with Key's song.

Union regiments always included brass bands. Attempts to save money by cutting the number of military musicians were met with fierce opposition. "Good martial, national music is one of the great advantages we have over the rebels," opined the *New York Herald.* "Are we going to relinquish our musical advantage? We might better give up Washington." At least one incident proved that bands could play a pivotal role on the battlefield itself.

Das Star-Spangled Banner song sheet, published by H. De
Marsan (New York), c. 1862–63.

Near Williamsburg on May 6, 1862, Union forces caught up to Confederates who had slipped away from the Siege of Yorktown. Outnumbered four
to one, without sleep and food, and running out of ammunition, Union
troops gained and lost the same ground four times over the course of the
day. Repeated calls for reinforcement went unanswered. At four p.m., however, as the Confederate line advanced yet again, a division led by Union
General Philip Kearny arrived, forestalling a Union retreat. A weary offi-

cer reported that Kearny "rallied our wavering ranks, in the name of the Union, and with his bands playing *The Star-Spangled Banner,* and his men yelling like savages, led his division to the attack on the double-quick." All the Union men sang along. "The effect was glorious," the officer recalled, "our division at once rallied, and the Confeds, falling back at all points, were soon fleeing everywhere."

Lyrical Evidence: Slavery and the Civil War

Some 450,000 German-Americans served in the Union Army, making up more than 20 percent of the force. Entire regiments, including the 32nd Indiana, 52nd New York, Ninth Ohio, 74th Pennsylvania, and Ninth Wisconsin, were formed of German immigrants and first-born German-Americans. Such units typically used German as the language of command, and their soldiers brought critical skills and experience to the Union ranks. Union recruitment needs thus benefited from the printing of Key's lyric in German translation. *Das Star-Spangled Banner* appeared in at least three editions, alongside a second Civil War–era German translation. These German versions of Key's text emphasize that speaking English was not a prerequisite for loyalty.

Many German-Americans favored abolition. A song sheet of *Das Star-Spangled Banner,* likely dating from 1862 or '63, seems calculated to appeal to the abolitionist cause. It features a colorized border of two U.S. flags linked by a central eagle taken from the Great Seal of the United States. Two figures stand on either side of the border's base. The one on the left wears a characteristic Union Zouave uniform with a blue coat and billowing red pants. The other is a muscular, shirtless Black man, suggestive of a freed slave. Tellingly, the translation uses the German word "Knecht" (servant) rather than "Sklave" (slave) for Key's third verse.

Union songs made it explicit and clear that ending slavery was the motivation for the Civil War, even before fighting began. A celebratory lyric written to the *Banner* tune and published immediately after Lincoln's 1860 election, for example, envisioned the abolition of slavery as a direct result.

The chorus of *The Triumph of Freedom* concludes: "Our mild, human Aegis in triumph shall wave, / O'er the homes of the Free—not the chains of the slave!" Written before South Carolina voted to secede, the lyric naïvely mocked the Southern threat to "break up the Union!" However, it also indicates that Lincoln's abolitionist supporters understood the stakes of his election and expected the new president to deliver on the promise of freedom.

When the war's first shots were fired at Fort Sumter on April 12, 1861, many in the North rallied to support the Union. To address the crisis in song, the physician and poet Oliver Wendell Holmes, Sr., wrote an additional verse to *The Star-Spangled Banner*. It would become the best-known stanza written to augment Key's text. Holmes explicitly identified slavery as the central conflict of the war, using the highest pitches of the melody to celebrate the "millions unchained" that would result.

The verse premiered at a benefit for Union volunteers at Boston's Howard Athenaeum on April 27, 1861, just two weeks after Sumter's fall. The Shakespearean dramatic actor Charlotte Cushman, who began her career as an opera singer, sang its premiere. The new lyric promised "our birthright" of freedom, even citizenship, to the enslaved, equating freedom with bravery by featuring the word "is" in its closing line.

> When our land is illumined by liberty's smile,
>   If a foe from within strike a blow at her glory,
> Down, down with the traitor that dares to defile
>   The flag of her stars and the page of her story!
> By the millions unchained when our birthright was gained
> We will keep her bright blazon forever unstained!
> And the Star-Spangled Banner in triumph shall wave
> While the land of the free is the home of the brave!

Holmes's verse was widely reprinted and frequently accompanied Key's text as a fifth stanza. It also appeared alongside yet another additional verse premiered at the same Boston benefit—one composed by sculptor Emma

Stebbins, Cushman's longtime romantic partner. The pairing suggests that Cushman may have commissioned both poets and that her own marketing savvy as a professional actor may have assisted in the distribution of the verses as a set.

After the war, Holmes revised his lyric slightly, changing line 5 to read: "By the millions unchained who their birthright have gained" to acknowledge emancipation. Many post–Civil War editions of Key's song incorporated Holmes's revised addendum, including bandmaster John Philip Sousa's influential collection *National, Patriotic and Typical Airs of All Lands* (1890). Holmes's verse appears up through World War II in some publications. It was even sometimes used as a replacement for Key's third verse, thus deleting its reference to "hireling and slave" in favor of a proclamation of Black freedom.

Holmes's verse offers a powerful complement to Key's text for students of American history and should be taught widely. It transforms Key's song into an abolitionist anthem. To know of it is thus to understand patriotism as dynamic and to recognize Key's lyric as part of an ongoing conversation about the future of the nation. The verse marks a turning point for the country, its people, and Key's song. All were changed fundamentally by the Civil War and the abolition of slavery. Holmes's new words affirm the potential of the nation's patriotic symbols both to inspire change and to undergo change. It shows that patriotic symbols are not immutable icons but markers and progenitors of history subject to transformation themselves.

While *The Star-Spangled Banner* was created during an era of legalized slavery, it can be considered symbolically redeemed by the Civil War, the Emancipation Proclamation, and the resulting Civil War amendments to the Constitution. The abolitionist Frederick Douglass proclaimed January 1, 1863—the day the Emancipation Proclamation went into effect—to be "the most memorable day in American annals." "The Fourth of July was great," he once explained, "but the first of January . . . is incomparably greater. The one had respect to the mere political birth to a nation, the last concerns the national life and character." Similarly, the birth era of *The Star-Spangled Banner* does not limit the song's later significance. That it

A Civil War recruiting poster, addressed to potential Black
soldiers, promises freedom, education, and prosperity
under the Stars and Stripes, 1863. Note that all the figures
represented appear to be African-American.

played a substantive role in the end of slavery has the potential to renew its
cultural character and unifying function.

At times Key's song helped the U.S. government manage the war's emotional turmoil. When the Military Draft Act was instituted in March 1863,
protests turned into class and race riots. The draft was not equal. Men of
means could pay a $300 commutation fee or hire a substitute. In New York,
the draft was to begin on July 13, but with news of heavy losses at Gettysburg, violence ensued. Protesters destroyed the draft office, and white rioters savagely beat and even lynched Black residents, blaming them as the

cause of the war. They burned to the ground the Colored Orphan Asylum as well as the homes of several Blacks and abolitionists. Four days of rioting resulted in the destruction of fifty buildings and more than one hundred deaths. Only federal troops could quell the mobs.

Two weeks later in Philadelphia, local authorities took musical precautions to avoid similar violence when draft lots were drawn. They tasked a blind vocalist with selecting the names. As soon as the lottery was complete, he began singing *The Star-Spangled Banner*. Those gathered echoed each chorus, and no violence resulted. A local paper claimed that the song's performance offered "the musical seal of condemnation of sympathizing traitors."

Key's patriotic song also supported the morale of Union prisoners of war. On July 4, 1864, a Union officer who was being held in a Confederate prison camp in Georgia began singing *The Star-Spangled Banner* after a comrade revealed a small silk flag he had kept secreted from the guards. Every Yankee prisoner joined in the chorus with "the full power of the lungs." Prayers and speeches followed, interspersed with songs and poetry, until a rebel officer broke up the celebration. Fellow prisoner Captain Joseph Ferguson of the First New Jersey Volunteers gave witness to the starvation, illness, and cruelty of the camps but remembered this spontaneous memorial as "one of the happiest days I ever spent in prison."

As the Union Army consolidated victories in 1865, *The Star-Spangled Banner* increasingly became a song of victory. After the fall of Richmond, Union bands played it and other patriotic tunes every evening in the city square. One historian called the Union's serenade a "requiem for buried Southern hopes." The city's defiant Unionist newspaper printed the lyrics to *Hail Columbia* and *The Star-Spangled Banner* in triumph. *The Star-Spangled Banner* was similarly performed in Philadelphia at a jubilee meeting to "celebrate the capture of Petersburg, Richmond, and the rout of Lee's army." In New York, ecstatic celebrants blocked city streets. They sang *Old Hundred*, the Doxology, *John Brown*, and *The Star-Spangled Banner*, repeating the chorus of Key's lyric "over and over, with a massive

roar from the crowd and unanimous wave of hats at the end of each repetition. . . . It seemed a revelation of national feeling."

Both song and flag, through these and other innumerable uses over
the course of the Civil War, became core icons of the Union Army and
its mission to preserve the Union and destroy slavery. The Civil War was
thus fought with ballads as well as bullets. In this sense, the Confederacy
was musically outgunned. The North produced some ten thousand songs,
while the South published only about six hundred. After Lee's surrender
at Appomattox Court House, a quartet of Union soldiers found themselves entertaining a group of former Confederate officers. Not wanting
to offend, they avoided patriotic songs. But the Southerners asked to hear
"your army songs," and the Northerners obliged, singing among other
selections the *Battle Hymn of the Republic, We're Coming Father Abraham,*
and *The Star-Spangled Banner* with gusto. "Many a foot beat time as if it
had never stepped to any but the 'music of the Union,'" recalled one of the
singers, and one enemy officer exclaimed, "Gentlemen, if we'd had your
songs, we'd have licked you out of your boots!" In parting, the most senior
Confederate officer shook hands with his former foes and said, "Well, the
time *may* come when we can *all* sing the *Star-Spangled Banner* again."

Peace and Remembrance: Toward a National Anthem

Following the Civil War, music was used to suture the wounds of division. In June 1869 the Union bandmaster Patrick Gilmore organized a
five-day National Peace Jubilee in Boston. Oliver Wendell Holmes, Sr.,
wrote a "Hymn of Peace" for the occasion, and the Boston drama critic
W. T. W. Ball contributed a new verse for Key's song. Its climactic
phrase proclaimed, "Not as North or as South in the future we'll stand, /
But as Brothers united throughout our loved land." To close the opening
half of the festival's first concert, a mammoth ensemble—a "full chorus
with grand orchestra, military band, drum corps, chiming of bells and
artillery accompaniment"—performed Key's full text with Ball's addi-

tional verse. The audience joined in the chorus for the final verse, rising "en masse in a state of high patriotic excitement." The New York reporter Kate Field captured the scene—"the *tout ensemble* of Gilmore, chorus, orchestra, drums, bells and canon were Fourth of July in a nut-shell. The audience went quite wild."

In former Confederate states, Key's song was played at government events, often in tandem with the Southern anthem *Dixie*, as if to honor those who fell in the South while asserting an overarching federal authority. A Republican convention in Atlanta celebrating the end of Reconstruction closed with pledges of loyalty and a band playing *The Star-Spangled Banner, Dixie,* and *Hail Columbia.* This process of musical repair would stretch over decades and focused increasingly on nostalgic patriotic events celebrating veterans. One such musical salve was presented at the New Orleans World's Fair in 1885. Its Connecticut Day celebration included a ceremony to return the battle flag of the Third Mississippi Regiment. The flag had been captured by Connecticut fighters more than twenty years before. At the ceremony, speeches were interspersed with music. An organ played the Union's *Marching Through Georgia*, then a band played "*Dixie,* the emblem of the Lost Cause." Finally, band and organ "united" to perform *The Star-Spangled Banner* and thus demonstrate the ability of North and South to work together.

Veterans organizations such as the Union's Grand Army of the Republic (GAR, founded 1866), its associated Women's Relief Corps (1879), and the United Confederate Veterans (1889), sustained the war's musical traditions through nostalgic encampments. The GAR songbook—*Odes, Hymns and Songs of the Grand Army of the Republic*—contained one hundred such "ballads of the war." It featured all four verses of *The Star-Spangled Banner* as well as its alternative lyric *The Flag of Fort Sumter.* The GAR did much to keep the promise of emancipation alive. It admitted Blacks as members, and its singalongs featured antislavery songs. The GAR also supported voting rights for Black veterans, promoted patriotic education, and advocated making Decoration Day, later known as Memorial Day, into a national holiday. The 1883 book *War Songs*—compiled for the GAR—

included Holmes's revised verse promising freedom to the enslaved in its version of *The Star-Spangled Banner*.

The rights gained by African Americans after the Civil War were soon rolled back. The Compromise of 1877—also known as the Great Betrayal— was an informal agreement among U.S. congressmen that decided the disputed 1876 presidential election. Republican Rutherford B. Hayes became president, but as a result federal enforcement of the Reconstruction amendments, and their guarantee of Black voting and citizenship rights, were disabled. The stakes of the election had been clear. One of Hayes's campaign songs, sung to the *Banner* tune, had proclaimed that the Republican candidate would "preserve what in battle was won!" and prevent a return to the "slave-driving ages." Instead, the disputed electoral result reversed these gains, with tragic consequences for Black Americans and the nation itself.

What ultimately restored patriotic fervor to a divided nation was U.S. military triumph. The decisive victories of the Spanish-American War in 1898 did much to unite North and South with feelings of both a common enemy and a powerful future. This unity, however, was built on the erasure of Black progress. The decisive U.S. entry into World War I would further solidify the status of *The Star-Spangled Banner* as the national anthem. It sparked a growing cult of the flag that enabled an ominous, coercive, and authoritarian patriotism that silenced dissent as much as it expressed unity.

On January 8, 1917, U.S. Army Regulations were amended to state: "The composition consisting of the words and music known as 'The Star-Spangled Banner' is designated the national anthem of the United States of America." Here for the first time, a federal agency officially linked the phrase "national anthem" to Key's song. The navy had led the way. Because of its need for music at international ports of call, it was the first to prescribe a musical identity for the nation. In 1889 it designated *The Star-Spangled Banner* for use in morning colors and *Hail Columbia* for each evening's ceremony. Navy personnel were directed to "face towards the colors and salute as the ensign reaches its peak . . . in hoisting, or . . . the ground in hauling down." It would take about a decade for Key's song to defeat *Hail Columbia* completely in the contest to represent the nation in military ritual. Until then, circumstance favored one song and then the other.

When John Philip Sousa completed his anthology of the world's anthems in 1890, he concluded that the "American national air has not yet been written." For Sousa, *Hail Columbia* was disqualified because its music was composed by a "German." Its composer, Philip Phile, is more accurately labeled a German-American. He wrote *The President's March* in Philadelphia for George Washington's first inauguration in 1789. Almost a decade later Joseph Hopkinson crafted the words of *Hail Columbia* to fit the melody. Sousa likewise dismissed Key's song, as its music was of English origin. When asked by foreign governments to name the national anthem, Sousa first chose *Hail Columbia* "because both music and words were written in this country." Yet when he was on tour with the Marine Band in 1891, he ended concerts with *The Star-Spangled Banner* in the position of honor.

William H. Santelmann, who took over Sousa's position as director of America's premier military ensemble in 1898, also featured *The Star-Spangled Banner* as the band's closing piece. He even had his musicians stand while they were playing it and encouraged audiences to do the same. By 1893, naval regulations identified *The Star-Spangled Banner* as "the national air," played for both morning and evening colors. Subsequent adjustments to the regulations, such as forbidding its performance as part of a medley or eliminating the repeat of the closing chorus, gave Key's song increasing official weight. While touring England in 1903, Sousa received word that King Edward VII was excited to hear the "American national anthem." His band played *The Star-Spangled Banner*.

To Stand or Not: Imagining Civilian Ritual

The earliest examples of listeners standing for *The Star-Spangled Banner* date from the time of the Civil War, when it was performed to express strength, resolve, and unity. Such examples were rare, however, and did not establish a tradition. Prior to 1900, renditions of Key's song were often boisterous and celebratory. The song was described as energetic and was performed at a faster tempo. Its renditions generated enthusiasm at political rallies, sometimes accompanied by cheers, applause, or waving flags. In 1893 a toast to President Grover Cleveland was drunk to the accompaniment of the national air. Yet the anthem ritual had already begun to change.

As Civil War veterans began to pass away, Key's song shifted in tone toward somber reverence and remembrance. In 1870 a *Banner* lyric written for the dedication of the Soldiers and Sailors Monument in Hingham Cemetery in Massachusetts reminded listeners that "their memory shall live, their names ever be bright, / For the earth and the heavens in their praise will unite!" Six years later another *Banner* parody appeared in Findlay, Ohio, for its Decoration Day ceremonies. *Our Soldiers' Monument* was sung following prayers, orations, and a benediction at the town cemetery. "Be sacred their memory for that is their due!" the lyric advised.

Veterans organizations such as the GAR began to ask audiences to stand for Key's song as early as 1891. In 1893 Civil War veteran Rossell G. O'Brien proposed a resolution to the Military Order of the Loyal Legion in Tacoma, Washington, that read:

> Resolved, That in future, and for all time, whenever the music of the "Star Spangled Banner" shall be played every member . . . shall immediately rise to his feet and uncover and remain standing until the music of its inspiring strains shall have ceased.

O'Brien installed similar GAR resolutions at the local, state, and national levels. The public, however, did not immediately adopt the practice. A 1902 article noted that a D.C. bandmaster failed to get Washington audiences "into the habit of rising to their feet" for *The Star-Spangled Banner* or *America*. In 1904 an observer at a band concert in Buffalo, New York, noted a shift in public sentiment when the audience that had typically "headed for home" during *The Star-Spangled Banner* instead remained in place and men bared their heads. Celebrating National Anthem Week in Buffalo a year later, thousands stood with "bared heads" to hear Key's song, then applauded the band so enthusiastically that it repeated the performance. A reporter concluded that the memory of Flag Day seemed to be "fresh in the minds of the people." Flag Day—the anniversary of the adoption of the official U.S. flag design by the Second Continental Congress on June 14, 1777—was not a sanctioned holiday until 1916, but it has roots in the 1880s and nurtured celebrations of both flag and song.

World War I: Pernicious Patriotism and Military Stylings

World War I not only intensified the nationalist associations of Key's song, it amplified patriotism's more pernicious dimensions. As war fervor and anti-German sentiment increasingly gripped the nation, fealty to *The Star-Spangled Banner* became a coercive litmus test not only of support for the war but of loyalty to the United States. In the summer of 1916, *The Washington Herald* reported that "the person who refuses to stand when the *Star Spangled Banner* is played is mighty lonesome these days." Still serving as U.S. Marine Band director, Santelmann now asked audiences explicitly to uncover their heads and remain standing during performances. He felt that honoring the anthem was a "patriotic duty." The song soon became a perilous test for the many American classical musicians who were of German descent, and even some native-born Americans who had trained overseas.

The American soprano and actress Geraldine Farrar became one of the first to run afoul of patriotic expectation in February 1917, when she remained seated during a performance of *The Star-Spangled Banner* at a New York theater. Having begun her career in Germany, her loyalty was called into question. A letter, supposedly written by her, soon surfaced in which she stated, "I am a Germanophile through and through." After press inquiries were met with terse peevish answers, the story spread nationally, and articles called for Farrar to be "rebuked" and "for the public to forget her." Other voices complained that patriotism was being confused for intolerance, but audiences boycotted her films. Farrar finally responded.

She declared to the press that she was "American first, last and all the time," and soon sang *The Star-Spangled Banner*, literally wrapped in a flag, at concerts in New York and Boston. The next year she was singing the anthem to promote the sale of war bonds. Farrar's controversy faded, but all were at risk. In March 1917, the student council of Hunter College petitioned its faculty to expel three fellow undergraduates for refusing to stand when *The Star-Spangled Banner* was sung at chapel exercises.

When the United States entered the war in April, patriotic pressure further increased. In December 1917 a Nevada school board dismissed a teacher for refusing to stand for Key's song. An editorial supporting the board's action remarked that war had identified "educators who disavowed nationalism—college professors, high school and grammar school teachers, even Christian preachers," who filled the heads of the young with "thoughts of peace and internationalism, certainly dangerous doctrine in these patriotic times." Such sentiments grew increasingly common. A pacifist in San Francisco was severely beaten by an army sergeant for refusing to stand for the anthem. The soldier remained free, while the pacifist was sentenced to ninety days in jail for disturbing the peace. In Pittsburgh, police arrested those who failed to stand. A Philadelphia actor was booked for the same offense, while a theater owner in Kansas purchased spotlights to shame patrons who failed to rise for the anthem.

Anti-German bias also rose to a fever pitch. Anything German was suspect. Rubella, or German measles, became liberty measles; hamburgers became liberty burgers. The violin virtuoso Fritz Kreisler, only recently discharged from the Austrian army, found his recitals picketed, boycotted, or suddenly canceled. He ceased performing until after the war. Orchestras and opera companies dropped German repertory, especially by living composers who would benefit from royalties. In Chicago, the musicians' union required all members be American citizens, immediately dismissing hundreds of Germans.

Most famously, the German conductor Karl Muck became embroiled in controversy when he failed to perform *The Star-Spangled Banner* with the Boston Symphony. A series of miscommunications and miscalculations fed a journalistic frenzy. Hearing of Muck's brouhaha, former president Theodore Roosevelt proclaimed that "any man who refuses to play *The Star-Spangled Banner* in this time of national crisis should be forced to pack up and return to the country he came from." Recent immigrants were put under surveillance and even interned in domestic camps under a policy of "arrest first and ask questions later." Muck as well as the Cincinnati Symphony Orchestra conductor Ernst Kunwald suffered the same fate. They were imprisoned in Georgia's Fort Oglethorpe and deported after the war.

Performing Key's air was now required concert fare. The St. Louis Symphony Orchestra began to play the anthem at every concert in November 1917. The San Francisco conductor Alfred Hertz overcame initial criticism of his *Banner* performances. Meanwhile Walter Damrosch, who had emigrated to the United States in 1871, created an influential arrangement that positively shaped public perceptions of his own loyalty. Having featured Key's air in his season opening concert, Damrosch criticized Muck's avoidance of the song as "cowardly." In contrast, Damrosch's version was praised in the press as "full chested and full voiced, manly, soldierly, fiery, aggressive, attacking the ear with shrilling reeds and loud proclaiming brass, while the roll and beat of the drums throng the veins . . . with quickening pulsations."

On the day the United States severed diplomatic ties with Germany, Damrosch gave an "impromptu" address to three thousand children at a Young People's Concert. Following a rendition of *The Star-Spangled Banner*, performed "reverently" by his musicians who stood while playing, the conductor instructed his young listeners:

> One of the noblest functions of music is to arouse patriotism. Our national anthem symbolizes to us the country we love, the United States of America. This comprises the North and the South, the East and the West. There is no dividing line. Whether we were born here or thousands of miles away, this is the country of our choice, and for which you and I must be ready at any moment to make any sacri-

fice. I want you, my young friends, to realize that what the flag symbolizes to the eye, the national anthem symbolizes to the ear, and
through the ear to the heart, demonstrating the great power of music
to awaken our deepest emotions and to ennoble us in the awakening.
We are proud of being citizens of New York, but we are still prouder
of the fact that we are all citizens of the United States of America.

His remarks were reprinted nationwide, serving as advance press for
an upcoming tour and burnishing his reputation as a loyal American. On
the other hand, his words also created much-needed rhetorical space for
immigrants to be accepted as loyal Americans.

REMARKABLY, DAMROSCH'S WARTIME fervor would come to define what
Americans think of still today as their traditional national anthem. In
the 1890s confusion had arisen about the precise musical identity of Key's
song. Because patriotic song was necessarily part of oral tradition, folk
practices continually reinvented its musical details. Two factors raised the
question of what was the proper version of *The Star-Spangled Banner*. First,
music teaching and its textbooks for school use became professionalized
in the 1890s. Second, the community singing movement encouraged the
singing of patriotic songs by groups, not soloists. When bands or people
assembled to sing, however, folk flexibility brought myriad musical details
into conflict, especially rhythms. The result was not a unifying experience
of social harmony but a musical realization of disunity.

As far back as the 1880s, public schools had become sites of national
rehabilitation through a politics of patriotic culture. Rather than a government effort, patriotic education was propelled by voluntary organizations, especially Civil War veterans' groups. Aimed at Americanizing
recent immigrants—both children and their parents—patriotic socializa-
tion made U.S. flags into essential classroom equipment. While students
began reciting the Pledge of Allegiance, most notably Francis Bellamy's
version first promoted for a simultaneous national celebration of Colum-

bus Day in 1892, they did not initially sing Key's song. What they lacked was a standard version.

Educators needed a regularized edition of *The Star-Spangled Banner* for classroom use—but what rhythms, which harmonies, what form, and what text were best? The question seems to have been asked first in 1907 by Elsie Shawe, director of music for the St. Paul Public Schools, who wrote to ask President Theodore Roosevelt to sanction "one authoritative version of our patriotic and national songs," as it was "impossible to have a chorus of children sing together these songs, that they have heard repeatedly, in different ways."

Consensus around the text arose first. The third verse—with its bloody imagery and its reference to "slave"—was not appropriate for children. Most, although not all, music books published for home or school use cut the verse. In 1912, after four years of committee meetings, the National Educational Association (NEA) adopted an official musical arrangement of *The Star-Spangled Banner* for school use. It likewise expunged the third verse. Intended as it was to be sung by an entire class of students, the NEA arrangement also dropped the traditional choral echo. This made each verse shorter and more efficient for schoolday ritual. The new version, however, had a fatal flaw. Its snappy rhythms were also regularized to even quarter notes. The result was easy for children to sing, but created a plodding repetitiveness that destroyed the song's patriotic verve.

When published by the Music Supervisors National Conference in the 1912 booklet *Eighteen Songs for Community Singing*, the NEA version elicited immediate complaints from music educators, and a new committee was appointed in 1916 to address its problems. In March 1917 the music supervisors published a revised version of Key's song with a single small adjustment to the melodic rhythm and four-part harmony throughout. Before the end of the same year, however, their collection was expanded and reissued, adopting a militaristic aesthetic that introduced further changes to the anthem arrangement. The snapped, dotted rhythms were fully restored, and performance instructions gave Key's concluding cho-

The initial community singing arrangement of *The Star-Spangled Banner* by the Music Supervisors' National Conference, March 1917.

rus a triumphant quality by broadening the tempo and asking the singers to sing fortissimo. The words "free" and "brave" now rang out more powerfully. Published as the "Service Version," this battle-born arrangement became standard, and not only for military use: from this point forward, it defined the American public's general understanding of the anthem. In

The revised "Service Version" arrangement of *The Star-Spangled Banner* by the Music Supervisors' National Conference, published later in 1917. This version shows the musical impacts of World War I.

October 1918, the supervisors issued a special "Liberty Edition" of their songbook "to stimulate and advance the new, virile American spirit created by our part in the war."

Ironically, the music supervisors based their Service Version on the theory that *The Star-Spangled Banner* was a folk song, if one that they had regularized. Thus, the musical arrangement was rooted not in historical sources but in the way Americans realized Key's song in everyday life. The supervisors asked community song leaders to become musical anthropologists, gathering groups of singers, starting a performance of *The Star-Spangled Banner,* and allowing the singers to continue without a conductor or accompaniment. The researchers were to notate the version "as it emerged from the masses." One conclusion was Americans' preference for dotted rhythms: the rhythmic simplifications of the NEA version and its even rhythms had actually made the anthem more awkward to sing. At least that was the music supervisors' conclusion, as such even rhythms were "foreign to our natural tendencies." Another conclusion was that Americans performed the song in unison, with the collective singing the melody as one. This made a suitable harmonization a matter of conjecture, rather than tradition. The final publication aimed to be "sensible, dignified, and simple." Even this version, however, generated complaints and controversy.

At this same time, the U.S. Bureau of Education acted on a parallel and long-neglected 1914 request from the NEA to make its earlier version official. In May 1917 the bureau established an all-star committee boasting bandmaster John Philip Sousa, New York Symphony director Walter Damrosch, musicologist Oscar Sonneck, and two music educators—Arnold Gantvoort, who had chaired the original NEA committee, and a fresh voice, Will Earhart, as chair. The committee worked through Key's song, voting measure by measure on the proper pitches and rhythms, to revise and affirm the NEA arrangement. With Sousa's vote delayed until the last minute and publication and performance deadlines pressing, Earhart assembled a final version of the melody himself and asked Damrosch to polish the harmonization using Sousa's 1890 publication as a model.

Instead, Damrosch created his own arrangement, borrowing from his 1898 realization of the tune for a celebratory cantata titled *Manila Te Deum,* composed in response to the U.S. victory in the Spanish-American War. Damrosch reported being quite happy with the patriotic hyperbole of the result, as his orchestration "developed into quite a climax on the last two lines of each verse." This new version was put into press immediately, without further review. The result was disastrous and lasting. Precisely the artistic features that pleased Damrosch, including a running bass line at the climactic chorus, made the arrangement's use for community singing difficult. Incomplete chords along with nonstandard harmonic progressions and voicings put Damrosch's version out of range of amateur singers. Gantvoort and other educators were livid.

More than one hundred years later the Damrosch and Service Version arrangements continue to function as the prototypical arrangements of the national anthem. In this sense, their mission to standardize Key's song was successful, even as they perpetuate the jingoistic fervor of World War I. Yet the attendant complaints about each version also speak to the impossibility, if not the undesirability, of the task. The expressive power of Key's song lies in its musical flexibility. To standardize the anthem is to standardize patriotism itself.

Chapter 5

Play Ball!

The *Banner* in Sports

The playing of the National Anthem should be as much a part of
every game as the kick-off.

—*NFL commissioner Elmer Layden (1945)*

Any Stadium, USA

The tradition's origins have long been forgotten, but today American sports events from sea to shining sea begin only after players, coaches, officials, and spectators pause to perform the national anthem. The ritual is so deeply ingrained in American culture that "Play Ball!" is the classic comic punch line to the question "what are the final words of *The Star-Spangled Banner*?" Details vary from game to game, sport to sport, and amateur to professional leagues, but the fundamentals remain constant: an announcement calls the assembly to attention, and then for about one hundred seconds (give or take), unity in song triumphs proud and strong as participants stand, hand over heart, to share in a ritual of nation.

Only the first verse of Francis Scott Key's lyric is performed. In a gesture of respect, hats are removed, and all turn to face the flag. Members of the military typically stand at attention and salute. Coaches may instruct players to strike a standard pose, helmets under arm or caps uniformly covering their hearts. All sing or stand silently to enact a performance of community. Moments later opposing teams will battle in the athletic equivalent of war. Wearing uniforms of competing colors, their fan proxies will cheer, groan, shout, protest, mock, and celebrate the results of each score or skirmish. One side will depart the battlefield ecstatic in victory, the other humbled in defeat. Yet before a winner can be crowned, all present are musically enfolded as one nation through song.

This powerful ceremony of unity is characterized by variety. The scene includes name-brand sports superstars and anonymous fans, wealthy patrons hidden in luxury boxes, extended families arrayed in end zones and bleachers, coaches, players, reporters, stadium security, and other workers. At high-profile events, the song may be sung by a chart-topping vocalist. Participants may be U.S. citizens or foreign visitors—the young and old, men, women, trans, gay, straight, or gender diverse. They may have contrasting racial and ethnic heritages; some of these identities may be visible and others not. Yet the game-day singing of *The Star-Spangled Banner* overwrites difference. It forges all into one.

The ritual's pedagogy teaches everyone how to be American. Children mimic adults as game after game repetition permeates the memories of those raised in the tradition. Even those who protest are participating, making a commitment to belonging and expressing hope that the nation can better meet their needs. Loyalty is rehearsed. In song, nation and sport reinforce the patriotic credibility of one another in sonic circularity. Community arises without the need for a handshake. The ceremony instills a belief in patriotic unity that transcends place, space, and time, connecting Americans to one another in a national imagination. All assume that ritual and song are timeless, unchanging, and have always been precisely so. The sheer success of the game-day anthem is signaled by how little its participants know or even care to know about its history. Tradition is all that matters.

Sporting lore features patriotic tales of stirring, breathless renditions. Yet only a thin and treacherous boundary separates performances praised as authentic expressions of patriotic devotion from those rejected as meaningless, self-indulgent stylizations. Artistry matters, but context can tip the balance as well. Americans experience the anthem differently during times of war or social strife than during times of peace. A rendition gone awry through a failure of voice or memory can tarnish a singer's reputation forever. In a celebrity culture fueled by print and more recently social media, a singer who forgets Key's lyrics plunges into unerasable infamy. Knee-jerk fan reactions can reveal bias, if not overt racism, as when a singer's dress or musical style fall outside expectations. At times, artists have courted, if not intentionally incited, controversy with activist arrangements that draw attention to society's political fault lines. Celebrity athletes can likewise harness the anthem's ritual focus as a platform to call for change.

There is no one way or only way to sing *The Star-Spangled Banner*. From a historical perspective, the anthem has been sung at tempos fast and slow, in triple and duple time, with effusive ornamentation and with austere, unadorned simplicity. Debating who has the right to sing the anthem and how can reveal much about the social issues in play at a particular historical moment. Claims that a specific rendition certainly is or is not "traditional" generally turn on the perceived sincerity of the performer. Whitney Houston's 1991 Super Bowl performance, for example, is regarded by many as the anthem's definitive statement, but it was far from orthodox. Even so, many experienced her impassioned delivery—particularly in the context of the First Gulf War—as both wholehearted and powerfully expressive of national identity.

As America's secular religion, sports play a crucial role in the construction of patriotic sentiment, even belief in the idea of the United States itself. Patriotism is the expression of love and devotion to country, whether realized in celebration of the nation or expressed in the hope of protest. The very possibility to choose between these modes makes patriotism valid. Sports give the nation the opportunity to make that choice every day. Thought by some to dilute or cheapen the anthem, the every-game anthem holds the potential to build community from the ground up. The story of how the *Banner* came to be a central feature of American sports is a drama of the ever-shifting communal understanding of what it means to be a nation. This story begins in New York with a local alliance of Civil War–era "base ball" clubs.

The *Banner* Up to Bat
May 15, 1862, Brooklyn, New York

On May 15, 1862, in Brooklyn, a live brass band played *The Star-Spangled Banner* to open the Grand Inauguration of the Union Base Ball and Cricket Grounds. Club flags decorated the stands, but at this time of Civil War, the clubs' colors were "o'er shadowed by the nation's ensign." Promoter William H. Cammeyer had leased the field to three athletic and social clubs— Eckford, Putnam, and Constellation—each sharing rights to the field two days a week. A fence enclosed the grounds, not (as is sometimes reported) to allow for tickets to be sold, but rather to provide a safe environment "where ladies can witness the game without being annoyed by the indecorous behavior of the rowdies." This was possible because the fence created the possibility of throwing unruly male spectators outside the gate. After nine innings featuring what must have been some remarkably ineffective pitching, Manolt's side defeated McKinstry's 17 to 15. Between two and three thousand spectators attended, helping to kick off what was soon described as the "present furor for this manly sport."

In the nineteenth century, before the advent of audio recording and public address systems, performing *The Star-Spangled Banner* at a baseball game required hiring a brass band. But the expense of hiring musicians made music unusual at sports events. Opening day was the occasion most likely to feature a live ensemble. One typical example was a beautiful April day in 1897, when the baseball season opened in Philadelphia. The players themselves raised the United States' forty-five-star flag, "while the band played 'The Star-Spangled Banner.'" Mention of such performances in newspapers was sporadic at best, suggesting not that they were rare but rather that they were common enough to be routine and thus not newsworthy.

Some teams featured a multipart musical ritual on opening day. At Manhattan's Polo Grounds in 1898, for example, a brass band led the players of both teams to the spectators' grandstand in two lines side by side, "what the 'rooters' termed the opening march to victory." As the music started, fans in the bleachers began to clap, and their applause burst "into a roar" when the athletes arrived at home plate. The teams then parted, and the players, "doffing their caps, retired to the bench." Still at home plate, the musicians waited for the cheering to subside, and then played *The Star-Spangled Banner*. Rituals varied from team to team. The following year at an opening day in Brooklyn, "the players and the band went to centre field for the usual opening march to the grand stand. . . . The crowd was very quiet until the players formed in line . . . [and] headed by the band, playing 'The Star-Spangled Banner,' began the march."

Collegiate football was just beginning to take hold of the public imagination in the 1890s, but an early anecdote reported coast to coast helped arouse patriotism among Americans generally. The "inspiring incident" occurred before the 1899 Army-Navy football game—only the fifth meeting in what is now a storied rivalry. On this day, the Midshipmen's band played *The Star-Spangled Banner* before the game, apparently surprising both players and fans.

> At once every cadet within sound of the music, whether sailor or soldier, stood at attention and uncovered, as he was bound to do by regulation. Every other military man present obeyed the instincts of his training immediately. Then all present followed this example and the assemblage of nearly 25,000 persons stood in silence and in the attitude of respect until the stirring sounds ceased.

The writer goes on to lament that "the people of the United States are sometimes lacking in their show of respect for national symbols," especially an "apparent indifference in pose and manner when the national air is played or sung." Not only was the 1899 Army-Navy Game a vehicle for the transfer of military custom to civilian behavior, but the news article

BACK TO BOSTON!

"O LISTEN TO THE BAND."

Newspaper caricatures of band musicians participating in
the pageantry of baseball's first World Series, 1903.
(Boston Globe, Oct. 11, 1903)

itself served as a didactic tool. As it concluded, "the incident . . . reminded the American public, in a spectacular way, of their duty and privilege when the Star Spangled Banner is played or sung."

The 1918 World Series has long been touted in baseball lore as the moment when the every-game anthem entered sporting ritual, but Key's song had, in fact, been a regular part of World Series pageantry from the championship's origin in 1903. Both teams that first year hired bands to support their players and excite the crowd. Boston's Cy Young, the legendary hurler for whom baseball's top pitching award is still named, played a pivotal role in this inaugural World Series by beating the Pirates 7 to 3 to take the series back to Bean Town. Yet before a single ball or strike had been thrown that day, the teams' bands waged their own contest in sound. A newspaper described the pregame musical action, as Boston's players warmed up on the field:

The Boston band played the "Star Spangled Banner" and the crowd cheered. As an offset, the Pittsburg[h] band struck up the "Wearing of the Green" and the crowd cheered from one end of the field to the other. As Capt. Clarke led his Pirates out for practice, the Boston band struck up "America," and the immense crowd arose to its feet and cheered wildly. The Pittsburg[h] band responded with the "Star Spangled Banner." Boston came back with a "Medley of Yankee Doodle" and "Away Down South in Dixie." This musical contest went on until the game was called.

The two bands' musical rhetoric is more comprehensible when we realize that Boston's American League team was not yet known as the Red Sox. Instead, they were called the "Boston Americans" or the "Amerks." By playing *The Star-Spangled Banner,* the Boston band used patriotic song to celebrate their team and its hometown where the American Revolution had begun. As the Pirates took the field, Boston's band offered another sonic challenge by playing *America*—celebrating both their team and the upstart American League.

Representing the National League, Pittsburgh's musicians retorted with what was either a musical salute or an ethnic slur, playing the Irish Catholic ballad—*The Wearing of the Green*—at a time when Boston had the largest Irish community in the United States and anti-Irish, anti-Catholic prejudice remained strong. The musical volleys continued to the crowd's delight, inspiring a rare second rendition of Key's song. A cartoon accompanying the newspaper's account shows how these musical and sporting battles intertwined. Back in Boston three days later, the players would settle the dispute on the field. The "Amerks" became baseball's first "world champions," defeating the Pirates to win the inaugural series in eight games, 5 to 3.

What created the star-spangled tradition of American sports, however, was not patriotism but economic self-interest. Opening day 1917 followed the U.S. entry into World War I by only a matter of weeks. This accident of timing, more than a savvy plan, inspired patriotic ballpark pageantry. In the nation's capital, the Washington Senators enlisted Assistant Secretary of the Navy Franklin D. Roosevelt to lead the home team in a mock military drill

Patriotic pregame drill, opening day at Griffith Stadium, Washington, D.C., April 20, 1917. Franklin D. Roosevelt, then assistant secretary of the navy, accompanies players from the Washington Senators (carrying bats over their shoulders, like army-issue rifles) to show baseball's support for the war effort.

in which bats replaced the doughboys' rifles. Roosevelt then supervised the raising of the nation's flag to the strains of Key's song, and Vice President Thomas Marshall threw out the ceremonial first pitch to start the season.

To curry public favor, baseball owners assigned military drill instructors to each professional team, supposedly in an effort to prepare athletes for wartime service on the battlefield. Such token exercises were more show than substance, however, as the leagues had no intention of surrendering their talent to the military. Baseball executives failed to anticipate, however, that war would soon present American professional sports with a nearly existential crisis.

The 1917 World Series was marketed as the "Star Spangled World Series," and Chicago's White Sox faced New York's Giants. Red, white, and blue bunting decorated Chicago's Comiskey Park, while New York's Polo Grounds featured ribbons of American flags. As the American League champions, the Sox literally wore patriotic pride on their sleeves. Owner Charles Comiskey decorated the team's uniforms in stars, flags, and span-

"President Wilson Throwing Out Ball at the Opening of the American League Season at Washington" (1916), a photo featured on the 1917 World Series program book cover.

gles and promised to donate part of the team's earnings to the Red Cross. Military servicemen were given free tickets.

That year *The Star-Spangled Banner* sounded before each World Series game—the first time Key's song can be documented to have been played for a full sequence of games. Before game one, the band played George M. Cohan's wartime hit *Over There*, and afterward men removed their hats for the anthem. Chicago's band entertained the crowd before game two by "jazzing up 'America,'" but it performed *The Star-Spangled Banner* "in all sincerity" and without "the jazz notes." For games three and four in New York, the song again preceded the first at bat, but it was played during warm-up. For game four, Giants players also gathered at second base and marched toward home plate carrying flags of the U.S. allies, while the band played *My Country 'Tis of Thee*. Notably, fans stood solemnly with bared heads for each of the anthem renditions. No account mentions singing.

The 1917 series's program book amplified the league's patriotic promotional strategy. The cover featured a photograph of President Woodrow Wilson throwing out the first pitch of the season, with the caption, "A big enough boy to enjoy the national game—and—a man big enough to guide our country through its greatest crisis." At once, the program claims baseball as America's "national game" and shows the nation's leader, standing confidently behind the flag's stars and stripes, smiling and enjoying baseball even during a time of war. But the image is a chronological fiction. The photo had been taken on opening day 1916, a year before the United States entered the war. In fact, the demands of war had caused Wilson to cancel his 1917 opening day appearance. However, the message of the 1917 cover was clear: baseball was patriotic, good for the war effort, and sanctioned by the nation's leader. In actuality, the president's actions soon signaled that the "national game" was of only secondary importance.

In 1918 baseball's argument that the sport was patriotic crumbled. Token drills, donations of money, and a "bats and balls fund" to provide equipment for the troops did not counteract the feeling that baseball had failed to do its part. On July 19 secretary of war Newton Baker announced that professional baseball would be classified as "non-essential" under the federal Work or Fight Order. Baseball players of draft age were thus required either to enlist or to work for the war effort in a more productive occupation. As a result, all players twenty-one to thirty years of age faced immediate induction into the army. Unless a compromise could be reached, professional baseball would be devastated. The first-place Chicago Cubs would lose all but two of their players; St. Louis would retain only three, Pittsburgh four, and Philadelphia's Nationals would also lose all but two.

Secretary Baker allowed the league to keep playing through September, but baseball executives were forced to embrace his decision. John Tener, president of the National League, who had argued just a month before that baseball "is essential to the morale of the people," now meekly conceded that "we will most gladly make sacrifice of our business interests in the country's welfare." The regular season was cut short, and military enlistment culled athletic talent from the league. The World Series, famous then as now as the "October Series," ended in mid-September.

While the 1918 championship did not inaugurate the tradition of play-ing *The Star-Spangled Banner* in American sports events, the song nev-ertheless played a dramatic role in game one. Its rendition may deserve credit for being the first time fans are known to have sung along. Another first may have been the airborne stunts performed by military aviators over the ballpark before the game.

The series began in Chicago's Comiskey Park as it had the year before, but this time the Cubs were the city's championship contender. "Home Run King" Babe Ruth pitched the opening game for Boston's Red Sox, but fans were reportedly distracted by the war. Attendance was down. Both the weather and the country's mood were bleak. During the seventh-inning stretch, a twelve-piece band surprised the crowd by playing *The Star-Spangled Banner*. Fans and players alike snapped from their stupor, removed their caps, and turned toward the band. Red Sox third baseman Fred Thomas—on leave from the navy to play in the series—offered a strik-ing military salute, "with his eyes set on the flag fluttering at the top of the lofty pole in right field." As *The New York Times* described it, "First, the song was taken up by a few, then others joined, and when the final notes came, a great volume of melody rolled across the field." A huge cheer erupted. Recent commentators have suggested that a tradition was thus born. It makes for a great story. Unfortunately, the claim is mainly hyperbole.

In fact, *The Star-Spangled Banner* had little effect on the success of the 1918 series and, if anything, confirmed for league executives the value of patriotism as an example of what might have been. Attendance was abys-mal, down one-third from 1917. Ticket revenues—the kitty from which players, leagues, and teams were paid—totaled less than half the previous year. To make matters worse, a strike by players angry at new pay rules delayed the start of game four. It further soured public support.

For 1919, baseball's prospects seemed even more bleak. The whole sea-son might even have been canceled, casting the sport into an existential crisis of potentially lethal duration. But fate smiled on baseball. Germa-ny's surrender on November 11, 1918, saved the upcoming season. Athletic talent and fans returned. Still, executives had learned an important lesson. Baseball would never again be declared "non-essential." Patriotism and the economic success of professional sports were now strategically intertwined.

International Competition and Anthem Diplomacy

International competition brought new value to the musical symbols of nations. When teams from different countries clashed, paired anthems sounded a message of identity, respect, and friendship that crossed barriers of language, place, and culture. During World War I, for example, French commissioners attending a football game at the University of Michigan were honored with a rendition of the French national anthem *La Marseillaise* by the school's marching band. Playing a foreign anthem on U.S. soil required, then as now, that America's own anthem follow, and indeed, the French visitors remained standing for *The Star-Spangled Banner*.

Because its leagues included both U.S. and Canadian teams, ice hockey made use of anthem diplomacy as early as the 1920s. When in 1924 the Royal Military College of Canada met the U.S. Military Academy on a rink in Ontario, "the audience stood with bared heads as the Star Spangled Banner and God Save the King were played before the game started." For the opening of Madison Square Garden in 1925, the Montreal Canadiens defeated the New York Americans 3 to 1. Before the game began, each team's band played its respective national song—*God Save the King* first, then *The Star-Spangled Banner*. It is conventional that such dual anthem performances begin with the foreign visitor's musical symbol.

Anthem diplomacy also inspired one of the more spectacular musical displays of nationalism in sporting history—a twenty-two-anthem marathon. On April 14, 1931, little more than a month after he signed the bill making Key's song the official U.S. anthem, President Herbert Hoover opened the 1931 baseball season in Washington by throwing the season's ceremonial first pitch. Coincidence, however, had combined baseball's traditional opening with Pan-American Day. The U.S. Army Band, flanked by players from the Washington Senators and the Philadelphia Athletics, marched to the diamond's flagpole. The Mexican flag was run out on a horizontal cable and was then saluted by artillery blasts from cannons stationed along the third-base line. The band then played the Mexican national anthem. The flags of twenty other Latin American countries were raised in sequence, each saluted by cannon fire and its national anthem. Finally, "the Stars and Stripes were run up last, greeted by another blast that came from the cannon as the band played 'The Star-Spangled Banner.'"

In 1896 the Olympic Games were revived, and while the medal ceremony has since become the emotional catharsis of every Olympic event, initially the modern games did not include a medal ceremony. At these first modern games in Athens, flags identified each nation's team on parade, but the emphasis was on international cooperation. There were no anthems and no medal podiums. The *London Graphic* reported that American champions, after winning a series of track and field events, were "loudly cheered by the strong American contingent present, who waved star-spangled banners and raised that curious college shout 'Ra-ra-ra!'"

It was not until 1924, at the first-ever winter games in Chamonix, France, that formal musical salutes to Olympic winners were made. Medals were presented en masse at the closing ceremonies, and the anthem of each champion's homeland was played. *The Star-Spangled Banner* was heard only once—for Charles Jewtraw, who won America's lone gold in 500-meter speed skating. Six months later, at the 1924 Paris summer games, the United States would take a dominant total of forty-one golds. It was here that the now-traditional Olympic medal ceremony was born. When the United States won the games' first gold in rugby, a forty-piece band performed Key's song.

These first medal ceremonies were not necessarily solemn occasions. As an American correspondent reported:

> It is a custom of the Olympic games that at the end of each competition the flag of the countries placed first, second, and third are raised, and the national anthem of the winning country is played. A large number of the people after the diving contests refused to stand up

during the playing of "The Star Spangled Banner," and kept up their hooting and yelling during it. It was really shocking.

Although the Olympics are now broadcast internationally and feature recorded arrangements of each nation's anthem, the medal ceremony has changed little since 1924. In keeping with the international spirit of cooperation that characterizes the games, however, Olympic musical arrangements tend to minimize the sonic features of militarism in favor of a polite nationalism. Slower tempos, less martial rhythms, softer harmonic substitutions, and orchestrations that feature not brass and percussion but winds and strings are typical.

Still, Olympic medal ceremonies are by definition overtly nationalist and thus political. During the Cold War, the battle to win the overall medal count became a proxy war between capitalism and communism, the United States and the Soviet Union. This battle has continued in the twenty-first century with China's gold medal strategy. Yet rule fifty of the Olympic Charter proclaims, "No kind of demonstration or political, religious or racial propaganda is permitted in any Olympic sites, venues or other areas." Historically, this rule has been used to sanction athletes, often of color, who leverage the games' global platform as a stage for protest.* From another perspective, however, the Olympics themselves are inherently political. While the games showcase international cooperation, they also express national power and economic privilege. The games further serve as a form of advertising for the host country. Organizers can claim a distinction only between political goals that are sanctioned and those which are not.

World War II and the Every-Game Anthem

Two inventions made the every-game anthem possible: audio recording and public address systems. Thomas Edison's successful experiments with

---

* The 1968 Olympic protest by American sprinters Tommie Smith and John Carlos is examined in Chapter 8.

his tin-foil phonograph date from 1877, and recording technology developed rapidly from wax cylinders (c. 1896–1915) to lacquer disks (from 1910). The fidelity of audio recording was good enough to reproduce music convincingly well before the availability of technology to amplify it for a large crowd. Not until the 1920s did electric amplifiers and speakers make it feasible to broadcast sound to a stadium full of spectators. One of the earliest uses of live amplification was for an Armistice Day Celebration at the Los Angeles Memorial Coliseum on November 11, 1923. The *Los Angeles Times* reported that "thousands who were there rose to their feet as Dr. Hiner's band sent out the opening bars of the 'Star Spangled Banner.' The Western Electric public address system installed . . . reproducing with tremendous volume the program broadcast by KHJ." Amplification was subsequently used for prominent public events such as presidential speeches and state fairs, but only gradually in sports—first in boxing and football, and then in track and field.

Baseball was reluctant to follow the trend, as spectators could understand the game visually without distracting decibels of commentary. Experiments with amplified announcements began at stadiums in the late 1920s, first at New York City's Polo Grounds for a game between the Giants and the Pirates on August 25, 1929. The novelty here was that umpire Cy Rigler had a microphone inside his mask to broadcast balls and strikes. For musicians, however, such systems posed a professional threat.

In October 1930 no band was hired for the World Series. Instead, music was amplified throughout the stadium from phonograph records. *Hail to the Chief* sounded as President Hoover arrived, and *The Star-Spangled Banner* was "ground out by a talking machine." A newspaper correspondent lamented that "the color and glamor has departed from . . . the world's series." Recorded music for film, radio, and sports events made the late 1920s and '30s a terrible period for professional musicians, many of whom lost jobs. But even though it was now technologically and economically feasible to broadcast *The Star-Spangled Banner* before every professional sporting event, it was not yet socially imperative. The every-game anthem was still on the horizon.

WORLD WAR II would be the inflection point, but the ubiquity of *The Star-Spangled Banner* in sports was more gradual than sudden. It prepared America for war as much as it responded to war. After Congress made it the official anthem of the United States on March 3, 1931, civic events of all kinds came to feature Key's song. As tensions in Europe increased, the anthem's sense of pride and confidence offered a reassuring antidote to the anxiety of war engulfing the globe. Nonsporting rituals led the way.

The Star-Spangled Banner was first broadcast on radio in February 1922, as performed live by the Paul Whiteman Orchestra. Such early renditions were singular celebrations of American ingenuity, that is of radio technology itself. In 1935 Indiana representative Virginia Jenckes was concerned that *The Star-Spangled Banner* was rarely heard on the radio, so she suggested to the chairman of the Federal Communications Commission (FCC) that American shortwave stations "sign off with 'The Star-Spangled Banner.'" She was inspired by the anthem sign-offs of stations in England, France, and Germany. "British broadcasting stations are so punctilious," she emphasized, that their "national anthem is heard after every program."

In July 1935, Station WHO in Des Moines, Iowa, took up Jenckes's charge, using Key's song to end the broadcast day. A supportive radio critic called upon the FCC to require all U.S. stations to do the same, arguing that "anyone hearing the 'Star Spangled Banner' would recognize it as a sign-off and its moral effect on the people of this country could not be doubted." The following year an Associated Press bulletin noted that *The Star-Spangled Banner* was now heard on NBC radio an "average of three times a day."

By 1939, WNYC in New York was not only opening and closing its daily schedule with the national anthem but had switched from playing an instrumental version to a choral rendition—"to familiarize listeners with the words." Movie theaters screened reels of choral renditions with captions to teach Americans the lyric. On July 11 of the same year James Petrillo, president of the American Federation of Musicians, ordered all of its 138,000 members to play the anthem at both the beginning and end of every program.

Baseball had joined the patriotic effort by July 1941. That month a widely reprinted news item confirmed the ubiquity of playing *The Star-Spangled Banner* at baseball games. A reporter criticized the then New York City franchise for the poor quality of its well-worn recording of Key's song: "The Giants should purchase a new record of the national anthem. The one played over the loudspeaker before every game sounds like it is overcome with patriotic emotion." Baseball's "every game" anthem was thus firmly in place in the summer of 1941, some six months before Pearl Harbor.

Japan's preemptive attack on December 7, 1941, shocked the nation, not only rousing the U.S. military from its isolationist bunker into World War II, but inflaming a fervid nationalism that relied on the nation's anthem. Less than a month later, *The New York Times* noted a new sense of American unity and identified Key's song as one cause of the transformation.

Danger and bad news are widely credited with unifying the nation since Pearl Harbor; but "The Star-Spangled Banner," that grand old national anthem, has had a mighty part in the welding. Never has it been played and sung more often in so brief a period. . . . It opens every public gathering; the opera and the football game, the play, the fight and the dance, the banquet and the town meeting. Easily forgotten in days of peace, like the Army, the Navy, the Marines, and even the flag, it now becomes, all of a sudden, a tremendously precious and important thing.

Professional sports would quickly come to rely on its new alliance with patriotism. During World War II the rationing of food, fuel, rubber, metal, and other raw materials devastated many American businesses. The manufacturing of pianos, for example, was illegal because it used too many vital resources. The famed Steinway factory shifted to producing planes, along with a few lightweight "G.I. Pianos" that could be airdropped to troops in Europe. Rationing also affected sports, as automobile and motorcycle racing were ordered suspended to save fuel and tires.

President Harry Truman (left) is presented with a pass to any game by
NFL commissioner Elmer Layden (center) and Washington Redskins
owner George Marshall, at the White House, August 22, 1945.

Athletes were again prime candidates for the military draft, which tar-
geted men ages eighteen to thirty-five. The boxing champion Joe Louis,
like many other top athletes including baseball's Joe DiMaggio, Ted Williams, Yogi Berra, and Jackie Robinson, found himself in army-issue kha-
kis. As during World War I, many colleges canceled their football seasons.

But professional baseball thrived. Whereas in 1918 the sport lost its
argument claiming to be vital to domestic morale, World War II would be
different. On January 15, 1942 (just a month after Pearl Harbor), President
Franklin D. Roosevelt signed a "Green Light Letter," indicating that "it
would be best for the country to keep baseball going." Some five hundred
professional ballplayers served in the military, draining the athletic talent pool, but the game went on. Baseball's legitimacy allowed football and
other professional sports to continue as well. The leagues would carry this
success forward.

On August 22, 1945, a week after Japan's surrender ended World War
II, there was a symbolic meeting at the White House. National Foot-

ball League commissioner Elmer Layden, accompanied by George Marshall, owner of the Washington Redskins, gave President Truman a gold, engraved pass to any professional game. Although Truman had attended a Redskins game as a senator, no American president had ever attended a football game. Now that peace had arrived, however, the league seized the opportunity for a publicity stunt and photo. Layden then announced that he would instruct all teams to make *The Star-Spangled Banner* a permanent part of football. "The playing of the National Anthem should be as much a part of every game as the kick-off," he told the president. "We must not drop it simply because the war is over. We should never forget what it stands for." Football's 1945 promise became the first official mention by any professional league that *The Star-Spangled Banner* would be performed at each and every game. A tradition was born.

The every-game anthem is today a structural component of American professional sports. Baseball has used the ritual since 1941 (1942 in the minors), and the NFL and collegiate football since 1942. The National Basketball Association has opened games with the anthem since its founding in 1946. The National Hockey League also started playing the anthem in 1946, although in the 1970s teams often substituted "God Bless America." Major League soccer in the United States has likewise featured the pregame anthem since its founding in 1996. The patriotic temperature of the ritual has ebbed and flowed over the decades as public opinion has shifted, wars have been declared, and protests became common, yet sports' pregame anthem ritual has never ceased.

Football's Super Bowl Anthems

Whitney Houston's 1991 rendition of *The Star-Spangled Banner* at Super Bowl XXV is for many—fans and singers alike—the greatest performance of the U.S. national anthem in sports history. Singers from Beyoncé to Lady Gaga have cited it as an inspiration. Responding to unanticipated public demand, Arista Records released an audio and home video version of the performance. Profits were donated to the American Red Cross Gulf Crisis

Fund. Ten years later, two weeks after New York's Twin Towers fell, the recording was released again; proceeds supported the New York firefighters and police disaster funds. In 1991 Houston's anthem hit number twenty on the *Billboard* Hot 100 chart; in 2001 it reached number six. Houston's performance is brilliant, poignant, and powerful. It offers a case study in anthem aesthetics—how performers convey meaning with both voice and choreography, and how contemporary events shape audience reception.

Super Bowl XXV featured a pregame anthem ritual that had long become emblematic of football's championship, but this day it carried added weight. Operation Desert Storm had begun just ten days earlier, and already the America-led coalition in Kuwait was overwhelming Iraq's military. Military success inspired national pride. Fans waved seventy thousand American flags distributed by the NFL. Nevertheless, security for the game was tight, and many feared a terrorist attack. SWAT teams patrolled from the roof of Tampa stadium, and the Goodyear Blimp was grounded as a precaution. Although patriotic fervor in sports had diminished in the 1980s, military themes were especially evident around Houston's performance that day. Her performance of the anthem marked a turning point.

The video of Houston's performance begins with announcer Frank Gifford welcoming Houston and inviting fans to sing along, while reminding them of the stakes for America's military abroad: "And now to honor America especially the brave men and women serving our nation in the Persian Gulf and throughout the world, please join in the singing of our national anthem." Martial snare drums, punctuated by a bass drum and a cymbal crash, introduce a brief trumpet fanfare as Houston begins the lyric with its snappy triadic descent.

Houston's brisk vocals are accompanied by the musicians of the Florida Orchestra, wearing formal black. She wears a sporty white track suit with red and black accents and a white shirt and pants. A matching headband pulls back her natural curls. Her Afro styling, three decades removed from its associations with Angela Davis and the Black Panther Party, nevertheless pays quiet homage to Black pride and the civil rights era. The outfit disguises her sensuality.

Whitney Houston performs *The Star-Spangled Banner* at Super Bowl XXV, January 27, 1991. Musicians of the Florida Orchestra are in the background.

"O say can you see?"—the first phrase of the anthem is proud and strong. Houston sings in full voice with the orchestra reinforcing each note. She arrives on certain words—"light" and "twilight," for example— slightly ahead of the accompaniment, adding urgency to her expression. Brief snippets of lyric bass line and a cymbal crash on beat four punctuate the sturdy pride of the opening lines.

The mood of the second phrase—"Whose broad stripes"—shifts as Houston anticipates and lingers over the first syllable with emotional intimacy. A change of vocal color makes what is actually a simple musical repetition sound new. Her now soft, expressive introspection is enhanced by the gently sustained chords of the orchestral accompaniment. Only Houston's voice intones the melody.

As she continues, the television camera leaves the close-up views of the singer to pan the crowd. A Black soldier, featured before, now salutes the flag with steel-eyed precision. A woman in the crowd, hand over heart, recognizes the camera, smiles, and waves a miniature American flag. Elsewhere, fans unveil a full-size flag, its stars in a field of blue seeming to illustrate Key's lyric.

"And the rockets' red glare"—Houston's voice opens up, delivering the powerful, illustrative lines of Key's lyric as vocal fireworks. She again arrives on the downbeats in anticipation of the accompaniment, giving the words "glare" and "air" an impassioned emphasis followed by the echoing accent in the orchestra. The camera focuses on the twenty-seven-year-old singer's face, as she closes her eyes and throws her head back to sing the melody's highest pitches. She is radiant.

With cinematic precision, the screen dissolves as Houston sings "our flag was still there" to feature a sustained shot of an American flag flying above Tampa Stadium. Orchestral horns add a lyrical cry of triumph. Ensemble and singer then align for the lyric's climactic close. "O'er the land of the free"—Houston emphatically sustains the word "free," ecstatically flipping up a bluesy fourth to signal both her vocal prowess and her apparently unabashed joy as she spreads her arms wide and throws her head back on the highest note of her performance. Houston now sticks to the unadorned melody—"And the home of the . . ."—marking each word and closing each hand into a fist. For the climactic word "brave," she raises first her right arm and then her left to punctuate the final word of Key's song with determined reiteration. Her gesture echoes the 1968 "Black Power" salutes of Tommie Smith and John Carlos combined, but now with an exultant smile.

The camera soon features the cheering crowd: signs reading "God Bless America" and "Go USA" boast of wartime optimism. As Houston jumps down from her platform, cheers replace her triumphant voice. Four F-16 jets from the 56th Tactical Training Wing at Tampa's MacDill Air Force Base scream overhead in a V formation. The whole alloy of sound, song, and visuals has been magisterially orchestrated for patriotic effect. The running back Kenneth Davis, who played in the game for the Buffalo Bills, remembered, "We were in the middle of a war in Iraq, when she sang and the jets flew over, it put chills in your body." The Bills special teams standout Steve Tasker said, "She moved me to tears." General H.

Norman Schwarzkopf, stationed at the command center in Saudi Arabia, was "touched very, very deeply" when he watched Houston's performance later on videotape.

Only in retrospect does one realize that this performance, which feels so traditional, stirring, and patriotic, is in fact surprisingly unconventional. Key's original song is in a clear triple meter, characteristically notated in 3/4 time. Houston's performance, however, is in 4/4 time, an extra beat having been added to each measure by her producer and longtime musical director Rickey Minor. The added beat would "allow Houston to open up her lungs and 'breathe.'" NFL executives, especially Commissioner Paul Tagliabue, were nervous that Houston's rendition was not traditional enough, especially in a time of war. Their complaint, recalled Jim Steeg, who worked in NFL productions from 1979 until his retirement in 2004, was that Houston's anthem was "too slow and difficult to sing along with." Steeg was told to call Houston's manager, her father, John, to ask for a new version. "The conversation was brief," Steeg said. "There would be no re-recording."

The shift of musical time, from the waltz-like 3/4 to a slow, reflective 4/4, had a profound impact on the mood of Key's song, forging it anew as a sacred hymn. That the result *feels* traditional signals the anthem's metamorphosis from a rollicking song of victory in 1814 through the pugilistic militancy of World War I to a sacred hymn of patriotic devotion here. Houston has also added a considerable number of gospel-tinged ornaments: extra pitches, melismata, passing tones, and appoggiaturas. The most extensive additions are on the words "yet wave," which feature the alternating pitches of a trill that seems to illustrate a flag fluttering in the breeze. While similarly ornamented pop renditions have been dismissed as in poor taste, the perceived sincerity of Houston's performance allows it to be heard as traditional and true, even in her highly personal signature performance.

EACH SUPER BOWL rendition of the anthem is unique, yet analyzed together, they offer an object lesson in patriotic procedure. The Super Bowl uses a recurring set of standardized, designed-for-television components that serve as a base structure for the pregame ritual. Often a military color guard marches onto the field, featuring soldiers from the local area representing each of the U.S. military services and each carrying a flag. They are flanked by snare drummers, who perform a cadence. The singer or singers, always American, step to a microphone to perform a personalized arrangement of the anthem. Like its half-time performers, Super Bowl anthem singers are never paid a fee; only their expenses are covered. A giant American flag typically decorates the field, supported by hundreds of volunteer handlers. There is a quick introduction, and then Key's text is delivered clearly. Every singer adjusts pitches and rhythm, adding ornamentation and even shifting the melody's expressive contour. Female singers are likely to flip up a fourth on the climactic word "free," demonstrating their range and power, while the most extensive additions are usually reserved for the word "brave" that brings the song to a close. Cher sang this final word three times.

For years, it was common for singers to lip-sync their performances, and the NFL, in fact, insisted upon having a recording made in advance of the game. While Houston was singing, and the video is utterly convincing, she was in fact singing into a dead microphone. Others who performed to recorded tracks include Diana Ross, Barry Manilow, Neil Diamond, Faith Hill, and Jennifer Hudson. For Houston, the use of the recording solved balance and amplification challenges caused by the full orchestral accompaniment. Another worry, in live performance, is the possibility of screeching feedback. Singers typically spend two hours the Friday before the game rehearsing the anthem. Despite such rehearsals, not all singers can pull off the role convincingly while lip-synching. Jewel's disengaged mimicry in 1998 is among the most egregious deceptions. On the TV broadcast, we hear her voice before she opens her mouth to sing. Recent improvements in field amplification systems have made lip-synching unnecessary.

The Friday rehearsal is also a time for the television crew to practice its camera work. Their imagery helps articulate the patriotic spirit of Key's words. Cameras start with the singer, pan the crowd, cut to fireworks illustrating the "rockets' red glare," and typically show a flag flying somewhere in the stadium when the lyric reminds the listener that "our flag was still there." The climactic phrase returns the camera's focus to the singer, often with a final cut to jets flying overhead.

As a collection, the Super Bowl *Banners* from 1966 to 2021 offer a cultural history of the pregame ritual. These first fifty-five renditions feature two marching bands, four trumpet solos, and a duet of trumpet and spoken lyric (Super Bowl IV, 1970), six choral versions, two vocal duets, a trio, a quintet, and thirty-eight solo vocal renditions (26 by women, 12 by men). One arrangement intermixes the lyrics of *The Star-Spangled Banner* with *America the Beautiful* (SB XXVIII, 1994), and at one game the anthem was not sung at all but was replaced by *America the Beautiful* (SB XI, 1977). Only Billy Joel (1989 and 2007) and Aaron Neville (1990 and 2006) have sung it more than once, while the disability activist Marlee Matlin has performed three times (1993, 2007, 2016) as the American Sign Language (ASL) interpreter. Absent for the ritual's first twenty-five years, ASL has been featured at every Super Bowl since 1992 and often celebrates a prominent leader or musician associated with disability rights.

While the average length of a Super Bowl anthem is one minute and fifty-one seconds, performances have averaged over two minutes since Whitney Houston came in at precisely that length in 1991. The longest Super Bowl rendition to date—which clocked in at two minutes and forty-four seconds—was sung by Alicia Keys in 2013, but even this performance fails to rival Aretha Franklin's stunning four-and-a-half-minute rendition for a 2016 Thanksgiving Day football game in Detroit. Neil Diamond's 1987 performance for Super Bowl XXI is the shortest among the first fifty-five, at only one minute and four seconds.

Remarkably, the anthem has been sung in all twelve musical keys. By far the most common is B-flat major (thirteen times), but the next most popular are surprises: G and G-flat major (six), F and A-flat major (five), E and A major (four). Two keys have been used only one time: B major (by Billy Joel, for SB XXIII in 1989) and E-flat major (by Cher, for SB XXXIII in 1999).

Although Houston was the first to sing Key's song in 4/4 time at the

Super Bowl, later singers have followed suit, such as Luther Vandross (SB XXXI), Aaron Neville/Aretha Franklin (SB XL), Jordin Sparks (SB XLII), Jennifer Hudson (SB XLIII), and Pink (SB L). Others, including Faith Hill (SB XXXIV), Beyoncé Knowles (SB XXXVIII), Renée Fleming (SB XLVIII), and Jazmine Sullivan/Eric Church (SB LV), started in 4/4 and ended with a driving 3/4. The drum line under Kelly Clarkson (SB XLIX) added beats to an underlying 3/4 pulse that thus mixed in 4/4 and even 5/4 measures. Luke Bryan's unaccompanied rendition (SB LI) is effectively unmetered.

The most transformational Super Bowl performance may have been delivered by Diana Ross at 1982's Super Bowl XVI in Detroit; she had not only a local Motown connection but star power. Before her performance, Super Bowl anthems had a haphazard, regional flair. Performers included solo trumpeters and college marching bands. Television broadcasts often mixed in the sound of the crowd singing along with the usually excellent but less-known singers. The principal trumpeter of the National Symphony, Lloyd Geisler, performed the anthem at Super Bowl III, while ten years later a university men's a cappella chorus—the Colgate Thirteen—sang. Charley Pride was a bona fide country star when he sang the anthem in 1974 at Super Bowl VIII, but Diana Ross demonstrated the advantages of featuring a multichart celebrity. Steeg, who recruited Ross, remembered that it "transformed everything; once a star of that magnitude did it, other people decided it was OK." Every Super Bowl singer since then has been a performer with a national following and the recipient of multiple awards.

Lyrical mishaps at the Super Bowl are mercifully few, but mixing up the words can destroy an otherwise stellar performance, as Christina Aguilera experienced in 2011. If not for a simple error, Aguilera's passionate delivery would rival the best. Harry Connick, Jr., was reportedly so anxious about muffing the words that he had his father mouth the lyrics from the sideline.

Several singers have found ways to add political overtones to their Super Bowl anthems, often by manipulating Key's words. In 1994 Natalie Cole sang part of *America the Beautiful*—"America, America, God shed His grace on thee"—while the chorus behind her stuck to Key's script. The chorus then repeated "O'er the land of the free" three times while Cole echoed "the free" twice and finally shouted "I'm so glad I'm free" on the song's highest pitch. Sung with fierce determination and gospel flair by an African American soloist and chorus, this celebration of freedom was especially potent. The climactic repetitions of the lyric "home of the brave" leveraged special meaning here since the game took place in Atlanta, the "home" of civil rights leader Martin Luther King, Jr., thirty years after the 1964 Civil Rights Act was signed into law. As a musical and political statement, Cole's rendition of the anthem was artistically and socially stunning.

The choice of performer also carries messages about race and inclusion, especially in a sport where the majority of players are African American. At Super Bowl I in 1967, *The Star-Spangled Banner* was performed by two marching bands, from the University of Arizona and Grambling College. While the student instrumentalists from Arizona were predominantly white, the musicians from Louisiana's historically Black college were mainly Black. The 450 musicians combined symbolically on the field to form an American flag. In total, about a third of the anthem's performers have been of African American heritage, and about 15 percent are of mixed race. Mariah Carey (2002), Christina Aguilera (2011), and Demi Lovato (2020) have been Latino. Thus overall about half of the championship's first fifty-five anthem singers were musicians of color, proportionately greater than their representation in the overall U.S. population.

Voices Against the Anthem in Sports

The early 1970s mark the one period to date when there was a serious threat to the use of *The Star-Spangled Banner* in American athletics events. In those years, three social forces conspired to call the anthem ritual into question: opposition to the Vietnam War, the continuing struggle for civil rights, and political controversy over protest itself. Minor protests during renditions of the anthem became common, in which some fans would not participate in the ritual, refusing to stand and sing or just ignoring it entirely. Other fans found this behavior disrespectful. For example, in September 1970 in Skokie, Illinois, a high school football player refused to remove his helmet in protest of U.S. military action in Vietnam and Cambodia. The team suspended him. The school principal appealed to reinstate him, but the coach refused. When players voted with the coach, the school's football season was canceled.

Controversy broke out nationally in January 1973, when the U.S. Olympic Committee, likely in hopes of denying Black athletes the opportunity to protest, decided to skip the anthem altogether for a track meet to be held at Madison Square Garden. Director Jesse Abramson explained, "There is no rule or regulation about playing the anthem at sports events. We saw no relevance between the anthem and a track and field meet. Nobody has to prove his patriotism at sports events." The public outcry, however, was immediate. "Irate calls from all over the country" overwhelmed the organizers. Some called for a boycott. Twenty members of the New York City Council sponsored a bill to require the anthem before all sports events at which admission was charged. Organizers reinstated the anthem.

What may have begun as an attempt to wrap athletics in the flag is now an ideological straitjacket. Any attempt to stop or limit the pregame anthem ritual results in criticism that threatens the economic prosperity of the sport. Recent controversies over kneeling during the national anthem have provoked similar fan backlash and calls for boycotts.

The end of the Vietnam War in 1975 reduced pressure on the anthem ritual, and the American Bicentennial celebrations of 1976 seem to have restored a simpler, if overly commercialized, patriotic sentiment. During the 1980s and '90s, as the Cold War thawed and the Berlin Wall came down, patriotism became less urgent, and its associated sporting rituals lost their intensity. The onset of the First Gulf War, however, turned the tide, and the 9/11 terrorist attacks and subsequent War on Terror that followed raised the temperature of patriotic rhetoric still higher. More recently, while the Black Lives Matter movement has again made the ritual controversial, its ubiquity has not yet been significantly impacted. The NBA's Dallas Mavericks initially skipped the song to start their 2021 campaign before reversing course, while the NFL opened its 2020–21 season by counterbalancing Key's anthem with *Lift Every Voice and Sing,* a song often called the Black or African American national anthem.

Patriotism relies on sincerity. Paid patriotism is thus an oxymoron. Love of country should not be bought and sold for cash, but the boundary between marketing and patriotism can blur. In 2015 Arizona senators Jeff Flake and John McCain released a report, titled "Tackling Paid Patriotism," that identified more than $53 million in federal marketing contracts with sports teams. It detailed $6.8 million in payments made by the Pentagon to professional football, baseball, hockey, and soccer teams between 2012 and 2015. This was likely a small fraction of the phenomenon.

Such pay-for-patriotism spectacles frequently involved the pregame anthem. Military personnel might be invited to sing the anthem (solo or in chorus), join an on-field color guard, or be part of a field-flag detail. The report details twenty-eight such instances involving the anthem. "Fans should have confidence that their hometown heroes are being honored because of their honorable military service, not as a marketing ploy," McCain said. In response, the NFL returned $724,000 and issued guidance to its teams to separate paid advertising from "programs that honor members of the military and their families."

Complaints about the sheer ubiquity of the every-game anthem also arise. Pro-anthem devotees feel the pregame ritual is a vital marker of community and a cherished opportunity for Americans to show respect to the nation and military. Those who would reduce or eliminate the singing of the anthem at sports events, however, do not fall into a single political camp. Some see the anthem as a force of coercive militarism and nationalist propaganda. Others fear that too frequent repetition dilutes the song's ability to express patriotism at all. In June 1972, claiming that *The Star-Spangled Banner* was his favorite song, Kansas City Royals owner Ewing Kauffman announced that the anthem would be performed only on Sundays and holidays in order to counter "indifference to the flag." Less than two weeks later, following hundreds of fan complaints, he restored the every-game ritual.

During this same era, TV sports commentator Howard Cosell offered one of the more provocative indictments of the pregame ritual. An anonymous, indifferent patriotism, he said, risked debasing the very idea.

I don't equate professional football, major league baseball or any other sport in this country with motherhood, apple pie, and patriotism. . . . How is it an evidence of patriotism to sing or hear the national anthem played before a game? That's a cheap and easy thing, and 200 million Benedict Arnolds could subscribe to it and it still wouldn't make them patriots.

The Star-Spangled Banner has become inseparable from American sports. It plays a multilayered role. On the business side, it is both a patriotic advertisement and a vaccination against wartime's economic constraints. On the practical side, it calls fans to attention, playing a functional role in crowd control as an acoustic signal that the game is about to begin. For some fans, however, the overarching purpose of the pregame anthem is spiritual, as a civic ritual of commitment to nation.

In any regard, organized sports have become the most regular opportunity for Americans to sing and experience *The Star-Spangled Banner*. The every-game anthem is thus a potent force in the construction of a shared sense of nation. While repetition has its flaws, it also has power— the power to create and recreate a sense of community through song. For some, this concord offers a feeling of belonging, while for others, it may sound an alienating discord. For all, it is a reminder that the social project of America is just that, a project, and one that—as the history of the anthem in sports affirms—is in a state of continual transformation, debate, and reinvention.

Chapter 6

Singing Citizenship

A Tradition of Dissent

I love America more than any other country in the world,
and, exactly for this reason, I insist on the right to criticize her
perpetually.

—*James Baldwin (1955)*

Lyrics of Patriotism and Protest

Patriotic symbols are potent tools of protest, direct conduits to the nation's collective sense of history, values, and ideals. While patriotism trades on the immutable and timeless, the nation that it invokes is always in flux and subject to change. As any nation confronts new challenges, a reflective, critical patriotism reminds a people of their guiding principles and ideals. In a thriving democracy, patriotism should be a complicated and contested space. To disrupt patriotic harmony is to demand change, to call attention to the unmet needs of the community's constituents, often by pointing to suffering and injustice. As democracy grapples with the uncertainty of the present, patriotism roots the resulting choice in a collective sense of purpose. Critical patriotism is thus where the nation's challenges meet its aspirations.

As its affiliation with the nation deepened, *The Star-Spangled Banner* became increasingly effective as a vehicle for protest. Key's lyrics built on, contributed to, and further propelled an ongoing commentary in song about the future of the United States. From 1790 to 2021, more than 575 lyrics were written to the tune that is remembered today as only *The Star-Spangled Banner*. Alternative words sung to the melody were particularly common in the nineteenth century up through World War I. More than four hundred such lyrics were written after Key's famous song was published. Often paraphrasing Key's original for rhetorical effect, they called on the nation's patriotic pride to demand that it live true to its ideals. Not all such lyrics were protests—many celebrated or affirmed the status quo—but all expressed a vision, all served to guide and to shape the nation.

Beginning in the 1840s, protest lyrics written to the tune of *The Star-Spangled Banner* addressed themes of injustice and inequality. They have recounted stories of domestic violence and the devastation that alcoholism wrought upon a family. They have drawn attention to slavery's horror, unfair labor practices, and the denial of suffrage to women. They have tackled dozens of social issues: temperance, abolition, freedom of the press, labor rights, monopoly capitalism, monetary policy, international relations, peace, war, piety and Christian service, public education, imperialism, and military justice reform, among others. They amplify social dissonance, making audible the needs of the nation's people, often those denied the power to otherwise speak for themselves. By paraphrasing *The Star-Spangled Banner*, protesters recruited the patriotic sentiment of Key's song in service of a fundamental argument that the nation should do better. It is a tradition of American citizenship that stretches over two centuries.

Among the first lyrics of explicit protest written to the *Banner* tune was *The Song of the Flogged Sailor* (1845). Published in Baltimore, one of America's most important port cities and the birthplace of *The Star-Spangled Banner*, the lyric accompanied a dramatic newspaper account of U.S. Navy seamen who suffered punishments described as "a disgrace to the service." The article proclaimed that the "abominable and barbarous practice of flogging ought to be done away with" and offered three verses beginning:

Ye men of the shore, in kind mercy extend
Your ear to the woes of the sons of the ocean,
From the last of the tyrant we pray you defend

The tars who'd fight for you with fondest devotion.
    We fear not the storm
    In its mightiest form,
We've nothing to dread from the voice of the wave,
    But the flesh cutting lash
    Of the tyrant so rash,
Gives grief and dismay to the heart of the brave.

On nineteenth-century U.S. Navy vessels at sea, discipline was brutal. It was physical and corporeal, usually flogging with a whip called a cat-o'-nine-tails. As early as 1808, the surgeon Edward Cutbush decried the practice, and naval regulations limited punishment to twelve lashes. Yet flogging continued and often exceeded that limit. Aboard ship, a captain was judge, jury, and appeals court. The navy carpenter Samuel F. Holbrook offered several horrifying accounts of shipboard discipline in his autobiography:

Here were three hundred men, boys and marines, assembled round the old hulk to see these two young men nearly flayed alive, for going over to New York without leave. When all had assembled, the two prisoners were brought from their place of confinement, more dead than alive. The first was stripped and seized up. On these occasions, every man and officer stands with hats off, and perfectly silent, in order to show the *supremacy* of a law that cuts a man's flesh to pieces. Capt. Chauncey, standing on a slight elevation, and with a stentorian voice, addressed the crowd: *"Men! what the law allows you, you shall have, but by the eternal God if any one of you disobeys that law, I'll cut your back bone out."* "Go on with him, boatswain's mate and do your duty, or by God, you shall take his place."

The result could be fatal.

The Song of the Flogged Sailor makes a vivid case for the eradication of flogging. Its use of the *Banner* melody emphasizes the patriotism of the sailor who serves his country, just as it invokes the patriotic duty of the reader to protect naval servicemen. Despite the threat to health of Amer-

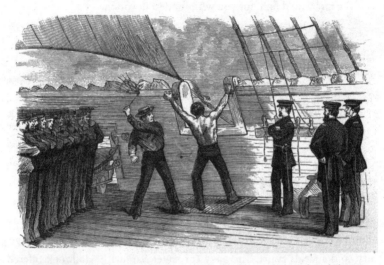

A nineteenth-century flogging, from the diary of U.S. Navy sailor Edward Shippen.

ican sailors and the sheer barbarity of the practice, flogging aboard U.S. naval ships was not fully outlawed until July 1862.

A Women's Rights Anthem

Third in frequency, after only Fourth of July lyrics and political campaign songs, many lyrics paraphrasing Key's patriotic song addressed issues critical to women. They were widely printed in newspapers, songsters, and even as sheet music. Most are temperance songs, attacking the evils of alcohol and its impact on the family, but others advocate for women's suffrage and confront violence against women. *The Factory Maid*, written in 1833, recounts in seven verses the story of Sarah Maria Cornell, a woman found dead on December 20, 1832. Sung to the *Banner* tune, its first verse runs:

> Oh list the sad tale of the poor Factory Maid,
>   How cheerful she went when the day's work was over,
> In cloak and in bonnet all simply arrayed,

To meet a dark fiend in the shape of a lover.
How gladsome and gay she tript on her way,
But alas! on her path the foul murderer lay.
Oh! weep for Maria, the poor Factory Maid—
So charming, so fair, and so basely betrayed.

Cornell, first deemed to have committed suicide, was discovered to have
been pregnant at the time of her death. Evidence pointed to the already
married Reverend Ephraim K. Avery as both the father and the murderer.
Avery's lengthy trial heard testimony from almost two hundred witnesses
and garnered national attention. The prosecution depicted him as emblematic of a corrupt Methodist clergy, protecting its reputation at all costs. The
defense characterized Cornell as mentally unstable, immoral, and promiscuous. Lurid details convinced the court of public opinion that Avery was
guilty, but the jury found him innocent. That was when the song appeared.
It offered a sympathetic view of Cornell, referred to as "Maria," and represented her lover as a false serpent who broke vows to both wife and church.
By echoing Key's song, the lyricist argued that violence against women was
a national concern. Printed in newspapers and as broadside song sheets, the
song is both a murder ballad and a morality tale. It is also a lyrical weapon
of vigilante justice that condemns Avery to social banishment. When the
courts failed, the song delivered both verdict and punishment.

To celebrate the Fourth of July in 1840, Catherine H. Waterman penned
a *National Temperance Ode* to the *Banner* melody. It celebrates the virtues
of "pure water"—what in the war against alcoholism was both an alternative beverage and a symbol of health and purity. Premiered by a choir at a
temperance convention in Philadelphia, the lyric references both *Adams
and Liberty* and Key's repeated refrain to celebrate a life alcohol "free."

Come, sons of Columbia, while proudly and high,
Every bosom with freedom and glory is swelling,
While our Eagle's bright Eyrie's still built in the sky,
And tyran[n]y's death-song is heard in each dwelling,

Come, the bright chalice drain—and again and again,
Let our pledge, and our toast, in a far-sounding strain,
Be water—pure water, bright sparkling with glee,
That flows like our life's blood, unfettered and free.

Waterman's song was published in sheet music form, arranged for three
voices, and is an example of the most common protest lyric associated
with the *Banner* melody—the temperance song.

Music was a primary vehicle of temperance meetings, alternating with
sermons and speeches. Hymns, sentimental songs, and patriotic parodies
were especially popular. That the *Banner* melody would be used as the
basis for songs arguing against the use of alcohol suggests that by 1840,
its association with London's Crown and Anchor Tavern or memories of
the drunken skits through which the English original was introduced to
American audiences had been, if not forgotten, then overshadowed by
the tune's effectiveness as a vehicle for national commentary. If irony was
intended, it was meant not as a joke but as a serious attempt to rehabilitate
American identity around the notion of abstinence. In temperance songsters, Key's lyrics were often printed before such anti-alcohol paraphrases.

The history of the temperance movement is the story of growing activism among American women. With such titles as *Come Home, Father*
(1864), *Father's a Drunkard, and Mother Is Dead* (1866), *Sign the Pledge for
Mother's Sake* (1867), and *Please Sell No More Drink to My Father* (1884),
temperance songs reveal the interweaving of domestic issues of neglect
and violence into the anti-alcohol crusade. In an era when men, both as
husbands and as fathers, were the economic and legal lifeline connecting
a family to the public sphere, alcoholism was associated with both physical abuse and abject poverty. *Banner* variants lamented the tragedies that
resulted. In 1843 *The Cold Water Magazine* offered a vivid alternative lyric
to Key's song to inspire the zeal of temperance activists. A husband or
father falling victim to alcoholism was, these lyrics argue, not only a personal struggle but a family catastrophe and a national tragedy.

1. Oh! who has not seen by the dawn's early light,
   Some poor bloated drunkard to his home weakly reeling,
   With blear eyes and red nose most revolting to sight;
   Yet still in his breast not a throb, of shame feeling!
   And the plight he was in—steep'd in filth to his chin,
   Gave proof through the night in the gutter he'd been,
   While the pity-able wretch would stagger along,
   To the shame of his friends, 'mid the jeers of the throng.

2. To his home when he came, half frantic with ire,
   That his poor wife had dared, while he revell'd, to sleep,
   Though wretched and faint 'neath miseries dire,
   She had striven, all in vain, her sad vigils to keep,
   And tears, gushing, chase down her wo-begone face
   In the furrows which sorrow and suffering trace,
   To see her loved lord like a wild demon rave,
   To the vilest of sins, a beast and a slave.

3. But thanks to that band who so faithfully swore,
   That the havoc of rum and the bottle's confusion
   Our home and our country should ravage no more
   If aught might o'ercome the foul curse and pollution.
   They are striving to save the victim and slave,
   From th' horrors of guilt and th' drunkard's dark grave,
   And the temperance banner in triumph shall wave,
   O'er the land of the free and the home of the brave.

Oh! Who Has Not Seen?, an 1843 temperance lyric that paraphrases *The Star-Spangled Banner.*

The opportunity to supply thousands of temperance societies with music drove a fervid industry of temperance publishers to create sheet music and convention songsters. At least twenty-two sets of temperance lyrics used the *Banner* melody. *The Washington Banner* was written for a precursor of Alcoholics Anonymous, a self-help group called the Washingtonians. Three additional 1842 lyrics directly paraphrase Key's—*Defence of Fort Temperance*, the *Temperance Banner*, and *The Star of Temperance*. Later variants included *The Clarion* (1859), *The Banner of Temperance* (1867) by gospel lyricist Fanny Crosby, *The Spotless White Banner* (1874), *The Foe of Church and Freedom* (1884), and *The No-License Banner* (1909). This explosion of temperance parodies reflects the increasing scope and energy of the temperance movement, which culminated in the ratification of the Eighteenth Amendment in 1919 and thus America's Prohibition Era (1920–33).

Women's Suffrage

The suffrage movement developed in tandem with temperance and abolition, as winning the vote for women was a strategy to elect leaders who would support both causes. Written by the Reverend C. C. Harrah, *The Equal-Rights Banner* (1888) connects women's suffrage to the nation's very survival.

1. Oh say, have you heard of the new, dawning light,
Bringing hope to our land, and its foes all surprising?
Our banner still floats, as the emblem of right,
And the day breaks upon us, for women are rising.
And with ballots in hand, at the right's dear command,
They'll be true to the flag and will rescue our land;
And ever the EQUAL-RIGHTS BANNER shall wave
O'er the land of the free and the home of the brave.

While suffrage songsters feature hundreds of lyrics set to the music of American patriotic songs for use at conventions and street protests, parodies of *The Star-Spangled Banner* are conspicuously rare. The 1909 *Suffrage*

United States ! Your banner wears
Two emblems—one of fame ;
Alas, the other that it bears
Reminds us of your shame.

The *white* man's liberty in types
Stands blazoned by your *stars* ;
But what's the meaning of your *stripes* ?
They mean your *negro's scars.*   THOMAS CAMPBELL.

Illustration of an enslaved Black man with U.S. flag and liberty pole with cap,
from the 1843 *American Anti-Slavery Almanac.* Note how the flag's stars are
divided into white and black, representing North and South, free and slave.

Song Book, for example, contains twenty-eight lyrics sung to such tunes
as *America,* the *Battle Cry of Freedom, Dixie, Marching Through Georgia,*
Maryland, My Maryland, and *Auld Lang Syne.* No fewer than eight appear
for the *Battle Hymn of the Republic,* adding an air of religious fervor and
moral righteousness to the cause. However, the collection contains no lyrics composed to the Anacreontic tune. This absence suggests that by the
early twentieth century, the role of Key's song in American life was shifting—it was becoming a sacred national hymn. It seems tactical then that

women seeking the right to vote treated *The Star-Spangled Banner* not as a vehicle for parody and protest, but as something iconic and immutable. This musical show of respect seems calculated to demonstrate that suffragettes were not radicals but conscientious citizens who understood and deserved the vote.

An Abolitionist Anthem

The back cover of the *American Anti-Slavery Almanac* of 1843 presents a striking image of patriotic contradiction. A rough rope hangs from a liberty pole topped with its traditional liberty cap. The rope binds two things fast—a United States flag and an enslaved Black man. It is a contrast of freedom and bondage, a challenge to America's ideals. Abolitionist poets noted the fraudulent irony of a patriotic song asking if the nation's flag still waved "o'er the land of the free." For the enslaved, the nation had never earned such distinction.

In 1843 some 2.5 million Black men, women, and children were held captive in heritable servitude in the United States. This number would rise to 4 million before the Civil War. Proclaiming liberty as the nation's guiding principle, *The Star-Spangled Banner* served both as a symbol of aspiration and a marker of a stark, continuing failure. Abolitionist poets wrote alternative lyrics to Key's song, including what may be the most viscerally gripping set of words every paired with the *Banner* tune—*Oh Say, Do You Hear?* (1844).

1. Oh say, do you hear, at the dawn's early light,
    The shrieks of those Bondmen, whose blood is now streaming
From the merciless lash, while our Banner in sight,
    With its stars, mocking Freedom, is fitfully gleaming?
Do you see the backs bare, do you mark every score
Of the whip of the driver trace channels of gore:
And say, doth our Star Spangled Banner yet wave
O'er the land of the Free, and the home of the brave?

2. On the shore, dimly seen thro' the mists of the deep,
    Where Africa's race in false safety reposes,
   What is that which the breeze, o'er the towering steep,
    As it heedlessly sweeps, half conceals, half discloses?
   'Tis a slave ship that's seen, by the morning's first beam,
   And its tarnish'd reflection pollutes now the stream:
   'Tis our Star Spangled Banner, O, when shall it wave
   O'er the land of the Free, and the home of the Brave!

3. And where is the Band, who so valiantly bore
    The havoc of war, and the battle's confusion,
   For Liberty's sweets? We shall know them no more:
    Their fame is eclips'd by foul Slavery's pollution.
   No refuge is found on our unhallow'd ground,
   For the wretched in Slavery's manacles bound;
   While our Star Spangled Banner, in vain boasts to wave
   O'er the land of the Free, and the home of the Brave.

4. Shall we ne'er hail the day, when as freemen shall stand,
    The millions who groan under matchless oppression?
   Shall Liberty's shouts, in our heav'n-rescued land,
    Ne'er be shar'd by the slave in our blood-guilty nation?
   Oh, let us be just, *e're in God we dare trust,*
   Else the day will o'er take us, when perish we must;
   And our Star Spangled Banner at half-mast shall wave
   O'er the death-bed of Freedom—the home of the Slave.

Oh Say, Do You Hear?, an 1844 abolitionist commentary on Key's lyric, is one of the
most cogent and forceful protest lyrics written to the anthem melody.

The lyric's author was Dr. Edwin Augustus Atlee, an agent of the underground railroad in Battle Creek, Michigan. In July 1844, possibly com-
menting on the Independence Day holiday, he published these words as a

"New Version of the National Song" in the *Signal of Liberty,* an abolitionist newspaper printed in nearby Ann Arbor. Atlee's lyric featured graphic imagery—sonic, visual, and physical—to deliver a visceral argument to abolish slavery in the United States.

Key's original lyric breaks through Atlee's in four parallel verses. The opening of each invokes the well-known lines of Key's text, but Atlee shifts their imagery to argue against slavery. Rather than the foul footsteps of the British soldiers, for example, the foul "pollution" that must be washed out here is slavery itself. Atlee's final verse trades upon Key's appeal to piety in order to echo a divine hope—"Oh, let us be just, ere in God we dare trust." Its searing closing image is both poignant and powerful. The nation's flag still waves, but at half-mast. It mourns for racial justice, not above the land of the free and brave, but over the "death-bed of Freedom—the home of the slave." Atlee's lyric called out the acrid lie of an ensign of freedom flying over a nation that condoned slavery. Less than two months later his lyric gained both a prominent endorsement and a national audience when it was republished in William Lloyd Garrison's abolitionist weekly *The Liberator.*

In 1858 *The Liberator* would again publish an antislavery lyric composed for the Anacreontic tune—*The Patriot's Banner.* This new lyric was printed just below the four verses of Key's lyric. Remarkably, *The Liberator* offers no comment about the word "slave" in Key's third verse. Some abolitionists, in fact, embraced Key's song as a statement of freedom's promise, singing it at antislavery meetings and festivals. The Massachusetts Anti-Slavery Society, for example, had long sponsored an annual Anti-Slavery Celebration of the Fourth of July that also served as a mass abolitionist meeting.

Other contemporary accounts, however, make it clear that Key's song elicited conflicted feelings in the Black community. A Civil War–era concert at New York City's Black Zion Baptist Church in 1862, for example, was to feature *The Star-Spangled Banner* as its grand finale. Before the concert concluded, however, the master of ceremonies J. W. Jacobs announced that "so long as there was a slave in the United States, that was no song for colored people to sing." *Where Liberty Dwells, There Is My Country,* a song honoring New York's Seventh Regiment then serving in the Union Army, was sung instead.

The first presidential campaign lyric sung to the tune of *The Star-Spangled Banner* to call for the end of slavery was *The Dawn of Liberty*, supporting the first-ever Republican Party candidate John C. Frémont in 1856. It would be the next Republican candidate, however, whose fate it would be to change the nation. In 1860 Abraham Lincoln won both the popular vote and Electoral College with only 39.8 percent of ballots cast because the overall vote was split among four candidates. Three songs written to support Lincoln's candidacy were sung to the *Banner* tune: *Honest Abe of the West*, *Old Abe the Rail-Splitter*, and *The Banner of Freedom*. These argued musically that Lincoln was the patriotic choice who would preserve the union. Ironically, one other *Banner* lyric assisted Lincoln's victory, but it was composed in support of John Bell, the presidential nominee of the Constitutional Union Party.

The Progressive Banner

After the Civil War, industrialization accelerated. American progressivism was one response to its economic impacts, including monopoly capitalism and labor strife. A core question of American political life was thus the fundamental balance between business and labor. The nation's identity was at stake, and public debates incorporated newspaper ballads sung to the *Banner* tune. They addressed topics such as the value of labor, the importance of education, and the economic impact of corporate trusts. *Rouse, Ye Heroes!* (1882) called on Americans to fight the tyrant "grim Monopoly" and "break the bonds that again are our people enslaving." Such lyrics often invoked slavery to describe workers denied fair wages and respect for their work.

Progressive lyricists focused not only on urban labor but on farm labor as well. The *Kansas Alliance Songbook* of 1891, for example, celebrated "all kinds of toil" and called upon family farms to unionize, using this verse sung to the *Banner* melody.

Farmers, stand to your rights; the time has now come
When we must take the lead in the oncoming battle.
By the right of your suffrage put good men and true
To lead us to vict'ry and give the death rattle
To all future efforts to grind workmen down
To worse than the slave, or acknowledge a crown,
Let our Star Spangled Banner once more proudly wave
O'er a "Land of the Free" made by men that are brave.

As late as 1922, the *Oklahoma Union Farmer* published a *Banner* lyric asking "Oh, say, does that same Farmers' Union yet stand / To protect farmers' rights from the sharks of the land?"

Other *Banner* paraphrases focused on issues of factory labor, using patriotism's call as inspiration for workers to unionize. Founded in 1905, the Industrial Workers of the World (IWW) envisioned a pan-industrial union. In 1909 the IWW published a pocket-size songster soon known as *The Little Red Songbook*. Subtitled "Songs to Fan the Flames of Discontent," this book of lyrics included *The Banner of Labor* to be sung to the tune of *The Star-Spangled Banner*. Its chorus shouted the rallying cry— "And the BANNER OF LABOR will surely soon wave, / O'er the land that is free, from the master and slave." Such pro-labor parodies were not found only in radical publications. In 1905 *The Land of the Trust* appeared in *Life Magazine,* demonstrating that progressivism was also a middle-class movement.

Among the criticisms of *The Star-Spangled Banner* as an anthem is its celebration of militarism. Also troubling to pacifists is the song's effectiveness as a wartime rallying cry. Such associations, however, offered pacifists the opportunity to recast the love of country as a love of peace. Several of the earliest Anacreontic lyrics celebrated peace as a benefit of the national compact. *Adams and Liberty* (1798) used the word "peace" three times. *A Navy Forever!* (1799) called for a strong navy as a guarantee of peace, while an 1801 lyric posited that Thomas Jefferson's election as president had forged a nation "united in peace." In 1808 the *Banner* lyric *Embargo and Peace* preferred economic sanctions to war. Key's song itself envisioned a nation "blessed with victory and peace," and at least six separate lyrics sung to the Anacreontic tune celebrated the coming of peace after the War of 1812. Following the Civil War, in contrast, only W. T. W. Ball's peace lyric appeared and then not until four years after the war had ended. This inability to heal reflected an enduring Civil War wound in the nation's identity.

In the late nineteenth century, as the United States exercised its territorial ambitions, annexing Hawaii and seizing Spain's colonies in 1898, *Banner* lyrics amplified both sides of the resulting debate over American imperialism. *The New Star-Spangled Banner* of 1900 celebrated these territorial additions and cast the nation's flag as a signal of liberation. "Oh, say, let the star-spangled banner be waved," the widely reprinted lyric proclaimed, "O'er the lands we have freed and the people we've saved." As Philippine resistance continued, however, a 1902 lyric criticized the violence being used to bring "liberty" to its people, concluding, "O'er their heads the proud Star Spangled Banner shall wave, / Even though every head may be down in a grave." The U.S. military government in Manila went so far as to pass a law requiring that *The Star-Spangled Banner* be performed if the rebel anthem *Aguinaldo's March* was played. In 1903, despite claims that anti-American passions had passed, Philippine audiences continued to cheer the revolutionary general's march while booing *The Star-Spangled Banner.*

In 1905 the United States hosted a peace conference between Russia and Japan, earning President Theodore Roosevelt the Nobel Peace Prize. The conference was celebrated with the song *The Star-Spangled Banner of Peace,* the first fully anti-war lyric written to the melody. Composed by the Alabama educator and prison reformer Julia S. Tutwiler, the lyric expressed hope "that man's blood nevermore by man's hand shall be shed." As World War developed in Europe, the lyric was used for anti-war conventions, Peace Day celebrations, and Fourth of July demonstrations. It appeared in U.S. papers in 1911, 1915, 1918, and even as late as 1933.

After World War I began, the New York City public school principal

Kate Devereux Blake addressed teachers across the nation on "The Duty of
the Teacher Towards Peace." She also offered an original anti-war parody
of *The Star-Spangled Banner* for their students to sing. Used as a second
and final verse to Key's song, it made vivid the stake that children—and
thus teachers—had in the war.

> Oh, say can you see, you who glory in war,
>   All the wounded and dead of the red battle's reaping?
> Can you listen unmoved to their agonied groans,
>   Hear the children who starve, and the pale widows weeping?
>   Henceforth let us swear
>   Bombs shall not burst in air
>   Nor war's desolation wreck all that is fair.
> But the Star Spangled Banner, by workers unfurled,
> Shall give hope to the nations and peace to the world.

A newspaper respondent mocked Blake's verse, noting that "until the
world is wholly gentled, the people who make national anthems . . . of
the *Twinkle, Twinkle, Little Star* type will not have a country of their own
long." Blake's words thus became part of America's debate over its role in
the emerging global conflict. Such peace lyrics—sung to a melody being
used by most Americans as a pro-war cry—offered a contrasting argument. Another *Banner* lyric even called for the formation of what would
soon be the League of Nations, and thus for a way that nations could solve
their differences without the need for war.

The Star-Spangled Banner—which in 1917 was deemed the "national
anthem" of the American military—increasingly became a contested
symbol and political weapon. At a 1917 peace meeting, anti-war speakers were forced to abandon their speeches when soldiers in the audience
began singing *The Star-Spangled Banner* to drown them out. A pro-war
Banner lyric written by Helen Gray Cone, a pioneering English professor
at Hunter College, celebrated the U.S. intervention in Europe as a defense
of freedom.

Oh, say, can you see, on the torn fields of France,
The fair flag of hope over brown legions flying,
With its broad stripes that blaze, and its bright stars that dance,
The pride of the living, the faith of the dying?
Yes, the red-white-and-blue, borne in battle anew,
Gives proof to the world that our hearts are still true;
And the Star-Spangled Banner shall fearlessly wave
For the cause of the free, in the ranks of the brave!

In conversation with the lyrics by Tutwiler and Blake, Cone's words illustrate the potential of *Banner* lyrics to facilitate public debate.

In the twentieth century, enabled by the ubiquity of recording and broadcast media technologies, political expression using Key's song shifted from writing alternative lyrics to the rhetorics of performance style. But the tradition of writing political lyrics to the *Banner* tune never died out completely. Recently the internet has allowed politically engaged poets to share these lyrical arguments, even though they are no longer typically published in newspapers. The twenty-first century has thus witnessed a revival of Anacreontic lyric, written for political, sentimental, and humorous effect. Subjects range from Fourth of July celebrations of military heroism to frustrations with technology and high health insurance premiums. Other *Banner* lyrics mock the anthem mishaps of Roseanne Barr and Christina Aguilera, while a vein of sports parody denounces the "Star Cranked-Up Batters" of baseball's steroid era, laments the playoff woes of the New York Mets, and examines Colin Kaepernick's NFL protest from both sides of the debate. Political lyrics criticize every recent president—Bush, Obama, Trump, and Biden—and address issues such as immigration, government bailouts, and the War on Terror. Anacreontic poetry remains alive and well.

Chapter 7

Nation in Translation

Language and the Politics of Belonging

Our National Anthem is a powerful and beautiful statement regardless of the language in which it is recited or sung.

—*Voices United for America (2006)*

Nuestro Himno
April 28, 2006, Latinx Radio

In a simultaneous premiere over Latin radio stations nationwide, *Nuestro Himno*—a Spanish-language, Latin-pop arrangement of *The Star-Spangled Banner*, exploded on the airwaves. It fueled protests on immigrant rights and sparked a conservative backlash. To translate the anthem is always a political act. Even at its most literal and reverential, to sing the anthem in another language is to extend a claim of belonging, to assert that American identity is multiple and expansive, rather than singular and narrow.

The 2006 track, the title of which means "Our Anthem" in Spanish, was produced by New York's Urban Box Office Records as a message of solidarity timed to coincide with immigration rights marches planned for May 1 of that same year. The protests—labeled The Great American Boycott or A Day Without Immigrants—leveraged the annual May Day workers' commemoration to highlight the contributions of immigrants to the U.S. economy. A punitive immigration bill then under debate in the U.S. Senate had inspired the demonstrations; advocates instead called for the creation of a legal path to full citizenship for the undocumented.

Musically, *Nuestro Himno* carries the markers of sincere patriotic devotion. "It has the passion. It has the respect," explained the producer Adam Kidron, who organized the project. The steady beat of an insistent snare drum underlies the lyric from beginning to end, expressing a resolute march feel that evokes the anthem's traditional military associations. The lyric, accompanied by guitars and strings, is delivered as a soaring pop ballad by a procession of two dozen Latinx vocalists, featuring the Dominican trio Voz a Voz, the Mexican singers Kalimba and Gloria Trevi, New York's Tony Sunshine, the Cuban-American rapper Pitbull, the Haitian singer Wyclef Jean, and the Puerto Rican musicians Carlos Ponce, Olga Tañón, and Ivy Queen, among others. This vocal parade weaves a sonic

Producer Eduardo Reyes (center) with *Nuestro Himno* artists Voz a Voz and Reggaeton Niños at Ellis Island, New York, May 30, 2006.

tapestry of Latinidad—the Latin American family of nations. Tracks had been recorded in New York, Puerto Rico, Miami, Mexico City, Los Angeles, and Madrid and then were mixed together into a single performance. The Spanish lyric was borrowed from a 1919 translation of *The Star-Spangled Banner* commissioned by the U.S. government. Titled *La bandera de las estrellas*, this singing translation of Key's text had been realized by Frank Haffkine Snow, a professor of modern languages at the U.S. Naval Academy. In a moderate 4/4 tempo, Snow's lyric is realized using the contour of the traditional *Banner* melody, even as each vocalist makes the melody more personal by using every opportunity for expressive ornament. The full recording clocks in at three minutes and twenty-one seconds. It offers a full statement of Key's opening verse plus a second verse that mostly repeats the first, with substitutions for the opening three lines. This repetition allowed producers to include more artists on the track and to add vocal commentary. For example, Snow's 1919 translation ends with the word "sagrada," but here it is sung twice, emphasizing a "sacred" patriotic devotion to the nation.

Nuestro Himno inspired both broad press coverage and a predictable furor. Some Americans heard it as a hostile protest song and objected to the very notion of translating the anthem at all. To do so suggested that Spanish-speaking Americans were equally American and raised the specter of a bilingual nation. One blogger called it the "Illegal Alien Anthem." Charles Key, a descendant of the lyric's author, helped fuel the backlash, saying, "I think it's a despicable thing that somebody was going into our society from another country and change our national anthem." The album's producer, who was British but had lived in the United States for sixteen years, reported receiving "more hate mail in the last 24 hours than I've experienced in my whole life."

President George W. Bush, who spoke in Spanish on the campaign trail to court Latino voters, responded saying, "I think the national anthem ought to be sung in English, and I think people who want to be a citizen of this country ought to learn English." Kidron suggested that the president should instead "embrace the opportunity to teach a wider audience about the American Dream." Part of the song's motivation, he claimed, was to amplify patriotism among protesters. "There's no attempt to usurp anything," he explained. It would even help immigrants understand the anthem, the flag, and the "ideals of freedom that they represent." One reporter called the whole controversy "much ado about nothing." Others noted that the national anthem had long been sung in translation. No one noticed that the track's translation was itself a U.S. government creation. The State Department even had four Spanish translations on its website at the time, but they soon disappeared from view.

Nuestro Himno was overtly political for two reasons: context and added content. Its release at a time of public debate over immigration offered a direct commentary on American identity and values. It argued that the nation should be welcoming, that historically the nation had been built through immigration, and that Spanish-speaking Americans were no less patriotic than others. It simultaneously called on Spanish-speaking Americans to unite for political power. Additions to the translation made this intent clear. From the track's outset, Ivy Queen calls to *"Latinos, Latinas, hermanos, hermanas,"* invoking a collective solidarity. An interlude between the statements of Key's verse has Wyclef Jean exclaim, *"La libertad, somos iguales, somos hermanos en nuestro himno"* (Liberty, we are equals, we are brothers in our anthem). Jean's words parallel Key's "land of the free," but in the revolutionary spirit of the French motto *"Liberté, égalité, fraternité,"* which is also (and perhaps not coincidentally) the tripartite motto of Jean's own nation of Haiti. Most overtly, Pitbull inserted a call to action: *"Mi gente sigue luchando, Ya! es tiempo de romper las cadenas"* (My people, keep fighting; It is time to break the chains).

When the full album *Somos Americanos* (We are Americans) was released in June, it contained an extended remix with an additional rap by then twelve-year-old P-Star, the stage name of Priscilla Star Diaz. Her lyric added two layers to the song. First it brought to the fore the needs of children caught in the immigration battle. Second, it expanded the cause of undocumented Latino workers to include workers of all races and ethnicities.

Immigration hard-liners created alternative lyrics to the anthem tune to add their own voice to the debate. Frustrated with the government's failure to pass more stringent immigration laws, the Philadelphia talk radio personalities Steve Bryant and Tony Polito penned "the last National anthem you'll ever need," a parody of *The Star-Spangled Banner* asserting that the undocumented found financial comfort on welfare and that liberal politicians just wanted their votes, while Congress was "blind" and President Bush "doesn't care." Conservative Senator Lamar Alexander of Tennessee introduced a nativist English-only anthem resolution. He worried that a Spanish-language anthem "adds to the celebration of multiculturalism," eroding "our understanding of our American culture." A parallel resolution stalled in the House Judiciary Committee, but not before inspiring a multilingual response.

A group calling itself Voices United for America found the notion of an English-only mandate inconsistent with free speech. They issued a recording that presents Key's lyric in a mix of ten languages: Italian, Spanish, Swedish, Bulgarian, German, Arabic, Japanese, Tagalog, Korean, and English. Their musical enactment of American diversity avoided the jingoism of Key's central stanzas and focused instead on the courage, freedoms, and devotion of the original text's first and last verses. It was also accompanied by a written manifesto:

> Our National Anthem is a powerful and beautiful statement regardless of the language in which it is recited or sung. Immigrants arriving in our country today seek the same freedoms and liberties as did our forefathers. The talents and diversity of people of all backgrounds do not diminish nor destroy American values, rather they add color and texture to the American Portrait.

Key's song had once again become a flashpoint for debate. It asked who was American, and who should be. In sounding difference within American identity, it made the nation's Anglo-European center more audible. It empowered those who were often written out of the American story to make their presence heard, to claim their patriotism, and to assert their belonging—in sum, the recording told a more complex and expansive American story.

An American Tradition

Translating *The Star-Spangled Banner* into other languages is an American tradition. Since 1851, more than one hundred translations of Key's lyric have been published in at least forty languages. These include Albanian, American-Samoan, American Sign Language, Arabic, Armenian, Cherokee, Crow, Czech, Dakota, Esperanto, French, Gaelic, Scots-Gaelic, German, Greek, Hawaiian, Hebrew, Hungarian, Indonesian, Italian, Japanese, Lakota, Latin, Lithuanian, Mandarin, Navajo, Ojibwe, O'odham, Polish, Portuguese, Russian, Serbian, Spanish, Swahili, Swedish, Tagalog, Turkish, Ukrainian, Umatilla, and Yiddish. Claims that *Nuestro Himno* represented the first commercial recording of the anthem in translation were incorrect. The baritone František Pangrác recorded Key's song in Czech in 1918, the pop vocalist Patrick Dickson recorded it in Hawaiian in 1983, and the educator Katherine Duncum recorded a Navajo version in 1988. In 1999, the French translation *La bannière étoilée* was released, and the Cherokee National Youth Choir recorded it in their tribal language in 2002. More recordings have followed.

Translation necessarily requires shifts in poetic imagery, as even words denoting the same meaning in two languages never have precisely the same connotations. Literal translation reduces such shifts, but in translating a song for performance, one is confined not just by meaning but by melody, rhythm, and rhyme, making the translation of song an art form unto itself.

Nearly all translations of *The Star-Spangled Banner* are singing translations—like the *Bandera* text used in *Nuestro Himno*. Singing translations attempt to realize the words of another language into a parallel lyric that can be sung to the original melody. Rhythms are readily adjusted to accommodate syllables added or subtracted, but the practical challenge of conveying metaphor in a singable lyric necessarily inspires the translator to exchange one poetic conceit for idiomatic equivalents, even if the intended result is the same.

A common line of attack against translations of Key's lyric is to dismiss them as attempts to "change" the nation's anthem. This argument is easy to "prove." The new lyric is simply reverse-translated back into English and inevitably found awkward and wanting. An Associated Press story, for example, translated the opening verse of *Nuestro Himno* back into English as beginning "The day is breaking, do you see it?" and concluding "The voice of your starry beauty is still unfolding, / Over a land of the free, the sacred flag?" But to invert a poetic translation using a cold literal approach misrepresents the translator's art, resulting in fragmented, inelegant gibberish that predictably offers only distorted mumblings and distant echoes of the original.

Historically, translations of *The Star-Spangled Banner* have been motivated by the desire to make the song accessible to and expressible by an additional American community. Anthem translations welcome, facilitate, and celebrate an expanded sense of American-ness itself. As the German-speaking soldiers who fought for the Union Army demonstrated so valiantly, loyalty to the United States is not expressed in English only. On the most basic level, translations have allowed more Americans to claim their love of the nation in ways that speak most sincerely to their experience.

The first known translation of Key's lyric appeared in Galveston, Texas, as *Das Star-Spangled Banner*. This German text was first published in 1851 and was likely created by Hermann Seele, a German immigrant who worked as a teacher in the New Braunfels settlement and later became its mayor. He favored the U.S. annexation of Texas and each year sang *The Star-Spangled Banner* and gave a speech at a local celebration of the Fourth of July. Niclas Müller, a poet and refugee from Europe's 1848 revolutions who established a New York print shop, created a second German translation. Both could be sung to the original tune, and both were published and republished during the Civil War, serving the expressive needs of German-speaking troops in camp and their families on the home front.

In 1876 Brazil's last emperor, Dom Pedro II, translated Key's lyric into Portuguese while touring the United States. That same year a third German translation—*Das Sternenbanner-Lied*—was published in celebration of the nation's centennial. Translated by Baltimore journalist Edward F. Leyh (1840–1901), the text would appear in Leyh's own *Die Deutsche Correspondent* as well as other American German-language newspapers. It was sung at the 1903 Nord-Oestlicher Saengerfest in Baltimore "by the entire audience, standing." Leyh's moving commentaries reveal a deep pride in the contributions of the Pennsylvania Dutch (that is, German immigrants) to their adopted nation and suggest that *The Star-Spangled Banner* was well known, even beloved, among many nineteenth-century German Americans.

Anthem translations emphasize the nation's multilingual past. Immigrant communities in the United States frequently published Key's text in non-English newspapers, songsters, and church hymnals, expressing ethnic pride while pursuing Americanization and integration into the prevailing culture. Father Eugene O'Growney, a progenitor of the Gaelic language revival in Ireland, translated Key's lyric in 1898 as *An Bhratach Gheal-Réaltach*. Fleeing anti-Jewish pogroms from the 1890s, Jewish settlers in the United States created a vibrant New World community, particularly in New York. In 1898 a singing translation of Key's song was published in Hebrew as *Degel hakokhavim*. The translator, Gerson Rosenzweig, explained that Jewish Americans who had escaped to freedom in the United States held the notion of liberty dear: "To no one can the 'Star Spangled Banner' hold out more promise than . . . to those who have suffered for centuries because they held holy the right of freedom of worship." A version in Swedish—*Den stjärnströdda fanan*—was published in 1903.

Forging Allies: World War I and Beyond

World War I–era translations of *The Star-Spangled Banner* into French and Italian carried America's heroic tune to Europe and helped unite the Allies. These lyrics show little fidelity to the Key's original but used his poetry as a point of departure to inspire courage, instill hope, build trust, and facilitate international cooperation. In 1917 the Parisian publisher E. Gaudet issued a French version by Victor Meusy as *La bannière étoilée*. Intended for live performance, it was available in five versions: full orchestra, fanfare ensemble, male quartet, piano solo, and voice with piano. The following year *L'étendard étoilé: Hymne national américain* appeared among the imprints of E. Dupré in Paris. While the text is credited to Alfred Delbruck as a "translation," it merely evokes Key's original. Literally, it calls upon the French to redouble their military efforts. The lyric envisions the U.S. flag— joined in battle with the French—as a source of manly inspiration to conquer barbarity. Its cover illustration shows a resolute soldier draped in the American flag and backed by a fierce American eagle.

Captain Frank A. Perret of the American Red Cross created the 1917 Italian lyric—*Il vessillo stellato*—to fit the anthem tune. It was less a translation than a new song created to inspire the Italian populace to trust Americans.

These World War I sheet music covers of *L'étendard étoilé* (1918), a French version of the U.S. anthem, and *Il vessillo stellato* (1817), an Italian version, show American soldiers as valiant protectors of Europe.

Taught to children and sung at Red Cross events, the lyric describes *"nostro vessillo stellate"* (our, that is—America's, starry banner) as *"il simbolo fiero di nostera speranza"* (the proud symbol of our hope) for *"un popolo sogni la sua libertade dal fiero oppressor"* (a people that dreams of their freedom from the fierce oppressor). A New York publisher issued *La bandiera stellata*, a more literal singing translation, the next year. Dedicated to President Wilson, who is celebrated as a *"Campione della democrazia,"* the translation appeared side by side with Key's original, expressing the dual loyalty of Italian Americans. A similarly inspired Polish translation by Karol Wachtel appeared in 1918 as *Nasz Sztandar Gwiaździsty.*

Foreign language translation also served as a flashpoint of anti-immigrant distrust and resentment, particularly during the anti-German hysteria of World War I. In May 1917 following the U.S. entry into the war, a self-proclaimed American Rights Committee demanded of the Indianapolis school board that the singing of American patriotic songs in German by pupils in German language classes be "abandoned forthwith and never resumed." Such translations had been a tool for teaching English-speaking Americans how to speak German. Nevertheless, the school board unanimously agreed.

Frank Snow's 1919 Spanish translation was a World War I-era, U.S. government project. It had been commissioned by Lieutenant F. Eugene Ackerman, director of the Bureau of Latin-American Affairs for the Committee on Public Information (CPI). Established by President Wilson's April 1917 executive order, the CPI mobilized public opinion in support of U.S. involvement in the war. It was the first large-scale propaganda agency of the U.S. government. After the war, Ackerman facilitated the distribution of Snow's translation in "thousands of copies" sent to South and Central America through the Spanish edition of *Export American Industries,* a trade magazine of the National Association of Manufacturers. Ackerman's goal was to advance American business interests in Latin America. Snow's translation was also published for domestic use under the auspices of the U.S. Bureau of Education, adapted to its official edition of Key's song featuring Walter Damrosch's harmonization. With Key's English text printed on the back, the Spanish-language edition served the needs of the U.S. government's Americanization strategy to transform immigrants into Americans.

Remarkably, the language that inspired the greatest number of translations of Key's text, at least prior to the close of World War II, was Yiddish. American Jews, witnessing the horrors of the Holocaust in Europe and increasingly unwelcome at home, seemed to use Key's song to make audible the fact that they were already loyal, patriotic citizens of the United States. No less than five Yiddish versions of *The Star-Spangled Banner* suitable for singing appeared in 1943, marking the one-hundredth anniversary of Key's death. Translations by Leivick Hodes, Aaron Nissenson, and Leon Feinberg appeared in the collection *Lider fun der milkhome, antologye,* while Berl Lapin's lyric appeared in a Yiddish bulletin, and another version by Abraham Asen was published as a song sheet by New York City's Educational Alliance.

As World War II raged, the State Department's Division of Cultural Cooperation called for singing translations of *The Star-Spangled Banner* in both Spanish and Portuguese to distribute throughout Latin America. The project was an extension of Franklin D. Roosevelt's "Good Neighbor Policy." Translating the U.S. anthem was another way to build trust and prevent the Axis powers from gaining a foothold in the region. Clotilde Arias was awarded the State Department's contract. Born in Peru, she had come to New York in 1923 to study music and became a U.S. citizen in 1942. Arias combined skills as a translator, composer, and lyricist with a deeply held belief in pan-Americanism. She worked through ten drafts to complete the artistically compelling Spanish lyric—*El pendón estrellado*—on February 19, 1945. Arias's work then became the basis for the subsequent Portuguese translation. There is no evidence that either lyric was ever distributed. Later donated to the Smithsonian, her manuscript became available in 2014 and was premiered by the Latino chorus Coral Cantigas. In 2020 the Puerto Rican singer Jeidimar Rijos recorded Arias's translation for the We Are All Human Foundation to recognize the "role of the Hispanic Community fighting the COVID-19 pandemic."

As the Cold War deepened after World War II, U.S. diplomatic policy shifted, but its use of anthem translations continued. In 1957 a sheet music edition of *The Star-Spangled Banner* with English lyrics and a literal Spanish translation was published by the U.S. Information Service (USIS) in Santiago, Chile. In January 1958, USIS in Djakarata (now Jakarta, Indonesia) published a sheet music edition of Key's anthem with a lyric as well as the story of Key's authorship in Indonesian. Five thousand copies were printed and distributed. Like every sanctioned U.S. government version since 1918, these State Department imprints dropped Key's more militant third verse and its reference to "slave."

Native American Lyrics and Recent Translations

Native Americans have a vexed relationship with U.S. identity. They are citizens of a country that was an enemy in war, annexed tribal lands, pushed First Nations people onto reservations, and discouraged tribal cultural practices including use of their native language. New World settlers and later the U.S. government itself routinely ignored and abused Indigenous rights. It was not until 1924, for example, that most Native Americans were recognized as U.S. citizens, and many states delayed their accompanying right to vote until 1957. Yet Native Americans have historically exhibited extraordinary patriotic devotion, serving in and alongside the U.S. military in numbers far above their percentage of the population. World War II's Navajo code talkers are among the most celebrated. Family heritage, limited access to other educational and financial opportunities, and in some tribes, a celebrated warrior culture all contribute to this devotion to military service.

Key's anthem has been translated into many tribal languages, including Cherokee, Crow/Apsaalooké, Dakota, Lakota, Navajo, O'odham, and Umatilla. In 1988, as we have seen, Dr. Katherine Duncum translated and recorded *The Star-Spangled Banner* in Navajo. An elementary school teacher and later a professor of Navajo culture and language, Duncum was motivated in part by the mission to preserve the Navajo language through

Delegates stand as Michael Enis and Alicia Childs of the Tohono
O'odham nation perform *The Star-Spangled Banner* in their
traditional language via satellite during the Democratic National
Convention, Boston, July 27, 2004.

a tuneful pedagogy. In 2004, at the Democratic National Convention,
Alicia Childs and Michael Enis sang the anthem in their Native language,
Tohono O'odham. Credited to Albert Alvarez, the translation had been
sung since 1991 at civic events in Arizona. While serving as a symbol of
diversity at the convention, tribal members hoped the anthem would
inspire young Native Americans to learn and preserve their language. As

nation chairwoman Vivian Juan-Saunders remarked, "Our language is a sacred element of who we are as a people."

Translations of Key's text have indeed inspired several Native American students to engage more deeply in their tribal language. Lorna Her Many Horses, while growing up on the Rosebud Reservation in South Dakota, created a literal singing translation in Dakota, a Lakota dialect, as part of her own language study. She had to invent a word for "rocket," as there was no Lakota equivalent. Her project to distribute her translation in print and audio recording to Native American military veterans led to a presidential citation and the opportunity to sing her translation at the White House Tribal Nations Conference in 2011. Steven Wilson, a member of the Oglala Lakota people, was in turn inspired by Her Many Horses and began singing *The Star-Spangled Banner* in Lakota at high school sports events in 2015. For Wilson, singing the anthem in a Native language serves to recognize a "people who have gone without a voice." When singing, he feels he is sharing a message of "unity and diversity" that he intends "to represent everyone, not just Native Americans."

While the internet has made First Nations translations more readily discoverable, evidence indicates that translations of Key's song were made both much earlier and in additional tribal dialects. An Ojibwe lyric in Anishnaabemowin, sung loosely to the anthem's tune, has roots that predate the American Civil War. It is preserved today by the women's hand-drum group Miskwaasining Nagamojig. Rather than a simple translation, it recounts a long history of the Ojibwe people, first examining the historic division of the Lakota and the Ojibwe and then addressing their nineteenth-century wars with the U.S. government. The text offers lyrical commentary on the relationship of the Lakota people to the United States, intertwining the histories of both nations. The linguistics professor Margaret Noodin, herself of Anishinaabe descent, explains that it "came to represent not only the battles against the Chimookiman [Long-Knives, or Anglo-Americans], but also the battles fought alongside them. The song was likely sung when Lincoln signed the execution papers for thirty-eight Dakota warriors in Minnesota, and it was likely sung by the all-native membership of Company K, who fought for the North during the Civil War."

Key's song has been translated into other Native American languages as well. Winona Beamer's Hawaiian translation was first performed at a University of Hawai'i homecoming football game in 1982, sung in 4/4 time by Patrick Dickson. In January 2006 leaders of American Samoa, the Pacific island territory that is the southernmost point of the United States, proposed recognizing a Samoan translation of Key's text by Namulau'ulu Dr. Pouesi Pouesi, Jr., as the official local version. Samoa has the highest rate of military enlistment of any U.S. state or territory.

In 1999 the radio and record executive David Émile Marcantel created the French translation *La bannière étoilée* to mark the second Acadian World Congress, hosted in Louisiana. It celebrated the distinctive American culture of some three thousand French Acadians or Cajuns, who were expelled from Canada's maritime provinces after 1755 but found refuge in Louisiana. A subsequent recording was used as a signoff for KJEF 1290AM, at that time the only French-language radio station in the United States.

In 2001 the Philippine activist and songwriter Joey Ayala recorded *Bagong Hinir,* a tribute to the Philippine-American experience, written to the tune of *The Star-Spangled Banner* in the islands' native Tagalog language. Ayala was drawn to the melody as for him it captured the essence of an anthem. Rather than a translation, Ayala created a new song. His single verse speaks to the "pure hope and happiness" of Philippine immigrants in quest of "freedom to prosper in a peaceful land." In citing the "bridge of war" that forged the connection between the two peoples, Ayala acknowledges both the 1899–1902 Philippine-American War and World War II, when Filipinos and Americans fought side by side.

Ayala wrote and recorded his anthem in California, when he served as deputy director of the Philippine-American Pusod Community Center in Berkeley. The song helped him confront homesickness and grapple with "that feeling of being alien, of being far away." Accompanied only by guitar, Ayala's plaintive vocals are ultimately optimistic but remain unsettled and questioning. Overdubbing his voice to evoke a sense of community, his lyric concludes, "Here we now stand, migrant natives all, in this newly chosen land, we forge our history." Rather than end the song here, however, he repeats the *Banner* melody's opening phrase, leaps to a higher final note, and stops on a diminished seventh chord, suspending the listener without a conclusion. Like Ayala's own relationship to America, his song remains unresolved.

Translation is never a dispassionate act. Even the most literal rendering of *The Star-Spangled Banner* is political because it makes American identity more accessible. It is an expansive act to recognize, acknowledge, and connect. It is also an expression of devotion and belonging. None of the translations examined here pose a threat to the priority of Key's English original. No translator professes any intent to replace it. Instead, translations celebrate, grapple with, and build upon a community's historic relationship to American identity. To recognize the more than 170-year history of translating *The Star-Spangled Banner* brings a panoply of American voices to the fore in U.S. history. Translation both facilitates and invites a bigger nation to express its devotion in a manner that is personally authentic, true, and meaningful. Translation makes the anthem stronger and enhances the song's ability to call all Americans together.

Chapter 8

The Anthem and
Black Lives

An American History

*These protests are not about making people feel comfortable. . . . It's
about promoting the discussion.*

—Sociologist Harry Edwards (2019)

By the Dawn's Early Light
September 13, 2017, Baltimore, Maryland

In the early morning hours of September 13, 2017—203 years to the day
after the British bombardment of Fort McHenry began—unidentified
protesters used red and black paint to revise the Francis Scott Key
Monument in Baltimore. They spray-painted the words "racist anthem" in
black on the statuary's base, and inscribed quotes from Key's third verse
on the sidewalk nearby. It read: "NO REFUGE COULD SAVE HIRELING
OR SLAVE, From terror of flight or gloom of grave." The pool of water
surrounding the statue was stained red with paint, creating a bloodstain
allusion to slavery's violence and suffering. If anyone missed the point,
the words "Blood on his hands" were inscribed on the pool's exterior wall.

Erected in 1911 in anticipation of the lyric's centennial in the city of its
birth, the memorial depicts the ecstatic moment when Key caught sight
of McHenry's flag and knew the nation was saved. Recontextualized

by paint, however, the memorial called something different to mind. It reminded the public of Key's slave-owning past and connected the anthem to a broader public debate over the nation's historical monuments. What should be remembered and how? Who decides? Should American history be told differently? Some described the act as "vandalism" and the words as "graffiti." Others saw it as an informed protest disrupting a standard historical narrative that denies the American legacy of racial violence and oppression. Baltimore's mayor promised to restore the statue.

Three years later activists in San Francisco used ropes to topple the statue of Francis Scott Key in Golden Gate Park. They spray-painted the caption "Slave Owner" in red below the opening where the bronze likeness of the poet writing his famous lyric had reclined since 1888. Occurring symbolically the day after Juneteenth, the protest again called attention to Key's ownership of slaves and again sparked a public debate both for and against. ABC news broadcast interviews with local residents, documenting their conflicting reactions. One called the protest "shameful," while another said he was "not sad," because "statues like this tend to make heroes of people without any real conversation about the full picture of what they did in their lives." One Black resident said he hoped that toppling the statue would "wake up some people," so "they can understand where we're coming from." The mayor promised a full review of public art in the city.

These reconsiderations of the nation's symbols and their connection to racial injustice today had been inspired by the Black Lives Matter movement. The reexamination of the anthem—specifically, the interrogation of both the lyric and the lyricist and their relationship to slavery—had been inspired, if indirectly, by the bold actions of another then local resident, NFL quarterback Colin Kaepernick. Particularly traumatic for Kaepernick was the death of Mario Woods, who had been shot twenty times by five San Francisco police officers on December 2, 2015.

It took three games for anyone to notice. Then on August 26, 2016, a picture of the San Francisco 49ers sideline, taken during a seemingly routine rendition of *The Star-Spangled Banner* at this third pre-season football game, caught fire in the media. The image showed Kaepernick sitting

alone during the patriotic ritual. The reporter who posted the picture did
not intend to highlight any one player, just the overall scene of a sideline
in disrespectful disarray. The result, however, was both intensely personal
and of national scope. In a postgame interview, Kaepernick revealed that
his comportment was no accident: by sitting, he was taking a stand:

> I am not going to stand up to show pride in a flag for a country
> that oppresses Black people and people of color. To me, this is bigger
> than football and it would be selfish on my part to look the other
> way. There are bodies in the street and people . . . getting away
> with murder.

It was not the first time a Black American had leveraged the star-spangled ritual to sit in protest. As early as December 1860, a Black woman
remained seated for a *Banner* rendition being performed by a Black choir.
It was a critical moment in U.S. history. Abraham Lincoln had just been
elected president, and the South Carolina legislature was leaning toward
approving a declaration of secession. With the Union at a breaking point,
a charitable concert was given for the benefit of Boston's Joy Street Baptist
Church and its abolitionist minister, John Stella Martin, who himself had
escaped slavery in 1856.

Writing for a Black newspaper, an unnamed Black woman noted that
the concert's selections were all "well executed, except the *Star-Spangled
Banner,* which grated harshly upon my ears." She explained that her reaction was due not to the quality of the singing but to the contrast between
the song's lyrical promise and lived reality. "This song always appears to
me to be out of place when sung by colored people," she protested, proclaiming that the words " 'O long may it wave, O'er the land of the free, and
a home of the brave' should never be pronounced by Anglo African lips,
so long as a single child of God clanks a fetter upon the American soil."
Although the audience was asked to rise in honor of the song, she stated
proudly, "I kept my seat, as a protest." By refusing to stand, she exercised
her own freedom. By amplifying her actions in the Black press, she drew

attention to the critical question facing the country. Would the nation finally end slavery, or would it yet again compromise and accommodate? Her protest was extraordinary. In that era, there was no prescribed ritual for performing a national song like *The Star-Spangled Banner*. Thus, the refusal to stand required an explicit request to do so.

For Kaepernick, the situation was different. Patriotism and American professional sports had long ago merged into a strategic alliance, even as its emphasis ebbed and flowed with public sentiment. Since the 2001 terrorist attacks that felled New York's World Trade Center, football, with its large crowds, pregame pageantry, and extensive television coverage, had become an especially potent stage for increased patriotic fervor.

During times of war, patriotic ritual becomes a social litmus test of loyalty. Dissent is scorned. When the nation faces a common existential threat, singing the anthem is interpreted as a pledge and promise to pull together as one. Such unity can be critical for national survival, and Key's song has long served to inspire military service and sacrifice. To sit, kneel, or raise a fist—to do anything at all different during the anthem ritual—is to call attention to the fragility of national unity. In a country as large as the United States, the nation is necessarily a concept that lives more in the mind than in experience. It is an imagined belief made real in ritual and visible in symbol that the notion of "we the people" is America's strongest form. As a result, to use the anthem for protest can be perceived as a threat not only to national unity but to the nation itself.

Kaepernick's protest was not about the anthem. Rather, he used the communal focus of the anthem ritual to call attention to the killings of Black men and women by police. The deaths of Woods, Oscar Grant, Rekia Boyd, Michael Brown, Tamir Rice, Laquan McDonald, Sandra Bland, and Freddie Gray urged him to action and inspired him to create the Know Your Rights Camp initiative. Kaepernick vowed to continue his protest, until the American flag "represents what it's supposed to represent." He stated clearly, "I'm not anti-American. I love America." Embittered fans nevertheless reveled in Key's song at high volume as they burned their Kaepernick souvenir jerseys.

The history of anthem activism by Black athletes may well begin with Eroseanna "Rose" Robinson, the 1958 U.S. high jump champion. She is thought to be the first prominent Black American athlete to refuse to stand for the national anthem in protest during an athletic event. At the 1959 Pan-American Games in Chicago, she remained seated during the opening ceremonies. As with many female athletes who have protested, her actions were largely unnoted by the press. In 1960–61, Robinson finally became front-page national and international news when she was jailed for her anti-war and civil rights activism, specifically for refusing to file an income tax return and for attempting to desegregate a whites-only diner.

The Star-Spangled Banner also played a supporting role in America's civil rights movement, even as anthems such as *We Shall Overcome* and *This Little Light of Mine* led the way. American flags and renditions of the national anthem were important touchstones for the movement, asserting that Black Americans too were Americans, deserving of their constitutional rights. Their battle for civil rights did not seek to overthrow the government but demanded a social and legal revolution of recognition, reform, and representation. In July 1963 in Brooklyn, Black protesters lay down in front of heavy construction machinery and sang *The Star-Spangled Banner* as police attempted to remove them. Their peaceful protest halted work on a hospital site to demand an end to hiring discrimination in the construction industry. That August Camilla Williams sang *The Star-Spangled Banner* on the steps of the Lincoln Memorial to mark the start of speeches at the March on Washington for Jobs and Freedom. Martin Luther King, Jr., delivered his "I Have a Dream" speech soon afterward. The *Banner* also steeled Black protesters facing violent resistance. In 1965 in Selma, Alabama, following the "Bloody Sunday" police beatings of protesters attempting to cross the Edmund Pettus Bridge, four hundred activists sang *The Star-Spangled Banner* at dawn after spending the night on the streets as part of an all-night prayer vigil.

At the 1968 Summer Olympic Games in Mexico City, the American runner Tommie Smith won the 200-meter sprint in the world record time of 19.83 seconds. His teammate John Carlos was edged at the tape by

The human rights salute during the playing of *The Star-Spangled Banner* at the medal ceremony for the 200-meter men's sprint competition at the 1968 Olympic Games in Mexico City, October 16, 1968. Pictured are (from left): Australia's Peter Norman (silver) with Americans Tommie Smith (gold) and John Carlos (bronze). Smith and Carlos share a single pair of black gloves between them, so Smith raises his right arm, while Carlos raises his left.

Australia's Peter Norman but took bronze. A half hour later all three wore Olympic Project for Human Rights badges in solidarity as they approached the medal podium for the playing of *The Star-Spangled Banner*.

The Americans had designed the symbols of their protest carefully. As during the final sprint itself, they wore black dress socks rather than white athletic socks to draw attention to the issue of race. Smith, who was the son of a sharecropper, and Carlos also carried their shoes to the medal podium as a marker of Black poverty. Smith wore a black scarf and Carlos a beaded necklace, hoping to remind viewers of the murderous lynchings of Black Americans. Carlos kept his jacket open, a breach of etiquette, to show solidarity with the working class, both Black and white. He also wore a black T-shirt to hide the "USA" emblazoned on his jersey. Smith had considered turning his back to the Stars and Stripes as the anthem played but instead chose to address the flag "with pride, but . . . with a black accent." Having served in the ROTC, Smith told Carlos, "the national anthem is sacred to me. This can't be sloppy."

When the band began the U.S. anthem, both men thrust a black-gloved fist into the air and bowed their heads. The fist was a symbol of strength through unity, fingers brought together in a gesture of power. Each held his arm aloft and immobile until the anthem had finished. Smith later explained this "silent" protest:

> We did it with pride, and we wanted it to represent everybody without making a statement for anybody, just a silent gesture for anyone to interpret their way. . . . The gesture I made represented my father, for all the times he worked those fields and endured everything he did, who didn't speak much . . . but let his actions speak for him. . . . I wanted the gesture to represent him. I wanted it to embody that pride and love for what America is supposed to be. With those two gloves, we were able to do it all.

The International Olympic Committee demanded that Carlos and Smith be suspended, or the entire U.S. team would be banned from further competition. The U.S. Olympic Committee issued an apology for the "discourtesy displayed by two members of the U.S. team in departing from tradition" and violating "basic standards of sportsmanship and good manners." Such criticisms of the act served to distract from the protest's purpose, focusing on the behavior alone to undercut the need to address the underlying issues it raised. Smith saw things differently. Rather than a violation of etiquette, their protest was an act of responsibility:

> To use the Olympic Games as a platform for political protest was a no-no. What I believed, instead, is that you take what you do best, which for me was running track and field, and use it as a platform for something good. . . . Most people don't agree. . . . They think that it was needed but that the Olympics was not the place to do it. I disagree; if you are one of the world's greatest in a particular field . . . , you have an avenue, and you have a responsibility to use it, especially if you have something to say about society and how people are treated, [for] people who are not in the position to say it themselves.

Denver Nuggets guard Mahmoud Abdul-Rauf stands and prays
during the anthem before an NBA basketball game against the
Chicago Bulls, Chicago, March 15, 1996.

Smith and Carlos were suspended from the U.S. team and evicted from the athletes' village. They did not lose their Olympic titles or medals. Carlos summed up their position soon after: "All we ask for is an equal chance to be a human being."

In 1996, as the anthem played before some sixty Denver Nuggets basketball games, the point guard Mahmoud Abdul-Rauf (who as Louisiana State University star Chris Jackson had embraced Islam in 1991) stretched on the sidelines or hid in the locker room. Again, a reporter was the first to notice. In explaining his protest, Abdul-Rauf decried racial discrimination and described the U.S. flag as a "symbol of oppression, of tyranny." The National Basketball Association issued a suspension, claiming Abdul-Rauf was violating his contract, specifically Player/Team Conduct Rule J, paragraph two, which stipulated that "players, coaches and trainers are to stand and line up in a dignified posture along the sidelines or on the foul line during the playing of the National Anthem." Abdul-Rauf forfeited $37,707 in salary, but his suspension was lifted after one game when he agreed to stand with his team during the ceremony. He continued his protest by closing his eyes and praying silently into his hands as the anthem played. Fans booed, but a robust debate for and against his right to protest occurred in the press. A rising star who remains among one of the game's greatest free-throw shooters, Abdul-Rauf was traded the next season and was out of the league within two years.

In contrast, Colin Kaepernick's protest broke no NFL rule, yet his actions became part of the nation's culture war, attracting the vitriol of presidential candidate Donald Trump. In response, in 2018 the league adopted a new rule that imposed fines for kneeling during the anthem. Players were allowed to remain in the locker room instead. The NFL rule was legal. First Amendment protections of free speech serve to check only the government, not a private enterprise. Nevertheless, the rule made no one happy and created its own backlash. In the end, it remained on the books but was not enforced. Kaepernick, however, was soon out of a job. The 49ers released him at the end of the 2016–17 season, and he has not returned to the league.

The Star-Spangled Banner amplified all these protests. Rather than an abuse of either the Anacreontic melody or Key's song, the use of the anthem as a vehicle for protest is core to its very tradition. This tradition began with Francis Scott Key himself, as his 1814 lyric described a vision for the nation not as it existed but as he hoped it would be—a people strengthened by a strong federal government, a shared religious piety, and patriotic unity. Smith and Carlos extended this tradition by disrupting the comfortable imagined unity asserted by the Olympic Games' medal ritual: that their athletic achievement was an uncomplicated manifestation of national greatness and a symbol of an untroubled global harmony. Instead, by expressing hope that sport, nation, and world could live up to their professed ideals, they pointed out that all were currently falling short.

Today the vital question concerning *The Star-Spangled Banner* is not if but how Key's words and attitudes concerning slavery and race affect the experience of his song. Can the song function as an anthem for all Americans? Might the full acknowledgment of Key's story—both his complicity in slavery as well as his antislavery efforts—help repair an American history that too often diminishes or even denies the persistence, scope, and impact of racism in its past? What did his words mean in 1814? Does the phrase "hireling and slave" refer to Black Colonial Marines, white British soldiers, or something else? Does the anthem lyric explicitly support slavery or not? Does it matter?

Reconsidering "Hireling and Slave"

In 1836 the American Anti-Slavery Society published a remarkable broadside poster. It decries slavery in the District of Columbia, proclaiming the seat of the U.S. government as the "Slave Market of America." To call attention to the nation's betrayal of its founding ideal of freedom, it uses two illustrations with titles that trade on the popularity of Key's already well-known chorus. The first illustration, titled "Land of the Free," shows America's all-white founding fathers reading the Declaration of Independence aloud in 1776. The second, titled "Home of the Oppressed," shows a contemporary scene: a white overseer leading a group of enslaved Black men past the Capitol. Two U.S. flags fly atop the building. Recognized not as citizens nor as deserving basic rights, the enslaved men nevertheless raise their arms in salute to the symbols of freedom, the caption suggesting that they sang or shouted "Hail Columbia." Theirs is a patriotic cry that calls upon the nation's leaders to fulfill the promise made by the Declaration of Independence that "all men are created equal."

The fundamental contradiction between the nation's celebration of freedom, including symbols such as *The Star-Spangled Banner*, and its history

Illustrations from an anti-slavery broadside poster titled *Slave Market of America*, American Anti-Slavery Society, New York, 1836.

of racist policies resides at the core of American democracy. Historians credit Black Americans and their often frustrated but insistent demands for equality as driving much of the progress in civil rights for all Americans. Today such legal battles—for example, over gay marriage—are often based not on the Constitution or its Bill of Rights but on three post–Civil War amendments, especially the Fourteenth. Ratified in 1868, the Fourteenth Amendment guaranteed, for the first time, equal protection under the law for all Americans. As Nikole Hannah-Jones has proclaimed, "Our democracy's founding ideals were false when they were written. Black Americans have fought to make them true."

The phrase "hireling and slave" in Key's third verse creates a dissonance in the national lyric, yet it has long eluded explanation or evaluation. But now that the internet has made all four verses of Key's song more readily accessible, the question has come to the fore. What does the word "slave" in the anthem lyric mean? Some argue that it prevents Key's song from functioning as a truly unifying statement. Can a song that appears to embrace the notion of slavery serve as an expression of national harmony, especially for those descended from enslaved Americans?

There are three credible readings of the phrase "hireling and slave." Each broadens our understanding of American history, and each makes specific what certain Americans in 1814 might have understood by Key's words. The first reading would have struck many Black Americans and abolitionists with virulent irony; the second identifies how most white Americans would have understood Key's lyric in 1814; the third speaks to what likely inspired Francis Scott Key himself to use the phrase.

In 2014 students at Baltimore's historically Black college Morgan State University created a pioneering and provocative documentary film. "The third verse decries the flight of Blacks from slavery to the British side to serve in the British army," notes their professor DeWayne Wickham. In the film, students are shown Key's third verse. Confronted by the word "slave," they express shock and concern not only about its intent but about the reason for their unfamiliarity. "There's obviously a reason why they left it out," says one student, "because a lot of people wouldn't be willing to say it anymore, if they knew that this was a key component." Another student remarks, "I'm taking it as that *The Star-Spangled Banner* wasn't intended for Black people," while yet another finds the lyric "contradictory to the song, because it is about freedom and they are talking about slavery." Considering the impact of this new knowledge, this same student suggests, "I probably wouldn't sing it anymore, . . . or I wouldn't give it as much respect as I do now." The film purports to reveal the "hidden truths about the third verse of the song" and ends with a powerful choral performance of Key's complete lyric. The students' responses are honest and insightful.

This historical reading of "hireling and slave" asserts that Key's phrase refers to British enemy soldiers, specifically Redcoat regulars (hirelings) and Colonial Marines (slaves). Colonial Marines were Black men who had escaped slavery in the United States and then volunteered to fight with the British. They were among Britain's most valuable soldiers in the War of 1812.

In April 1814, British Admiral Alexander Cochrane released an official proclamation that "all those who may be disposed to emigrate from the UNITED STATES will, with their Families, be received on board of His Majesty's Ships. . . . They will have their choice of either entering into His Majesty's Sea or Land Forces, or of being sent as FREE Settlers to the British Possessions in North America or the West Indies." The proclamation said nothing of slavery, but the word FREE in all capital letters made the message clear. Some four thousand emancipated themselves and fled slavery aboard British ships—a small fraction of the region's enslaved population, which numbered in the hundreds of thousands.

Britain's offer of freedom, however, was not purely altruistic. It was an act of war, intended to disrupt the Chesapeake economy and instill fear among white Americans of a violent uprising. The proclamation was also a strategic recruitment tool. Colonial Marines provided needed manpower and essential local knowledge. They helped British ships navigate American waterways and guided British troops along unfamiliar overland routes. Unlike British regulars, they were unable to desert, and they were highly motivated to fight their former captors. Some two hundred Colonial Marines fought in the battles at Bladensburg and Baltimore. Their service helped make possible Britain's more aggressive Chesapeake campaign of the summer of 1814.

Given the fear that Colonial Marines induced, some Americans who heard Key's third verse in 1814 certainly may have interpreted the word "slave" as a specific reference to these formidable Black fighters. Key himself was a slaveholder, and although none of his own slaves fought for the British, he would have witnessed the impact of Cochrane's proclamation firsthand. Hundreds of enslaved people in the Georgetown region had escaped to the British following the burning of Washington. Claims that Key's third verse glories in the blood of escaped slaves are overstated, however. If Key intended to refer to Colonial Marines, his choice of words was a poor one. The purpose of Key's lyric was to unify a divided nation. Invoking the word "slave" in reference to those who were actually held in forced labor would have served to divide. In early America, the issue was so toxic that those drafting the Constitution, the nation's governing document, avoided the word "slave" entirely and instead wrote euphemistically of "other persons." By using the word "slave" in this way, Key would have inspired division, not unity.

A historical irony of *The Star-Spangled Banner* is that Key, in praising the defenders of Fort McHenry, celebrated the heroism of Americans both white and Black. Black men fought on the American side of the War of 1812. Reports and payment receipts confirm that free and enslaved Black men assisted in Baltimore's defense. They dug trenches and served as substitutes in Baltimore's fire brigade. Such service was not without its own insults—Black workers were paid half the wages of whites— but Key was certainly aware of such Black participation in Baltimore's defense. Before departing on his mission to rescue Beanes, Key would have observed the city's frantic preparations for the British assault. That Black workers would have helped build earthworks and other defenses was both expected and typical.

Black men had assisted in the defense of Washington the month before, a fact that Key again would have witnessed firsthand. On August 21 a general proclamation required Washington's civilians, including "all free men of color," to help build defensive works. Further, as a frequent visitor, Key knew that Baltimore had a large and growing free Black population. In the early 1800s, the need for skilled labor in Baltimore's shipyards created what one historian has called a "refuge city," in which free Blacks and enslaved "quasi-freedmen" could find both work and some level of social independence. In its 1810 census, Baltimore City counted 10,343 Black residents, making up more than 20 percent of the total population. Of these, 5,671 or nearly 55 percent were free.

Other Black men were specifically among the defenders of Fort McHenry. One of them was Charles Ball, who escaped slavery and declared himself a "free man of color" and later served in Joshua Barney's Chesapeake Bay Flotilla. During the War of 1812, Barney's motley collection of gunboats and barges harassed the British fleet with rare effectiveness, at least until they were forced to scuttle their boats during the fall of Washington. In his 1837 memoir, Ball also wrote of being among the defenders of Baltimore that repulsed the midnight British feint outside Fort McHenry. He had even manned a cannon at the Battle of Bladensburg. Although certainly not side by side, Key and Ball thus fought together in Washington's defense.

Men like Ball, who escaped slavery and served in the U.S. military, played a remarkable role in the War of 1812. They risked capture and a return to slavery, even as their service provided a protective cover identity. They also reveal the complex nature of patriotism, as they chose devotion to the country of their enslavement. Ball, for example, had other options. In his autobiography, he wrote of being aboard a British ship in the Chesapeake between the battles of Bladensburg and Baltimore. Offered passage to the West Indies with a group of freed slaves, he declined and instead returned to Baltimore to rejoin his American unit. He remained in Baltimore after the war, finding work "as a free black man."

That free Blacks were involved in America's defense in both Washington and Baltimore invites reconsideration of the word "freemen" in verse four of *The Star-Spangled Banner*. Today we might hear the word "freemen" as a generic synonym for Americans. In 1814, however, it was a technical term that reported a vital distinction. When one could be enslaved, being among the freemen meant everything. In proclaiming "O! thus be it ever when freemen shall stand, / Between their lov'd home, and the war's desolation," Key was ostensibly praying for the right of all free men, potentially those both Black and white, to defend their nation. His own legal representation of Blacks who were suing for their freedom in court, beginning in 1806, might have made this issue especially vivid for him. He had freed the first of his own slaves in 1811, three years before the Battle of Baltimore and thus three years before writing his famous lyric.

It is nevertheless hard to believe that Key's 1814 lyric celebrated an inclusive vision of American identity that welcomed Black Americans. As both poet and lawyer, Key was never casual in his use of language, so most likely his use of the words "freemen" and "slave" would have fallen squarely within the stereotypical understandings of the day. Such language was in fact common in the era's patriotic lyric and political discourse. The words' meaning, however, rested on a now out-of-date distinction between Europeans and Americans—that is, between those who were subject to a king and those who were not.

More than two centuries later it is difficult to appreciate, but in 1814 most Americans would likely have understood the phrase "hireling and slave" to refer without complication to the British enemy, who were both professional soldiers and vassals of King George III. These "slaves" were primarily white. The notion that in 1814 most Americans would have understood Key's use of the word "slave" to refer to whites was an indication of their deep assumption of Black inferiority. It is a legacy of pervasive white supremacy. In the United States of 1814, only white men mattered.

American sentiments during the War of 1812, often called the Second War of Independence, echoed the sentiments of the Revolutionary War three decades earlier. Key's word "hireling" is intended to discredit British fighters as mere mercenaries, motivated by desire for the spoils of war and not by honor. In this same sense, by referring to the British soldier as a "slave," he mocks their fealty to a monarch. In contrast to the British, Americans answered the call to wartime service as free volunteers.

In fact, the question of forced military service was among the irritants that had caused the War of 1812. In the run-up to the war, British press gangs routinely boarded U.S. and other merchant ships in search of "British deserters"—including newly minted Americans of English heritage. In effect, they kidnapped American seamen and forced them into servitude in the Royal Navy. An enemy fighter, conscripted or impressed into the British military, could readily be considered a "slave." A Fourth of July lyric published in 1813 and sung to the Anacreontic tune makes explicit the connection between naval impressment and the War of 1812. Its final verse emphatically uses the word "slaves" in reference to white Americans:

> Be true to ourselves, nor shrink back in alarms
>   At the dreams of despair, or the hypocrite's rattle;
> Tis the cause of your Seamen commands you to arms,
>   And the God of your Fathers shall aid you in battle.
>   Then unite heart and hand,
>   And immoveable stand,
>   And disdain e'er to sheathe in the scabbard your brand,
> Till Vict'ry, bright Vict'ry, proclaims o'er the waves,
> That your COMMERCE IS FREE, and your SEAMEN NOT SLAVES.

Key's lyric, of course, would not have attacked Americans forced against their will into British military service. Theoretically, his use of the word "slave" may have referred to British conscripts, but the word "slave" in U.S. patriotic poetry proves to be both more common and more general.

Many American patriotic songs of Key's era and before feature the word "slave" in the general sense of a subject who owes allegiance to a king. *Adams and Liberty* (1798), the Federalist anthem that popularized the Anacreontic melody in America, features the word "slaves" in the repeated chorus for each of its nine stanzas:

> *For ne'er shall the sons of Columbia be slaves,*
> *While the earth bears a plant, or the sea rolls its waves.*

Here the "sons of Columbia" are the descendants of America's revolutionaries who won independence from Britain. In the political context of the 1790s, the song calls on these descendants to resist the influence of the French and their king and thus not become "slaves." Key must have known this popular lyric well. *Adams and Liberty* is the most likely model for his song *When the Warrior Returns,* which in turn was the model for *The Star-Spangled Banner* (see Chapter 3).

That early American patriotic songs celebrated "freedom" and "liberty" in a land that condoned slavery is initially incomprehensible. But the use of the word "slave" in patriotic lyrics to refer mainly to white Americans was so typical as to make it by far the most likely explanation of Key's use and meaning. It was a well-worn trope, almost a cliché. Americans today, for example, remember that in 1775 Patrick Henry cried "Give me liberty or give me death!" to inspire a declaration of independence. Rarely quoted, however, is his preceding line: "Is life so dear, or peace so sweet, as to be purchased at the price of chains and slavery?" By invoking "slavery," Henry was talking about himself and his white Richmond, Virginia, listeners being subject to King George, not to the evil of people bought and sold in the American colonies as labor.

In another example, an 1813 newspaper lyric similarly referenced the American Revolution of 1776, remembering "When Tyrant George assail'd our shore, / And thousands of his Slaves sent o'er." No Black fighters were "sent o'er" from Britain during the Revolutionary War. These "slaves" were the British regulars. Dozens of later American lyrics written after *The Star-Spangled Banner* use the same poetic device, referring for example to white Confederates as "slaves" of Abraham Lincoln. Such uses were not ironic. The bitter reality that many Black Americans were in fact enslaved was simply overshadowed by the era's racist ideology.

A THIRD POSSIBLE meaning of the word "slave" in Key's lyric may well be the most likely to reflect the lyricist's own thinking. Since the phrase "hireling and slave" is singular, as opposed to the plural references to the British enemy that immediately precede it, the phrase may refer to an individual British soldier. The British soldier particularly deserving of Key's patriotic venom would have been Major General Robert Ross. Key was disillusioned by Ross and by the "illiberal, ignorant and vulgar" British officers, who he found were "filled with the spirit of malignity against every thing American." Ross had led the attack on Washington and had personally ordered the burning of the White House and the Capitol. He was also personally responsible for the imprisonment of Beanes. Of signal importance, Ross was the most prominent British soldier killed in the attack on Baltimore, information that reached Key's ears while he was still aboard ship and writing his lyric.

Held at anchor aboard his truce vessel in the battle's aftermath, Key knew precious few specifics about what had happened. Following the bombardment, however, the U.S. agent for prisoners John Stuart Skinner shuttled between Key's ship and the British command vessel. Skinner's official reports reveal that Admiral Cockburn, who was with Ross when he was mortally wounded, had informed Skinner of Ross's death. Skinner in turn would have shared such news with Key. Cockburn had even told Skinner that in a desperate attempt to get life-saving medical care, Ross had been "jolted down . . . in a cart" rather than carried more gently on a litter to return to the British ships. Cockburn surmised that the violence of the trip had sealed Ross's death.

It is thus feasible that for Key, Ross alone experienced the "terror of flight" and the "gloom of the grave." Key's aesthetic and sense of propriety would have prevented him from identifying Ross by name in his lyric. But trained as a lawyer, Key used language with careful precision. Thus his use of the singular in the phrase "hireling and slave" is not likely accidental. Both a paid, professional soldier and a vassal of George III, British General Robert Ross alone is the most likely object of Key's lyrical scorn.

Key and Slavery: An American Legacy

Even as *The Star-Spangled Banner* has taken on new uses and meanings over time, the circumstances of its creation continue to shape its contemporary reception. Origins matter with patriotic symbols, which are in essence scraps of national myth distilled into image, idea, or, in this case, a song. Francis Scott Key's record concerning slavery and race is thus relevant to the anthem story, even more so because it is checkered and contradictory. How are we to understand a man who owned people in bondage but professed a universal right to freedom, who both fought for the freedom of Blacks and facilitated their sale in his legal work, who prosecuted abolitionists in court, and who called slavery "the only blot that dim'd the lustre of his Country's fame"?

A lay minister of the Episcopal Church, Key professed that slavery was a moral wrong and argued provocatively in court that "by the law of nature all men are free." But nothing he said or wrote that survives in the historical record suggests that he believed Blacks could ever be equal to whites. For the full course of his life, the racial bigotry characteristic of the era's political mainstream lay beneath his professional efforts. At the very least, he was complicit in white supremacy and was confined professionally by the status quo. In 1833, appointed district attorney for the District of Columbia by the pro-slavery president Andrew Jackson, Key was charged with enforcing the laws of the nation's capital, where slavery was legal and its very practice was a political symbol. Key was likewise accommodating in his fundraising speeches for the American Colonization Society. His calls for freedom can be heard on two levels—one calling loudly for voluntary emancipation, the other quietly activating white fears of Black insurrection and racial "amalgamation."

Still, many of Key's actions, both in his legal career and in his personal philanthropy, fall on the antislavery side of the political divide. He spoke against slavery and undertook antislavery activities, which he certainly saw as such. He asserted that slavery was a "great moral and political evil." He repeatedly called for the destruction of the international slave trade, declaring it "inhuman," a "pestilential crime," and "abominable and detestable beyond all epithets." He was especially concerned with the kidnapping of free people to feed the trade's bottomless appetite for human chattel. Yet at home, in the United States, Key supported only a voluntary manumission, in which slave owners freed the enslaved by choice. He also advocated for what in retrospect was sheer fantasy—a gradual, peaceful end to slavery.

Key professed a theory that "no slave State adjacent to a free State can continue so" and argued that economic pressures would inevitably transform every border slave state into a free state, resulting in a domino effect that would end slavery. In Key's mind, when Maryland, which bordered the free state of Pennsylvania, was forced to also become free, Virginia would follow, and then North Carolina and Tennessee, until all American slavery died a gradual if inhumanely slow death. In an 1829 fundraising pitch for the American Colonization Society, he buttressed his theory with census and economic data.

Key claimed to be working to hasten this cascade of liberty by accelerating voluntary emancipation through colonization. In 1816 he was among the founders of the American Colonization Society (ACS), and he remained a passionate champion of its contradictory cause to the end of his life. The organization's stated goal was to create a Black protectorate in Africa to serve as both a haven and a removal area for those who were liberated from the American slave system. He gave his most passionate public efforts—as a leader, donor, fundraiser, speaker, and writer—to the cause of colonization. He wrote part, if not all, of the society's constitution, was a longtime member of its board of managers, and volunteered as a fundraising spokesman for more than a decade. Professing pragmatism, he argued that colonization produced real results—southern slave owners who willingly freed their slaves. At the same time, he vehemently opposed the "madness of abolition." He asserted that Blacks freed suddenly would be condemned to poverty and suffering. He left unspoken the loss of social and economic privilege that emancipation would cause white slave owners.

Key's seemingly incompatible beliefs in both slaveholding and emancipation were not as exceptional in American history as might first appear. Benjamin Franklin not only owned enslaved people but sold them at his store. He later became affiliated with abolitionist causes and wrote boldly about the integration of Blacks into American society. John Jay, the Supreme Court's first chief justice, founded and served as president of New York's Manumission Society in 1785, yet he continued to own people into the 1810s. Others who professed freedom while affirming slavery included Supreme Court justice Gabriel Duvall, Key's uncle Philip Barton Key, and even Key's brother-in-law, the future Supreme Court justice Roger B. Taney. Taney, who has been justly vilified by history, authored the Supreme Court's notorious 1857 *Dred Scott* decision eliminating Black claims to citizenship, yet he had emancipated all his own slaves by 1822 and likewise supported the enslaved plaintiffs in the *Amistad* case in 1841.

Key was not a major slaveowner as is sometimes claimed. He lived a life of words—law, poetry, and prayer—instead of life on a plantation. In August 1811 he was obliged to purchase his father's indebted estate, Terra Rubra, at auction to prevent his parents from being turned out of their home. The estate's few enslaved laborers might have become his property at this time, or if not, this may have happened later by inheritance. Key may have been romanticizing his own situation when he described in court how a son who had inherited debt along with his father's slaves "sees, among these afflicted and faithful creatures, his old kind nurse who has loved him as her own child—the old man who watched over his childhood and made his play things—their children, the playmates of his youth . . . and he can't sell them. He gives bonds for the debts—and goes to work." For Key, Terra Rubra was an idyllic summer family retreat, not a working farm.

Key owned more than a dozen people as slaves during his lifetime and reportedly paid wages to Black servants as well. The U.S. Census of 1820 documents that five enslaved people resided in his Georgetown home. His letters reveal that he likely considered himself a benevolent slaveholder, concerned with the health and welfare of the enslaved. Along with his wife, Polly, he followed the Key family tradition of referring to household slaves euphemistically as "servants." Key freed at least seven of his slaves during his lifetime and the remainder in his 1837 last will and testament. Their emancipation came into effect only after both he and his wife passed away.

Key rationalized his continued slaveholding on what he argued were humanitarian grounds. "I am still a slaveholder," he would explain to an abolitionist minister, "and could not, without the greatest inhumanity, be otherwise. I own, for instance, an old slave, who has done no work for me for years. I pay his board and other expenses, and cannot believe it a sin in doing so." Under Maryland law, those enslaved over age forty-five were not eligible for emancipation, so Key's moral and ethical compromise was to assert that slavery was not only acceptable but the preferred alternative to poverty in freedom. Key was the paternalistic arbiter of this preference.

Both friends and rivals knew Key by the racist epithets "the Black's lawyer" or, less politely, "The N***er Lawyer," because of his legal work representing Blacks unjustly enslaved. In August 1835, as will be discussed later in this chapter, a white mob rioted against Washington, D.C.'s, free Black population, looting and burning Black churches, schools, and businesses. Key feared that his own family's residence, just a few blocks from Capitol Hill, would be ransacked. He whisked his wife and young children out of town and hired armed guards to protect his home. Key's reputation as a Black advocate and thus his fear of personal attack was real. It requires interrogation and qualification, but it was a reputation earned over some four decades.

Key's record of supporting Black men, women, and children who were seeking freedom through legal action is more substantial than typically recognized. While his legal career was a long one, no single lawyer is affiliated with more freedom petitions in the District of Columbia than Key. Between 1806 and 1840, Key filed petitions in at least 106 cases on behalf of Blacks seeking freedom. One historian has called the thousands of such freedom petitions a "public counterpart of the Underground Railroad." Key won at least twenty-eight of these cases, resulting directly in the freedom of fifty-eight men, women, and children. He lost at least two dozen other cases, representing thirty-four people who thus remained enslaved. His most impactful freedom case began in 1825. Key's relentless legal efforts on behalf of the victims of the *Antelope* slave ship would result in the freedom of 131 others.

Key reportedly made "a great many enemies" as a result of his freedom work. He filed freedom petitions against influential academic, legal, and political leaders, such as Father Francis Neale, a Jesuit priest and the president of Georgetown University; North Carolina congressman Lemuel Sawyer; and Supreme Court Justice Gabriel Duvall, in front of whom Key would argue cases for the remainder of his career. Key won the case against Duvall, lost to Neale, and eventually settled out of court with Sawyer. If Key's primary goal had been financial and political success, he would have done well to follow his uncle's example and forswear freedom cases.

Key's antislavery attitudes may date from as early as the 1790s, when he was apprenticed in law to Jeremiah Townley Chase (1748–1828). Although Chase owned people as slaves himself, he was one of just eleven delegates at Maryland's 1788 state convention to vote against ratification of the U.S. Constitution because it permitted slavery. Speaking of freedom cases, Key said that he "considered every such cause as one on which all the worldly weal or woe of a fellow creature depended," and that he "had tried no causes with more zeal and earnestness." He professed that "never was his success in any contests so exulting as when, on these occasions, he had stood forth as the advocate of the oppressed." Key, however, also represented slave owners in court and facilitated the sale of enslaved persons as mere property.

Key first filed a petition on behalf of a Black person seeking freedom from slavery on September 17, 1806. In June 1811, after five years of legal maneuvers, multiple appeals, and a retrial, the man known as "Negro Ben" was finally and forever free. Less than ten days later, Key signed his first set of manumission papers to free one of the enslaved people he owned—a six-year-old girl named Kitty. Key owned the girl jointly with the Washington merchant Alexander McCormick. The men filed a writ in U.S. District Court to set Kitty free, stating that she "was the daughter of Henny, a free woman." Less than a month later, Key signed a second deed of manumission promising to free "my Negro boy named James, two years old last April, and Negro boy named Joe, about six months old," when they "attained the age of 25 years." It was illegal in Maryland at this time to free an enslaved minor, until they came of age or were otherwise financially supported.

In December 1815 Key was contacted by Jesse Torrey, Jr., a Philadelphia physician and antislavery activist, for aid in three petitions for freedom. Torrey had heard a remarkable story: an enslaved woman, awaiting sale in D.C., had jumped from a third-floor attic window onto a stone street below. She was in despair at her family being broken apart, and in fact, she would never see her two daughters again. Later identified as Ann Williams, she fractured her spine and both arms, yet somehow she survived the fall. Unable to walk until she healed, she was sold to George Miller, the owner of the slave pen in which she had been imprisoned.

Torrey not only located Williams but was given permission to interview her. It seemed that her new owner felt himself beneficent for having taken on the responsibility of her care. During the interview, however, Torrey discovered three additional Black captives in Miller's pen: a twenty-one-year-old man secured in irons and a young widow with her infant child. All three had been born free, kidnapped, and were being sold illegally into slavery. Subsequent court documents identify them as John Parker and Rosanna Brown and her daughter, Mary Eliza.

As Torrey would report, Key "volunteered his own services as attorney, gratis," and filed emergency petitions and injunctions with the D.C. court preventing the captives from being removed from Washington until their cases were settled. Key also drew up a charitable "subscription" that raised "between one and two hundred dollars." Such money was used to pay jail fees, which prisoners owed in this era. Tragically, legally free Blacks held in jail—even for their own protection—were commonly sold into slavery to pay the debts on such fees. Parker and the Browns, for instance, would be held for six months, as Torrey traveled to Delaware to gather "unequivocal proof of the legal right of the captives to their liberty." All three were successfully freed.

Not long afterward Torrey and Key became congressional witnesses. In 1816 they provided sworn statements to a Select Committee to Inquire into the Existence of an Inhuman and Illegal Traffic in Slaves in the District of Columbia, as part of an investigation sponsored by Key's close friend, the Virginia congressman John Randolph of Roanoke. In his deposition, Key testified that people of color were being brought illegally to D.C. from

Maryland and Delaware to be sold to traders from Georgia and Carolina. He noted that the trade "has been greatly increasing" and reported seeing abuses, even while "omitting those acts of inhumanity committed in confining & transporting them," such as "separations of husband & wife, parents & children, & the frequent seizure of free persons who are hurried off in the night, brought to the city, & transported as slaves." Highlighting the violence and emotional trauma of this illegal trade, he reported on the desperation of some captives:

> A woman was sold to a trader a week or 10 days ago, who has a husband in George Town. She had lived for nearly a year near my house. Her master who lives in Maryland told me that she was a most faithful servant, . . . that he had wanted to sell her but would not sell her away from her husband. She was taken by the Trader into the City in a hack and I am credibly informed and believe that she attempted to kill herself by cutting her throat.

He also gave evidence that a "negro woman," sold to one of these traders, took "up a cleaver . . . [and] chopped off one of her hands; upon which the trader refused to take her." Key's accounts of such horrors documented for Congress the day-to-day violence and suffering of the enslaved that was typically ignored or suppressed.

Finally, Key recounted under oath a dramatic personal confrontation with a trader that soon became a rescue. The trader was "carrying off a number of negroes," including "a woman who was unquestionably free." Key and a local magistrate approached the house where the group was detained. "We were refused permission to see the negroes," Key reported, "and while a man, concerned with the trader, kept us in conversation in the front of the house, the other attempted to carry off the woman (with other negroes) through the back yard into another street. We overtook him leading his horse with the woman by his side, and a pistol in his hand. He left the woman, leaped on his horse, and rode off at full speed." Several of these anecdotes, along with the tale of the three freed from slavery, were soon featured in Torrey's 1817 antislavery book *A Portraiture of Domestic Slavery.*

Remarkably, Key kept in contact with Ann Williams. Nearly thirteen years after her jump, he filed a freedom petition on behalf of Ann and three new children—Tobias, John, and Ann Maria. Despite being legally owned by Miller and his son, Williams had been living independently and added to her family. Likely the Millers' main interest in her was the hope of selling her children for profit. After Key took up the Williamses' case, the Millers ignored a series of court summons, delaying the case for four years. By the later 1820s, ignoring court orders was an increasingly viable defense strategy in freedom suits. To ignore such orders was to claim that they had no legal authority. The slave owner defendant thereby asserted that legal protection applied only to a person and that the enslaved were mere property. Williams's case finally came to trial when the Millers smuggled her twelve-year-old son out of the district to be sold. In May 1832, a jury decided in favor of Ann and her children. They were free. Key himself paid the jury fee, suggesting that the Millers had not shown up or had simply walked out of court.

Key's most impactful courtroom success in releasing the enslaved from bondage came through the American Colonization Society (ACS), in particular the case of the *Antelope,* an illegal slave ship captured off the coast of Spanish Florida on June 29, 1820. Key became involved in the troubled case only as it reached the Supreme Court after five years of litigation. During his opening arguments, Key asserted that "by the law of nature, all men are free." The Court, however, voted to return the slave ship *Antelope*'s human cargo to slavery. Despite this initial setback, Key filed continuing legal maneuvers that would eventually free most of the slave ship's prisoners. In July 1827, 131 *Antelope* victims who had been established as free by the courts boarded the *USS Norfolk.* The ACS settled them in Liberia. Sixteen years later the case would provide an important legal precedent for the case of a more famous slave ship, the *Amistad,* its human cargo, and the question of freedom. Key would play a behind-the-scenes role, both in the *Amistad* case and in the eventual return of its victims to Africa.

KEY'S PRO-SLAVERY REPUTATION, both in his lifetime and more recently, stems largely from his response to the Washington City race riot of 1835, also known as the Snow Riot. His professional overreach in prosecuting a local abolitionist was legally flawed and factually incorrect. It also had tragic unintended consequences, exacerbating if not precipitating white violence upon the district's Black community. With the South already rattling the saber of Civil War and abolitionists demanding the immediate end to slavery in the nation's capital, Key's long-sought vision of a peaceful end to slavery dissolved before his eyes. The riot precipitated a professional, philosophical, and personal crisis for Key. He questioned his commitment to Black freedom suits and subsequently took only cases in which those to be freed had family support or professional prospects to protect them from poverty.

This violence against Washington's Black community occurred against a backdrop of white fear rooted in memories of Nat Turner's rebellion, economic depression, and the rabid success of the Anti-Slavery Society's national pamphlet campaign. Tension in the district was already acute when, in the early hours of August 5, the enslaved Black youth John Arthur Bowen, "aged about 19 years," entered the bedroom of his sleeping mistress with an ax. Bowen reportedly was drunk and may have been influenced by attending an abolitionist meeting earlier in the evening. Forced from the house by his mother, who was also enslaved to the household, Bowen reportedly shouted "I will have my freedom. . . . I have as much right to freedom as you do," then escaped into the night. Bowen was later captured and jailed.

News of the incident sparked rumors of a pending Black racial insurrection, and a mob of white men streamed into Judiciary Square, around the District of Columbia's City Hall. They demanded that Bowen be released to face the crowd's "justice." Key himself got caught up in the drama and made it worse.

As district attorney, Key assembled a grand jury to hear from neighbors who had been keeping an eye on a recent Northern arrival in town, Dr. Reuben Crandall. A witness described an antislavery pamphlet of "the most incendiary and insurrectionary character" inscribed by Crandall with the handwritten instruction "read and circulate." This evidence alone convinced the grand jury of Crandall's guilt, and fatefully Key issued a warrant for his arrest. Rather than appease the white mob—soon estimated to number three thousand—Crandall's arrest only fed its fury. For five days the mob demanded to lynch Bowen and Crandall. Key and others refused. Then, frustrated, the mob took out its anger on the district's Black population with devastating effect. Among the rioters' first targets was the Epicurean Eating House, owned by a Black man, Beverly Snow, after whose name the riot is known.

Key next bungled the prosecution of Crandall, in part because the defendant's legal team successfully compared Key's own antislavery activity to Crandall's and, in effect, put the district attorney himself on trial. Key's words preserved in the trial record seem overly personal. He is not simply prosecuting Crandall but defending himself and his beloved ACS as an organization. Crandall was found innocent, and the abolitionist press justly vilified Key for bringing the charges. One Northern newspaper, however, defended Key, writing that he "was pledged to the people to procure the conviction of Crandall, for without that assurance they would have torn him to pieces."

Key undoubtedly detested abolition and defended the legality of slavery. But a balanced account of the Snow Riot notes that Key defended Black interests as well. He also prosecuted the white rioters who had destroyed Black property. In the fall of 1835, he brought nineteen such cases, winning ten. The next spring he took on one additional case against seven of the mob's white leaders. In *United States v. Fenwick et al.*, defense attorneys made deft moves concerning the definition of the charges themselves, the evidence, who could testify, and even the very possibility of guilt of leaders for a mob action. Key overcame these objections to secure a conviction.

IN 1937 AND as recently as 2012, a horrific racist quote has been attributed to Key, suggesting that he said that Blacks "would constitute a distinct and inferior race of people, which all experience proves to be the greatest evil that could afflict a community." This quote does not represent Key's direct, first-person comments. It is, instead, his third-person description of the thinking of "colonizationists" in reply to a questionnaire mailed to him by abolitionist minister Benjamin Tappan in 1838.

Tappan's questionnaire sought to understand the thinking of pious Southerners on the topic of slavery. Its fourth question asked Key about the beliefs of colonizationists who insisted that emancipated Blacks leave the United States and emigrate to Africa. Key replied in a manner that repeats the racist views of colonizationists, while establishing strategic distance between those views and his own. Key answered—somewhat awkwardly given the number of pronouns involved:

> It is, I believe, universally so thought by them [colonizationists]. . . .
> This opinion is founded on the conviction that their [free Black]
> labor, . . . could not be secured, but by a severer system of constraint
> than that of slavery—that they [emancipated Blacks] would constitute
> a distinct and inferior race of people, which all experience proves to be
> the greatest evil that could afflict a community. I do not suppose, how-
> ever, that they [colonizationists] would object to their [emancipated
> Blacks'] reception in the free States, if they [such free states] chose to
> make preparations for their comfortable settlement among them.

Key attributed this opinion to "them," suggesting that his personal views differed. Of course, Key was a supporter of colonization, and he failed to clarify his own opinion for Tappan.

Key had made a similarly slippery statement at Crandall's trial, one that also traded on ambiguity and hid Key's own thinking. Key's personal position was further obscured by his role as a spokesman for the ACS, which tried to forge a political middle ground between slavery and abolition. It may have been strategic for Key to hide his personal views, however complicated. On the surface, Key's "letter" responding to Tappan gives the illusion of being a revealing and unfiltered personal communication between acquaintances. It is more accurately seen as an institutional propaganda piece, soon published in the ACS's own monthly journal and reprinted in newspapers from Maine to North Carolina.

Key's actions may offer stronger evidence of his beliefs than his rhetoric. When he freed those he owned, he never made removal to Africa a precondition. He provided those he freed in his lifetime with training in a skill that would enable them to achieve financial independence. Such training necessarily signaled a belief—contrary to ACS doctrine—that free Blacks could live and remain productively in the United States. Key further volunteered as a teacher at a no-cost "colored Sabbath school," established in 1816 as an extension of the Georgetown Lancaster School that he had helped to found in 1811 and for which he served as president.

Despite such efforts, Key argued that Blacks would never find equality in the United States, at least as part of his ACS rhetoric. Even in a free state such as Pennsylvania, Key claimed that free Blacks "cannot be adequately protected in their personal, much less in the exercise of the civil rights allowed them, . . . they have but the name of liberty." One observer found Key's concerns for Black rights to be manipulative at best. Writing of his speech at an 1829 ACS fundraiser in New York, a reporter for an antislavery paper criticized his description of the "degraded situation of the free coloured people" and found Key's assertion that "they must always be . . . oppressed, free but in name," to reflect Key's own bias, noting that "prejudice dwelt in his little heart, which cannot be bigger than a cherry."

Key died in January 1843, eighteen years before the start of the Civil War and nearly twenty years before the Emancipation Proclamation went into effect. Today, more than two centuries after he wrote his national lyric, racism continues to be exposed as a core failure of the United States in living up to its foundational ideals. Key's personal life, legal career, and role in government service were characterized by a fundamental and false compromise between slavery and freedom—two incompatible systems that were bound together in order to unite the states of America. Key was on the wrong side of history, and his words and actions cannot be excused. He imagined and supported only a chimerical path by which slavery could end peacefully. His devotion to the nation's founding bargain to accommodate slavery became his own personal, professional, and patriotic compromise.

But Key's life also reveals that a balanced account of the past resists the clear categorizations of the present. His attempts to find a pragmatic solution to slavery exposes a more chaotic struggle, one at odds with a simple narrative of slavery's acceptance. It is likewise the messy, tumultuous, and evolving story of America, and one that would lead to his song becoming a rallying cry of the Civil War.

Celebrating Dissonance

Recent critiques of *The Star-Spangled Banner*—its lyric and its author— have given voice to urgent calls to replace it as the national anthem or even to discard the use of national anthems across the globe. Replacement could occur when a new song arises in public consciousness as an effective alternative or when the social dissonance created by performing Key's song simply becomes too damaging to national unity. For some, that point has already arrived. But the dissonance made audible by Key's song also has value. It places the issue of equality at the center of national discourse. The anthem's ritual celebration of American idealism, emphatically clashing with the discrimination experienced by too many Americans, is an alarm bell. It warns that the nation's quest for equality remains incomplete. Colin Kaepernick's protest tapped into the Black Lives Matter movement and amplified it. But without the platform of the NFL's symbolic anthem ceremony, his protest would never have garnered national attention.

The best possible response to the social dissonance created by Key's song is to fulfill the promise of equality in the lives of all American citizens. When the words "land of the free" and "home of the brave" ring true for all Americans, then the anthem's associations with slavery will serve as an important reminder of struggles overcome to deliver on its promise of equality and justice for all. More immediately, protests and provocative op-eds about the anthem's connection to slavery expose the failures of a purely triumphalist reading of American history. To recover Francis Scott Key's story of slave ownership and to remember the role of the Colonial Marines in the War of 1812 is to restore the importance of slavery not only to American history but to its legacies in the American present.

For Juneteenth 2021—coincidentally, the first time the holiday was officially recognized by the federal government—350 "ancestral sculptures" comprising the work *Monumental Reckoning* by the African American artist Dana King were unveiled in San Francisco's Golden Gate Park. Made of steel with different sizes of spiraling vinyl tubing, the four-foot tall black statues encircled the base of the Francis Scott Key plinth. They served to memorialize those Africans stolen from their homelands and transported for the Atlantic slave trade aboard the ship *San Juan Bautista* in 1619. Among these men, women, and children were those who would be sold into the English colonies at Point Comfort, Virginia. Their arrival marked a turning point in American history.

The sculptures' vigil called on the public to commune with American history across time and place. King suggested that her ancestors "stand in judgment, holding history accountable to the terror inflicted on the first group of enslaved people brought here in 1619 to the last person sold to another, all victims of chattel slavery." San Francisco mayor London N. Breed stated that the work would "serve as an example of how we can honor our past, no matter how painful, and reflect on the challenges that are still with us today." King agreed, saying, "The memory of African descendants deserves to be told truthfully and publicly. . . . Even though the business of enslavement ended long ago, it still resonates generationally for African Americans and forms the bedrock from which systems of oppression proliferate today." This chapter argues that Key's song too invites us to tell the story of the United States, no matter how painful, and to reflect both on today's challenges and on tomorrow's possibilities.

The empty Francis Scott Key Memorial in San Francisco, surrounded
by some of the Black ancestral figures of *Monumental Reckoning*, a public
sculpture by Dana King, July 2021.

Chapter 9

Performing Patriotism

Musical Style as Social Symbol

I oftentimes think of *The Star-Spangled Banner* as something that
synthesizes the history of America warts and all.

—*Jon Batiste (2021)*

Devotion and Protest: The *Woodstock Banner*
August 18, 1969, New Bethel, New York

Arguably the most powerful, searing rendition of the anthem ever
recorded, Jimi Hendrix's 1969 *Woodstock Banner* should not have
happened. Delays plagued the Woodstock Music and Art Fair, so
instead of closing the event Sunday night as planned, Hendrix performed
first thing Monday morning. After playing for more than an hour, he
announced his regular concert-closer, *Voodoo Child (Slight Return)*. As the
festival's headliner, the superstar psychedelic guitarist seemingly intended
to shut Woodstock down, thanking the crowd "for giving us . . . your ears
and your hearts," as he continued to jam. He introduced the members of
his new band—Gypsy Sun and Rainbows—and signed off, saying "thank
you very much and goodnight. I'd like to say peace, yeah, and happiness."
But anthems were on his mind. In fact, he had introduced *Voodoo Child*
just a few minutes earlier as "the new American anthem until we get one

together." As he sustained a closing chord, strumming to a climactic finish, he nodded to the band, reset his effects pedals, and began to play *The Star-Spangled Banner.*

Hendrix had been thinking about anthems at least since 1967 and the Monterey Pop Festival that marked his triumphant return to the United States. In London he had joined forces with Mitch Mitchell on drums and Noel Redding on bass to form the pioneering power trio The Experience. Now back in the States as Monterey's next-to-last act, he went to extremes to avoid being upstaged by the closing act—The Who. He squirted lighter fluid onto his guitar while performing *Wild Thing* and infamously set the instrument on fire. Combined with his effortless virtuosity, such antics put him on the front page of American rock magazines, serving to launch an incandescent career. Unremarkable at the time, however, he had introduced *Wild Thing* as "the English and American combined anthem together."

Hendrix's trip to England had not only provided him with a new artistic direction but had forged a new personal perspective about his own identity as an American. *Wild Thing* was itself a symbol of this transatlantic journey. The U.K. band The Troggs had scored a hit with the song in 1966, but it was not an original. It had been composed by American songwriter Chip Taylor and recorded by a New York–based band named The Wild Ones. By performing *Wild Thing* at Monterey, Hendrix made his own transatlantic travels audible. Here was an American musician performing in a rock trio formed in London playing an American song made famous by a U.K. band.

At Woodstock, Hendrix again found himself at a major festival, marking a historic moment with a new anthem. Launching into a personal take on Francis Scott Key's song, he created one of the most iconic musical visions in rock history. Fortunately, it was preserved on film in Michael Wadleigh's Academy Award–winning documentary, for which it serves as both an artistic and a spiritual climax. Hendrix's *Woodstock Banner* offers a profound statement of cultural synthesis not only of music's potential for protest but of the social upheaval of the 1960s. As one critic proclaimed, "It was the most electrifying moment of Woodstock, and it was probably the single greatest moment of the sixties."

The *Woodstock Banner* defies simple analysis in its elegant synthesis of patriotism and protest. Hendrix sounds the melody proudly: in full, in time, and in tune. In effect, he sings the words through his guitar. Even his feedback-strewn psychedelic departures serve to bring lyrical phrases like "the rockets' red glare" and "bombs bursting in air" to musical life. While Key's words paint a picture of the Battle of Baltimore in 1814, Hendrix illustrates and updates this imagery for 1969. The result is often misunderstood. Hendrix does not insult or dismantle the anthem, he amplifies it.

The guitarist's cataclysmic departures from the traditional melody are at once displays of instrumental virtuosity and sonic portraiture—musical sketches of rockets and bombs, sirens and gunfire, riots and war—that recast the anthem as a raging commentary on a jungle war in Vietnam and a street war at home for civil rights. Following these illustrations, Hendrix inserts a somber quotation of *Taps*—a melody used since the time of the Civil War to honor the ultimate sacrifice of military service. It is a remembrance of war's inevitable consequence—the death of those on the front lines. Hendrix himself had friends in Vietnam. He had served in the U.S. Army's 101st Airborne, earning his "Screaming Eagles" patch as a paratrooper before escaping the army to pursue his musical career.

Hendrix's musical explication of the anthem ends with a surprising message of affirmation. As his guitar lands on the word "wave," he sustains the pitch for some fourteen seconds and uses the whammy bar to produce a deep, undulating vibrato to animate in sound a picture of America's ensign fluttering in the breeze. His guitar answers Key's question and shows that yes, "our flag was still there." Sustaining this vibrato with an effects pedal through the remainder of the song, Hendrix extends the pitch for the word "free" for some six seconds, then rounds out the anthem with a muscular, final cadence, emphatically underscoring the word "brave." His rendition is both stunning and profound, critical and hopeful.

Often considered a singularly inspired improvisation, Hendrix's *Woodstock Banner* is more accurately thought of as just one way station in an ongoing compositional process. All told, his anthem obsession lasted two full years, with Woodstock as its midpoint. Hendrix performed the anthem at least seventy times, first combining *The Star-Spangled Banner* with *Taps* in an outro to *Wild Thing* on August 16, 1968, just over a year before Woodstock. He continued to perform the anthem up through and after Woodstock, silenced only by his untimely death. His last known anthem performance was almost a year after Woodstock, in Hawaii, on August 1, 1970.

For Hendrix, Key's song was a musical snapshot of the nation, picturing both American dreams and American failures. In this vein, he sometimes introduced Key's song with the title "This Is America." His anthem arrangement was flexible, responding to his feelings at any particular political moment. It could be as short as three minutes or as long as six and a half. Always built off the traditional melody, it might feature unabashed musical pride. One such example is a March 1969 solo studio recording made at New York's Record Plant. This anthem is an ecstatic sonic fireworks display with twenty-four layers of patriotic trills and melodic passing tones layered atop one another using multitrack engineering magic. It entirely avoids Woodstock's violent, pealing mimicry of bombs falling and the screams of human suffering.

At the Los Angeles Forum in April, in contrast, Hendrix grows frustrated onstage as he sees venue security manhandling his fans. In response, he introduces the anthem as a "song that we was all brainwashed with." Offering a clean, quiet, unfiltered version of the melody, he unexpectedly detunes on the words "bright stars," dimming Key's patriotic pride by playing flat. Then after sounding the pitches for the words "gallantly streaming," Hendrix offers his own commentary on the moment, muttering a derisive "bullshit." He knew how to use the anthem as social critique.

Hendrix's most dystopian renditions were intoned at San Francisco's Winterland Ballroom in October 1968. Seeming to express the rising tide of anti-war protests while visiting this hotbed of youth activism, he performs the anthem four times in six sets. Each begins with dark atmospheric improvisations punctuated by Mitch Mitchell's explosive drums. A distorted, mistuned anthem melody follows, sometimes interrupted by raucous advertising jingles, that devolves into the *Taps* eulogy and breaks off in despair. The anthem melody is abandoned, incomplete, unfinished, unresolved. These brooding tone poems demonstrate that if Hendrix wanted to burn the anthem musically, he knew how.

At Woodstock, in contrast, Hendrix offered a complex interweaving of protest with pride, revolution with reverence. On one hand, the Woodstock festival had been a logistical nightmare. It was one big traffic jam that had prevented artists from making it to the stage; its oversize crowd exceeded expectations, trampled the gates, and made a paid festival free; and all this was mixed with rain, mud, and physical misery. On the other hand, the music was epic, and more important, the attendees pulled together as a community. The predicted public health disaster never materialized. Woodstock was thus a social triumph; its mantra of peace, love, and music proved true in practice. The festival pointed to a better future, guided by America's youth, guided by music. Hendrix's *Woodstock Banner* celebrates and affirms this optimism, while marking another step in the mixed-race guitarist's own practice of citizenship. By extending his set that Monday morning, Hendrix offered not just a song of protest and patriotism, but expressed a belief in a better future.

THE POLITICAL STORY of *The Star-Spangled Banner* in the twentieth century is a tale not of new lyrics but of transformative performances. High-profile events, sometimes broadcast nationally—such as baseball's World Series or political conventions—offer a platform to launch a musical statement. However, controversy can arise in the smallest of venues. Every performance of the national anthem offers a social message. Those participating are imagined in national unity and patriotic devotion. The performers in turn affirm their own American identity. Musical style and instrumentation, even when supporting the most traditional of versions, convey meaning. A rendition by the Boys Choir of Harlem has a social resonance different from that of a rendition by the St. Louis Symphony. The anthem played by country and bluegrass fiddler Charlie Daniels speaks differently than one performed by the Mormon Tabernacle Choir or Beyoncé.

Link Davis, Jr., created the "Star Spangled Banner, Cajun Style," to express a regional patriotism, while the jazz bandleader Carla Bley explored her own patriotism in a twenty-minute anthem suite in her album *Looking for America*. The banjoist Bela Fleck responded spontaneously in the studio to the 1990 Gulf War, while EDM artists created a "Power House Edition" dance-mix of Key's song following 2001's 9/11 attacks to speak to American youth.

While national symbols evoke a timeless connection to American history, the music of *The Star-Spangled Banner* has changed over time. Throughout the nineteenth century, Key's song was sung by soloists who performed all four verses and sometimes additional ones. Audience members sang only the song's chorus, the final two lines of each verse. Twentieth-century complaints that Americans did not know the words to their signature song reflect this nineteenth-century performance tradition. Americans did not need to memorize words they simply echoed back. Military regulations, governing primarily instrumental renditions, eliminated the repeated chorus in 1905, and as the song shifted to use in group singing, the repeated chorus became redundant and obsolete. To sing or perform the anthem today is thus not to sing it the way it was experienced by Francis Scott Key.

U.S. law lacks any requirement about how the national anthem is to be performed; nor do any legal mandates dictate how civilian audiences are to behave during the anthem ritual. All such expectations are customary and voluntary. During World War I, attempts to specify an official patriotic code arose but focused on norms for display of the flag. A two-day meeting sponsored by the American Legion in 1923 recommended only that Key's song be granted "universal recognition as the national anthem." Slightly revised in 1937, the flag code was adopted by Congress in June 1942 but does not mention the anthem. A parallel Code for the National Anthem of the United States of America was developed in April 1942. It recommended the Service Version in A-flat as the preferred edition.

However, Congress soon added a brief addendum to the 1931 law naming Key's song the anthem titled "Conduct during Playing." It states—in its most recent version—that nonmilitary persons present:

should face the flag and stand at attention with their right hand over the heart, and men not in uniform, if applicable, should remove their headdress with their right hand and hold it at the left shoulder, the hand being over the heart; and when the flag is not displayed, all present should face toward the music and act in the same manner they would if the flag were displayed.

Initially adopted in 1942 and subsequently adjusted, this statement codified cultural practice, but the operative word "should" fell short of a legal mandate. Creating such a mandate—and as a result, legal jeopardy around performances of the anthem—would be a patriotic mistake.

While controversial renditions of *The Star-Spangled Banner* can inspire calls for regulation, any such legal requirements would have the unintended consequence of making sincere patriotism impossible. If to sing the anthem is to express love of country, then using law to govern this expression would make its performance not an expression of patriotism but an act of obedience. It would be impossible to distinguish between a rendition inspired by true devotion and one crafted to avoid punishment. For this reason, no law should be passed to specify how the national anthem or any patriotic song is to be performed. To do so would be to undercut the very possibility of patriotism. The musical arrangement and expressive details of the song must be left open to the artistry and intent of the performer. The price of sincere patriotism is thus the potential for protest.

The success or failure of an anthem performance instead pivots on artistry. If a rendition is perceived by listeners as artful, emotionally compelling, and authentic, significant departures from tradition can be received as patriotic, even exceptionally so. Whitney Houston's 1991 Super Bowl performance is one example. The other end of the spectrum is marked by Roseanne Barr's performance at a baseball game one year earlier, a performance so widely condemned as to permanently damage Barr's reputation. Context makes a difference. A political event, such as a war or a public controversy, that surrounds a performance can transform how it is received and interpreted. Artistry also matters. A musician with the skills to say something in song can share a profound message.

A case study both in context and in artistic intent was set in motion in 1968 in Detroit, at the apex of the Vietnam War and just one year after the city's devastating riots.

José Feliciano's Musical Revolution
October 7, 1968, Detroit

Some ten months before Woodstock, another popular recording artist addressed an unorthodox rendition of the anthem to America's youth. Broadcast live nationally, it created a much larger firestorm of controversy. The Puerto Rican singer and guitarist José Feliciano, an ardent baseball fan, had readily accepted the invitation to open game five of the 1968 World Series in Detroit. Accompanying himself on guitar, Feliciano offered a

José Feliciano performs the anthem at game five of the 1968 World Series in Detroit. Note that the backing band is standing at attention but not performing.

sweet soul, gospel-tinged interpretation of the anthem, singing all of Key's words precisely, but to an unexpected, original melodic variation.

The play-by-play broadcaster Ernie Harwell, who would later become a Tigers radio legend, had unwittingly risked his young career when he booked Feliciano. A songwriter himself, Harwell was attuned to popular music trends. Feliciano had emerged onto the national scene that summer with a hit record, a laid-back, soul version of The Doors' 1967 hit *Light My Fire*. Not only did this cover hint at what Feliciano would do with the anthem, but Harwell invited Feliciano to perform in part because of his personalized take on Key's song. "I had heard from people in music whose opinion I respect," noted Harwell as the controversy blossomed, "that he had an interesting version of the national anthem."

Tigers management had asked Harwell to find singers for each game the team would host. Singer Margaret Whiting (game three) and Motown heartthrob Marvin Gaye (game four) stirred no controversy with their performances. Ironically, Harwell remembered being forced to ask Gaye to temper his R&B stylings: "They were worried about Marvin because of his Motown connection," Harwell remembered. "They told me to . . . ask him to sing it a little more traditional." Indeed, Gaye delivered text and melody in his typical style, accompanied by a brass band in center field that prevented him from going too far afield of the expected. As Gaye sang, however, he slowed down, extending the drama and pathos of the song and giving special emphasis to its concluding celebration of freedom. If he intended this as social commentary, no one objected.

Feliciano's "hippie" anthem, however, inspired immediate criticism, as complaints lit up telephone switchboards around the country. "Storm Rages over Series Anthem" exclaimed the front page of the *Detroit Free Press* the next morning. "It's disgraceful," complained one observer. "It was just a desecration to hear it sung that way," said another. "I didn't stand up," a fan at the ballpark claimed, "that wasn't the national anthem he was singing." At one veterans' hospital, angry ex-servicemen reportedly hurled shoes at the singer's image on TV. Harwell received "a couple thousand letters," he remembered, "people called me all sorts of names, saying

I was a Communist." Harwell, however, defended the singer: "I feel a fellow has a right to sing any way he can sing it . . . the way he feels it."

Baseball executives had not anticipated Feliciano's soul-tinged approach. As preserved on the original broadcast tape, the stadium announcer asks fans to "join in the singing of our national anthem," an impossibility given the unconventional melody Feliciano would use. Further, the announcer introduced not only the singer but Merle Alvey's band as the song's performers. Blind since birth, Feliciano was unaware of the band until he was asked what musical key he would use. He replied that he'd just accompany himself on guitar. The band's traditional arrangement was wholly incompatible with the singer's plans. For starters, Feliciano sang in 4/4 time rather than the traditional 3/4 meter. Band members thus stood dumbfounded behind Feliciano as he sang. Light applause followed. News outlets reported fans booing, but little can be heard on the broadcast tape. Fans seemed more stunned than angry.

"I was afraid people would misconstrue it and say I'm making fun of it," Feliciano explained, "but I'm not. It's the way I feel." He also admitted that he intended to update the anthem for a new era. "America is young now, and I thought maybe the anthem could be revived. . . . I wanted to contribute something to this country, express my gratification for what it has done for me. I love this country very much. When anyone knocks it, I'm the first to defend it." A few days later he explained further: "I came to New York from Puerto Rico as a very poor boy, . . . [and] America has been extremely good to me. I didn't set out to defame the anthem. . . . I don't feel anything unless I can do it as you heard." He soon began opening all his U.S. concerts with his version of the anthem.

A *Detroit Free Press* editorial entitled "Why All the Furor?" defended the singer. While preferring "a standard rendition," editors noted that Feliciano "brought a special kind of meaning to the song . . . too rarely felt in our national and patriotic institutions. . . . Feliciano was saying that nothing is static, that nothing lies beyond examination or change, that this too is America." The Tigers' star catcher Bill Freehan offered an insider's view: "I met José Feliciano five minutes before he went out to sing. He is a baseball fan and he was proud and nervous about being asked. I can't condemn the rendition because I know how much he wanted to be accepted. . . . I know one thing: He made Marvin Gaye . . . sound like a square."

Younger listeners flooded radio stations with requests to hear Feliciano's *Banner* again, and bootleg acetates appeared on the streets of New York the day after the game. RCA Victor rushed to release a 45-rpm single. A single-sided promo copy was quickly sent to DJs, while a commercial 45 was announced in *Billboard*'s "Spotlight Singles" on October 23. Its B-side featured Feliciano's cover of the Beatles' *And I Love Her,* possibly as a clever answer to questioning critics who doubted Feliciano's true feelings about his native land.

The record registered immediately on *Billboard*'s Top 100 chart. Feliciano felt he had reinvigorated patriotism among America's youth. "The song had practically passed into oblivion. Now it's back in every home as it should be," he remarked. Feliciano's rendition indeed marked a historic turning point. It shattered the anthem's musical orthodoxy, opening new artistic possibilities for pop stylists to offer sincere, personal arrangements of Key's song. His was also the first broadcast performance to use 4/4 meter. Although loosely inspired by the original Anacreontic tune, Feliciano's vocal line does not feel derivative. Its opening descent is traditional, but rhythmic displacement and tuneful ornamentation not only keep the melody flowing but establish an original soulful feel. Remarkably, Feliciano actually stretches the melody's compass. It is one pitch wider than traditional.

More than his musical interpretation, it was the political events surrounding Feliciano's anthem that distorted its reception. It hit the airwaves in a year when public opinion was shifting against the Vietnam War and protesters were taking to the streets. The nation was also reeling from violence—the assassination of Martin Luther King, Jr. (April 4), subsequent riots in Washington, Chicago, and Baltimore, and the assassination of presidential candidate Robert F. Kennedy (June 5).

Feliciano did not sing another pregame anthem until 2003—a thirty-five-year hiatus—when he appeared at game five of the National League Championship Series in Miami. As the Tigers were in 1968, the Marlins were behind three games to one in the seven-game series, but they rallied to win the pennant and the World Series. Feliciano appeared again in San Francisco for game one of the 2012 National League Championship. Although the Giants lost to the Cardinals that day, they would go on to win the World Series, ironically sweeping the Detroit Tigers in four games. Given the undercurrent of superstition in baseball, teams would be wise to invite Feliciano to perform whenever they reach the postseason. His anthem is a proven winner.

Aretha's Gospel Anthems
August 26, 1968, Chicago

Feliciano's World Series anthem was not the first to be received as controversial, even unpatriotic. Two months before at Chicago's 1968 Democratic National Convention, Aretha Franklin's opening rendition was bitterly dismissed, often in racist language, as a "soul version" or even a "Congo version" of the nation's song. Partially preserved on an archival broadcast tape, Franklin sings to a traditional musical accompaniment. Accounts that suggest she used an "unusual" or "jazzed-up" arrangement are simply false. Instead, she sings the expected text and tune, while taking modest expressive liberties with the rhythm. As she sings the second phrase—"Whose broad stripes and bright stars"—she raises both arms and signals attendees to join singing. When they do, however, she offers a kind of gospel solo response to the traditional call of the crowd's performance. She takes a deep breath before "ramparts" and draws out the first syllable as a gospel shout. She then allows the audience to carry the song, entering late and pressing forward on the words "were so gallantly streaming," ending before the crowd but in idiomatic soul style. Some newspaper accounts criticized her vocal abilities, reporting that she couldn't hit the high notes. This is wholly

Aretha Franklin sings the national anthem at the Democratic National
Convention, Chicago, August 26, 1968.

incorrect. Instead, she delays the high notes slightly, creating drama and
emphasis. A simple mix-up of the words follows, as she accidentally repeats
the lyric's opening "O say can you" instead of singing "O say does that" to
begin the lyric's final couplet. She quickly and smoothly corrects herself.

Misinformation about Franklin's version metastasized, spurred by the many controversies and protests saturating the nominating convention itself. Her lyrical stumble was magnified, and since no recording was publicly available at the time to document what had actually occurred, exaggeration piled on outrage. Franklin was soon accused of intentionally leaving out the climactic word "free" as a message of protest. Others insisted she sang the climactic phrase. The soul singer's manager tried to quash any misunderstandings: "The main difficulty was that Aretha was at one end of the hall and the band at the other, so that she was unable to hear it. On top of that, she was terribly nervous and may have stuffed over some of the words. But I am sure she did not leave out any word or phrase intentionally."

The surviving recording suggests that Franklin was aiming for a respectful and traditional rendition of Key's song. She sings the standard melody and does not add notes, syllables, or ornament. Her gentle adjustments to pacing are wholly typical of gospel or soul and do not appear to deliver any special political statement, other than to underscore the singer's own legitimate and sincere Black identity. That in 1968 a Black woman was singing at a national political convention was itself a political statement. No musical enhancement was needed. Eventually, Aretha herself responded to the controversy: "All I know is I sing like Aretha Franklin. . . . If they asked me to tackle the anthem again, I'd sing it exactly the same."

Indeed, the Queen of Soul would be invited to sing the anthem many times, but in truth she never sang it exactly the same way twice. Her later performances, for which she often accompanied herself on keyboard, include extensive melodic ornaments—melismata, lyrical repetitions, and gospel-infused vocal extensions—that go far beyond her 1968 rendition. She never lip-syncs to a prerecorded track, as her style is too spontaneous. She performed for the 1987 light heavyweight title fight of Detroit's Thomas "Hitman" Hearns, the 1992 and '96 Democratic conventions, the 1993 World Series, the 2003 NFL National Kickoff, the 2009 National Mall July Fourth, baseball's 2011 American League Championship Series, the 2014 Harvard Commencement, and Super Bowl XL, along with other events. In 2016 she gave what appears to be the anthem's longest-ever broadcast version at Detroit's traditional Thanksgiving Day Lions football game.

Comedian Roseanne Barr sings *The Star-Spangled Banner* at a
San Diego Padres game, July 25, 1990.

Roseanne Barr: Bursting "On Air"
July 25, 1990, San Diego

The actress and comedian Roseanne Barr sat atop of the media world
in 1990. A "television mega-star," she was the creative force behind the
most-watched television sitcom in the United States, *Roseanne*. Barr's
portrayal of the show's namesake—an outspoken, iconoclastic working-
class mother—made her an object of public fascination, especially as the
identities of character and actress merged in the public imagination. She
was the anti-Hollywood Hollywood star, the subject of tabloid exposés
and academic critique. Voters for the People's Choice Awards named her
the favorite female TV performer. Activist and best-selling author Barbara Ehrenreich praised her as the icon of "the hopeless underclass of the
female sex: polyester clad, overweight occupants of the slow track; fast-
food waitresses, factory workers, housewives, members of the invisible
pink-collar army; the despised, the jilted, the underpaid."

When Barr botched the anthem in front of 24,744 major league baseball fans and a national TV audience in possibly the song's worst perfor-

mance ever, listeners believed it was either a bad joke, a tasteless publicity stunt, or an intentional attack on the nation's values. Only a limited audience caught the performance live, but afterward her disaster was replayed coast-to-coast ad nauseam. The backlash was so severe, it rocked Barr's personal and professional life.

Her rendition is painful to experience. On the broadcast tape, Barr can be heard saying, "Tell me when I have to start," just before she launches into a brisk opening presentation of the melody. She starts out fine. Her tone is shrill but certainly within bounds for a vocal amateur. By just the sixth note, however, her voice begins to crack, and she is nearly a quarter-step flat on the word "see." While she sings each word clearly and correctly, her pitch wobbles. Her second phrase repeats the faults of the first. After she squeezes out the highest notes once again, she aspirates a self-conscious chuckle, seemingly recognizing that her performance is failing. Fatefully, she forges ahead.

On "RAM-parts" Barr's voice frays, with the most difficult parts of the song still to come. It is here that the melody jumps up in tessitura to its highest pitches—notes that even professional singers approach with care. Barr screams out the phrase "And the rockets' red glare." Pushing far above her vocal range, she fails to reach the correct pitches, and her tone narrows sharply to a painful, razor-wire screech. The crowd now audibly turns on her. Stunned silent until this moment, fans begin to jeer, interpreting her performance as not just bad but intentionally insulting—a failed attempt at her trademark humor. The crowd's negativity soon becomes deafening but still fails to drown out the singer's amplified wailings.

Barr's voice recovers a bit for the anthem's final phrase, given its lower pitch level. She even adds decorative passing tones to the words "banner yet wave," suggesting she has practiced the song in advance. However, she has lost the crowd, even as she fights back against the onslaught of boos. She remains determined. On the word "free," her voice disintegrates, yet she extends the pitch dramatically for some three full seconds, as the chorus of hecklers grows fierce.

Barr is no longer Roseanne Barr the relatively effective singer of her stand-up act; she has shifted gears to become "Roseanne"—the brash,

damn-polite-society character from her TV series. Her performance of
the word "free" is a shout of liberation, from baseball tradition as well as
demure femininity. Her anthem is a sonic middle finger targeting the stadium's almost thirty thousand fans in retaliation for their vitriol. Barr's
final vocal gasp is no better. The word "home" wobbles between pitches.
She lifts her shoulders and lowers them emphatically on the word "brave."
Catcalls fill the stadium. Barr steps back, grabs her crotch, and spits on the
ground, crassly imitating a baseball player. She then struts toward the visitors' dugout, throwing her head back and raising her arms wide, seeming
to embrace the crowd's hostility. As she exits the field, the broadcast tape
records her plea to stadium personnel: "Get us out of *here!*"

Barr's anthem threatened to derail her career. It was featured on
national television news, radio talk shows debated it, and newspapers
fanned the flames of controversy. If the quality of her singing had been
the main criticism, the ruckus would likely have faded. Instead, her pro-
fane gestures became the impossible-to-ignore focal point. Letters to the
editor called for a boycott of her show, while others collected complaints
to mail to advertisers. The Padres' promotions director Ron Seaver made
an initial attempt at damage control, claiming that Barr's rendition had
been marred by an echo delay in the sound system and that the actress had
intended no insult to the game or the nation. Interviewed by San Diego's
KFMB-TV news, however, Barr doubled down. "I think I did great and
people wanted more," she proclaimed.

Friends assured Barr that the furor would "roll over and die," but it did
not. Front-page articles and more letters poured in. The American baritone Robert Merrill, known since 1969 for his prototypical anthem renditions at Yankee Stadium, said, "This woman, who obviously has no taste
at all, went out to sing the national anthem and distorted the song. It was
to me like burning of the flag." Padres players joined the critical chorus.
"I thought it was disgusting," said the star outfielder Tony Gwynn. The
pitcher Eric Show commented, "It was an insult to the song and all the
people who have died for what we have left of our freedom." Much was at
risk for the Padres. Since World War I, their hometown had been the site

of a major navy base, and the addition of Marine and Coast Guard units gave San Diego the nickname "martial metropolis." Many of the team's fans had deep military connections.

Barr began receiving death threats, and upcoming professional projects were canceled, including a girls' empowerment cartoon titled "Little Rosey." She later said that she could not go out "in public for about one full year without being spit on in restaurants." She reported having Los Angeles Police Department officers "stand up on my roof and protect my life and my kids for two years." Barr has since claimed that she was attempting to deliver a respectful, traditional performance that day. "I was singing in my act at the time—and I am a good singer," Barr said twenty-five years after the event. "I was flattered and fully intended to sing a good version of the song." But with no sound check at the stadium and no musical accompaniment to keep her on pitch, a small initial mistake became a major disaster. Barr claimed that she had been warned in advance by talk show host Johnny Carson, who told her "Whatever you do, don't start too high." Nevertheless Barr "started too high. I knew about six notes in that I couldn't hit the big note. So, I just tried to get through it." The recorded evidence suggests that she was telling the truth.

Twenty-one years after her infamous shrieks, Barr again sang the anthem on a baseball diamond. This time it was for a low-key girls' softball game in Hawaii. The performance was filmed for the first season of her cable reality show *Roseanne's Nuts*. After considerable drama and considerable rehearsal, Roseanne successfully performed the anthem in a strong mezzo voice, using falsetto to hit the high note on "free." The crowd cheered. On the recording, her voice is smooth, and she successfully navigates the same gentle passing-tone ornamentation on "banner yet wave" that she attempted in 1990. For the most part she stays on key, and when she gets off, she gets back on. The telling difference is her starting pitch. Here she sings in the key of G-flat, a full half-octave below the C-major starting pitch of her previous attempt.

In her successful repeat performance, Barr saw implications both personal and patriotic: "I proved to myself what I wanted to prove, which was that I'm not going to be a slave to fear. I live a free life. I live a life of freedom because this is the United States of America and we are free." Key's song had taught her a lesson about herself as well as the nation.

Igor Stravinsky's "Illegal" Anthem
January 15, 1944, Boston

Before the internet, a spurious black and white "mug shot" of the Russian émigré composer Igor Stravinsky circulated in blurry photocopies among classical music aficionados. It was accompanied by a scandalous tale of Stravinsky's arrest for desecrating the U.S. anthem.

At first glance, the image's nefarious overtones seem genuine. A haggard, expressionless portrait of the composer with cavernous eyes lends credibility to the story of legal misadventure, as does a sign hanging crookedly around his neck that reads "Boston Police / 5474 / 4 15 40." This last line, however, exposes the myth. It indicates the date of the photo—April

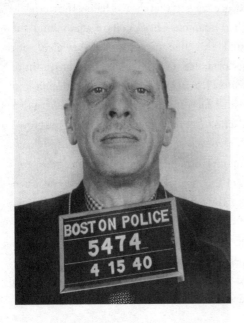

Igor Stravinsky's "mug shot" is
actually a photo from his 1940
visa application.

15, 1940, which coincides not with Stravinsky's 1941 anthem arrangement nor with his 1944 appearance in Boston to conduct it, but with his successful 1940 visa application for permanent U.S. residency. Despite the obvious falsehood, however, the legend offers echoes of truth.

The tale is rooted in a real event—a January 15, 1944, "all-Stravinsky" concert by the Boston Symphony Orchestra. Stravinsky's anthem arrangement was to open the evening, and the composer himself would conduct live at Symphony Hall and over national radio. An Associated Press preview story had primed the controversy. It featured a photo of Stravinsky peering at the first page of his new spangled score, over a provocative caption: "STRAVINSKY REVISES NATIONAL ANTHEM." Stravinsky hoped the coast-to-coast broadcast would allow his arrangement finally to be recognized as the standard version of Key's song. His hope would be dashed.

Stravinsky and the Boston Symphony had already performed the arrangement without incident, twice in fact: first, in Cambridge on Thursday, January 13, and again the next afternoon in Boston. As was his custom, Stravinsky turned about on the podium to conduct the audience singing along. One reviewer described the result: "At the start, the audience began to sing with the orchestra in the customary manner, but soon the odd, somewhat dissonant harmonies ... became evident. Eyebrows lifted, voices faltered, and before the close practically everyone gave up even trying to accompany the score." This negative review, during a time of war, led to the invocation of a little-known 1917 Massachusetts law. The law, which is still in effect, reads in full:

> Whoever plays, sings or renders the "Star Spangled Banner" in any public place, theatre, motion picture hall, restaurant or café, or at any public entertainment, other than as a whole and separate composition or number, without embellishment or addition in the way of national or other melodies, or whoever plays, sings or renders the "Star Spangled Banner", or any part thereof, as dance music, as an exit march or as a part of a medley of any kind, shall be punished by a fine of not more than one hundred dollars.

Stravinsky reported that "just before the ... concert, a police commissioner appeared in my dressing room. . . . He said that policemen had already been instructed to remove my arrangement from the music stands." The Saturday-night broadcast thus began with the announcer explaining: "Mr. Stravinsky will play the Star Spangled Banner in its customary version, . . . he will readily conform to the Massachusetts law." Despite claims to the contrary, he was not arrested.

Ironically, Stravinsky's controversial arrangement is rather beautiful. It was written in the summer of 1941, and the composer mailed a bound version of his score to President Franklin D. Roosevelt with his handwritten dedication to the American people:

Searching about for a vehicle through which I might best express my gratitude at the prospect of becoming an American Citizen, I chose to harmonize and orchestrate as a national chorale the beautiful sacred anthem The Star Spangled Banner. It is a desire to do my bit in these grievous times toward fostering and preserving the spirit of patriotism in this country that inspired me to tender this my humble work to the American People—Igor Strawinsky [sic] / 1941

In the context of World War II, however, the composer's conception of Key's song as a lush national hymn fell flat. Listeners desired a virile, reassuring musical statement that depicted a powerful nation capable of defeating any threat. Stravinsky's version, a hymn rather than a call to arms, was too serene. Less than two months after its premiere, the attack on Pearl Harbor brought the United States into World War II, and the more militaristic resonance of Key's song captured the national ethos. Wartime fervor overruled artful reinvention. Yet the composer, his supporters, and certainly his publisher all maintained hope that Stravinsky's setting would become the anthem's official version. All failed to comprehend the social dynamic that doomed the project to failure.

The claim that Stravinsky changed no melodic note requires a small but significant qualification. He changed no pitch, but he did adjust the rhythm to create a more symmetrical contour that emphasizes the tune's opening "O-o say" impulse—that is, the snapped rhythmic motto of a dotted-eighth plus a sixteenth note. He artfully emphasized this motto's stately rhythmic gesture and alternated its propulsive drive with three even quarter notes in two-bar pairs. The result is more lyrical and hymn-like. The snapped figure is typically associated with a military march, but Stravinsky's slow tempo is transformative. The expressive result is not bellicose but majestic, evoking just the "noble American national chorale" that the composer described as his intent.

The nontraditional feel of Stravinsky's version is most apparent at the lyric's dramatic high point, but not because of modernist experimentation. Here Stravinsky dropped the volume from loud to soft and smoothed out the rhythmic contour to present the phrases "rockets' red glare" and "bombs bursting in air" with reverential awe. This austere shift creates a sonic oasis of peace and simplicity. The orchestral accompaniment emphasizes this effect even further as lush strings take over the melody, whereas trumpets and brass had dominated until then. The result is musically compelling—translucent and delicate—but an associated effect is that the high notes become that much harder to sing. At the very moment in which amateur singers need firm support to seek out the topmost pitches, the accompaniment pulls away.

The climax of Stravinsky's musical vision is instead the concluding chorus—the lyric's final two lines. Here the dotted rhythms and strong forte dynamic return. Rolling eighth notes in the bass line drive to the traditional hold on the word "wave," using a conventional dominant triad that would normally push the harmony back to the comforting reassurance of the home key. Here, however, Stravinsky's harmonization avoids the norm. Rather than arrive on an affirming tonic, the composer substitutes a dissonant B-flat minor seventh chord on the words "land" and "free." The would-be singer's sense of arrival is thus undercut, offering not harmonic confidence but uncertainty. As a result, many amateurs singing along simply stop. Stravinsky may have intended this dissonance to create a more dramatic sense of resolution when the song finally cadences on the word "brave." Indeed, the effect on this final word is especially powerful in his conception. He emphasizes unity as each SATB part ends firmly on the home pitch of B-flat in a stunning unison. The result is undeniably artful, but if most singers have dropped out before reaching the melody's conclusion, it is severely compromised.

A recording of Stravinsky conducting his anthem arrangement with a professional choir survives. Not released until 1972, the impassioned 1964 recording underscores the problems with the composer's conception. His slow rendition becomes ever slower. The recording begins at a relatively brisk pace of almost 100 beats per minute (bpm) before settling into a tempo of about 85–90 bpm for the opening phrases. The third phrase on "rockets' red glare" slows even a bit more to 75–82 bpm, while the final phrase pulls back dramatically to a stately 60 bpm with additional slowing from there. The whole verse lasts about one minute and eighteen seconds. The recording demonstrates that experienced singers, schooled in the specifics of Stravinsky's interpretation, could render it as a powerful musical statement. The same was not true of an unrehearsed public.

Stravinsky's *Banner* failed for more than one reason. Even if it had been a musical triumph, it would have been undercut by the increasing anti-Russian sentiments of the Cold War. Critics soon accused the composer of a "lack of respect" toward the nation and even "subversive intentions." But Stravinsky's primary error was mismanaging the song's social function as a participatory ritual of national communion. It failed to serve the needs of amateur singers and thus, despite its musical beauty, failed as the nation's preferred setting of the anthem.

Lift Every Voice and Sing: African American Reconceptions
July 1, 2008, Denver

On July 1, 2008, the jazz singer and Denver resident René Marie approached the podium to set the stage for the mayor's annual "State of the City" address. Invited to sing *The Star-Spangled Banner*, the child of civil rights activists performed "my version of the national anthem." She sang the traditional Anacreontic melody using the words from the first verse of James Weldon Johnson's *Lift Every Voice and Sing*, often referred to as the Black national anthem. The song's three verses, according to their author, express the story of "the American Negro, historically and spiritually." Set to original music by his brother, J. Rosamond Johnson, the lyric had premiered more than a century earlier, sung by some five hundred schoolchildren in Jacksonville, Florida. The year 1900 marked a critical era in U.S. race relations. Discriminatory Black Codes increasingly undermined the rights gained by Black Americans through the Fourteenth and Fifteenth amendments. The Supreme Court's 1896 decision in *Plessy v. Ferguson* further sanctioned racial segregation and its inequalities.

Marie's performance was musically compelling. The live audience applauded, somewhat uncertain about what had occurred. Controversy arose afterward, in the media. Although she had sung this same arrangement before, at public events in Denver, with some of the same city officials present, Marie was accused of deception and of failing to sing the national anthem at all. She apologized to the mayor for "distress that may have resulted" but not for her song. Marie believes that art is necessarily a form of social activism. "I believe personal action is the key to social change," she explained, "It is personal action that preceded every major advancement in this country, including the very establishment of the United States of America itself." She proclaimed that "this is the aspect of being American that gives me the greatest sense of pride."

Her fusion of the two songs is artistically powerful. Both lyrics speak to a pivotal moment in the nation's history and address the founding ideal of liberty. Her slow, free-form interpretation of the melody avoids a sense of pulse, allowing her to adapt rhythm and pitch to stark differences in syllable count. The *Banner* melody's highest and most dramatic pitches underscore the "faith," "hope," and optimism of Johnson's lyric. His final two lines map elegantly onto the triumphal conclusion of the anthem melody: "Facing the rising sun of our new day begun, / Let us march on 'til victory is won." Marie's rendition was an expression of patriotic devotion that highlights the history of Black America and thus the nation's unfinished quest to realize its ideals.

The synthesis was inspired by Marie's experiences in singing both songs as a child, growing up in a segregated, southern town. "It seemed apparent to me early on," she noted, "that the sentiments expressed in each song are diametrically opposed to one another." *The Star-Spangled Banner* spoke proudly to many, but "that sentiment was not a reality for black folks living in a town with Jim Crow laws, where the flag often hung from buildings they could not enter." She observed that "nobody but black folks found comfort in *Lift Ev'ry Voice and Sing*." "I loved singing both songs, but each seemed to have their own aspects of exclusivity and segregation." Her goal was thus to "marry the two ideologies musically by melding the two songs into one harmonic thought." She later adapted the arrangement into a full six-part jazz suite titled *Voice of My Beautiful Country* (2011) that incorporates settings of *America the Beautiful* and *My Country 'Tis of Thee*. The suite concludes with a lyrical prayer, repeating the climactic phrase of Johnson's lyric—"Let us march on 'til victory is won. Let us march on." Her example of musical fusion has led the way for other African American artists to find a personal path to express their patriotism.

The composer and violinist Jessie Montgomery has also imagined compelling musical alloys of *The Star-Spangled Banner* and *Lift Every Voice and Sing*, first in 2009 in a work titled *Anthem* with lyrics by sixteen-year-old Kirby Vasquez, and then in 2014 in a work for solo string quartet and chamber orchestra titled *Banner*. Montgomery began her professional career as a violinist in the Providence String Quartet, the resident ensemble of a nonprofit educational initiative known as Community MusicWorks (CMW) that provides free music instruction to urban youth as a vehicle of community empowerment. Inspired by Barack Obama's election as president, CMW asked Montgomery to create a musical anthem celebrating the civil rights movement. An original theme sets a quotation from the preamble to the Constitution and soon invokes the nation's youth as its future. Written for a string ensemble including CMW faculty and students, the work asks performers to both sing and play, developing into a setting of the Black anthem in counterpoint with allusions to *The Star-Spangled Banner*. Five years later the Sphinx Organization commissioned Montgomery to commemorate the two-hundredth anniversary of Key's song. The composer admitted being "personally conflicted" by the commission because as an "African American person living in the United States," she "never felt that the song actually applied to me." Montgomery had previously even protested by remaining seated during anthem performances. To navigate the work's personal and political implications, she envisioned a kaleidoscopic remix for the twenty-first century, transforming Key's song into a multicultural American rhapsody. Its high-energy opening sets up an introspective central episode featuring the *Lift Every Voice* melody in the solo string bass. Echoes of twelve folk songs and anthems are heard, drawn not only from the United States but from its cultural neighbors. Quotations include *Mexicanos, al grito de Guerra* (Mexico), *This Land Is Your Land* (United States), *Lo Eterno* (Cuba), *La Boriqueña* (Puerto Rico), the Appalachian folk song *Cumberland Gap* (a reference to the Confederacy), and a musical setting of the Pledge of Allegiance.

Montgomery deftly crafts the whole into a Sousa-like march form, juxtaposing contrasting strains and a slower trio section to invoke the patriotic American genre. A percussive interlude combines military rolls and the strings' hip-hop scratching with African-inspired hand drumming on the wooden sides of the string basses. The whole then spins into a propulsive, celebratory finale built from layers of the Anacreontic melody. "The Star Spangled Banner is an ideal subject for exploration in contradictions," she explains, "For most Americans the song represents a paradigm of liberty and solidarity against fierce odds, and for others it implies a contradiction between the ideals of freedom and the realities of injustice and oppression. . . . A tribute to the U.S. national anthem means acknowledging the contradictions, leaps and bounds and milestones that allow us to celebrate and maintain the tradition of our ideals."

To reopen the COVID-delayed 2020 NBA season, the jazz pianist Jon Batiste created a more inclusive, racially just arrangement of the anthem, responsive to the Black Lives Matter movement. He layered the traditional anthem tune, played by piano, atop the melody of *Lift Every Voice and Sing*, sounded by a cello as both bass line and countermelody. For the New Orleans–born Batiste, the triplet feel of *Lift Every Voice*'s 6/8 rhythms sounding against the dotted sixteenths of the anthem created a 3 versus 4 polyrhythm that evoked American music's connections to Africa. "It's a tonal allegory," he explained. A contrasting New Orleans bounce beat entangled the threads of this musical synthesis. Switching to electric guitar, Batiste continued in homage to Jimi Hendrix, using distortion to depict the lyric's "bombs" and "rockets." He even imitated Hendrix's deep vibrato on the whammy bar to illustrate that "our flag was still there." All the while the melody of *Lift Every Voice* continued dissonantly underneath. Batiste then returned to the keyboard to finish the anthem melody, enriching the harmony with a florid series of scales and arpeggiations that created a spiritual, almost celestial coda. "When you put music in that context," he later reflected, "at . . . the reopening of the NBA season, all of the players kneeling in arms, representing so much of what we're dealing with in that moment. I truly believe that's music that exists at its highest potential, it's not about commodification, it's not about anything but capturing the moment and really helping it to reflect truth."

Like Hendrix, Batiste performs the anthem a bit differently on each occasion, drawing on a range of musical symbols to comment on the American experience. Released in 2013 as a bonus track on the album *Social Music*, Batiste presented a solo piano rendition, which would serve as the basis for later anthem performances in concert, at voter registration rallies, and at protests. Harmonies both from the gospel church and from Gershwin infuse its opening phrases. He thus acknowledges the Black and white genesis not only of American music but of America itself. The lyric's bombs and rockets are depicted as a flood of pianistic sounds, what Batiste terms a "lion's roar"—a series of rich chords and pounding runs sounded with the piano's damper pedal lifted off the strings so that they ring and blend. Batiste later explained that in creating this musical climax, he tried to evoke a portion of James Weldon Johnson's lyric for *Lift*

Every Voice, specifically the words "Let it resound loud as the rolling sea." "That's the resounding sound of freedom," Batiste explained. "That's our people standing up, all people standing up, all Americans who believe in the ideal of what America is meant to represent. That's the feeling that I wanted to ignite."

The Nigerian-American artist Ekene Ijeoma created a different feeling— one of reflection and reckoning—with *Deconstructed Anthems*. The work uses sound, or maybe more accurately its absence as silence, to bring attention to the 2.3 million people imprisoned in the United States. Over the course of twenty or so minutes, the anthem melody is repeated multiple times. With each reiteration, notes are removed from the iconic tune. These gaps represent "those who have been systematically removed from their families and communities," those "whose voices have been silenced, and those whose system has failed them." Ijeoma creates site-specific editions for each city in which *Deconstructed Anthems* is produced. The work can be performed live by a solo pianist or jazz trio, or it can be automated using a computer-controlled piano. Silences are determined by an algorithm drawing upon historical incarceration data, with the number of repetitions tied to the discrepancy between white and Black incarceration rates.

For the work's 2017 premiere, Ijeoma placed the performers inside a twenty-foot-square, ten-foot-tall architectural box outlined by thirty-six rectangular panels that evoked the physical and spiritual bars of a jail cell. Each panel was covered in two-way mirror film and bathed in a sharp white internal light. When external lights flashed to mark the music's melodic gaps, the clear panels became solid mirrored bars. These mirrors invited the audience to use the silences as an opportunity for reflection. By the thirteenth repetition, only a single pitch—C, the tonic or home pitch of the arrangement's musical key—remained. The final two iterations of the tune were completely silent—an extended and uncomfortable period of contemplation for audience and performers alike. On the one hand, this silence offered an acknowledgment that the nation had failed to live up to its ideals. On the other, the emptiness was a blank canvas of possibility onto which a new story of freedom could be written. Ijeoma thus deployed the anthem melody as a social tool in *Deconstructed Anthems*—an alloy of sound and incarceration data that presents a measurement of national well-being, "a social barometer for how well our society is doing."

History proves that re-composing *The Star-Spangled Banner* is far from exceptional. As early as 1816 or '17, the American composer James Hewitt wrote a completely new tune to convey Key's lyric. Hewitt knew of the Anacreontic melody's British origins and sought a more appropriate "native" setting. In the twentieth century, musicians have imagined a series of "singable" variations of the melody, narrowing its range to make it more vocally accessible. In 1979 the American rocker Lou Reed, an outspoken social and environmental critic, recorded Key's lyric to a wholly original, upbeat melody as the song *America*. Known for their transformational covers, the alternative band the Red House Painters retained Key's lyric but reimagined the music for Generation X in 1993. Their anthem has been described as everything from "a feedback strewn desecration" to "a sexy, romantic song."

Dozens of lyricists have also attempted to paraphrase, modify, and revise Key's words to expand the lyric's focus beyond a single battle and create a more encompassing national statement. As early as 1897, Edmund Holbrook proposed new words with the title *Our National Flag—The Star-Spangled Banner*. Another revision sought to interweave words by Key and Abraham Lincoln with original contributions. Compared with the well-worn familiarity of Key's original, such alternatives feel stilted at best. None have made a lasting contribution.

THE PERFORMANCE HISTORY of *The Star-Spangled Banner* as surveyed here reveals much about the song's expressive range. All its performances make identity claims, some boldly modifying text or tune while others delivering the expected with a surprising stylistic accent. As a patriotic act, every performance is on some level political. To sing the anthem is to position oneself in relation to the nation, even if one's message is a call for change. To perform the anthem is to express belonging, a declaration that enlivens the expressive range of Key's song, while affirming its function to build national unity. Given the hundreds of different lyrics that Key's song has inspired, its alternative melodies, and the many varied musical settings to which the lyric has been sung, the characteristic of the American national anthem that most deserves recognition is its resilience. *The Star-Spangled Banner* has given voice to a range of competing ideas in a range of musical styles, yet it maintains both a core musical structure and an essential message of community devotion. If history is a guide, neither revision, variation, translation, reinterpretation, nor error proves an existential threat to the song or its role in American society. Like the nation itself, *The Star-Spangled Banner* sometimes speaks in a determined dissonant cacophony rather than in a harmonious unity. This resilience is arguably both the anthem's and the nation's true strength.

Postlude

Composing Nation

E pluribus unum (Out of many, one)

—*Motto from the Great Seal of the United States (1782)*

Song as Citizenship

On that August 6, 1834, day, when Francis Scott Key toasted the defenders of Fort McHenry who had inspired his already famous song, the lyricist lawyer concluded his speech by presenting his audience with a vision for the future of patriotic lyric. In retrospect, his words are surprising. He did not predict or even hope that *The Star-Spangled Banner* would become the national anthem. Instead, he called on Americans to live up to their founding ideals. To do so, he said, would inspire new heroes whose deeds would inspire new songs. As the account of Key's speech concludes:

> if a nation's songs were of any importance to it, there was but one way of providing a supply of them. . . . If national poets, who shall keep alive the sacred fire of patriotism in the hearts of the people, are desirable to a country, the country must deserve them; must put forth her patriots and heroes, whose deeds alone can furnish the necessary inspiration; when a country is thus worthy of the lyre, she will command its highest efforts.

The Star-Spangled Banner was never intended to be the country's singular musical symbol. Key did not write a national anthem, he wrote a patriotic lyric inspired by the deeds of one set of heroes in order to inspire heroism by future generations of Americans. Key undoubtedly hoped for and enjoyed the song's success, but in no way had he intended it as a conclusive statement. *The Star-Spangled Banner* was published into a vibrant culture of political songwriting in which new lyrics were sung to old tunes and shared on a daily basis. Singing and composing was an act of citizenship, a means of sharing, shaping, and debating ideas to guide the nation's next steps.

Key's lyric has been printed and reprinted, sung, recorded, and performed at literally countless sports events, graduations, military ceremonies, concerts, Fourth of July parades, and other civic celebrations. While the song became the "official" anthem of the United States only in 1931, it had functioned as the national anthem long before that. It was referred to as "the" or "our" national anthem as early as the 1830s. When in 1900 Congress first received a petition to designate Key's song as the official national anthem, a newspaper noted that "it is regarded as such already whether congress acts upon the petition or not." The resulting 1931 act was thus belated—it merely recognized what had been increasingly true of American ritual practice.

Time and repetition have burrowed Key's words and Stafford Smith's melody deep within the collective American psyche. For those who embrace the song, it offers a sense of belonging. Its words recall a moment of collective courage in selfless defense of the nation; its wide-ranging melody is an emotional hook that signals America's bold, adventurous spirit. Their combination sparks a proud aural image of what Americans hope they are, can be, and will ever remain. Reinforced by more than two centuries of use, the sheer weight of this cultural legacy is the song's most powerful asset.

No song enjoys a stronger claim to represent the United States. Nevertheless, the meanings of the past can shift. Cultural practices change. New songs appear. Certainly, the musical and associative strengths of Key's song would make it difficult to dislodge, yet its history is likewise mired in the complexity of the nation's own story. Its connections to slavery, coercive nationalism, and anti-immigrant jingoism make it hard for some Americans to feel welcomed by the song's patriotic embrace. As an anthem functions to unite, the question remains—can *The Star-Spangled Banner* bring all Americans together?

Anthem Alternatives

Objections to *The Star-Spangled Banner* as anthem predate its official recognition. Pacifists rejected the lyric's military inspiration. Prohibitionists lamented the melody's association with drink. Nationalists opposed the tune's English origins, and music teachers grumbled, finding it too hard to sing. In 1918 the singer and social activist Katharine Cheatham published the protest pamphlet *Words and Music of The Star-Spangled Banner Oppose the Spirit of Democracy which the Declaration of Independence Embodies*. But none of these complaints could counter the momentum of American cultural practice. The question had long been settled.

The Star-Spangled Banner arguably became the nation's sonic signature during the Civil War. From the war's outset, flag and song functioned as powerful symbols of union—an idea worth fighting and dying for. After four bloodstained years of sacrifice, the war ended chattel slavery and preserved the Union, making it the nation's defining historical, political, and social crisis and affirming freedom and equality as its guiding principles. At long last, the United States seemed to fulfill the promise of Key's lyric as truly a "land of the free and the home of the brave."

Unmentioned in 1931 but urgent today are the song's connections to slavery. Francis Scott Key owned enslaved people of African descent, represented slave owners in his legal practice, and vehemently opposed abolition. In stark contradiction, he also freed his slaves, worked to end slavery, prosecuted white-on-Black rioters, and fought at least 107 cases in court on behalf of enslaved men, women, and children, winning freedom for more than 180 people. Yet Key's willingness to compromise the most basic of human rights placed him on the wrong side of history. Further, the third verse of his lyric features the word "slave." If an anthem's role is to create unity, the inclusion of that word—regardless of its meaning—erects a barrier that makes it more difficult for the song to function as an anthem. If the nation desires a patriotism that more readily inspires all Americans, what might be done?

One solution would be to replace Key's anthem with a more inclusive song. This would be more difficult than simply writing new legislation, however. The 1931 bill identifying the anthem recognized a status that Key's song had already achieved, so the naming of a new anthem would require less an act of lawmaking than a shift in social practice. Passing a law proclaiming another song the anthem would likely fail. Any alternative song would first need to displace Key's lyric in national spirit to unify all Americans. Such a shift has happened before, namely when Key's song replaced *Hail Columbia* after the Civil War. Nevertheless, the new song would have to have enough emotional power to convince people to unify around it. It would become the anthem only if all Americans used it as such.

The song most frequently proposed as an anthem alternative is *America the Beautiful*. Originally titled "Pikes Peak," this 1893 poem by Katharine Lee Bates was later matched with Samuel A. Ward's 1882 hymn tune *Materna*. The combination strikes a compelling chord. The melody's graceful contour presents a timeless and peaceful confidence that is nationalistic without being militaristic. Bates's lyric avoids the social flashpoints of Key's original, while its later verses reference freedom, law, liberation, and brotherhood—all post–Civil War themes of unity and equality. It is a very effective peacetime anthem, but it has not been sung historically at times of national crisis. It is instead *The Star-Spangled Banner* that has served as a national rallying cry.

Unknown until 1938, *God Bless America* was not even an anthem candidate seven years earlier. However, it has another significant limitation: it is still under copyright. The song should enter the public domain in 2035, but until then, it is out of the running as the national anthem. Copyright protection would similarly disqualify any recent or newly composed song, unless it were specifically released into the public domain and could be copied, arranged, and performed freely.

Another fix would be to have Congress clarify the 1931 law naming Key's song as the national anthem. Its text simply states that: "The composition consisting of the words and music known as The Star-Spangled Banner is the national anthem of the United States of America." In 1931 the phrase "words and music known as The Star Spangled Banner" would have referred specifically to the two prevailing and nearly identical government-sanctioned publications of the song then in circulation. One was the so-called "Service Version" and the other was a version commissioned by the Department of Education. Both versions expunged Key's third verse, including its reference to "hireling and slave." It would seem appropriate today for Congress to adopt this sanctioned, three-verse version of Key's lyric as its official text. This would relieve the lyric of the word "slave" and thus allow the song to better represent all Americans.

Historically, songs other than *The Star-Spangled Banner* have been used as unifying expressions in American civic rituals. To treat the nation's musical symbol as plural rather than singular, as a collective repertory rather than a single song, would provide options to better address community needs. Imagine if the NFL season kicked off with *The Star-Spangled Banner*, while in week two *America the Beautiful* was performed before individual games. In subsequent games *Lift Every Voice, God Bless America, This Land Is Your Land,* and *My Country 'Tis of Thee (America)* could all accompany the raising of the flag. There is historical precedent for such a repertory. In 2001 the shock and mourning of the 9/11 terrorist attacks temporarily substituted *God Bless America* for *The Star-Spangled Banner* in national ritual. But on October 7 of the same year, when cruise missiles launched to begin the Global War on Terrorism, *The Star-Spangled Banner* returned to rally the nation.

The single best response to the use of *The Star-Spangled Banner* as a vehicle for racial protest in the United States is to address any underlying discrimination, bias, or injustice that plagues the nation. As Martin Luther King, Jr., said in 1968, at what tragically would be his final speech, "All we say to America is, 'Be true to what you said on paper,'" referencing the Constitution. America could likewise be true to its anthem. Protests use the national anthem ritual but are not generally about Key's song. Simply replacing the song would not address the nation's underlying social conflicts. Some NFL athletes recognized this in 2020 when they refused to take the field for either *The Star-Spangled Banner* or *Lift Every Voice*. As these Miami Dolphins players asserted, "If we could just right our wrongs, we wouldn't need two songs."

History Lessons

It is not the purpose of history to make one either love or reject the past. Instead, history offers us an understanding of the past to inform the present. *The Star-Spangled Banner* is a surprisingly rich archive offering insight into the conflicts and complexities that forged the United States. Especially audible is the struggle to balance competing interests to realize America's ideal of freedom and its corollary of equality. The story of Francis Scott Key, slave owner, anti-abolitionist, and advocate for the enslaved, as well as the tales of his song, its more than 575 different lyrics, and its countless political performances can inform our understandings of pivotal moments in American history. To know the abolitionist lyrics of an E. A. Atlee or Oliver Wendell Holmes, Sr., is to understand patriotism as a process of negotiation and change.

The musical and textural flexibility of the nation's anthem is a feature rather than a flaw. Flexibility makes Key's song emotionally responsive to moments of national import, from war and peace to injustice, tragedy, and triumph. Fortunately, *The Star-Spangled Banner* has proven robust and resilient both as a song and as a social practice, such that translations, alternative lyrics, and performances that stretch its very definition have not undercut its ability to unify but have instead strengthened its symbolic connections to community.

Singing *The Star-Spangled Banner* enables unity when content and expression harmonize with their social and political backdrop. When its performances instead elicit dissonance—for example, by calling for unity at a time when one group of Americans has been singled out as disadvantaged—our sense of being one nation is instead disrupted, creating a crisis in patriotism. For democracy to function well, such community dissonance must be heard, recognized, and resolved. It is through this potential to make social dissonance audible and thus to demand change that *The Star-Spangled Banner* exercises its social power.

Historically, performances of *The Star-Spangled Banner* that brought dissonance to the fore have often encountered resistance. Demands for change can be ignored or denied. More typically, the response is indirect— to critique the act of protest itself, complaining that disrupting national unity is itself disloyal. Protesters are dismissed as un-American, and protest is deflected without addressing its substance. Often called "blind patriotism," this unquestioning patriotism is in fact a blinding tactic that protects other interests. Constructive patriotism, in contrast, sees good faith critique as an attempt to make the nation stronger by exposing factors that weaken civic unity. In this sense, an anthem lyric like Key's that celebrates the nation's ideals while carrying the burdens of its contradictory history—both its triumphs and struggles—may be an advantage, helping to chart a path forward.

To understand *The Star-Spangled Banner* as merely an icon is to limit the nation to an impoverished patriotism. Key's song is not only an allegory of democracy; it serves as a primary document, a living record of the American experiment in flux. It is an act of civic creativity that came to serve as a symbol of the nation. By treating it as a timeless object, rather than as always contemporary, we misunderstand patriotism as a thing rather than a process—as something inherited and taken for granted rather than as something shared and earned. An anthem, like patriotism itself, must necessarily be a contested but inclusive space in which devotion to the whole is put into practice. It is inherently political, but it can never be the sole possession of any one viewpoint, party, or faction. Patriotism must be accessible to all as a shared dedication to make the nation better. As a result, singing the anthem becomes interactive and communal. It is not just a symbol of unity but a concerted effort to bring people together.

As a historian of Key's song, I have come to embrace its contradictions and to celebrate its controversies. The ability of Americans to practice democracy successfully depends not on editing our past but rather on understanding our missteps, biases, and flaws, along with our acts of heroism, compromise, sacrifice, and problem solving. All these together make the nation possible. America's shortcomings give its triumphs meaning. To sing Key's song today is necessarily to understand how in the past the American nation has confronted the horror of racism, the bias of gender discrimination, the toxicity of anti-immigrant jingoism, the pangs of economic inequality, and the suffering caused by virulent nationalism and how the community must continue to challenge every such injustice. It is also to understand the moments of bravery, integrity, and sacrifice that have kept the nation viable and intact. To sing Key's song most fully is to embrace a reflective and constructive patriotism, to remember history in such a way as to allow the past to inform and generate new acts of courageous citizenship. For this reason, to replace *The Star-Spangled Banner* may be a mistake. It would discard the power of history, the use of both the troubles and the triumphs of Key's song as a compass navigating toward a more constructive future.

To understand *The Star-Spangled Banner* is to know its fantasies and flaws, the bias and privileges of its era and its author, and its dreams of future possibility. Key's song is not an endpoint but a contribution to an ongoing conversation about the country and how it might aspire to realize its potential. As music, Key's words were empowered to reach the heart alongside the mind. But it is vital that Americans today and tomorrow understand that his intent was not to inspire endless repetition of a static symbol and its unchanging story, but rather to task Americans with the responsibility of composing the nation's future. Key's lyric is less a call to sing than a call to compose; *The Star-Spangled Banner* is an invitation to citizenship.

Acknowledgments

I t seems fitting that a book about how music forges community took
a community to put together. Friends, family, and colleagues—both
personal acquaintances and scholars whose work I know only through
their writings—have made my book possible. Writing is always a journey,
and writing about *The Star-Spangled Banner* takes on special challenges
given its wide chronological scope and the sheer amount of material to
consider. While doing historical research can feel like searching for the
proverbial needle in the vast haystack of time, studying Key's song seems
more akin to sorting and making sense of the hay. There is too much information. To all those who have helped me make sense of *The Star-Spangled
Banner*, I offer a deep and sincere thank you.

O Say Can You Hear? builds on a foundation of painstaking research
and rigorous interpretations by generations of scholars. Some readers may
be surprised that a whole book could be written about a single song. In
fact, a half-dozen books about *The Star-Spangled Banner* precede mine.
Such studies begin with Oscar Sonneck and his successors in the Library
of Congress, particularly Richard S. Hill and William Lichtenwanger.
The rigor of their work was both essential and inspiring. The comprehen-

sive and insightful surveys authored by George Svejda and Marc Ferris pointed me to vital sources and allowed this book to focus on specific themes. I further built on the work of Joseph Muller, P. William Filby, Edward G. Howard, Vera Brodsky Lawrence, Kate Van Winkle Keller, David K. Hildebrand, Simon McVeigh, Steve Vogel, Martha Jones, Kristin Hass, Charles Garrett, Patrick Warfield, Stephanie Shonekan, Shana Redmond, Laura Lohman, and Billy Coleman. Jefferson Morley's pioneering examination of Key's response to the 1835 Washington Race Riot raised critical questions for further examination. The recent Francis Scott Key biographers Sina Dubovoy and especially Marc Leepson cataloged myriad details and provided richer understandings of the lyricist's life, while the freedom suit database created by William G. Thomas III opened up a new view into Key's legal advocacy.

Archives and expert archivists have been essential to this work as well, including those at the American Antiquarian Society, the British Library, the London Metropolitan Archives, the Marine Band Library, the Maryland Historical Society, the University of Maryland, the University of Michigan's Clements Library, and the Library of Congress. I am especially grateful for the tireless assistance of Clayton Lewis, Jayne Ptolemy, Kira Wharton, Loras Schlissel, Ray White, and James Wintle.

My work was generously supported by fellowships from the University of Michigan's Humanities Institute and the Public Scholar Program of the National Endowment for the Humanities. A one-term sabbatical from the University of Michigan's School of Music, Theatre & Dance allowed me to complete the manuscript. Financial support for research travel came through the University of Michigan's Office of Research, along with funding to create the accompanying recordings. Jerry Blackstone conducted the choral recording sessions, which resulted in the release of the album *Poets and Patriots*. I am especially grateful for the artistry of its student singers as well as colleagues James Kibbie, Scott Piper, Scott VanOrnum, producer Andrew Kuster, and engineer Dave Schall. These performances deeply informed my understanding of Key's song.

My partners in creating the Star Spangled Music Foundation, Susan

Key and Michael Pratt, have been engaged interlocutors, supportive friends, and unfailing collaborators. At the Poets and Patriotism recital at the Library of Congress, the artistry of Thomas Hampson opened my ears to the power of alternative lyrics sung to the anthem melody. I am likewise grateful for the questions and insights of the teachers who participated in our 2014 NEH Banner Moments Institute, exploring the anthem's potential for the K-12 classroom. Faculty collaborators for that project included Sheryl Kaskowitz, Alejandro Madrid, Maureen Mahon, Christian McWhirter, David Prather, Anne Rubin, and Patrick Warfield. The passion and creativity of our master teacher Dan Tolly provided daily inspiration. The fall 2014 exhibit at the University of Michigan Library—*Banner Moments: The National Anthem in American Life*—advanced my thinking and would not have happened without the support of Jamie Vander Broek, Bettina Cousineau, Luciana Nemtanu, and designer Grace Rother.

Dozens of colleagues and friends offered feedback on drafts. My gratitude goes to Peter de Boor, Susan and Bill Booth, Christie Finn, Charles Garrett, Joseph Horowitz, Laura Jackson, Charlotte McConnell, Michael Pratt, William G. Thomas, and Peter Witte. Other colleagues provided timely and vital advice, including Walter Kamphoefner, Stefano Mengozzi, Margaret Noodin, Michael Ochs, and Steven Whiting. Several provided insights into the many translations of Key's song. My colleagues in the Singing Justice Coalition provided pivotal guidance at a critical moment in the manuscript's development. The conversations I shared with Naomi André, Stephen Berrey, Tyrese Byrd, Christie Finn, Thomas Hampson, Caroline Helton, Cody Jones, Traci Lombre, Olga Panteleeva, Louise Toppin, and Samantha Williams were both joyous and transformative.

My students at the University of Michigan helped inspire this book, and their honest feedback and questions helped shape it. I am especially grateful to those who searched for alternative lyrics and other details through U-M's Undergraduate Research Opportunity Program. These assistants include Kayla Gonyon, Logan Jacobs, Elizabeth Nesbitt, Steven O'Neill, Christopher Pumford, Daniel Reed, Jacob Silver, Liz Stover, Julia

Triezenberg, and Samuel Waldron. All made substantive contributions. Christina Holder-Rodriguez, Sophia Janevic, and Lisa Keeney provided additional help in proofing and cataloguing alternative lyrics.

Many informants gave of their time and insights to bring original materials to this study. I am especially grateful to multidisciplinary artist Ekene Ijeoma, the composers Kris Bowers and Jessie Montgomery, and the Super Bowl producer Jim Steeg.

My research on the *Woodstock Banner* first appeared in the *Journal of the Society for American Music*. The suggestions of editor Mark Katz and assistant editor Will Robin advanced both my thinking and the quality of the writing. My initial forays into alternative lyrics and musical arrangements were first published in Clague and Kuster's *Star Spangled Songbook*. My coeditor, Andrew Kuster, contributed his artistic insights, engraving talents, and project management skills in bringing that project to press.

This book would not have come to fruition without the patient, persistent, and sage advice of my editor, Chris Freitag, at W. W. Norton. His push for clarity, shape, and concision made this book better. I am further in the debt of assistant editor Julie Kocsis and especially copyeditor Janet Biehl, for the final level of clarity and precision she brought to the text. The artistry of cartographer Gene Thorp and his willingness to experiment brought insight to the illustration of Key's movements during the Battle of Baltimore.

I am also grateful to my musicology department colleagues at the University of Michigan, who have modeled excellence in scholarship and teaching throughout my career: James Borders, Christi-Anne Castro, Gabriela Cruz, Inderjit Kaur, Joseph Lam, Charles Lwanga, Stefano Mengozzi, Mackenzie Pierce, Louise Stein, and Steven Whiting. My friend and fellow Americanist Charles Garrett is a personal inspiration and graciously read drafts and covered my required courses when I was on leave. Dean David Gier insisted that my scholarly research continue, even as my administrative portfolio expanded.

Thinking back, it was my family's annual summer driving trips up and down the eastern seaboard that planted the seed for this work. Spurred by my parents' love for American history, we hiked seemingly every battle-field connected with the Revolutionary and Civil wars. I wish I could say I was always enthusiastic, but my father had the last laugh as those visits to Plymouth Rock, Bunker Hill, Concord, Roanoke, Gettysburg, Antietam, Appomattox Court House, and Stone Mountain made deep impressions on me about the vision and sacrifice that brought the idea of America to life. I am likewise grateful to my children—Hannah, Michaela, and Ronan—for their love and willingness to listen to me drone on ad nauseam about every lyrical variant and freedom case. To my wife, Laura, in particular, I will be forever grateful for your unwavering support and for your insistent opti-mism that this project was not only worthwhile but would someday come to an end. As usual, you were right.

Thank you all for making this book possible.

Notes

Prologue

ix "My country, right": Carl Schurz (R-MO), Remarks in the Senate, 42nd Cong., 2nd sess., February 29, 1872, in *Congressional Globe* 45, 1287.

ix "men who had exhausted": Western Associated Press, "The Great Storm at Samoa," *Indianapolis Journal*, April 14, 1889, 1–2. Throughout, page numbers for newspaper citations are provided when available for the assistance of the researcher but may represent only one of the paper's editions on a particular day.

x "I think that was": *Spokesman-Review* (WA), October 21, 1968, 1.

x "El charro": De La Cruz's performance is archived on YouTube at http://youtu.be/8GivmO32OSk.

xi "Why is a foreigner": Cindy Y. Rodriguez, "Mexican-American Boy's National Anthem Sparks Racist Comments," CNN, September 16, 2013. The tweets are archived at http://publicshaming.tumblr.com/post/52763976629/racist-basketball-fans-pissed-a-mexican-american-boy.

xi "wider anger": René A. Guzman, "Little S.A. Singer Proves He Is a Class Act," MySA, June 12, 2013, www.mysanantonio.com/news/article/Little-S-A-singer-proves-he-is-a-class-act-4595773.php.

xii "Why are ppl": Snejana Farberov, "'I'm Just a Proud American': 11-year-old Mariachi Singer Shrugs Off Racist Backlash," *Mail Online*, June 13, 2013.

xii "belongs to all of us": Guzman, "Little S.A. Singer."

xii perform the anthem again: "Sebastien De La Cruz Returns for Encore, Cheered on by Obama," *HuffPost*, June 14, 2013.

xv **"patriotism of reflection."**: Alexis de Tocqueville, *Democracy in America* (1835), bk. 1, chap. 14, pt. 1, sec. 2.

xv **"constructive patriotism"**: Robert T. Schatz, Ervin Staub, and Howard Lavine, "On the Varieties of National Attachment: Blind Versus Constructive Patriotism," *Political Psychology* 20, no. 1 (March 1999): 151–74.

Chapter 1: American Dreams

1 **"The national air of"**: "Not One National Song," *New York Times*, August 25, 1889, 5.

2 **gave generously**: John T. Brooke, *Sketch of the Character of the Late Francis Scott Key* (Cincinnati, 1843); also in *African Repository* 19, no. 5 (May 1843): 144–50. Sina Dubovoy, *The Lost World of Francis Scott Key* (Bloomington, IN: Westbow Press, 2014), 346.

2 **his law practice**: Biographical details are from Marc Leepson, *What So Proudly We Hailed: Francis Scott Key, A Life* (New York: Palgrave Macmillan, 2014), 13, 16, 114.

2 **To "Francis Scott Key"**: Edward S. Delaplaine, *Francis Scott Key: Life and Times* (Brooklyn, NY, 1937), 378.

3 **"You have recalled"**: Francis Scott Key, "At a Political Meeting," in *Poems of the Late Francis Scott Key, Esq.*, ed. Rev. Henry V. D. Johns (New York: Robert Carter & Brothers, 1857), 195–203, quoted as realized in Delaplaine, *Life and Times*, 378–81.

4 **met George Washington**: Leepson, *What So Proudly*, 9.

5 **soon published**: Key's speech is reprinted in *Washington: First in the Hearts of His Countrymen*, ed. William Buckner McGroaty (Richmond, VA: Garrett & Massie, 1932), 217–35.

5–6 **mother's ancestors**: Dubovoy, *Lost World*, 2–5.

6 **Light Dragoons**: Leepson, *What So Proudly*, 3–4.

6 **English law**: Dubovoy, *Lost World*, 89.

6 **one of his six sons**: Leepson, *What So Proudly*, 24, 88.

7 **Key served in**: Ibid., 43–49.

7 **Key set sail**: P. W. Filby and Edward G. Howard, *Star-Spangled Books: Books, Sheet Music, Newspapers, Manuscripts, and Persons Associated with "The Star-Spangled Banner"* (Baltimore: Maryland Historical Society, 1972), 43. See also William Lichtenwanger, "Richard S. Hill and 'The Unsettled Text of The Star Spangled Banner,'" in *Richard S. Hill: Tributes from Friends*, ed. Carol June Bradley and James B. Coover (Detroit: Information Coordinators, 1987), 84.

7 **family doctor**: Polly Key was the youngest of seven siblings, with one brother and five other sisters.

7 **cared briefly for Key**: Dubovoy, *Lost World*, 180.

7 **ship whose name**: Steve Vogel, *Through the Perilous Fight* (New York: Random House, 2013), 260. The ship may have been named the *President*, but it was certainly not the *Minden* as sometimes reported. See Filby and Howard, *Star-Spangled Books*, 31.

7 **John Ferguson:** Vogel, *Perilous Fight,* 263. The crew as identified by Hill is in Lichtenwanger, "Richard S. Hill," 84.

7 **batch of letters:** Filby and Howard, *Star-Spangled Books,* 21; Vogel, *Perilous Fight,* 257.

7 **"unarmed and entirely":** Sam Meyer, *Paradoxes of Fame: The Francis Scott Key Story* (Annapolis, MD: Eastwind, 1995), 40.

7–8 **Beanes was being treated:** F. S. Key-Smith, *Francis Scott Key: Author of The Star-Spangled Banner, What Else He Was and Who* (Washington, DC: Key-Smith & Co., 1911), 66–67, cited in Meyer, *Paradoxes of Fame,* 37.

8 **The U.S. government:** Vogel, *Perilous Fight,* 255.

8 **"50 or 60" British cavalry:** J. E. Hall, *Report of the Trial of John Hodges, Esq. on a Charge of High Treason, Tried in the Circuit Court of the United States for the Maryland District, at the May Term, 1815* (n.p., 1815).

8 **burn the nearby town:** Meyer, *Paradoxes of Fame,* 35.

8–9 **"ruffian, patriot and philanthropist.":** John S. Skinner, "Incidents of the War of 1812," *Baltimore Patriot,* May 23, 1849, and *National Intelligencer,* June 4, 1849, repr. *Maryland Historical Magazine* 32, no. 4 (December 1937): 340–47; Vogel, *Perilous Fight,* 263–64.

9 **"mouth of the Potomac":** Skinner, "Incidents of the War," 342. Hill described the rendezvous point as "twenty-some miles south of Point Lookout." See Lichtenwanger, "Richard S. Hill," 84.

9 **"his application":** Roger B. Taney, "Letter Narrating the Incidents Connected with the Origin of the Song 'The Star-Spangled Banner'" (1856), in *Poems of the Late Francis S. Key,* ed. Rev. Henry V. D. Johns (New York: Robert Carter & Brothers, 1857), 13–28.

9 **With wine "in free circulation,":** Skinner, "Incidents of the War," 342–43.

9 **release Beanes:** Ross to U.S. General Mason, September 7, 1814, quoted in Delaplaine, *Life and Times,* 157.

9 **center of the action:** Taney, "Letter Narrating," 20–21.

12 **Unusually high tides:** The account of the Battle of Baltimore related here is based primarily on Vogel, *Perilous Fight,* 269–360, interwoven with items from Skinner, "Incidents of the War," Taney, "Letter Narrating," and various letters and newspaper accounts. Details not otherwise sourced are found in Vogel.

12 **their residence:** Skinner, "Incidents of the War," 347.

12 **"The admiral had intimated":** Key to John Randolph of Roanoke, October 5, 1814, in Lichtenwanger, "Richard S. Hill," 83.

13 **bold attack:** Skinner, "Incidents of the War," 341.

14 **Key had argued:** Dubovoy, *Lost World,* 192–95.

14 **saw smoke rising:** "Attack on Baltimore," *Niles Weekly Register,* September 24, 1814, 23.

14 **"all free people of color":** Gerard T. Altoff, *"Amongst My Best Men": African-Americans and the War of 1812* (Put-in-Bay, OH: Perry Group, 1996), 125–26.

14 **"forts, redoubts":** Vogel, *Perilous Fight*, 275.

14 **"a flag so large":** Ibid., 313.

14 **Grace Wisher:** See analysis by Stephen Whitman, "Grace Wisher Indenture, Short Analysis," n.d., http://www.flaghouse.org/wp-content/uploads/2020/03/Grace-Wisher -Indenture-Short-Analysis.pdf.

15 **"with every indication":** Vogel, *Perilous Fight*, 278.

15 **their own ship:** Skinner, "Incidents of the War," 347.

15 **"guns of a frigate":** *Defence of Fort McHenry*, broadside, September 17, 1814, preface (reproduced on page 5 of this book).

15 **precise location:** Skinner, "Incidents of the War," 347. For a discussion of possible locations of the ship, see Filby and Howard, *Star-Spangled Books*, 33, and Vogel, *Perilous Fight*, 284, 319–20.

15 **seaborne weaponry:** Scott S. Sheads, "H.M. Bomb Ship *Terror* and the Bombardment of Fort McHenry," *Maryland Historical Magazine* 103, no. 3 (Fall 2008): 257–67.

15 **"to annoy the coast":** Ibid., 257.

16 **"were forced two feet":** "Attack Upon Baltimore," *Niles Weekly Register*, September 24, 1814, 23.

16 **some 170 bombs:** Nancy Steenburg, "Attack on Stonington," *Connecticut Explored* (Summer 2012): 21.

16 **as happened in Alexandria:** Elting, *Amateurs to Arms!*, 223.

17 **"if it rained militia.":** Dubovoy, *Lost World*, 214.

17 **"there was not amongst us":** George Robert Gleig, *A Subaltern in America* (Philadelphia: E. L. Carey & A. Hart, 1833), 135–36.

18 **town aflame:** Donald E. Graves, *Sir William Congreve and the Rockets' Red Glare*, Historical Arms Series no. 23 (Bloomfield, ONT: Museum Restoration Service, 1989).

18 **American boat:** Lt. Henry Fisher of the 27th Maryland Regiment, *Battle of Baltimore*; see Vogel, *Perilous Fight*, 320.

18 **"double explosion.":** Details here and in following paragraphs are from "Attack Upon Baltimore," *Niles Weekly Register*, September 24, 1814, 24, and Altoff, *"Amongst My Best Men,"* 129.

19 **"The balls now flew":** Vogel, *Perilous Fight*, 324.

20 **"It was the universal belief":** Ibid., 333.

21 **1,800 shells:** Sheads, "H.M. Bomb Ship *Terror*," 263.

21 **"paced the deck":** Taney, "Letter Narrating," 25.

21 **"until the fleet was ready":** Ibid.

22 **General Ross's death:** Skinner, "Incidents of the War," 345.

22 **"At this time our":** Vogel, *Perilous Fight*, 339.

22 **"in the fervor":** Taney, "Letter Narrating," 25–26.

22 **returned to Baltimore Harbor:** Vogel, *Perilous Fight*, 347, suggests that they arrived between eight and nine p.m.

22 **"between 5 and 6 hundred":** Filby and Howard, *Star-Spangled Books*, plate 15, p. 44.

22 **"The enemy have not moved":** *United States Gazette* (Philadelphia), September 21, 1814, 6; also quoted in Filby and Howard, *Star-Spangled Books*, 47.

23 **"had written some lines":** Taney, "Letter Narrating," 26. Filby and Howard identify the hotel as the Indian Queen, in *Star-Spangled Books*, 51n27.

23 **Maryland Historical Society:** Harold Manakee and Beta Manakee, *The Star Spangled Banner* (Baltimore: Maryland Historical Society, 1954), 23–24.

23 **children were expected:** Elizabeth Key Howard to George Henry Preble, April 25, 1874, quoted in Oscar Sonneck, *The Star Spangled Banner* (Washington, DC: Government Printing Office, 1914), 91.

23 **"hanging matter":** Francis Scott Key, "At a Political Meeting," in *Poems of the Late Francis Scott Key, Esq.*, ed. Rev. Henry V. D. Johns (New York: Robert Carter & Brothers, 1857), 195–203, quoted in Delaplaine, *Life and Times*, 378–81.

24 **"Native Genius":** *Pittsfield Sun*, February 10, 1806; *Herald of the United States*, July 27, 1798; *Baltimore Patriot*, August 19, 1813; and *New York Journal*, August 16, 1787. See also "Parnassian Shrubbery," *Federal Galaxy*, March 10, 1797, 4.

24 **thirty-seven newspapers:** Filby and Howard, *Star-Spangled Books*, 113–14. To their list of twenty-two, I add: *Federal Republican* (Georgetown), September 22, 4; *Alexandria Gazette*, September 27, 2; *American Watchman* (DE), September 28, 1; *Petersburg Intelligencer* (VA), September 20, 2; *Long-Island Star*, October 12, 1; *Carlisle Weekly* (PA), October 14, 4; *Middlesex Gazette* (CT), October 20, 1; *Columbian Patriot* (VT), October 19, 4; *Norwich Courier* (CT), October 19; *Western Courier* (KY), October 19, 4; *New-Jersey Journal*, October 25, 4; *Natchez Gazette* (MS), October 26, 4; *Connecticut Courier*, November 2, 4; *Farmers' Repository* (WV), November 10, 4; and *Washingtonian* (Windsor, VT), November 14, 4.

24 **"beautiful and animating":** *Baltimore Patriot*, September 20, 1814, 2.

24 **"composed by Mr. Key":** Severn Teackle to Phillip Wallis, September 23, 1814, in Morgan Library, New York; see Filby and Howard, *Star-Spangled Books*, 157.

24 **"a versified and almost literal":** Skinner, "Incidents of the War," 347.

25 **first edition handbill print:** The evidence that this printing (shown on page 5) is in fact the first is circumstantial as the page itself gives no information about publisher or date. That a copy survived together with Key's handwritten fair copy in the family collection of Joseph Nicholson is perhaps the most compelling evidence supporting this particular print as the original first edition. Both documents are held by the Maryland Historical Society. The second known copy is held by the Library of Congress (ML1630.3.S69 1814 [case]). Three corrections have been made: (in verse 2) changing the "e" to "o" to create the word "now" (line 6) and adding a hyphen in star-spangled (line 7) and (in verse 3) adding a possessive apostrophe to the word "footsteps" (line 4).

26 **three opening pick-up notes:** The triadic descent appears first in 1843, see *The Star Spangled Banner*, arr. Francis H. Brown (New York: Atwill, 1843); Mark Clague and Andrew Kuster, eds., *Star Spangled Songbook* (Star Spangled Music Foundation, 2014), no. 34, pp. 119–22; reprinted in Muller, *Star Spangled Banner*, 91–96.

29 **"Never was a man more disappointed":** Francis Scott Key to John Randolph, October 5, 1814, 2, also in Lichtenwanger, "Richard S. Hill," 83.

30 **Key's later claims:** Key, "At a Political Meeting," 203.

31 **personal economic interests:** Billy Coleman, *Harnessing Harmony* (Chapel Hill: University of North Carolina Press, 2020), 41–47.

32 **"Sometimes, when I remembered":** Key to John Randolph, October 5, 1814, in Lichtenwanger, "Richard S. Hill," 83.

32 **"their merit":** *Analectic Magazine*, 4, no. 23 (November 1814): 433–34.

32 **"portentous" language:** "Odes, Naval Songs and Other Occasional Poems by Edwin C. Holland, Esq. Charleston," *Analectic Magazine* 3 (March 1814): 242–52. Filby and Howard surmise that Irving's service in the New York militia makes it unlikely that he was directly involved with the magazine's later publication of Key's song; *Star-Spangled Books*, 89.

Chapter 2: Origins of a Melody

34 **"Our national anthem":** Charles Braun, "Let's Waive 'The Star-Spangled Banner,'" *Fact* 2, no. 1 (January–February 1965): 3–7.

34 **funeral mass:** William Steif, "Hundreds Pray at Church of President," *Knoxville News-Sentinel*, November 23, 1963, 3.

35 **was composed by:** Although proposed by others before, researcher William Lichtenwanger was the first to unequivocally identify John Stafford Smith as the composer of *The Anacreontic Song*; see William Lichtenwanger, *The Music of "The Star-Spangled Banner" from Ludgate Hill to Capitol Hill* (Washington, DC: Library of Congress, 1977), 14–15.

35 **four songs and nine hymns:** It is not unusual to find Key's hymns *Lord, With Glowing Heart I'd Praise Thee* (1817) and *Before the Lord We Bow* (1832) in hymnals today; his lesser-known hymns include *If Life's Pleasures Charm Thee* (pub. 1826); *Behold the Grant, the King of Kings*; *Faith Is the Christian's Evidence*; *My God, My Father, May I Dare*; *Praise, My Soul, the God that Sought Thee*; *To Thee O God, Whose Awful Voice*; and *When Troubles Wave on Wave Assailed*. Key also wrote religiously inspired texts for then popular songs, including *The Home of the Soul* (1829, written to the song *Home, Sweet Home*) and two additional verses for the Irish love ballad *John Anderson, My Jo* (1842). *Warrior Returns* and the *Banner* make up Key's final two songs. See hymnary.org/person/Key_Francis and Clague and Kuster, *Star Spangled Songbook*, 133–143, 272–74.

35 **Society was founded:** See "The Catch Club" in Brian Robins, *Catch and Glee Culture in Eighteenth-Century England* (Suffolk, UK: Boydell & Brewer, 2006), 32–71. In 2016 I visited a contemporary London club, the Arts Club, www.theartsclub.co.uk/.

36 **"peers, commoners":** "History of the Anacreontic Society" (unsigned note to the editor), *Gentleman's Magazine* 50 (May 1780): 224.

36 **best instrumentalists:** "Anacreontic Meeting," *Times* (London), January 8, 1785, 3; see also Robins, *Catch and Glee Culture,* 74.

36 **Greek poet Anacreon:** Simon McVeigh, "Trial by Dining Club: The Instrumental Music of Haydn, Clementi and Mozart at London's Anacreontic Society," in *Music and Performance Culture in Nineteenth-Century Britain,* ed. Bennett Zon (Farnham, UK: Ashgate, 2012), 114.

36 **fifty-nine poets:** Michael Hilton, "The Anacreontea in England to 1683," 2 vols., Ph.D. thesis, Wolfson College, University of Oxford, 1980.

37 **Frivolity and farce:** Francis Scott Key was a member of a men's club founded in a similar pseudo-classical vein: Baltimore's Delphian Club (1816–22, 1824–25). He attended only occasionally and was never a full member. As one observer noted, attendees "indulged in pleasantries, in the manufacture of puns and epigrams and epitaphs and humorous stories." Key likely wrote the poem "On a Young Lady's Going into a Shower Bath," an erotic if metaphorical celebration of the pleasures of a woman's body, for the Delphians. See Leepson, *What So Proudly,* 100–1. The full poem appears in Delaplaine, *Life and Times,* 231; Ted Malone, ed., *The All-American Book of Verse* (New York: Garden City, 1948), 85; and David Lehman, ed., *The Best American Erotic Poems: From 1800 to the Present* (New York: Scribner, 2008), 1.

37 **four hundred people might attend:** Although newspaper accounts were prone to exaggeration, attendance figures for the Anacreontic Society mentioned in the *Times* include" "two hundred gentlemen" (November 16, 1787, 2), "two hundred and fifty, and before supper there were near three hundred" (December 21, 1787, 2), "upwards of two hundred" (February 1, 1788, 3), and "near four hundred strong" (February 3, 1789, 4).

38 **women were admitted:** For an account of women's participation in the society's meetings, see Katelyn Clark, "To Anacreon in Heaven: Observations on Gender and the Performance Practice of London's Anacreontic Society Song (c.1773)," *Early Music* 46, no. 4 (2018): 675–81.

38 **benches and tables:** McVeigh, "Trial by Dining Club," 108, 117–18.

38 **West End theaters:** Singers from the opera did not participate in Anacreontic meetings.

38 **toasts might occur:** "Anacreontic Meeting," *Times,* January 8, 1785, 3. Toasts mentioned specifically in the article are made to "the memory of departed members" and "the healths of the musical ladies."

38 **"salt box solos":** *Gentleman's Magazine* (1780), 224.

38 **"The president having left":** R. J. S. Stevens, *Recollections of R. J. S. Stevens: An Organist in Georgian London,* ed. Mark Argent (Carbondale: Southern Illinois University Press, 1992), 23–25.

38 *Non nobis Domine:* Sources conflict on where but not on when *Non nobis Domine* was sung. Most likely the work was performed in the dining room to signal the close of the meal and thus invite the company to relocate to the concert room

to begin the singing portion of the evening. "An Acreontic [*sic*] Dinner," *Times*,
October 9, 1788, 2; Stevens, *Recollections*, 25.

39 **"all the principal vocal performers":** "Anacreontic Meeting," *Times*, January 8,
1785, 3.

39 **sung by a professional:** Lichtenwanger, *Music*, 22.

39 **written in 1773:** John Marsh mentions that *The Anacreontic Song* was performed
as early as December 11, 1773; see Marsh, *The John Marsh Journals: The Life and
Times of a Gentleman Composer (1752–1828)*, ed. Brian Robins (Stuyvesant, NY:
Pendragon Press, 1998), 114–15.

39 **no year of publication:** Most sheet music of the period lacked composition and
publication dates; such information did not become common until it mattered for
copyright protection in the later nineteenth and early twentieth centuries.

39 **Ralph Tomlinson:** Lichtenwanger, *Music*, 8–9, 22. Note that Tomlinson's first
name is pronounced "Rafe" in English fashion.

40 **melody's composer:** Stevens, *Recollections*, 25, cited in Lichtenwanger, *Music*,
14–15.

41 **John Stafford Smith (1750–1836):** Engraving by Thomas Illman after a drawing by
William Behnes, in *The Apollo or Harmonist in Miniature*, vol. 2 (London, 1822),
frontispiece; see Lichtenwanger, *Music*, 18.

41 **William Boyce:** Robert J. Bruce and Ian Bartlett, "Boyce, William," *Grove Music
Online*, https://tinyurl.com/5uf9tbrp.

42 **Two of his original compositions:** Thomas Warren, ed., *A Collection of Catches,
Canons and Glees*, 11th ed. (London: Longman & Broderip, 1772). Stafford Smith's
contributions include a canzonet, *Stay Shepherd Stay*, 10–16, and a glee, *Sleep,
Sleep Poor Youth*, 32–37.

42 **canon prize:** Four prizes were given in most years, two for glees and one each for
a catch and a canon. A third work by Smith, a catch titled *Slaves Are They*, was also
printed in Warren, *Collection of Catches*, 12th ed. (1773), 32–33, but it did not win a
medal.

42 **five more times:** In 1774 Stafford Smith won for the glee *Let Happy Lovers Fly*,
a characteristic through-composed part-song in contrasting sections that begins
as a frivolous idyll but develops into a paean to love in death. In 1775 he would
again win twice, this time for the catch *Since Phillis Has Bubbled* and the aston-
ishingly beautiful glee *Blest Pair of Sirens*, a setting of the English poet John Milton's famous text celebrating the wonder of sacred music. The composer's final two
awards were for the glees *While Fools Their Time in Stormy Strife Employ* (1776)
and *Return Blest Days* (1777), after which Stafford Smith's name disappears from
the Catch Club's annual publications.

42 **ten guineas' worth:** One guinea equaled 21 shillings, while one pound equaled 20
shillings. Ten guineas was thus 10.5 pounds, and a middle-class family could be
sustained for between 40 and 100 pounds a year. See "Currency, Coinage, and the
Cost of Living," https://www.oldbaileyonline.org/static/Coinage.jsp.

44 **off to Rowley's:** A subscription advertisement for a collection of three-part songs by Battishill, organist at Christ-Church, lists "Mr. Rowley's, the London Coffee-house, Ludgate hill" as a registration address: *Public Advertiser* (London), December 22, 1775, 1. See also Sonneck, *Star Spangled Banner,* 39.

44 **"A fig for Parnassus!":** The later revised lyric reads "Away to the Sons of Anacreon we'll fly, / And there, with good Fellows, we'll learn to intwine," in lines 7 and 8 of verse 2 and thus removes the reference to Rowley's near Lud Gate.

45 **"old Lud":** The later revised lyric reads "From Helicon's Banks will incontinent flee" for line 2 in verse 3 to reflect the move of the society's meeting location from Ludgate Hill to the Crown and Anchor Tavern in the Strand. Sonneck, *Star Spangled Banner,* 40.

45 **"Whilst snug:"** A "snug" meeting in contemporary parlance was a private meeting for members of the club only.

46 **Original version:** "Song 566: Anacreontic Society," in *The Vocal Magazine; or Compleat British Songster* (London: Harrison & Co., 1781), 147–48. Page 147 is reprinted in Sonneck, *Star Spangled Banner,* plate V. This original version of the text was later updated.

46 **evergreen laurels:** In mythology, the laurel was immune to lightning.

46 **joy, community, and freedom:** According to Stevens, "all the Members, Visitors, and Performers, joined, 'hand in hand'"; Lichtenwanger, *Music,* 14. John Marsh reports that "in the last verse . . . we stood hand in hand all around the table"; Marsh, *Journals,* 115–16.

47 **illustration of the Anacreontic lyric:** Pictorial page from *Anacreontic Songs for 1, 2, 3 & 4 Voices, Composed and Selected* by Doctor Arnold (London: I. Bland, 1785). See also Lichtenwanger, *Music,* 10.

47 **social club scene:** See Marty Roth, "'Anacreon' and Drink Poetry; or, the Art of Feeling Very Very Good," *Texas Studies in Literature and Language* 42, no. 3 (Fall 2000): 314–45.

48 **French brandy:** William Purdie Treloar, *Ludgate Hill: Past and Present* (London: Griffith & Farran, 1881), 123.

48 **"unnatural mixtures":** Robins, *Catch and Glee Culture,* 60.

48 **Promenade Concerts:** Robert Elkin, *The Old Concert Rooms of London* (London: Edward Arnold, 1955), 51–56.

48 **"It's a club song":** Thomas Hampson, commentary from *"Poets and Patriotism" Recital,* July 3, 2014, Coolidge Auditorium, Library of Congress; video archived at youtube.com/watch?v=6XXgYTShtdk.

49 **private and public music making:** Many of these accounts are chronicled in McVeigh, "Trial by Dining Club."

50 **"When the company returned":** "Anacreontic Society," *Times,* November 16, 1787, 2, emphasis in the original. Sedgwick is identified as a bass singer in "Anacreontic Society," *Times,* February 3, 1789, 4.

50 **"the most respectable":** "An Acreontic [*sic*] Dinner," *Times,* October 9, 1788, 2.

51 the "celebrated Anacreontic Song": "Theatre-Royal, Drury Lane," *Times*, April 15, 1798, 1. This advertisement appears again on April 18, the date of the event.

51 "A Musical Entertainment": "Royalty Theatre," *Times*, September 19, 1788, 1.

51 "celebrated song.": "Theatre-Royal, Drury Lane," *Times*, May 22, 1798, 1.

52 Catch Club meetings: Robins, *Catch and Glee Culture*, 35.

52 "put the whole [meeting] into confusion": "Anacreontic Dinner," *Times*, October 9, 1788, 2.

52 judicial hanging: Maharaja Nandakumar (also called Nuncomar) was convicted of fraud and sentenced by India's first chief justice, Elijah Impey, a friend of Governor-General Warren Hastings, who had brought the charges.

52 *General Wolfe*: On the Death of General Wolfe (London: J. Fentum, 1785), H.1652.

54 The Dutch humanist Erasmus: See Erasmus, "My Achievements and Attributes," *The Folly Speaks* (1509), part 2.

54 "On Women": "Poets Corner," *Virginia Gazette*, September 6, 1770, 4; *Independent Gazetteer*, June 18, 1787, 3.

54 unpublished until 1951: Hopkinson's lyric is discussed and quoted in full in Richard S. Hill, "The Melody of 'The Star Spangled Banner' in the United States Before 1820," in *Essays Honoring Lawrence C. Wroth* (Portland, ME: Anthoensen Press, 1951), 155–56, enumerated as parody no.1, p. 164; Clague and Kuster, *Star Spangled Songbook*, no. 9, pp. 45–46.

54 "The late eighteenth century": Gordon S. Wood, *The Idea of America: Reflections on the Birth of the United States* (New York: Penguin Books, 2011), 57.

55 "may our Club flourish": "Poetry," *National Aegis* (Worcester, MA), August 21, 1805, 4; and *Baltimore Musical Miscellany* (Baltimore: Cole & Hewes, 1805), 1:26–29.

56 Smith died: Burial Records, London Metropolitan Archives.

56 "In memory of": The plaque's date is unknown, but it is certainly of twentieth-century origin, between 1931, when the anthem became official, and 1977, when a second plaque was added. This newer panel is located under the flags and reads: "USA flag given by Rotary Club of New York and British Flag by Rotarian H. G. Norman City High Sheriff to the Rotary Club of Gloucester 1920: Placed here on 26th August 1977 to mark the USA bicentennial year. Consider the world rotary movement's ideals of peace, goodwill, understanding and fellowship; Remember Arthur Newell of America and member of Gloucester Club who promoted these ideals between us."

Chapter 3: *Banner* Ballads

57 "One good song": James Lawrence Onderdonk, *History of American Verse (1610–1897)* (Chicago: A.C. McClurg, 1901), 90.

58 promoted-to-captain: Joshua E. London, *Victory in Tripoli* (Hoboken, NJ: John Wiley & Sons, 2005), 145–63; Alexander Slidell Mackenzie, *Life of Stephen Decatur* (Boston: Little, Brown, 1846), 64–82.

58 **host a dinner:** The dinner took place on Friday, December 6, in Georgetown. Other studies locate the dinner in Annapolis or give the incorrect date of November 30. That date was the planning meeting for the dinner. See "McLaughlin's Tavern," *Commercial Daily Advertiser* (Baltimore), December 14, 1805, 3. Additional information from *Charleston Daily Courier*, December 28, 1805, 2, which reports a toast to the recently deceased Federalist Alexander Hamilton.

58 **"When the Warrior returns":** *American and Commercial Daily Advertiser,* December 14, 1805, 3.

59 **the lyric's author:** Key's authorship is confirmed by the text's inclusion in *Poems of the Late Francis S. Key, Esq.,* ed. Rev. Henry V. D. Johns (New York: Robert Carter & Brothers, 1857), 34–36. Contemporary accounts note that the song "which had been prepared for the occasion about an hour before Dinner, by a Gentleman of George-Town, was sung in a superior stile, accompanied by two clarinets, and the company joining in the Chorus"; *Daily Advertiser,* December 14, 1805, 3. Abbreviated in other accounts, this comment has led to speculation that Key sung the solo himself or that he wrote its five verses in just an hour. More likely the song was carefully written before the event, was rehearsed in the hour before dinner, and was sung by an unnamed professional or otherwise skilled singer. The lyric does show signs of rushed construction in the repetitions of the first and last verse. Other weaknesses are the frequently slanted triple rhymes in lines 5 and 6 of each verse.

60 **No fewer than fifteen newspapers:** The lyric appeared in *Maryland Gazette,* December 19, 1805, 3; *American Citizen,* December 21, 2; *Republican Watch-Tower,* December 25, 1805; *Charleston Daily Courier,* December 28, 1805, 2; *Independent Chronicle,* December 30, 1805, 4; *Post-Boy,* January 7, 1806; *New-York Evening Post,* January 9, 1806, 2; *Freeman's Friend,* January 22, 1806, 4; *Carlisle Weekly Herald* (PA), January 24, 1806, 4; *Hampshire Federalist,* February 4, 1806, 2; *Pittsfield Sun,* February 10, 1806, 4; *Weekly Wanderer,* February 10, 1806, 4; *Vermont Gazette,* February 24, 1806, 4; and *Weekly Inspector,* October 25, 1806, 72.

61 **"It is a native production":** *Pittsfield Sun,* February 10, 1806, 4.

61 **"would not discredit":** *New-York Evening Post,* January 9, 1806, 2.

61 **credit Joseph Nicholson:** Rebecca Lloyd Shippen, née Nicholson, "The Original Manuscript of 'The Star-Spangled Banner,'" *Pennsylvania Magazine of History and Biography* 25, no. 3 (1901): 427–28. Shippen had previously sent an excerpt from Taney's 1856 letter to the magazine. It contained a postscript asserting Nicholson to be the one who matched text to tune; see *Pennsylvania Magazine* 22, no. 3 (1898): 321–25.

61 **"volume of flute music":** Nellie Eyster, "The Star-Spangled Banner: An Hour with an Octogenarian," *Harper's Magazine* 43 (1871): 254–58, esp. 257.

63 **too closely:** Kate Van Winkle Keller notes that Key's mixture of "olive" and "laurel" in the chorus of *Warrior Returns* seems an exchange for "myrtle" and "vine" in the Anacreontic original. See Keller, *Music of the War of 1812 in America* (Annapolis, MD: Colonial Music Institute, 2011), 108.

64 *The Social Club*: *The Baltimore Musical Miscellany* (Baltimore: Cole & Hewes, 1805), 2:158–60. The phrase "star-spangled" is found in verse two. The lyric reads: "Father Jove then look'd down, From his crystalline throne, / Which with **star-spangled** lustre celestially shone." See also Marc Ferris, *Star-Spangled Banner: The Unlikely Story of America's National Anthem* (Baltimore: Johns Hopkins University Press, 2014), 24.

64 **"Mr. Chambers"**: "By Authority," *Aurora General Advertiser*, January 8, 1793, 3. *Dunlap's American Advertiser*, January 9, 1793, 1, contains a listing of songs sung at this first-known performance.

65 **learned both song and skit**: George O. Seilhamer, *History of the American Theatre* (Philadelphia: Globe Printing House, 1891), 65. After the Old American Company continued to New York, Chambers remained in Philadelphia to sing at Alexander Reinagle's New Theatre. See "Grand Concert," *Aurora General Advertiser*, February 1, 1793, 1. He may have moved to Boston with Mrs. Chambers by 1796; see *Federal Orrery*, April 11, 1796.

65 **Mr. West**: "Mr. West's Night," *Weekly Museum*, June 1, 1793, 2; and "By the Old American Company," *Daily Advertiser* (NY), June 3, 1793, 2. The June 3 performance of *The Catch Club* was delayed from May 31, as announced in the *Daily Advertiser*, May 30, 1793, 3; Seilhamer, *History of Theatre*, 46.

65 *My Pipe*: *From Night to Morn*, in Charles H. Wilson, ed., *The Myrtle and Vine* (London: West & Hughes, 1800), 153; *'Twas You Sir*, in *The British Minstrel* (Glasgow: William Hamilton, 1843), 1:108; *Poor Thomas Day*, ibid., 1:34; *Here's a Health to All Good Lasses*, ibid., 1:122–23; and *With My Jug in One Hand*, in George Walker, ed., *The Flowers of Harmony* (n.p.: G. Walker, 1800), 38–39.

67 **signed "Julia"**: *Weekly Museum*, July 20, 1793, 2. "Julia" was a regular contributor of lyrics and poetry to the paper. Dated July 12, the lyric does not honor *Anacreon*'s distinctive internal rhyme in line 5, which may suggest that it was composed by ear rather than based on a printed source. See Hill, "Melody," 160 and no. 2, p. 164.

67 **pro-French song**: *La Marseillaise* would have been the more emblematic choice, but it was written only the year before, in 1792, and did not become the French anthem until 1795.

67 **titled *To Genêt***: *Columbian Centinel* (Boston), December 4, 1793, 4.

67 **rousing tune**: Also in 1793, an English poet penned an Anacreontic lyric critical of American revolutionary Thomas Paine, who was now supporting the French in breaking from their king. *Times*, September 28, 1793.

67 **"catches and glees"**: "Charleston Anacreontic Society," *City Gazette*, February 1, 1794, 3. The society met again a week later at Williams's "concert room"; *City Gazette*, February 8, 1794, 1. The group later changed its name to Harmonic Society; *City Gazette*, April 23, 1794, 3.

67 **Columbian Anacreontic Society**: Dorothy C. Barck, "The Columbian Anacreontic Society of New York, 1795–1803," *New-York Historical Society Quarterly Bulletin* 16, no. 1 (April 1932): 115–23.

67 **locus of musical excellence:** The last known notices of the society are from January 1803. *Evening Post*, January 31, 1803, 2, announces a meeting on February 1.

68 **singer-actor John Hodgkinson (1766–1805):** August von Kotzebue, *The East Indian: A Comedy in Three Acts* (New York: Charles Smith & S. Stephens, 1800), frontispiece.

68 **"regulations":** "A Card," *Daily Advertiser* (NY), February 26, 1795, 3, announces a meeting for that evening followed by "A Card." See also *Daily Advertiser*, April 14, 1795, 3; "Columbian Anacreontic Society," *Daily Advertiser*, April 23, 1795, 2; and "Columbian Anacreontic Society," *Daily Advertiser*, April 28, 1795, 5.

68 **"brothers":** "Anacreontic Society," *Daily Advertiser*, April 30, 1795, 3.

68 **John Hodgkinson:** Hodgkinson held the role of president into the elections of 1799. Barck, "Columbian Anacreontic Society," 116.

68 **"a great drum":** *Federal Orrery*, May 11, 1795, 1–2.

69 **"affectingly delightful":** Ibid.

69 *My Plaint:* *The New Vocal Enchantress* (London: C. Stalker, 1791), 3.

69 **"Not a false chord":** "Musical Jubilee," *Federal Orrery*, May 11, 1795, 1–2.

70 **Hodgkinson's repeated:** *Daily Advertiser*, June 12, 1795, 3; *Argus*, June 12, 1795, 3. The previous night Hewitt and Saliment also cashed in on the society's success, offering a benefit concert featuring instrumental concerti, an orchestral overture, and vocal music. The performance ended with Hodgkinson's encore recitation of "The Passions," now with new music composed by James Hewitt. Dancing accompanied by the orchestra brought the evening to a close; see "Concert," *Daily Advertiser*, June 6, 1795, 2.

70 *The Syren:* *The Syren* (New York: Berry & Rogers & John Reid, 1793), 60–62.

70 **Other printings followed:** *The Medley; or, New Philadelphia Songster* (Philadelphia: Neale & Kammerer, 1795), 206–8; *The Vocal Companion* (Philadelphia: Mathew Carey, 1796); *Dibdin's Museum* (Philadelphia: Charles, 1797); *The Sky Lark: or Gentlemen and Ladies' Complete Songster* (Worcester, MA: Isaiah Thomas, 1797); *The Syren, or Vocal Enchantress* (Wilmington, DE: Bonsal & Niles, 1797); and *The American Songster* (Baltimore: Warner & Hanna, 1799).

70 **many dozens more:** See Hill, "Melody," 161–62, 180–81.

70 **benefit skits:** "The Anacreontic Society," *Baltimore Patriot*, January 15, 1822, 2, with notices up to March 31, 1831, 2; "New York Glee and Catch Club," *National Advocate*, April 10, 1827. For the benefit skits, see *Alexandria Gazette*, August 17, 1810, 3; *Poulson's American Daily Advertiser* (Philadelphia), April 1, 1813, 3; *Albany Register*, April 13, 1813, 3; *Daily National Intelligencer*, August 14, 1815, 3; and others.

71 **Boston's Fire Society:** Henry H. Sprague, *A Brief History of the Massachusetts Charitable Fire Society* (Boston: Little, Brown, 1893), 17.

71 *Rise, Columbia:* Ibid., 53–54. *Rise Columbia!*, sheet music n.p., n.d. (1800?), Library of Congress, no. 2015563327.

71 **he was paid $750:** *Federal Orrery*, June 2, 1796, 50; and Sprague, *Brief History*, 54. Paine also wrote for the society's 1799 meeting; see *Russell's Gazette*, May 30, 1799, 2.

71 **printed music sold:** An advertisement for *Adams and Liberty* sets the price at 12.5 cents. *Federal Gazette* (Baltimore), June 20, 1798, 2.

71 **Six different music publishers:** Publishers of sheet music editions include Boston: Thomas & Andrews, June 1798; Boston: W. P. & L. Blake, June 1798; New York: W. Howe, 1798; *The American Musical Miscellany* (Northampton, MA, 1798), 211–18; New York: J. Hewitt's Musical Repository, 1798–99; second edition—corrected (Boston: Linley & Moore, 1798–99); third edition, corrected (Boston: P.A. von Hagen & Co., 1799–1800); New York: G. Gilfert, 1798–1801. See Oscar Sonneck and William Treat Upton, *A Bibliography of Early Secular American Music* (Washington, DC: Library of Congress, 1945), 2–4.

71 **keepsake:** See Vera Brodsky Lawrence, *Music for Patriots, Politicians, and Presidents* (New York: Macmillan, 1975), 148–49; Sonneck, *Star Spangled Banner*, plate 12; and Muller, *Star Spangled Banner*, 16–17. *Adams and Liberty* (both music and text) was also printed in *The American Musical Miscellany*, a widely distributed songster (Northampton, MA: Daniel Wright & Co., 1798), 211–18, in Sonneck, *Star Spangled Banner*, plate 10.

72 **Susanna Rowson:** Peter Leavensorth, "The Pursuit of a 'Just Proportion of Public Approbations': Rowson in Her Musical Context," *Studies in American Fiction* 38, nos. 1–2 (2011): 38.

72 **a new birthday song:** The text is included in Rowson's *Miscellaneous Poems* (Boston: Gilbert & Dean, 1804), 187–79, in which she dates the work to February 11, 1798. This is corrected by *Federal Galaxy*, March 10, 1797, 4, which contains the full lyric, identifies the performer, and dates its premiere to February 22 of that year. See also Clague and Kuster, *Star Spangled Songbook*, no. 15, pp. 63–64.

72 **five copies:** When Rowson published her *Miscellaneous Poems* in 1804, Paine subscribed for five copies. See Keller, *Music of the War*, 102n2.

72 **"Mr. Thomas Paine":** *Columbian Centinel*, May 26, 1798, 2.

72 **"To-morrow morning":** *Boston Price-Current*, May 31, 1798, 3.

72 **"in a style":** *Massachusetts Mercury*, June 5, 1798, 2.

73 **"Let Fame to the world":** *Pennsylvania Magazine*, May 1798, "Chorus" added. Leonidas was the victorious leader of Sparta against Athens.

74 **Artillery Company:** *Columbian Centinel*, June 2, 1798, 3, and *Columbian Centinel*, June 6, 1798, 2.

74 **Catherine Graupner:** *Salem Gazette*, June 5, 1798, 3. For other performances, see *Commercial Advertiser* (NY), June 7, 1798, 2, 3; *Philadelphia Gazette*, June 9, 1798, 3, and June 13, 1798, 2; and *Gazette of the United States*, June 16, 1798, 3.

74 **commencement dinner:** *Philadelphia Gazette*, July 24, 1798, 2. The commencement was on July 16. Hodgkinson also sang the song at Boston's Hay-Market Theatre. See *Russell's Gazette*, July 19, 1798, and *City Gazette*, February 26, 1800, 3.

74 **"the classic song":** *Columbian Centinel*, August 11, 1798, 2. A similar performance greeted the president at Milton Bridge the day before; *Federal Gazette*, August 18, 1798, 2.

74 **"voice of discord"**: "American Independence," *Gazette* (Portland, ME), July 9, 1798, 2.

75 **"No less delusive"**: Abraham Bishop, "Extracts from an Oration on the Extent and Power of Political Delusion," *Albany Register,* October 24, 1800, 2.

75 **"I wish Mr. Printer"**: *Independent Chronicle* (Boston), June 21, 1798, 1.

75 **"INTRIGUE and SEDITION"**: "The Fount," *Oriental Trumpet* (Portland, ME), July 18, 1798, 4, emphasis in original.

76 **Adams's birthday**: *New-Hampshire Gazette,* October 24, 1798, 3. Sonneck, *Star Spangled Banner,* attributes this lyric to Jonathan Mitchell Sewall, who also wrote *Columbia Exults!* in 1799.

76 **cited *Adams and Liberty***: These 1799 titles include "The Times," *Exeter Federal Miscellany,* February 9, quoted in Joseph T. Buckingham, *Specimens of Newspaper Literature* (Boston: Redding & Co., 1852), 334–36; *Massachusetts Spy,* July 7, 4; *Political Repository,* September 3, 4; *Otsego Herald* (NY), November 7, 4; and *Oracle of the Day,* November 9, 4. Another 1799 title was later called *The Gift of the Gods.* It is an American patriotic revision of an English poem without strong party affiliation; *City Gazette* (Charleston), August, 5, 1799, 3. A sixth pro-Federalist lyric likely appeared in late 1800. It begins "Columbia's brave Navy now floats on the main"; *Washington Federalist,* December 11, 1800, 3.

76 **"The Poets of our country"**: *Philadelphia Gazette,* November 20, 1799, 3, and *Gazette of the United States & Philadelphia Daily Advertiser,* November 21, 1799, 2. The "tuneful bard" was Mitchell Sewall.

77 **"FOR a few Elections back"**: "To the Independent Electors," *Independent Chronicle,* October 30, 1800, 2; emphasis in original.

77 **"AWAKE, ye Columbians"**: *Guardian,* January 16, 1801, 4.

78 **Jefferson & Liberty**: *Constitutional Telegraph,* January 28, 1801, 4.

78 **"we can now speak"**: *National Intelligencer* (Washington, DC), February 9, 1801, 4.

78 **Yeomen of Hampshire**: *Columbian Centinel,* June 3, 1801, 2; "New Patriotic Song," *Green Mountain Patriot* (Peacham, VT), October 15, 1801, 4.

78 **consul to Britain**: *Independent Chronicle,* May 9, 1803, 4. Other sources claim that this song was first performed in 1802, but the earliest newspaper account appears to be this one from 1803.

78 **Walt Whitman**: *Brooklyn Daily Eagle,* July 2, 1846, 2. See Walt Whitman, "Ode," in *The Uncollected Poetry and Prose of Walt Whitman,* ed. Emory Holloway (Garden City, NY: Doubleday Page, 1921), 1:22–23. The song was reprinted in the *Daily Eagle* on June 15, 1900, and in the *Eagle's* "Walt Whitman Centenary Number," May 31, 1919. See also *New York Times Magazine,* September 16, 1916, 14–15.

79 **"diffuse the same joy"**: *Aurora General Advertiser* (Philadelphia), January 9, 1796, 3.

79 **Verses to My Country**: *Balance* (Hudson, NY), November 11, 1806, 8.

79 **"From the deep"**: *Virginia Argus* (Richmond), July 12, 1808, 1.

80 **Battle of Queenston**: "A New Song," *Federal Republican,* December 28, 1812, 3.

80 **"Then unite, all ye sons":** *Virginia Argus* (Richmond), April 19, 1813; Hill, "Melody," no. 55, p. 173.

80 **party divisions:** *Virginia Argus*, April 19, 1813, 1.

80 **"Arouse! one and all":** *The Iron Greys*, in *Niles Register Supplement* (Baltimore), 1815–16. The text suggests that its creation date is likely earlier.

80 **"Shall the record":** *Newburyport Herald* (MA), July 14, 1812, 4.

80 *Rights of America: Carlisle Weekly Herald* (PA), January 15, 1813, 4.

80 **"Since now fairly":** *Baltimore Patriot*, August 19, 1813, 2.

81 *American Blues:* John Thomas Scharf, *History of Western Maryland: Being a History of Frederick*... (Philadelphia: Louis H. Everts, 1882), 1:180; *Newburyport Herald* (MA), December 25, 1812, 4; *Democratic Press*, January 9, 1813, 3; *Carlisle Weekly Herald* (PA), January 1, 1813, 4; and *Port-Folio Magazine* (November 1814), 516–18. Although *Port-Folio* published this lyric after Key's song, it was submitted by June 15 for the magazine's national song competition.

81 *The Battle of Baltimore:* For a rich analysis of the *Yankee Doodle* parody in comparison to Key's lyric, see David K. Hildebrand, "Bicentenary Essay: Two National Anthems? Some Reflections on the Two Hundredth Anniversary of 'The Star-Spangled Banner' and its Forgotten Partner, 'The Battle of Baltimore,'" *American Music* 32, no. 3 (Fall 2014): 253–71.

81 *The Battle of North Point:* William McCarty, *The United States Songster* (Cincinnati: U.P. James, 1836), 77–81; Clague and Kuster, *Star Spangled Songbook*, no. 28, pp. 103–105.

81 *The Victory at New Orleans: Baltimore Patriot*, March 4, 1819, 2; *National Advocate*, January 25, 1816, 5; *Essex Register* (Salem, MA), March 15, 1815, 1; *New-Jersey Journal*, May 9, 1815, 4.

81 **Key's Warrior Returns:** *Columbian*, September 17, 1813, 2; *Albany Register*, October 5, 1813, 3; *New-Jersey Journal*, January 11, 1814, 4; *National Aegis* (Worcester, MA), April 27, 1814, 4.

82 **"ALL hail to the BIRTH":** *Port-Folio Magazine* 3, no. 5 (May 1814): 496–98; *Port-Folio Magazine* 4, no. 1 (July 1814): 118–21, 129–31.

82 **No winner:** Richard Grant White, *National Hymns* (New York: Rudd & Carleton, 1861).

82 **"future American Anthem":** Jarmil Burghauser, "My Country, 'Tis of Thee," in *Dvořák in America*, ed. John C. Tibbetts (Portland, OR: Amadeus Press, 1993), 202–9.

82 *O Land of Mine:* Howard Pollack, *George Gershwin: His Life and Work* (Berkeley: University of California Press, 2006), 244.

83 **the song My Country:** *San Francisco Examiner*, April 27, 1919, 80.

Chapter 4: The *Banner* at War

84 **"Every rendition":** "The Unveiling of the Original Manuscript of the Star-Spangled Banner," *Maryland Historical Magazine* 49, no. 4 (December 1954): 265.

84 **seamen had suffered:** *Suburban Monthly*, September 6, 1898, 9.

84 **bloody third verse:** *Pittsburgh Daily Post*, March 20, 1898, 18 (five verses, incl.
Holmes); *Evening Star* (Washington, DC), April 9, 1898, 23 (three verses); *Knoxville
Journal & Tribune*, April 17, 1898, 10 (three verses); *Philadelphia Inquirer*, April 22,
1898, 8 (one verse); *Camden Daily Telegram*, April 28, 1898, 2 (four verses); *Lawrence Journal* (KS), April 30, 1898, 3 (five verses, incl. Holmes); and others.

85 **The band of the battleship *Oregon*:** *Harper's Weekly*, August 6, 1898, cover.

85 **The war had lasted:** G. J. A. O'Toole, *The Spanish War: An American Epic 1898*
(New York: W. W. Norton, 1986).

85 **"Never in the history":** *Amateur Record* 1, no. 6 (July 15, 1898): 2.

86 **"Dear Friends":** *Charleston Courier*, May 19, 1846, 2.

86–87 **"I believe war is":** "Miscellany. Speech of Mr. L. H. Sims, of Missouri, on the Bill
Making Appropriations for the Army," *Norfolk Democrat* (Dedham, MA), May 14,
1846, 1.

87 **"Up Texians":** William McCarty, *National Songs, Ballads, and Other Patriotic
Poetry Chiefly Relating to the War of 1846* (Philadelphia, 1846), 110–11. In the
twenty-first century, this lyric has been used to valorize the militia movement and
gun culture; see Dave Kopel, "Don't Mess With (Armed) Texas," *National Review
Online*, April 8, 2004, and Gregg Lee Carter, ed., *Guns in American Society* (Santa
Barbara, CA: ABC-Clio, 2002), 221.

87 **Davy Crockett:** *The Sons of Wyoming*, in *Lackawanna Citizen* (PA), April 24, 1847,
1; *The Death of Crockett*, in *Rough and Ready Songster* (New York: Nafis & Cornish,
1848), 167–69.

87 **The States of the Union!:** John Cameron, *Weekly Raleigh Register*, July 9, 1847, 1.

87 **toasts to "The Union":** *United States Gazette*, July 14, 1832, 1.

88 **"the greatest favorite":** *Daily Evening Bulletin* (Philadelphia), January 7, 1861, 2.

88 **"every verse":** "Affairs at the South," *Chicago Tribune*, January 4, 1861, 2.

88 **" 'Tis the star spangled":** "Academy of Music," *New York Daily Herald*, February 5,
1861. 5.

88 **"It was awful stuff":** *New Orleans Crescent*, February 13, 1861, 1.

88 **"The effect was electric":** *Chicago Tribune*, February 26, 1861, 2. The performance
Lincoln attended was on February 20 at the Academy of Music; *New York Daily
Herald*, February 21, 1861, 4.

89 **"Flag-raising was":** Abijah P. Marvin, *History of Worcester in the War of the Rebellion* (Worcester, MA, 1880), 24–25.

89 **single day:** *Richmond Whig*, April 6, 1865, 2.

89 **"anti-secession spirit":** "An Old Song for a New Occasion," *Civilian and Telegraph*, May 2, 1861, 1.

89 **"a large preponderance":** "A Pennsylvanian in Maryland," *Baltimore Sun*, June
21, 1861, 1.

89 **"A Parody":** *The New Confederate Flag Song Book* (Richmond, VA: A. Morris,
1864), 15–16.

90 **Key's own family, fled south:** Key's descendants served exclusively in the Confederate forces. He had eleven children and more than fifty grandchildren. The *Baltimore Republican* cited fifteen male descendants "liable to military duty" who served in the Southern army; see also *Connecticut Courant*, July 20, 1861, 2. These included grandsons Clarence Key, John Francis Key, William S. Key, McHenry Howard, and Billings Steele. In 1861 some sixty descendants of Francis Scott Key were living, and "every man, woman, and child was Southern," but none owned people as slaves; McHenry Howard, *Recollections of a Maryland Confederate Soldier . . .* (Baltimore: Williams & Wilkins, 1914), 3. See also Frank Key Howard, *Fourteen Months in the American Bastilles* (Baltimore: Kelly, Hedian & Piet, 1863), 4, 9.

90 **"all of us sung":** Dexter F. Parker, letter dated April 29, 1861, quoted in Marvin, *History of Worcester*, 50–51.

90 **poem *The Southern Cross*:** "Of Mrs. Ellen Key Blunt," *Boston Daily Advertiser*, July 31, 1861, quoted in Billy Coleman, *Harnessing Harmony: Music, Power, and Politics in the United States, 1788–1865* (Chapel Hill: University of North Carolina Press, 2020), 158; *Newark Daily Advertiser*, May 27, 1862; *Alexandria Gazette*, May 21, 1862; *Richmond Examiner*, June 11, 1862; and "Americans in Paris," *Baltimore Sun*, July 23, 1863.

90 **"stand for our Southern":** J. T. Mason Blunt, "A Patriotic Song from Across the Water," *Daily Selma Reporter*, November 4, 1862, 1; *Rebel Rhymes and Rhapsodies* (New York: G. P. Putnam, 1864), 287–89.

91 **many recruited his memory:** When George Pendleton ran for vice president on the Democratic ticket against Lincoln in 1864, the party claimed Key's song as its own. Pendleton was married to another of Key's daughters, Mary "Alice" Key. See Ferris, *Star-Spangled Banner*, 55.

91 **"I never could learn":** "The National Flag and Anthem," *Richmond Whig*, January 11, 1861, reprinted in "The National Airs and Songs," *Dwight's Journal of Music* 18 (January 12, 1861): 325.

91 **"as similar as possible":** "Provisional Congress," *Weekly Advertiser*, February 20, 1861, 4.

92 **fire on their compatriots:** Ferris, *Star-Spangled Banner*, 41.

92 **"O say does that Rag":** Edwin Heriot, *The Flag of the South*, in *Daily Morning News* (Savannah, GA), March 20, 1861; W. A. Haynes, *The Bars and Stars, Original Songs of the Atlanta Amateurs* (Atlanta, GA: Intelligencer, 1861), 6; *Rutland Weekly Herald* (VT), June 28, 1961, 3; *The Stars and Bars*, in American Song Sheets, Slip Ballads and Poetical Broadsides Collection, Wolf C167, Library Company of Philadelphia.

92 **"O, who ever knew":** *Richmond Dispatch*, May 14, 1861.

92 **titled *The Southern Cross*:** *Newbern Weekly Progress* (NC), April 23, 1861, 1, from *Southern Literary Messenger* 32, no. 3 (March 1861): 189. Sheet music edition: *The Southern Cross* (Richmond: George Dunn, 1863).

93 **"slaves of a traitor.":** *New Orleans Times*, February 5, 1865, 2.

93 **"black northern hordes":** *The President's Chair* (1863), in American Song Sheets, Slip Ballads and Poetical Broadsides Collection, Wolf C132A, Library Company of Philadelphia.

93 **Stonewall Jackson:** *The Jack Morgan Songster* (Raleigh, NC: Branson & Ferrar, 1864), 29.

93 **"Banner of States Rights.":** *Democrat* (Huntsville, AL), January 2, 1861, 4.

93 **"Oh, say can't you see":** *Richmond Dispatch,* October 24, 1861.

93 **"Oh, yes, I have seen":** *Star and Enterprise* (Newville, PA), March 6, 1862, 1

93 *Farewell to the Star Spangled:* Francis Hundley (lyrics), *Farewell to the Star Spangled Banner* (Richmond: John W. Davies & Sons, 1862); Clague and Kuster, *Star Spangled Songbook,* no. 58, pp. 200–1.

94 **"Till the foes of our Union":** *The Grand Army of the Republic Songster* (New York: Robert M. DeWitt, 1872), 176.

94 **"While a heart-throb":** *Ellsworth's Death,* in American Song Sheets, Slip Ballads and Poetical Broadsides Collection, Wolf 564, Library Company of Philadelphia.

94 **"great danger threatening":** J.W.D., letter dated April 1861, quoted in Marvin, *History of Worcester,* 52.

94 **Black fraternal organization:** Henry O'Connor, *History of the First Regiment of Iowa Volunteers* (Des Moines: State Historical Society of Iowa, 1862), 12–13.

94 **"Good martial, national music":** *New York Herald,* January 11, 1862, 4.

95 *Das Star-Spangled Banner:* Illustrated song sheet published by H. De Marsan of New York, c. 1862–63, copy held in Library of Congress, American Song Sheets, LC no. 113160.

96 **"rallied our wavering ranks":** James Fowler Rusling, *Men and Things I Saw in Civil War Days* (New York: Eaton & Mains, 1899), 244–45. Rusling also mentioned this event in an 1894 speech to a YMCA meeting; *Reading Times* (PA), January 29, 1894, 1.

96 **language of command:** Frank Baron, "Abraham Lincoln and the German Immigrants: Turners and Forty-Eighters," *Yearbook of German-American Studies,* supp. issue, vol. 4 (Lawrence, KS: Society of German-American Studies, 2012).

96 *Das Star-Spangled Banner: Das Star-Spangled Banner* (song sheet), (New York: H. De Marsan, c. 1862–63); Charles Magnus (New York, 1862), repr. Lawrence, *Music for Patriots,* 386, and Library of Congress, American Song Sheets, series 1, vol. 3. See also Clague and Kuster, *Star Spangled Songbook,* no. 55, pp. 191–93. A distinct translation is "The Star-Spangled Banner, The Song of the Patriot" (New York: Nic[las] Müller, c. 1861). See also Joseph Muller, *The Star Spangled Banner: Words and Music Issued Between 1814–1864* (1935; reprint, New York: Da Capo Press, 1975), 26.

96 **favored abolition.:** Walter D. Kamphoefner, "New Perspectives on Texas Germans and the Confederacy," *Southwestern Historical Quarterly* 102, no. 4 (April 1999): 440–55.

97 **"Our mild, human Aegis":** *The Triumph of Freedom,* in *Cleveland Daily Leader,* November 12, 1860, 3.

97 **Charlotte Cushman:** *Boston Evening Transcript,* April 27, 1861, 3.

97 **"When our land is illumined":** "The National Song—Corrected Copy," *Boston Evening Transcript,* April 29, 1861, 2. The lyric was likely printed first on April 28, but this issue is currently missing from the historical record. Holmes's text was often reprinted with small errors and is sometimes erroneously credited to Holmes's son, Oliver Wendell Holmes, Jr.

97–98 **Emma Stebbins:** *New England Farmer,* May 4, 1861, 4; *Daily Gate City* (IA), May 9, 1861; *Lewistown Gazette,* June 6, 1861, 1, confirm that both verses were premiered together. Stebbins's verse attacks the Confederate "traitors" but does not address slavery.

98 **"By the millions unchained who":** George Henry Preble, *History of the Flag of the United States of America* (1872; Boston: Williams, 1880), 730.

98 **influential collection:** John Philip Sousa, *National, Patriotic and Typical Airs of All Lands* (Philadelphia: Coleman, 1890), 14–15. See also *The Service Hymnal* (Philadelphia: Edward Stern, 1904) , 161–63.

98 **through World War II:** See *The Star-Spangled Banner* (Glenmont, NY: Edward John Smith, 1942), Library of Congress (ML1630.3.S69 1814 [non-case]).

98 **replacement for:** *The Service Hymnal* dropped Key's second and third verse and instead sandwiched Holmes's lyric between Key's first and last. See also *South Bend News-Times,* November 14, 1920, 17 and *The Wolf Point Herald,* December 23, 1920, 8, which refer to this substitution as a more general practice.

98 **"the most memorable day":** "January First 1863," *Douglass' Monthly* 5, no. 6 (January 1863): 1.

99 **A Civil War recruiting poster:** The text reads: "All slaves were made freemen. By Abraham Lincoln, president of the United States, January 1st, 1863. Come, then, able-bodied colored men, to the nearest United States camp, and fight for the stars and stripes." The back contains the lyrics to the song *John Brown's Body.*

99 **Protesters destroyed:** David M. Barnes, *The Draft Riots in New York* (New York: Baker & Godwin, 1863); "Battle Record for 1863," *New York Times,* December 31, 1863, 2.

100 **"the musical seal":** *Press* (Philadelphia), July 28, 1863, 2.

100 **"one of the happiest days":** Joseph Ferguson, *Life-Struggles in Rebel Prisons* (Philadelphia: Ferguson, 1865), 108–9.

100 **in the city square:** *Richmond Whig,* April 7, 1865, 3.

100 **"requiem for buried Southern hopes":** Rembert W. Patrick, *The Fall of Richmond* (Baton Rouge: Louisiana State University Press, 1960), 69.

100 **defiant Unionist newspaper:** *Richmond Whig,* April 6, 1865, 4.

100 **"celebrate the capture":** *Philadelphia Inquirer,* April 6, 1865, 8;

100 **"over and over":** George Templeton Strong, *The Diary of George Templeton Strong,* vol. 3, *The Civil War 1860–65,* ed. Allan Nevins and Milton Halsey Thomas (New York: Macmillan, 1952), 574–75.

101 **ten thousand songs:** Ferris, *Star-Spangled Banner,* 50, 53.

101 **"Many a foot beat time":** Carl Sandburg, *Abraham Lincoln: The War Years* (New York: Harcourt Brace, 1939), 4: 207–8, emphasis in the original.

101–102 **Ball's additional verse:** *New York Herald,* May 29, 1869, 12. Earlier versions of the lyric have "this broad" instead of "our loved." An article announcing Ball's 1899 suicide identifies him as a "well known newspaper man" of English origin who resided in Boston as a dramatic critic of the *Boston Traveler* and *Boston Herald. New Haven Register* (CT), May 22, 1899, 2.

102 **rising "en masse":** *Philadelphia Inquirer,* June 16, 1869, 4.

102 **"the** *tout ensemble***":** "Kate Field's Account of the Jubilee," *Providence Evening Press,* June 18, 1869, 3.

102 **A Republican convention:** *New Orleans Crescent,* February 23, 1869, 6.

102 **"***Dixie,* **the emblem":** *Vicksburg Herald* (MS), February 27, 1885, 1.

102 **"ballads of the war":** James H. Kyner, *Odes, Hymn and Songs of the Grand Army of the Republic* (Omaha, NE: Henry Gibson, 1880), 4, 107

102 **The 1883 book:** *War Songs, for Anniversaries and Gatherings of Soldiers* (Boston: Oliver Ditson, 1883), 36–37. Holmes's verse is given as an additional fifth verse.

103 **"preserve what in battle":** *Our Country, to Thee,* in *New Orleans Republican,* September 3, 1876, 6.

103 **"The composition":** *Army Regulations, Changes* No. 50, War Department, January 8, 1917, 1, paragraph 264, quoted in George J. Svejda, *History of the Star Spangled Banner from 1814 to the Present* (Washington, DC: National Park Service, 1969), 258.

103 **"face towards the colors":** General Orders and Circulars, no. 374, Navy Department, July 26, 1889, in Svejda, *History of the Star Spangled Banner,* 470.

104 **"because both music and words":** "National Anthems," *Evening Star* (DC), February 9, 1889, 6. See also Sousa, *Airs of All Lands,* 12.

104 **William H. Santelmann:** Svejda, *History of the Star Spangled Banner,* 228–29.

104 **"the national air":** *Regulations for the Government of the Navy of the United States* (Washington, DC: Government Printing Office, 1893), 39, in Svejda, *History of the Star Spangled Banner,* appendix G.

104 **"American national anthem":** Ferris, *Star-Spangled Banner,* 89–90.

104 **strength, resolve, and unity.:** *Brooklyn Daily Eagle,* April 22, 1861, 2. In World War I a widely reprinted but apocryphal tale credited then Secretary of State Daniel Webster with beginning the tradition of standing for Key's song in 1851 at New York's Castle Garden when Swedish soprano Jenny Lind performed Key's song. The story seems to be a distortion of events from a concert on December 18, 1850, in Washington, D.C. when Webster's gracious bow to Lind after she had performed *Hail Columbia* was noted in the press. See *Baltimore Sun,* December 20, 1850, 1.

105 **cheers, applause, or waving flags.:** *Lebanon Times* (KS), June 8, 1888, 1; *Pittsburgh Daily Post,* February 23, 1889, 1.

105 **toast to President Grover Cleveland:** *Burlington Free Press* (VT), March 8, 1893, 1.

105 **"their memory shall live":** Jas. H. Wilder, *Original Ode,* June 17, 1870, broadside, American Antiquarian Society.

105 **"Be sacred their memory":** *Findlay Jeffersonian* (Findlay, OH), May 26, 1876, 2.

105 **"Resolved, That"**: *Tacoma Daily Ledger,* October 19, 1893, quoted in Bessie Thompson Stephens, "They Stood Up for Him," *Daughters of the American Revolution Magazine* 105, no. 9 (November 1971): 796–98.

105 **"into the habit"**: "Americans and National Airs," *Washington Times,* October 25, 1902, 6.

105 **"headed for home"**: *Buffalo Express,* June 13, 1904, 7.

106 **"bared heads"**: "Huge Crowd Hears Concert at the Front," *Buffalo Courier,* June 19, 1905, 6.

106 **"the person who refuses"**: "Crowds Respond to National Air," *Washington Herald,* August 14, 1816, 3.

106 **"I am a Germanophile"**: *Philadelphia Inquirer,* February 14, 1917, 10; also *Macon Telegraph,* February 20, 1917, 4.

106 **"rebuked"**: *St. Louis Star,* February 13, 1917, 4; *Sapulpa Herald* (OK), February 22, 1917, 2.

106 **boycotted her films.**: *Chattanooga News,* February 14, 1917, 4; *Trenton Evening Times,* March 14, 1917, 14.

107 **"American first"**: *New-York Tribune,* March 13, 1917, 11; *Trenton Evening Times,* March 1, 1917, 6; *Trenton Evening News,* March 26, 1917, 2; "Fifth Ave. Pauses while Farrar Helps Loan," *New-York Tribune,* April 16, 1918, 6.

107 **Hunter College:** "Girls Won't Stand as Anthem's Sung," *Sun* (NY), March 18, 1917, 13.

107 **"educators who disavowed"**: "Weeding Them Out," *Reno Gazette-Journal,* December 14, 1917, 4.

107 **A pacifist in San Francisco:** *San Francisco Examiner,* March 6, 1918, 7.

107 **failed to stand:** *Pittsburgh Press,* April 24, 1917, 10.

107 **Philadelphia actor:** *Public Ledger,* April 3, 1918, 15.

107 **theater owner:** "Turn the Spotlight on the Unpatriotic," *Wichita Beacon,* May 2, 1918, 3.

107 **Fritz Kreisler:** "Fritz Kreisler Cancels Concerts," *Burlington Weekly Free Press,* November 29, 1917, 7.

107 **required all members:** "Chicago Musical Union Bars 'Alien' Players," *Musical America* 26, no. 3 (May 19, 1917): 52.

108 **"any man who refuses"**: "Send Dr. Muck Back, Roosevelt Advises," *New York Times,* November 3, 1917, 22.

108 **"arrest first"**: William B. Glidden, "Internment Camps in America, 1917–1920," *Military Affairs* 37 (1973): 137–41.

108 **Fort Oglethorpe:** Melissa D. Burrage, *The Karl Muck Scandal* (New York: University of Rochester Press, 2019); Edmund A. Bowles, "Karl Muck and His Compatriots," *American Music* 25, no. 4 (Winter 2007): 405–40.

108 **Alfred Hertz:** Leta E. Miller, *Music & Politics in San Francisco* (Berkeley: University of California Press, 2012), 53–55.

108 **"full chested"**: *Courier-News* (NJ), March 13, 1918, 9.

108 **"One of the noblest functions":** *Press and Sun-Bulletin* (Binghamton, NY), February 9, 1917, 3; *Champaign Daily News* (IL), February 16, 1917, 4; *Wichita Beacon*, February 19, 1917, 3; *Boston Post*, March 11, 1917, 45; and *Des Moines Register*, March 11, 1917, 25.

109 **Two factors raised:** See Patrick Warfield, "Educators in Search of an Anthem: Standardizing 'The Star-Spangled Banner' During the First World War," *Journal of the Society for American Music* 12, no. 3 (2018): 268–316.

110 **"one authoritative version":** Shawe to Roosevelt, October 28, 1907, Records Group 12, Entry 6, Historical Files, File Class 900, Box 68, National Archives and Records Administration; quoted in Warfield, "Educators in Search," 281. Shawe's name is sometimes spelled Shaw.

110 **cut the verse:** Examples include A. J. Gantvoort, *Gantvoort's School Music Reader* (New York: American Book Company, 1907), 196–97; McLaughlin-Gilchrist, *Fifth Music Reader* (Boston: Ginn, 1906), 216–17; and Charles Whiting, *The New Public School Music Course* (Boston: D. C. Heath, 1909), 100–1. There also seems to be a gendered component to the decision. Books for boys might contain the verse, like Edward Zeiner, *The High School Song Book for Boys and Mixed Voices* (New York: Macmillan, 1909), 56–57; but arrangements for girls did not, like John Shirley, *Part Songs for Girls' Voices* (New York: American Book Company, 1908), 17–18. The first publications to discard the third verse were religiously affiliated, including temperance songsters and hymnals. As early as 1854, *The National Temperance Songster* skipped verse three, while in 1857 a song collection for schools and seminaries titled *The Golden Wreath* also deleted it; *see* Silas W. Leonard and Rev. James Young, *The National Temperance Songster* (Louisville, KY, 1854), 163–65, and *The Golden Wreath* (Boston: Oliver Ditson, 1857), 184–85.

110 **expunged the third verse:** The NEA version was published as *Four National Songs* (New York: American Book Company, 1912). The composer was misidentified as Samuel Arnold. See Sonneck, *Star Spangled Banner*, 102–3. Anthem historians have long assumed that the third verse was dropped because of its anti-British rhetoric. Certainly, in World War I the United States and Britain were allies, but no direct evidence suggests this motivation. Likewise, no source mentions concerns over the word *slave*.

110 **new committee:** Business Meeting Minutes, *Journal of the Proceedings of the Music Supervisors National Conference* 9 (1916): 109.

110 **revised version:** *55 Songs and Choruses for Community Singing* (Boston: Birchard, 1917), 4.

110 **militaristic aesthetic:** *Twice 55 Community Songs* (Boston: Birchard, 1917), 3. The book also included songs from World War I allies Britain, France, Italy, and Russia. Note also the increased registral intensity to the chord supporting the word "free."

112 **"to stimulate and advance":** *55 Community Songs, Liberty Edition* (Boston: Birchard, 1918), inside cover. All German repertoire was removed and additional patriotic songs added.

113 **"as it emerged from the masses.":** "The Star-Spangled Banner," *Music Supervisors' Journal* 5, no. 2 (November 1918): 2–4.

113 **generated complaints and controversy.**: "That Service Version," *Music Supervisors' Journal* 5, no. 3 (January 1919): 3.

114 **"developed into quite a climax"**: Walter Damrosch, *My Musical Life* (New York: Scribner, 1926), 271.

114 **educators were livid.**: For more detail on the controversy, see Warfield, "Educators in Search," 296ff.

Chapter 5: Play Ball!

115 **"The playing of"**: *New York Times*, August 23, 1945, 19.

118 **Grand Inauguration**: All details of the first game are from "Out Door Sports," *Brooklyn Daily Eagle*, May 16, 1862, 2. Harold Seymour, *Baseball: The Early Years* (New York: Oxford University Press, 1960), identifies this rendition as the first documented performance of Key's song at a baseball game.

118 **three athletic and social clubs**: In this early era, "base ball" was a game not of teams but of clubs. Such clubs were as much social as sporting, in ways not dissimilar from the Anacreontic Society itself.

118 **"present furor"**: "The Base Ball Matches," *Philadelphia Inquirer*, July 1, 1862, 8.

118 **"while the band played"**: "Baseball Season Opened," *New York Times*, April 23, 1897, 5.

119 **"what the 'rooters' termed"**: "On the Baseball Field: Opening Game at the Polo Grounds Called on Account of Rain," *New York Times*, April 16, 1898, 10.

119 **"the players and the band"**: "Brooklyn Nine Defeated," *New York Times*, April 16, 1999, 8.

119 **"At once every cadet"**: Widely reprinted, the article appeared first as "The Star Spangled Banner," *Sun* (NY), December 8, 1899, 6.

119 **"the people of the"**: Ibid.

121 **"The Boston band played"**: *Boston Globe*, October 11, 1903, 1.

121 **Opening day 1917**: "Marshall Pitcher at Start of Game," *Washington Post*, April 20, 1917, 8; "Baseball Makes Bow with Patriotic Air," *Washington Herald*, April 21. 1917, 13. John N. Pistorio's band is described in its leader's funeral announcement in *Washington Times*, June 19, 1919, 5.

122 **token exercises**: "Corp. Hoffman Recruiter Here Is to Drill Boston Red Sox," *Green Bay Press-Gazette*, May 17, 191, 1.

122 **The 1917 World Series**: Hugh Baillio, "Day Dawns Cold, Aye," *Oregon Daily*, October 9, 1917, 10.

123 **Before game one**: "Flags and Khaki Popular at Comiskey Park Battle," *Lincoln Star*, October 7, 1917, 5.

123 **"jazzing up 'America'"**: Damon Runyon, "Chicagoans Are Patriotic," *St. Louis Star & Times*, October 8, 1917, 13.

123 **For game four**: "Giants Win Game by Five to Nothing," *Reno Gazette-Journal*, October 11, 1917, 6.

124 **caused Wilson to cancel:** "Flags and Khaki Popular at Comiskey Park Battle," *Lincoln Star,* October 7, 1917, 5."

124 **"bats and balls fund":** "Doff Hats to Foxey Griff," *Washington Herald,* December 25, 1917, 8. The fund was simultaneously a marketing ploy to spread baseball around the globe.

124 **"non-essential":** "Secretary of War Baker Decrees that Baseball Is Non-Essential Occupation," *Detroit Free Press,* July 20, 1918, 11.

124 **induction into the army:** In August 1918 the U.S. military draft was expanded to include all men, ages eighteen through forty five, but in November both the war and draft ended. Edward M. Coffman, *The War to End All Wars: The American Military Experience in World War I* (Lexington: University of Kentucky Press, 1998), 24–28.

124 **"is essential to the morale":** "Baseball Essential Says John K. Tener," *Evening News* (Wilkes-Barre, PA), June 25, 1918, 9.

124 **"we will most gladly":** "Professional Baseball Is Held To Be Non-Essential," *Decatur Herald* (IL), July 20, 1918, 4.

125 **the first time fans:** "Crowd Present Seemed To Take Little Interest in Work of Rival Athletes," *St. Louis Post-Dispatch,* September 6, 1918, 20.

125 **surprised the crowd:** "Bunched Hits in Fourth Gives Red Sox Victory," *Decatur Herald,* September 6, 1918, 4.

125 **"with his eyes set":** "One Run Gives Red Sox First Game of Series," *New York Times,* September 6, 1918, 14.

125 **Ticket revenues:** Revenues were down 58 percent, from $425,878 to $179,619. See "World's Series Facts," *Evening World* (NY), October 16, 1917, 16, and "Red Sox Beat Cubs 2 to 1 and Put World's Series of 1918 to Their Credit," *New York Times,* September 12, 1918, 12.

126 *La Marseillaise:* "Michigan Wins from Cornell by 42–0 Margin," *Chicago Daily Tribune,* November 11, 1917, A1.

126 **"the audience stood":** "Canadian Cadets Beat West Point," *New York Times,* February 17, 1924, S1.

126 **respective national song:** "Garden Is Opened in Blaze of Color," *New York Times,* December 16, 1925, 29.

127 **"the Stars and Stripes":** "Hoover Throws Out First Ball as Athletics Beat Senators in 11th, 5 to 3," *New York Times,* April 15, 1931, 37.

127 **"loudly cheered":** Quoted in "Here Is a Funny Story," *Harrisburg Telegraph,* April 27, 1896, 1.

127 **America's lone gold:** "French Committee Awards Prizes to Winning Athletes," *Press and Sun-Bulletin,* February 6, 1924, 18.

127 **first gold in rugby:** "Reports of Rugby Row in France Confirmed," *Woodland Daily Democrat,* June 14, 1924, 6.

127 **"It is a custom":** Julia Hoyt, "Americans in Olympics Prove Selves Good Sports of Whom Country May Be Proud," *Star Tribune,* August 19, 1924, 10.

128 **Slower tempos:** David Segal, "Tweaks to the Anthem Stir a Wave of Pique," *New York Times,* August 14, 2016, sports section, p. 6.

128 **China's gold medal strategy:** Hannah Beech, "The Chinese Sports Machine's Single Goal: The Most Golds, at Any Cost," *New York Times,* July 29, 2021.

129 **"thousands who were there":** "KHJ Peace Day Music Charms," *Los Angeles Times,* November 12, 1923.

129 **inside his mask:** Joe Price, "The Ritual Singing of the National Anthem," *Religious Studies News* 16, no. 3 (Fall 2001), 16; and Dan Schlossberg, *Baseball Gold: Mining Nuggets from Our National Pastime* (Chicago: Triumph Books, 2007). See also Associated Press, "Umpiring-Announcing: One and the Same Job," *Oshkosh Daily Northwestern* (WI), August 26, 1929, 13; this AP wire story was reprinted broadly.

129 **"the color and glamor":** Morris De Haven Tracy, "Color and Glamor Gone from Series," *Altoona Mirror* (PA), October 30, 1930, 23.

129 **terrible period:** The American Federation of Musicians campaigned against "canned" or "robot music." See Music Union's Ads Suppressed by Some Dailies," *American Guardian* (Oklahoma City), November 22, 1929, 4; and Bryant Putney, "Grace Notes," *Capital Times* (Madison, WI), October 5, 1930, 6.

130 **first broadcast:** *Fort Worth Star-Telegram,* November 16, 1941, 21.

130 **"sign off with":** For this widely circulated Associated Press story, see *Wisconsin State Journal,* February 12, 1935, 7. See also "The 31 and 49 Meter Bands," *St. Louis Globe-Democrat,* June 30, 1935, 38.

130 **"anyone hearing":** Darrell V. Martin, "WHO Idea is Commendable," *Pittsburgh Post-Gazette,* July 12, 1935, 12.

130 **"average of three times":** Associated Press, "Radio Programs," in *Daily Messenger* (Canandaigua, NY) May 9, 1936, 2.

130 **"to familiarize listeners":** Jo Ranson, "Radio Dial Log: News Notes," *Brooklyn Daily Eagle,* January 19, 1939, 22.

130 **teach Americans the lyric.:** "VFW Sponsors Move to Sing National Anthem," *Daily Notes* (Canonsburg, PA), March 10, 1939, 5.

130 **James Petrillo:** *Press and Sun-Bulletin* (Binghamton, NY), July 12, 1941, 5; United Press, "Orders Playing of National Anthem," in *News* (Paterson, NJ), July 12, 1941, 14. See also H. Colin Slim, "Stravinsky's Four Star-Spangled Banners and His 1941 Christmas Card," *Musical Quarterly* 89, nos. 2–3 (Summer–Fall 2006), 6.

131 **"the Giants should purchase":** The story was published in more than thirty newspapers under the headline "Today's Guest Star," including *Gettysburg Times,* June 7, 1941, 3, and *Reno Gazette-Journal,* June 7, 1941, 11.

131 **"Danger and bad news":** L. H. Robbins, "And the Song Is Still Here," *New York Times Magazine,* January 4, 1942, 17. Certainly, Japanese Americans who were put in camps during the war would not agree with Robbins's characterization of unity.

131 **"G.I. Pianos":** Ronald V. Ratcliffe, *Steinway* (San Francisco: Chronicle Books, 2002), 49–55; a vintage G.I. piano is held by the Musical Instrument Museum (AZ).

131 **save fuel and tires:** "Deadline of Auto, Cycle Racing Extended to July 31," *Metropolitan Pasadena Star-News*, July 8, 1942, 16.

132 **"Green Light Letter":** Roosevelt to Kenesaw Landis, baseball commissioner, January 15, 1942, Franklin D. Roosevelt Library, Hyde Park, NY. See also Gerald Bazer and Steven Culbertson, "When FDR Said 'Play Ball,'" *Prologue Magazine* 34, no. 1 (Spring 2002).

132 **symbolic meeting:** Harry S. Truman, Presidential appointment calendar, entry for August 22, 1945, Harry S. Truman Library and Archives, at Trumanlibrary.gov.

133 **"The playing of":** "Pro Football Pass for the President," *New York Times*, August 23, 1945, 19. Truman would attend the Army-Navy game in December 1942, but he never attended an NFL game. Nixon reportedly became the first sitting president to do so in 1969.

133 **founding in 1946:** "Minors Get Recording of National Anthem," *Scrantonian Tribune*, August 23, 1942, 26; Sport Podge, *News-Journal* (Mansfield, OH), September 22, 1942, 9.

133 **soccer in the United States:** Jaweed Kaleem, "In the 'Land of the Free,' Are You Fee to Sit Out the National Anthem?" *Los Angeles Times*, September 1, 2016

133 **Whitney Houston's 1991 rendition:** David Barron, "Musicians Hope to Score Big with Each Performance of the National Anthem," *Houston Chronicle*, February 2, 2017.

133 **Beyoncé to Lady Gaga:** Beyoncé interview, *The Oprah Winfrey Show*, April 5, 2004; Amrita Tripathi, "I Can't Wait to Come to India: Lady Gaga," CNN-IBN, February 15, 2011.

134 **hit number twenty:** Billboard.com. Houston's rendition also charted in 2012, reaching number forty-eight.

134 **America-led coalition:** Richard Lowry, *The Gulf War Chronicles: A Military History of the First War with Iraq* (iUniverse, 2008).

134 **security for the game:** Danyel Smith, "When Whitney Hit the High Note," *ESPN the Magazine*, February 1, 2016.

134 **marked a turning point:** Jim Steeg, interview by author, February 20, 2017.

134 **video of Houston's:** Houston's anthem performance is widely available on YouTube but was originally released on VHS tape as *Whitney Houston: The Star Spangled Banner as Performed at Super Bowl XXV* (Arista SW-5720, 1991 ©ABC Sports, Inc.).

136 **"We were in the middle":** Barron, "Musicians Hope."

136 **"She moved me":** Jill Lieber, "Blessings of Liberty Secured for Super Bowl XXV," *USA Today*, January 21, 2001.

137 **"touched very, very":** Ibid.

137 **extra beat:** The sheet music edition of *The Star-Spangled Banner* published as *Whitney: The Greatest Hits* (Van Nuys, CA: Alfred Music, 2000), 226–28, serves as a useful guide to Houston's ornamentation.

137 **"allow Houston":** Lieber, "Blessings of Liberty."

137 **"too slow and difficult":** Jim Steeg quoted in Smith, "When Whitney Hit."

138 **dead microphone:** Jim Steeg, interview by author, February 20, 2017.

138 **Recent improvements:** Ibid.

140 **5/4 measures:** Natalie Cole's rendition for Super Bowl XXVIII also appears to vary the meter but cannot be clearly identified aurally.

140 **"once a star":** Barron, "Musicians Hope."

140 **so anxious:** Steeg interview.

142 **behavior disrespectful.:** Virginia Pavette, "Americans Really Feel About Anthem," *Fort Myers News-Press,* January 30, 1973, 6.

142 **season was canceled:** Jack Mays, "Anthem Next?" *Franklin News-Herald,* November 11, 1970, 25.

142 **"There is no rule":** "Protest Causes Officials to Use National Anthem," United Press International, in *Raleigh Register,* January 18, 1973, 6.

142 **"Irate calls":** "Garden to Hear Anthem at Track Meet, After All," *New York Times,* January 17, 1973, 1.

142 **New York City Council:** Ibid., 29.

142 **Organizers reinstated:** "Sing Out, America!" *Cincinnati Enquirer,* January 17, 1973, 25.

142 **skipped the song:** "N.B.A. Says Teams Must Play the National Anthem," *New York Times,* February 10, 2021; "Scoreboard: Social Justice," *Courier* (Waterloo, IA), September 11, 2020, B2.

143 **"Fans should have":** John McCain and Jeff Flake, "Tackling Paid Patriotism: A Joint Oversight Report," at Mccain.senate.gov and Flake.senate.gov, November 4, 2015.

143 **"programs that honor":** Chris Isidore, "NFL to Return $724,000 that Taxpayers Spent on Patriotic Tributes," Money.cnn.com, May 19, 2016; McCain and Flake, "Tackling Paid Patriotism," 137.

143 **"indifference to the flag":** "Royals Resume National Anthem," *San Antonio Express,* June 21, 1972, 39.

144 **"I don't equate":** Paul Logan, "Flag, Anthem Have Place in Sport," *Daily Herald* (IL), September 7, 1972, 22.

Chapter 6: Singing Citizenship

145 **"I love America":** James Baldwin, *Notes of a Native Son* (Boston: Beacon Press, 1955), 9.

145–46 **more than 575 lyrics:** While many *Anacreontic* lyrics are discussed in this book, others are featured in sheet music form in Mark Clague and Andrew Kuster, eds., *Star Spangled Songbook* (Star Spangled Music Foundation, 2014); see Starspangledmusic.org for more information.

146 **"a disgrace to the service":** "Correspondence of the Baltimore Sun," *Sun* (Baltimore), April 9, 1845, 1. "Jack" and "Jack-tar" are generic names for a sailor, especially common in England. The rhyming variation is consistent and intentional.

147 **"Here were three hundred men"**: Samuel F. Holbrook, *Threescore Years: An Auto-biography* (Boston: James French & Co., 1857), 97–98, emphasis in original.

148 **A nineteenth-century flogging**: Edward Shippen, *Thirty Years at Sea: The Story of a Sailor's Life* (Philadelphia: J. B. Lippincott & Co., 1879), 32.

148 **not fully outlawed**: James E. Valle, *Rocks and Shoals: Order and Discipline in the Old Navy 1800–1861* (Annapolis, MD: Naval Institute Press, 1980).

148 **"Oh list the sad tale"**: *The Factory Maid*, in *Rhode-Island Republican*, August 7, 1833, 4; lyric credited to John Graham.

149 **promiscuous.**: "Trial of the Rev. Mr. Avery," *National Aegis* (Worcester, MA), January 30, 1833; "Trial of Ephraim K. Avery," *New-York American*, May 31, 1833, 4; "Avery's Trial," *American Repertory*, June 13, 1833, 1.

149 **"Come, sons of Columbia"**: Catherine H. Waterman, *National Temperance Ode* (Philadelphia: G.W. Hewitt, 1840); see also *Public Ledger* (Philadelphia), June 30, 1840, 2, and July 4, 1840, 3; also *Journal of the American Temperance Union* 4, no. 6 (June 1840): 128. The lyric was revised in three verses in four-part harmonization as *Come, Sons of Columbia*, in John S. Adams, *The Boston Temperance Glee Book* (Boston: Oliver Ditson & Co., 1851), 16–17. See also Clague and Kuster, *Star Spangled Songbook*, no. 52, pp. 179–81. The name "Waterman" may be a temperance-inspired pseudonym.

150 *Cold Water Magazine*: *Oh! Who Has Not Seen?*, in William A. Barrett, ed., *Temperance Annual and Cold Water Magazine for 1843* (Philadelphia: Drew & Scammell, 1843), 95, reprinted in Muller, *Star Spangled Banner*, 29–31; Clague and Kuster, *Star Spangled Songbook*, no. 44, pp. 153–54.

151 **temperance societies**: Anna Gordon's *The Temperance Songster* was priced individually, by the dozen, and discounted for orders "per 100" and distributed by the National Woman's Christian Temperance Union in Evanston, Illinois.

152 **Washingtonians**: Mary S. B. Dana, *The Temperance Lyre* (New York: Dayton & Newman, 1842), 48–49.

152 **additional 1842 lyrics**: A. B. Grosh, *Washingtonian Pocket Companion*, 2nd ed. (Utica, NY: Merrell, 1842), 75–76, 91–92, and A. Bensel, *Temperance Harp* (New York: Burnett & Allen, 1842), 24–25. Stephen Hubbard, *The Temperance Melodist* (Boston: Kidder & Cheever, 1852), 68–69, used the same text with new music, suggesting that at least one arranger felt it better to avoid the original melody's association with alcohol.

152 *The Clarion*: *The Union Temperance Song Book* (Boston: Oliver Ditson & Co., 1859), 54–55.

152 *Banner of Temperance*: William B. Bradbury, *Temperance Chimes* (New York: Stearns, 1867), 52.

152 *Spotless White Banner*: James Alexander Mowatt, *Mowatt's Temperance Glee Book No. 1* (NewYork: Hebbard & Munro, 1874), 6.

152 *Church and Freedom*: Horace B. Durant, *Prohibition Home Protection Party Campaign Songs* (Claysville, PA: Mrs. H. Abraham Durant, 1884), 28–29.

152 **No-License Banner:** Rev. O. R. Miller, "The No-License Banner" and "The Tem-
     perance Banner," in Elton R. Shaw, ed., *Stories of Hell's Commerce, or The Liquor
     Traffic in Its True Light* (Grand Rapids, MI: Shaw, 1909), 541–42. See also Paul D.
     Sanders, ed., *Lyrics and Borrowed Tunes of the American Temperance Movement*
     (Columbia: University of Missouri Press, 2006), 18–22. Among the fourteen songs
     cited by Sanders are the *Temperance Anthem* (56–57), *Prohibition Will Triumph* by
     William B. Marsh (59–60), and *Prohibition's Banner* by Samuel Jarden (60).

152 **"1. Oh say, have you heard":** Rev. C. C. Harrah, *The Equal-Rights Banner,* in *Report
     of the International Council of Women* (Washington, DC: National Woman Suffrage
     Association, 1888), 23. See also Danny O. Crew, *Suffragist Sheet Music: An Illustrated
     Catalogue of Published Music* (Jefferson, NC: McFarland, 2002), 96, 121, 149.

153 **no lyrics composed to the Anacreontic tune:** Henry W. Roby, *The Suffrage Song
     Book* (Topeka, KS: Crane & Co., 1909).

154 **4 million:** The 1840 census identified 2,487,355 enslaved Blacks in the United States.
     This number increased to 3.2 million in 1850 and almost 4 million in 1860.

154 **"Oh say, do you hear":** E. A. Atlee, "Poetry," *Signal of Liberty,* July 22, 1844, 1.

155 **Dr. Edwin Augustus Atlee:** Carol E. Mull, *The Underground Railroad in Michi-
     gan* (Jefferson, NC: McFarland, 2010), 64, 175. A homeopathic doctor, Atlee also
     founded Battle Creek's Swedenborgian Church. See A. D. P. Van Buren, "History
     of the Churches in Battle Creek," in *Report of the Pioneer Society of the State of
     Michigan* (Lansing, MI: George & Co., 1884), 5:323. Antebellum Battle Creek was
     a city with a strong progressive and abolitionist tradition. Atlee later moved to
     Philadelphia in 1847, became an ordained Swedenborgian minister, and passed
     away on March 8, 1852, at the age of seventy-six. *Journal of the Proceedings of the
     Thirty-fourth General Convention of the New Church in the United States,* June
     1852, 34.

156 **was republished:** E. A. Atlee, "From the Signal of Liberty," *Liberator,* September 13,
     1844, 148.

156 **The Patriot's Banner:** S. G. C., "The Patriot's Banner: A Parody," *Liberator,* April
     2, 1858, 56.

156 **Anti-Slavery Celebration:** *National Anti-Slavery Standard,* June 24, 1852, 2. Sim-
     ilar notices are found from at least 1846 up through 1861; see the issues of May 21,
     1846, 3, June 22, 1861, 2, and June 30, 1866, 2.

156 **Where Liberty Dwells:** "Grand Concert," *Pine and Palm* (Boston), February 13,
     1862, 4. The concert took place on February 5. See also Rev. G. S. Plumley, *Where
     Liberty Dwells, There Is My Country* (New York: Horace Waters, 1861).

157 **The Dawn of Liberty:** *The Freeman's Glee Book* (New York: Miller, Orton & Mulli-
     gan, 1856), 67; Clague and Kuster, *Star Spangled Songbook,* no. 46, pp. 159–62.

157 **patriotic choice:** Edmund O. Seedman, *Cleveland Daily Leader,* July 2, 1860, 2;
     Perrysburg Journal (OH), October 4, 1860, 4; *The Republican Campaign Songster,
     for 1860* (New York: Dayton, 1860), 27–28.

157 **John Bell:** "Bell and Everett," *Alexandria Gazette* (VA), August 11, 1860, 3.

157 **Rouse, Ye Heroes!**: Mary M. Cary, originally in *Chicago Express*, reprinted in *Independent* (KS), June 6, 1882, 1.

158 **"Farmers, stand to your rights"**: *Washington Republican* (KS), August 21 1891, 3, and *The Alliance Song Book* (Winfield, KS: Vincent, 1891), 12–13.

158 **"Oh say, does that same"**: *Oklahoma Union Farmer*, April 15, 1922, 9.

158 **"And the BANNER OF LABOR:** "The Banner of Labor," *IWW Songs* (Industrial Workers of the World, 1909), 11. The song was published previously in 1908 and credited to "D. Burgess"; see *Montana News*, December 3, 1908, 3. See also Clague and Kuster, *Star Spangled Songbook*, no. 61, pp. 210–12.

158 **The Land of the Trust**: John W. Brotherton, *Life Magazine*, June 29, 1905, 765; Clague and Kuster, *Star Spangled Songbook*, no. 60, pp. 207–9.

158 **A Navy Forever!**: *Oriental Trumpet* (Portland, ME), November 6, 1799; *Lancaster Intelligencer* (PA), March 11, 1801, 3.

159 **six separate lyrics**: *Peace and Honor*, in *Essex Register* (Salem, MA), March 15, 1815, 1; *Song*, in *Otsego Herald*, April 6, 1815, 4; *On the Restoration of Peace*, in *New-Jersey Journal*, May 9, 1815, 4; *Peace*, in *Western American* (OR), September 30, 1815, 1; *The Return of Peace*, Hill, "Melody," no. 78, p. 177; and *Commerce, War, and Peace*, in *Columbian* (NY), July 23, 1818, 2.

159 **peace lyric**: W. T. W. Ball, *New York Herald*, May 29, 1869, 12. See also Peace and Remembrance in Chapter 4 of this book.

159 **"Oh, say, let the star"**: *Reading Times* (PA), October 2, 1900, 4.

159 **"O'er their heads"**: *Detroit Free Press*, May 4, 1902, 11. The dialect of the original has been regularized here.

159 **Philippine audiences**: "Revolutionary Play Raided," *Hawaiian Star*, May 29, 1903, 5.

159 **Banner of Peace**: "Fourth of July by Summer School Students," *Journal & Tribune* (Knoxville, TN), July 2, 1910, 8; *Banner of Peace*, in *Birmingham News* (AL), May 18, 1915, 6.

160 **"Oh say, can you see, you who glory in war"**: *Journal of Education* 80, no. 10 (September 24, 1914), 269.

160 **"until the world is wholly gentled"**: "Not This Amendment of Our War Song," *Buffalo Enquirer*, September 14, 1914, 4; "New Author National Hymn to Speak Friday," *Topeka Daily Capital*, November 12, 1914, 4.

160 **League of Nations**: "The New Star-Spangled Banner," in *Parisian* (Paris, TN), August 13, 1915, 2.

160 **anti-war speakers**: "Star Spangled Banner Stops Peace Meeting," *Fort Worth Star-Telegram*, August 29, 1917, 5.

161 **"Oh, say, can you see, on the torn fields of France"**: Helen Gray Cone, "New Words to an Old Tune," *Indianapolis Star*, October 7, 1917, 43.

161 **revival of Anacreontic lyric**: The parody database at Amiright.com, https://tinyurl .com/9u2xc2ts, includes such Anacreontic lyrics as *The Peaceful Glorious Hero* (Fourth of July), *The New-Fangled Scanner* (technology), *The Nastiest, Anthem* (health insurance costs), *The Star-Spangled Beaver* (The Ballad of Roseanne Barr),

The Scarred Angled Banter (Aguilera), *The Star-Star Cranked-Up Batters* (steroids), *The Star-Mangled Ballclub* (Mets), *Oh Say, Did You See?* (NFL protests), *Bizarre Mangled Stammer* (Bush), *Obama the Best* [King of the West], *The Far-Mangled Spammer* (Trump), *Biden's Ill Manner, Those TARP-Dangled Bailouts,* and *The Muslim Superstate Song.*

Chapter 7: Nation in Translation

162 **"Our National Anthem":** Voices United for America, press release, May 18, 2006, text archived at https://johnpollard.com/track/2065454/the-star-spangled-banner.

162 *Nuestro Himno:* See also Charles Hiroshi Garrett, *Struggling to Define a Nation: American Music and the Twentieth Century* (Berkeley: University of California Press, 2008), 1–4.

162 **Great American Boycott:** "US Counts Cost of Day Without Immigrants," *Guardian,* May 1, 2006.

163 **"It has the passion.":** Jim Avila, "Spanish 'Star Spangled Banner'—Touting the American Dream or Offensive Rewrite," ABC News, April 27, 2006, https://abcnews.go.com/WNT/story?id=1898460.

164 **Latinidad:** María Elena Cepeda, "Media and the Musical Imagination: Comparative Discourses of Belonging in 'Nuestro Himno' and 'Reggaetón Latino,'" *Identities: Global Studies in Culture and Power* 16, no. 5 (2009): 548–72.

164 *La bandera: La bandera de las estrellas* (New York: G. Schirmer, 1919).

164 **"Illegal Alien Anthem.":** Michelle Malkin quoted in Christopher Shea, "Oy Vey, Can You See . . . Translating and Tweaking 'The Star-Spangled Banner' Is an American Tradition Almost as Old as the Anthem Itself," *Boston Globe,* May 7, 2006, E3.

164 **"a despicable thing":** Jim Avila, "Spanish." Charles Key was interviewed on camera and is identified as the lyricist's great-great-grandson.

164 **"more hate mail":** Oscar Avila, "Star-Spangled Anthem Delivery," *Chicago Tribune,* April 26, 2006, 16.

164 **"I think the national anthem":** *Chicago Tribune,* May 3, 2006, 13.

164 **"embrace the opportunity":** Laura Wides-Muñoz, "Spanish Anthem Draws Flak," *Herald-News* (NJ), April 29, 2006, A1, 6.

165 **"much ado about nothing":** "El Himno nacional?" *Knight Ridder Tribune Business News,* May 14, 2006, 1.

165 **the full album:** "Nuestro Himno" in *Somo Americanos* (CD), Urban Box Office, 2006, UBO 11000-2.

166 **"the last National anthem":** "Jose Can You See—New National Anthem," Phillytalk.com, May 23, 2007.

166 **"adds to the celebration":** *Congressional Record,* 109th Congress, 2nd Session, Vol. 152, No. 49, (Senate, May 1, 2006), S3770–71; 2006; "Anthem Translation Is Nothing New," *Arizona Daily Star,* May 3, 2006, 13.

166 **"Our national anthem is"**: Voices United for America, press release, May 18, 2006. The recording is available at *John Raymond Pollard,* johnpollard.com/track/2065454/the-star-spangled-banner. It was distributed free at YourNationalAnthem.com. The singers were all either U.S. immigrants or descendants of one, and all created the translations they performed. They included Dave Hall (Italian, Spanish, and Arabic), Chris Andersson (Swedish), Vlada Tomava (Bulgarian), Danny Katz (Japanese), Lydia Gaston (Tagalog), Susana Dé (German), and Stella Wixson (Korean). John Pollard to author, July 6, 2021.

167 **recording of the anthem in translation**: Pangrác's version, catalogued Victor 72116-A, August 5, 1918, is available at https://www.loc.gov/item/jukebox-30054. Dickson's is on *Patrick: No One Is Higher,* Island Song Records IR-004, 1983. Duncum's is on *American National Songs in Navajo and English,* audiocassette tape, 1988. *La banniere etoilee, Louisianne '99: Congress Mondial Acadien,* Musique Acadienne MACD-0010, 1999. And the Cherokee choir's is featured on *Building One Fire* (Tahlequah, OK: Cherokee Nation, 2002), CNYC004.

167 **More recordings**: More recent online video recordings are in Chinese, French, German, Hawaiian, Latin, Spanish, Yiddish, and other languages. *Das Star-Spangled Banner* and *La bandera de las estrellas* appear on the recording *Poets and Patriots: A Tuneful History of "The Star-Spangled Banner,"* Star Spangled Music Foundation, 2014.

168 **"The day is breaking"**: Associated Press, "Oh, Say, Does that Starry Beauty Yet Wave?," *Sioux City Journal,* April 29, 2006, 15.

168 **The first known translation**: *Galveston Zeitung,* December 5, 1851, 4. Walter Kamphoefner at Texas A&M University identified this source and suggests that the translator was likely Hermann Seele. Kamphoefner to author, December 23, 2019. The translation may have first been used in 1850; see "1850's July Fourth," *New Braunfels Herald-Zeitung* (TX), July 4, 2000, 1; and Shea, "Oy Vey."

168 **annexation of Texas**: Randy Rupley (Seele's descendant and family historian), interview by Julia Triezenberg, January 27, 2016.

168 **Niclas Müller**: "The Star-Spangled Banner, The Song of the Patriot" (New York: Nic[las] Müller, c.1861). See also Philip Allison Shelley, "Niclas Müller, German-American Poet and Patriot," *Studies in Honor of John Albrecht Walz* (Lancaster, PA: Lancaster Press, 1941), 1–20; "An Exchange of Letters with Longfellow," *PMLA* 60, no. 2 (June 1945): 611–13; and "Niclas Mueller," in Clifford Neal Smith, *Early Nineteenth-Century German Settlers in Ohio,* German-American Genealogical Research Monograph no. 20 (Baltimore: Clearfield, 2004), 28–29.

169 **Dom Pedro II**: "Our Yankee Emperor," *Louisiana Democrat,* May 10, 1876, 3.

169 **Das Sternenbanner-Lied**: *Pennsylvania Staats Zeitung* (Harrisburg, PA), January 20, 1876, 1.

169 **Die Deutsche Correspondent**: See Leyh's obituary in *New York Times,* July 1, 1901, 2; *Der Deutsche Correspondent,* September 13, 1895, 4, and August 11, 1898, 4.

169 **"by the entire audience,":** *Drei Uebersetzungen aus dem Englischen von Edward Leyh* (Baltimore: Verlag von Cushing, 1894), 22–23; *Baltimore and the Saengerfest: Official Program and Souvenir* (Baltimore: Saengerfest Association, 1903), 32g–32h.

169 **Pennsylvania Dutch:** *First Annual Report of the Society for the History of the Germans in Maryland* (Baltimore, 1887); *Pennsylvania Staats Zeitung* (Harrisburg, PA), January 20, 1876, 1. The "Dutch" are American descendants of German-speaking immigrants.

169 *An Bhratach Gheal-Réaltach:* "An Bhratach Gheal-Réaltach," trans. Eugene O'Growney, in *An Gaodhal* (The Gael) 13, no. 1 (July 1898): 5. See also Philip O'Leary, *The Prose Literature of the Gaelic Revival, 1881–1921: Ideology and Innovation* (University Park: Pennsylvania State University Press, 1994).

169 **"To no one can":** Gerson Rosenzweig, מזמרת הארץ/*Mi-zimrat ha-arets: American National Songs in Hebrew* (New York: 1898), preface. The translation also appears in Joseph Magil, *Collection of Zionist and National Songs*, 8th ed. (Philadelphia: Joseph Magil, 1909), T53, as well as the 10th ed. (1914) of the same text.

169 *Den stjärnströdda fanan: Evangelisches Gesangbuch* (Harrisburg, PA, 1895), 140; *Die Kleine Psalme* (1900), no. d117; *Nya Psalmisten* (three verses) (Minneapolis: Skoog & DeLander, 1903), 622.

170 *L'étendard étoilé:* Alfred Delbruck, *L'étendard étoilé* (Paris: Éditions Ricordi, 1918); Clague and Kuster, *Star Spangled Songbook*, no. 68, pp. 235–38. A third World War I–era French translation was published as *Le drapeau étoilé* (Paris: F. Durdilly / Ch. Hayet, n.d).

171 *"nostro vessillo stellate":* Charles Montague Bakewell, *The Story of the Red Cross in Italy* (New York: Macmillan, 1920), 51, 211–12; *Il vessillo stellato: Inno nazionale americano*, trans. Frank G. Parrett (Milan: G. Ricordi, 1917). Note that the middle initial as printed on the sheet music publication is in error.

171 *"Campione della democrazia":* **La bandiera stellata** (New York: Italian Book Co., 1918), at Library of Congress, Music Division Star-Spangled Banner (foreign language) research file.

171 *Nasz Sztandar: Nasz Sztandar Gwiaździsty* (Chicago: Polish Publishing Co., 1918), at Library of Congress, Music Division, Star-Spangled Banner (foreign language) research file. The translation was reissued by K. T. Barwicki in 1929 in Chicago and Poznàn.

171 **"abandoned forthwith":** "Opposes Singing Patriotic Songs in German Language," *Indianapolis News*, May 3, 1917, 14.

171 **"thousands of copies":** " 'Star Spangled Banner' Translated into Spanish for the South American," *El Paso Herald*, April 28, 1919, 10.

172 **Americanization strategy:** The sheet music edition of *La bandera de las estrellas* is copyright stamped "February 3, 1919," at the Library of Congress (ML1630.3.S69 1814 [non-case]); Clague and Kuster, *Star Spangled Songbook*, no. 69, pp. 239–41. Another Spanish translation can be found in the *Enciclopedia universal ilustrada europeo-americana* (1924), 22:589.

172 **Lider fun der milkhome:** I. Kissin, *Lider fun der milkhome, antologye* (New York: Bibliyotek fun poezie un eseyen, 1943), 9, 126, 234; *Pedagogishe bulletin*, no. 20 (October 1943); "The Star Spangled Banner in Yiddish" (New York: Educational Alliance, 1943), https://tinyurl.com/sw56rdyw. Asen's name also appears as Aysen or as Avrom Aisen. See also Uriel Weinreich, "The Star-Spangled Banner in Yiddish," *Yidishe Shprakh* 4, no. 2 (March–April 1944): 33–44.

172 **El pendón estrellado:** Manuscript held in the Clotilde Arias Collection, Smithsonian Archive, Washington, D.C.; Clague and Kuster, *Star Spangled Songbook*, no. 71, pp. 245–48. See also Leah Binkovitz, "At American History, Meet the Composer of the Spanish Language National Anthem," *Smithsonian Magazine*, September 27, 2012.

172 **Portuguese translation.:** Clotilde Arias, letter dated October 26, 1945, in scrapbook, Clotilde Arias Collection, Smithsonian Archive. The translator of the Portuguese adaptation is identified as a Mr. Soares.

172 **"role of the Hispanic Community":** "We Are All Human Foundation Revives 1945 Spanish Language Version of the U.S. National Anthem," Associated Press Newswire, April 14, 2020.

173 **U.S. Information Service (USIS):** U.S. Information Agency, Record Group 306, Entry P46 Field Publications, Container no. 156, National Archives and Records Administration.

173 **Five thousand copies:** Ibid., Container no. 23, folder 1-28-58, ARC no.1126039.

173 **devotion to military service.:** J. D. Simkins, "A 'Warrior Tradition': Why Native Americans Continue Fighting for the Same Government that Tried to Wipe Them Out," *Military Times*, November 15, 2019.

174 **tuneful pedagogy:** Katherine Duncum, *American National Songs in Navajo and English* (Arizona: Walk in Beauty Press, 1988), 10–11; Bill Donovan, "'Oh Say, Can You See' in Navajo?," *Independent* (Gallup, NM), March 25, 2005.

175 **"Our language is a sacred element":** Joseph Barrios, "Star-Spangled Moment for Two O'odham," *O'o*, July 28, 2004, 5; "O'odham Hope Anthem Translates into Youth Interest," *Arizona Daily Star* (Tucson), August 7, 2004, B1, B5.

175 **Tribal Nations Conference:** "Native Star Spangled Banner Gets White House Recognition," *Dakota Digest*, South Dakota Public Broadcasting, December 1, 2011; Dan Olson, "Native Tongue: Teacher Brings Lakota Language to 'Star Spangled Banner,'" Minnesota Public Radio, July 1, 2014.

175 **"people who have gone without a voice":** Danielle Ferguson, "Man Sings National Anthem in Lakota," *Argus-Leader* (Sioux Falls, SD), 1, 4; "USD Student Sings National Anthem in Lakota Language," *Sioux City Journal*, March 30, 2018, 1, 7; "Steven Wilson Sings the National Anthem in Lakota" (video), March 24, 2018, YouTube, https://www.youtube.com/watch?v=jk1LqWlZYOg.

175 **"came to represent":** Margaret Noodin, email correspondence with research assistant Steven O'Neill, 2014.

176 **Hawaiian translation:** Wayne Herada, "Chronicling the Isle Spirit . . ." *Honolulu Advertiser*, November 1, 1983, 34.

176 **Samoan translation:** Fili Sagapolutele, "American Samoa Translates 'Star Spangled Banner,'" *Samoa News*, January 25, 2006.

176 **KJEF 1290 AM:** David Marcantel, interview by author, November 24, 2020; *Album souvenir congrés mondial acadien 99*, Musique acadienne Records, 1999, MACD-0010.

176 **"pure hope and happiness":** "Pinoy Pod," episode 1, *San Francisco Chronicle*, May 23, 2006; Boying Pimentel, "Before 'America the Beautiful,' 'The Star-Spangled Banner' in Tagalog," Inquirer.net, February 10, 2014.

Chapter 8: The Anthem and Black Lives

178 **"These protests":** "Harry Edwards on Social Rights Activism in Sports," *Amanpour & Co.*, PBS, February 22, 2019.

178 **protesters used:** Colin Campbell and Sean Welsh, "Baltimore to Keep, Clean Defaced Francis Scott Key Statue," *Baltimore Sun*, September 13, 2017, and accompanying video interviews of Baltimore residents by Algerina Perna.

179 **bronze likeness of the poet:** For more on Key monuments, see Sam Meyer, *Paradoxes of Fame: The Francis Scott Key Story* (Annapolis, MD: Eastwind, 1995), 63–81.

179 **full review:** "Mayor Breed Calls for Review of Public . . . ," *ABC7 San Francisco*, June 21, 2020.

179 **Colin Kaepernick:** Martenzie Johnson, "Let's Take the National Anthem Literally, and the Songwriter at His Word," Undefeated.com, August 30, 2016; Mark Clague, "'Star-Spangled Critics' Miss the Point," CNN, August 31, 2016. One of the earliest sources to interrogate racism in the song itself was Jason Johnson, "Star-Spangled Bigotry: The Hidden Racist History of the National Anthem," *Root*, July 4, 2016.

179 **Mario Woods:** "Shooting Stirs Anger," *San Francisco Examiner*, December 4, 2015, A1, A9.

180 **overall scene:** "This team formation for the National Anthem is not Jeff Fisher approved. #HardKnocks." Jennifer Lee Chan, beat writer for NinersNation.com and NFLfemale.com, tweet, August 26, 2016.

180 **"I am not going to stand":** Steve Wyche, "Colin Kaepernick Explains Why He Sat During National Anthem," NFL.com, August 27, 2016.

180 **"well executed, except":** *Weekly Anglo-African* (NY), December 15, 1860, 3. The letter to the editor is signed "viator," but no name is given. The writer appears to be Black, referring to "our people" later in the text. No gender is given, but the text of a previous article about women's fashion with the same signature suggests that the correspondent was a woman; *Weekly Anglo-African*, June 9, 1860, 1.

181 **Camp initiative:** "Know Your Rights," *Paper* 36, no. 1 (Fall 2019): 22–25. Kaepernick hosted the first camp in 2016. It featured a set of ten fundamental human rights: to be free, healthy, brilliant, safe, loved, courageous, alive, trusted, and educated, and to know your rights.

181 **"represent what it's supposed to":** "Pissed Off Fans Burn Kaepernick Jersey After Colin Kaepernick Sits During National Anthem," August 29, 2016, YouTube, https://www.youtube.com/watch?v=Wyl59bVS7WI.

182 **1959 Pan-American Games:** "Ex-Track Star Continues Jail Fast," *Chicago Defender,* February 3, 1960, 4.

182 **largely unnoted by the press:** Harry Edwards, *The Revolt of the Black Athlete* (Urbana: University of Illinois Press, 2017), xxi–xxii.

182 **income tax:** *Green Bay Press-Gazette,* January 28, 1960, 1; "Pacifist Gets Year in Jail," *Vancouver Sun,* February 19, 1960, 46; "4 Negroes Held in Maryland in Restaurant Service Incident," *Philadelphia Daily News,* September 7, 1961, 3.

182 **hiring discrimination:** *St. Louis Globe-Democrat,* July 23, 1963, 2.

182 **four hundred activists sang:** "Selma Prayer Vigil: 400 Spend Chilling Night on Streets," *Ottawa Journal,* March 11, 1965, 1.

184 **black dress socks:** Tommie Smith and David Steele, *Silent Gesture: The Autobiography of Tommie Smith* (Philadelphia: Temple University Press, 2007), 28, 139–40. Unless otherwise noted, all details and quotations are from this source. Black athletic socks were not manufactured in this era. All the Black U.S. athletes wore black dress socks, unless they ran without socks at all.

184 **black scarf:** Tommie Smith, interview in *The 100 Greatest Sporting Moments* (documentary), BBC4, January 9, 2002.

184 **black T-shirt:** John Carlos and Dave Zirin, *The John Carlos Story* (Chicago: Haymarket Books, 2011), 120; Carlos's account differs from that of Tommie Smith in certain details.

184 **"with a black accent.":** Kenny Moore, "A Courageous Stand," *Sports Illustrated,* August 5, 1991, 76.

184 **"We did it with pride,":** *Smith and Steele, Silent Gesture,* 139–40.

184 **"discourtesy displayed":** "U.S. Apologizes for 'Discourtesy,'" *Cincinnati Enquirer,* October 18, 1968, 41.

185 **"To use the Olympic Games":** Smith and Steele, *Silent Gesture,* 35, 38.

186 **were suspended:** "Olympic Suspension Consummates 'Black Power' Dispute," Associate Press, in *Moberly Monitor-Index,* October 18, 1968, 9.

186 **Olympic titles:** Berry Tramel, "Tommie Smith & John Carlos Did Not Give Up Their Olympic Medals," *Oklahoman,* February 9, 2016.

186 **"All we ask":** *Not Just a Game: Power, Politics and American Sports* (documentary), Media Education Foundation, 2010.

186 **"symbol of oppression":** Dan Gartland, "A History of Athletes Protesting the National Anthem," SI.com, August 29, 2016.

186 **"players, coaches":** *Official Rules of the National Basketball Association,* 2013–14, 2016–17, NBA.com. The rule has since been renumbered as Rule H, Paragraph 2.

186 **forfeited $37,707:** *Philadelphia Daily News,* March 14, 1996, 76, 78.

186 **robust debate:** "Fans Boo, Abdul-Rauf Prays," *Great Falls Tribune* (MT), March 16, 1996, 21; Mike Lopresti, "Where Do You Stand on Player's Standing?" *Desert*

Sun (Palm Springs, CA), March 14, 1996, 23; Charlie Vincent, "Denver's Abdul-Rauf Doesn't Stand for Anything," *Detroit Free Press*, March 16, 1996, 19; and Jim Trageser, "A Matter of Conscience or Contract?" *North County Times* (Oceanside, CA), March 31, 1996, 53.

186 **not enforced.:** Tadd Haislop, "What Is the NFL's National Anthem Protest Policy?," *Sporting News*, September 20, 2020.

187 **"Slave Market of America":** "Slave Market of America," American Anti-Slavery Society, 1836, Library of Congress no. LC-USZ62-40900. Here the engravings are reoriented for vertical presentation.

189 **"Our democracy's founding ideals":** Nikole Hannah-Jones, "The 1619 Project," *New York Times Magazine*, August 14, 2019.

190 **students' responses:** Tim Reid and Duane Saunders, Jr., with Dean DeWayne Wickham, *What So Proudly We Hail*, May 16, 2014, Vimeo, https://vimeo.com/166881889.

190 **"all those who may":** Admiral Alexander Cochrane, "A Proclamation" (Bermuda), April 2, 1814. Fortunately, the British would honor their promise. The Treaty of Ghent, which brought the War of 1812 to an end, required Britain to return all people it had rescued. Britain instead paid $1,204,609 to U.S. slave owners in compensation for some four thousand who were liberated. Those freed from the Chesapeake region were relocated to Canada's east coast, specifically New Brunswick and Nova Scotia, where they created the town of Africville. Others were relocated to Trinidad, where their descendants today are known as "Merikans." See Vogel, *Perilous Fight*, 397–98. For more on the Colonial Marines, see Alan Taylor, *The Internal Enemy: Slavery and War in Virginia, 1772–1832* (New York: W. W. Norton, 2013).

190 **Colonial marines fought:** John R. Elting, *Amateurs to Arms!: A Military History of the War of 1812* (New York: Da Capo Press, 1995), 207.

191 **burning of Washington.:** Altoff, *"Amongst My Best Men,"* 125.

191 **glories in the blood:** Jason Johnson, "Star-Spangled Bigotry: The Hidden Racist History of the National Anthem," *Root*, July 4, 2016.

191 **paid half the wages:** John Davis to Edward Johnson, August 24, 1814, and Major General Samuel Smith to Baltimore's Committee of Safety and Vigilance, October 3, 1814. These documents and a list of Black men paid to dig the city's defenses (Maryland State Archives) are all available in Glenn Johnston, "Racism, Rhetoric, and Research: Francis Scott Key and Our National Anthem" (blog), posted May 1, 2019, https://tinyurl.com/7rs6w28s.

191 **"all free men of color":** Altoff, *"Amongst My Best Men,"* 122.

192 **"refuge city":** Christopher Phillips, *Freedom's Port: The African American Community of Baltimore, 1791–1860* (Urbana: University of Illinois Press, 1997).

192 **55 percent were free:** U.S. Census data reported by the Maryland State Archives as part of its online "Legacy of Slavery in Maryland" site at Slavery.msa.maryland.gov.

192 **In his 1837 memoir:** Charles Ball, *Slavery in the United States: A Narrative of the Life and Adventures of Charles Ball* (New York: Taylor, 1837), chap. 24.

192 **Men like Ball:** Another Black American fighter was "William Williams," a twenty-two-year-old man with light skin whose real name was Frederick Hall. He escaped slavery and may have passed for white and was thus able to serve as a private in the 38th U.S. Infantry. He died from wounds suffered in Fort McHenry's bombardment. Other U.S. Black soldiers and seamen mentioned are Michael Buzzard, George Roberts, Caesar Wentworth, and Gabriel Roulson. See Scott S. Sheads, "A Black Soldier Defends Fort McHenry, 1814," *Military Collector and Historian* 41, no. 1 (Spring 1989): 20–21 and Christopher T. George, "Mirage of Freedom: African Americans in the War of 1812," *Maryland Historical Magazine* 91, no. 4 (Winter 1996): 426–50.

192 **"as a free black man":** Ball, *Slavery,* 467–68, 471–73, 480.

193 **freed the first:** Helen Hoban Rogers, ed., *Freedom and Slavery Documents in the District of Columbia* (Baltimore: Gateway/Otterbay Press, 2007), 2:211.

194 **considered a "slave":** Free Blacks were commonly among the American sailors impressed by the British. In the 1807 *Chesapeake* affair, three of the four U.S. sailors captured were Black, and 15 to 20 percent of U.S. merchant seamen were Black; Altoff, *"Amongst My Best Men,"* xv, 9.

194 **"Be true to ourselves":** *Essex Register* (Salem, MA), July 7, 1813, 1, emphasis in the original.

194 *Adams and Liberty* **(1798):** See "The Political Thunder of *Adams and Liberty*" in Chapter 3.

195 **"Is life so dear":** William Wirt, *Sketches of the Life and Character of Patrick Henry* (Philadelphia: James Webster, 1817), 123.

195 **"When Tyrant George":** "The Death of Warren," *Lancaster Intelligencer* (PA), May 15, 1813, 2. The lyric seems to have been sung to the tune *Constellation.* See the songster *Sailor's Rights* (New York: Samuel Burtis, 1815), 50–52.

195 **white Confederates:** Frank Pinkney, *The Flag of Secession,* in American Song Sheets, Slip Ballads and Poetical Broadsides Collection, Wolf C53, Library Company of Philadelphia; Clague and Kuster, *Star Spangled Songbook,* no. 57, pp. 197–99. Francis Hundley (Mrs. Elijah Dupay Hundley), *Farewell to the Star Spangled Banner* (Richmond, VA: Davies & Sons, 1862); Clague and Kuster, *Star Spangled Songbook,* no. 58, pp. 200–201.

196 **"illiberal, ignorant and vulgar":** Key to John Randolph, October 5, 1814, 2, in Lichtenwanger, "Richard S. Hill," 83.

196 **British soldier killed:** Skinner, "Incidents of the War," 343. Additional textual evidence for this very narrow reading is in part the lyric's shift from plural to singular. The opening couplets of the third verse refer to the British enemy in the plural using the word "their" to identify both "blood" and "footsteps." In contrast, the reference to "hireling and slave" is singular. This could be a poetic use of the singular to imply the plural, but it is no less conceivable that Key intended the singular here to be restrictive.

197 **"the only blot":** Key's 1834 epitaph for American Colonization Society agent Jehudi Ashmun's graveside monument; Dubovoy, *Lost World,* 409.

197 **"by the law of nature"**: Key's courtroom oration in U.S. Reports, *The Antelope*, Vol. 23 U.S. (10 Wheaton) 66 (1825), 73.

197 **racial "amalgamation"**: "Mr. Key on the Colonization Society," *African Repository* 12, no. 11 (November 1836): 339. By "amalgamation" Key refers to the creation of mixed-race children.

197 **"moral and political evil"**: "Address of Francis S. Key, Esq.," in American Colonization Society, *The Proceedings of a Public Meeting* (New York: Protestant Episcopal Press, 1829), 23.

197 **"inhuman"**: "Mr. Key's Speech," *African Repository* 18, no. 9 (July 1842): 203–6, 207.

198 **peaceful end to slavery.**: "Address of Francis S. Key, Esq.," 23.

198 **"no slave State"**: Key to Tappan, *African Repository* 15, no. 7 (April 1839): 116.

198 **1829 fundraising pitch:** "Address of Francis S. Key, Esq.," 24. The invention of the cotton gin would make slavery so profitable as to upend Key's equation.

198 **most passionate public efforts:** In 1833 Key was temporarily forced from the board of managers and his fundraising activities ebbed, but he remained a staunch supporter; Dubovoy, *Lost World*, 408–9.

198 **"madness of abolition."**: "Mr. Key on the Colonization Society," *African Repository* 12, no. 11 (November 1836): 343; and Key to Tappan, *African Repository* 15, no. 7 (April 1839): 116.

198 **freed suddenly:** Key to Tappan, *African Repository* 15, no. 7 (April 1839): 117.

198 **Benjamin Franklin:** David Waldstreicher, *Runaway America: Benjamin Franklin, Slavery, and the American Revolution* (Farrar, Straus & Giroux, 2005); and David Waldstreicher, "Benjamin Franklin, Slavery, and the Founders: On the Dangers of Reading Backwards," *Common-Place* 4 (July 2004): 4.

198 **John Jay:** Jake Sudderth, "Jay and Slavery," (2002) in *The Papers of John Jay*, online at Columbia.edu/cu/libraries/inside/dev/jay/JaySlavery.html.

199 **Roger B. Taney:** William G. Thomas III, *A Question of Freedom* (New Haven, CT: Yale University Press, 2020), 205; *United States v. Amistad* 40 U.S. 518 (1841).

199 **father's indebted estate:** Dubovoy, *Lost World*, 147–48.

199 **by inheritance:** Key's father died in 1821 and his mother in 1830; Leepson, *What So Proudly*, 97–98, 125.

199 **"sees, among these"**: "Mr. Key on the Colonization Society," *African Repository* 12, no. 11 (November 1836): 349–50.

199 **Terra Rubra:** Key sold and leased land rather than manage the property himself; see Delaplaine, *Life and Times*, 431, and Dubovoy, *Lost World*, 435.

199 **dozen people:** Dubovoy, *Lost World*, 345.

199 **five enslaved people:** Records archived at Ancestry.com, cited in Johnston (2019).

199 **benevolent slaveholder,:** Leepson, *What So Proudly*, 38, 131.

199 **"servants"**: According to one family story, Key's grandmother Ann Arnold Ross Key was blinded when she attempted to aid an enslaved woman trapped by fire; Leepson, *What So Proudly*, 8. See also Dubovoy, *Lost World*, 85.

199 **freed at least seven:** Dubovoy, *Lost World,* 419. Copies of Key's will are held at St. Johns College, the Maryland Historical Society, and the Library of Congress.

199 **came into effect:** Leepson, *What So Proudly,* 26, 190–91. Mary Tayloe Key died on May 18, 1859, according to her gravestone.

199 **"I am still a slaveholder":** Key to Tappan, *African Repository* 15, no. 7 (April 1839), 117. Key described for Tappan his own experiences in emancipating seven of his slaves. As of 1838, six of the seven were alive and "supporting themselves comfortably and creditably." He explained that freeing his enslaved laborers had been an intentional process. It began by providing vocational training during a transition period "of a few years in favorable circumstances," so that "when emancipated" they were "fitted for the duties and trials of their new condition."

200 **"the Black's lawyer":** Reuben Crandall to his father, cited in Jefferson Morley, *Snow-Storm in August: Washington City, Francis Scott Key, and the Forgotten Race Riot of 1835* (New York: Doubleday, 2012), 188; quoted in Marvis O. Welch, *Prudence Crandall: A Biography* (Manchester, CT: Jason, 1984), 117. See also *Cincinnati Daily Gazette,* July 11, 1870, cited in Leepson, *What So Proudly,* 26.

200 **white mob:** "Correspondence of the Boston Courier," *Liberator,* April 20, 1836, 3; Leepson, *What So Proudly,* 176; and Morley, *Snow-Storm in August,* 114.

200 **hired armed guards:** Leepson, *What So Proudly,* 107.

200 **freedom petitions:** Earlywashingtondc.org/people/per.000001. See also Jesse Torrey, Jr., *A Portraiture of Domestic Slavery, in the United States* (Philadelphia: John Bioren, 1817), 52. Key claimed that he had "only heaven's smile his fee" in such cases; "Mr. Key on the Colonization Society," *African Repository* 12, no. 11 (1836): 348.

200 **"Underground Railroad":** Thomas, *Question of Freedom,* 9.

200 **"a great many enemies":** Reuben Crandall to his father, January 29, 1836, quoted in Dubovoy, *Lost World,* 395, and Welch, *Prudence Crandall,* 117.

201 **settled out of court:** See *Priscilla Queen v. Francis Neale* (1810), https://earlywashingtondc.org/cases/oscys.caseid.0025; *William Jordan v. Lemuel Sawyer* (1823), https://earlywashingtondc.org/cases/oscys.caseid.0050; and *Thomas Butler et al. v. Gabriel Duvall* (1828), https://earlywashingtondc.org/doc/oscys.case.0212.001; and Leepson, *What So Proudly,* 107.

201 **If his primary goal:** Thomas, *Question of Freedom,* 68. In 1794 Philip Barton Key signed a retainer with Georgetown College leaders, in effect agreeing to a truce to stop representing the enslaved suing for their freedom.

201 **permitted slavery.:** Jon L. Wakelyn, "Jeremiah Townley Chase," *Birth of the Bill of Rights: Encyclopedia of the Antifederalists* (Westport, CT: Greenwood Press, 2004), 1:42–43. Key stated in his 1838 letter to Tappan that he "was born in Maryland, and have always lived in a slave State," yet "for forty years and upwards, I have felt the greatest desire to see Maryland become a free State." Subtracting forty-plus years from the letter's date, Key's first thoughts on the issue were during his time as an apprentice to Chase; Key to Tappan, *African Repository* 15, no. 7 (April 1839): 115.

201 **"considered every such cause"**: "Mr. Key on the Colonization Society," *African Repository* 12, no. 11 (1836): 348.

201 **represented slave owners**: In the 1825 settlement for *Jordan v. Sawyer*, Key and his opposing counsel granted power of attorney to Tench Ringgold, the U.S. marshal of the District of Columbia, to sell Jordan; Key might have agreed to the sale of his client in order to control a private sale (as opposed to an auction) and thus manage both to whom and where Jordan would be sold. See *National Intelligencer* of 1825: May 24, 3; May 27, 1; May 30, 1; May 31, 1; June 1, 4; and June 3, 1.

201 **"Negro Ben"**: *Ben v. Sabret Scott,* court documents, archived at http://earlywashingtondc.org/cases/oscys.caseid.0001. Some sources report incorrectly that Ben's case was lost, e.g., Leepson, *What So Proudly,* 26.

201 **"was the daughter of Henny"**: Dorothy S. Provine, ed., *District of Columbia Free Negro Registers, 1821–1861* (Bowie, MD: Heritage Books, 1996), 214. It is not clear how Key came to own Kitty, but later in his life he suggested that in some cases, the best strategy to free the enslaved was to raise funds charitably to purchase them, e.g., regarding the Antelope case and the 1837 case of Dorcas Allen; see "'Horrible Barbarity' Accounted For," *Liberator,* September 29, 1837, 4.

201 **"my Negro boy named James"**: Helen Hoban Rogers, ed., *Freedom and Slavery Documents in the District of Columbia* (Baltimore: Gateway/Otterbay Press, 2007), 2:211. Note that because Maryland law did not recognize Blacks as legal personalities, such documents were deeds of gift, not contracts. Once filed in court, they could not be revoked without challenge. See T. Stephen Whitman, *The Price of Freedom: Slavery and Manumission in Baltimore and Early National Maryland* (New York: Routledge, 1997), 98.

202 **Ann Williams**: Thomas, *Question of Freedom,* 195–96. For additional information on the regional importation of the enslaved to Washington for sale at higher prices, see Walter C. Clephane, "The Local Aspects of Slavery in the District of Columbia," *Records of the Columbia Historical Society of Washington, D.C.* 3 (1900): 224–56.

202 **John Parker and Rosanna Brown**: Petitions filed for Freedom, *Rosanna Brown and Mary Eliza Brown v. Bennett* (1815), https://earlywashingtondc.org/doc/oscys.case.0034.001; and *John Parker v. Offutt* (1815), https://earlywashingtondc.org/cases/oscys.caseid.0035.

202 **"volunteered his own services"**: Torrey, *Portraiture,* 46–53.

202 **debts on such fees**: "Slave Market of America," 1836. Key would later raise funds to facilitate the purchase of Dorcus Allen and two children, setting them free; see Alison T. Mann, "'Horrible Barbarity': The 1837 Murder Trial of Dorcas Allen, a Georgetown Slave," *Washington History* 27, no. 1 (Spring 2015): 3–14.

202 **successfully freed**: Torrey, *Portraiture,* 53.

202 **John Randolph**: *Annals of Congress, House of Representatives* (1816), 14h Cong., 1st Sess., 1115–17.

203 **"carrying off a number":** Select Committee on Illegal Traffic in Slaves in D.C., Deposition of Francis S. Key, April 22, 1816, Earlywashingtondc.org/doc/oscys. supp.0002.003.

204 **antislavery book:** Torrey, *Portraiture*, 44–45.

204 **Williams's case finally:** *Ann Williams et al. v. George Miller and George Miller, Jr.* (1832), at Earlywashingtondc.org/cases/oscys.caseid.0105.

204 **the Antelope:** John Thomas Noonan, *The Antelope* (Berkeley: University of California Press, 1977), 31.

204 **"by the law of nature":** U.S. Reports, *Antelope* 23 U.S. (10 Wheaton) 66 (1825), 72–73.

204 **ACS settled them:** Dubovoy, *Lost World*, 297–305.

204 **Amistad case:** Former president John Quincy Adams successfully defended the fifty-three African captives in the 1841 case. His diaries report that Key warned him emphatically about the *Antelope* precedent, fearing that the "best thing that could be done was to make up a purse and pay" for their freedom. At Key's suggestion, Adams studied the *Antelope* case thoroughly. His opening oration lasted nine hours and, as published, filled 132 pages. Forty of them concerned the *Antelope* appeal. Even after the *Amistad* victims were freed, Key used his influence in Congress to return those freed to Africa at government expense. They set sail for Sierra Leone on November 26, 1841. See John Quincy Adams, diary entry for January 14, 1841, in *The Diaries of John Quincy Adams: A Digital Collection* (Boston: Massachusetts Historical Society, 2004), 41:218, at www.masshist.org/jqadiaries; also Dubovoy, *Lost World*, 440–44.

205 **"aged about 19":** Newspaper reward notice, cited in Morley, *Snow-Storm in August*, 129.

205 **"I will have my freedom":** Ibid., 126.

206 **vilified Key:** "Trial in Washington for Circulating Incendiary Publications" and "Correspondence of the New-York American," *Liberator*, April 30, 1836, 3, and "Acquittal of Dr. Crandall," *Liberator*, May 7, 1836, 3.

206 **"was pledged to the people":** "Crandall's Trial," *Hampshire Gazette* (Northampton, MA), May 4, 1836, cited in Leepson, *What So Proudly*, 181.

206 **nineteen such cases:** Leepson, *What So Proudly*, 187.

206 **secure a conviction:** *United States v. Fenwick et al.*, April 7, 1836, case 15,086, in Cranch, *Reports . . .* (Boston: Little, Brown, 1852), 4:675–81, quote from 4:678. See also Earlywashingtondc.org/cases/oscys.caseid.0180.

207 **"a distinct and inferior race":** Delaplaine, *Life and Times*, 449, cited in Morley, *Snow-Storm in August*, 40.

207 **Benjamin Tappan:** Tappan's letter and Key's replies were printed as "Correspondence between Mr. Tappan and Mr. Key," *African Repository* (Washington, DC: American Colonization Society) 15, no. 7 (April 1839): 113–25, and reprinted in Elijah Paine, *A Collection of Facts in Regard to Liberia* (Woodstock, VT: Augustus Palmer, 1839), 17–36. Born in 1788 in West Newbury, Massachusetts, this Benjamin

Tappan is not the district judge and U.S. senator from Ohio born in 1773, who was
the brother of abolitionists Arthur and Lewis Tappan. See biographical note in
Alexander McKenzie, *An Address Delivered on Christmas Day, at the Funeral of
Rev. Benjamin Tappan, D.D.* (Augusta, ME: Kennebec Journal Office, 1864), 4.

207 **similar slippery statement:** "Mr. Key on the Colonization Society," *African Repository* 12, no. 11 (November 1836), 345–46.

208 **monthly journal:** "Correspondence between Mr. Tappan and Mr. Key," *African
Repository* 15, no. 10 (June 1839): 164, mentions reprints in the *New Hampshire Gazette*
(May 14) and the *Christian Mirror* (Portland, ME), (May 16); reprints are also found
in *Vermont Mercury*, May 31, 1839, 1, and *Newbern Spectator* (NC), May 31, 1839, 1.

208 **remain productively:** Key to Tappan, *African Repository* 15, no. 7 (April 1839), 117.

208 **"colored Sabbath school":** "Schools and Education of the Colored Population,"
American Journal of Education, ed. Henry Barnard 3 (1870): 193ff., esp. 298.

208 **never find equality:** "Address of Francis S. Key, Esq.," 25.

208 **"cannot be adequately protected":** "Mr. Key's Address," *African Repository* 4, no.
10 (December 1828): 300.

208 **"degraded situation":** "American Colonization Society," *Rights of All*, October 19, 1829,
47–48.

209 **calls to replace it:** Joshua Kosman, "Beyond Ramparts and Rockets: It's Time to
Rethink the National Anthem," *San Francisco Chronicle Datebook*, July 1, 2021.

210 *Monumental Reckoning*: Described at MonumentalReckoning.org.

210 **"serve as an example":** San Francisco Mayor's Office, press release, May 7, 2021.

Chapter 9: Performing Patriotism

212 **"I oftentimes think":** Jon Batiste, interview by Terry Gross, *Fresh Air*, March 11, 2021.

212 **"for giving us . . .":** Concert quotes are from "And Now for Our Next Song," *Just
Ask the Axis*, www.justasktheaxis.org.uk/anfons/1120.asp.

213 **"the English and American combined":** D. A. Pennebaker, dir., *Jimi Plays Monterey*, Criterion Collection, DVD-CC1624D, 2006, 37:00ff.

213 **documentary:** Michael Wadleigh, dir., *Woodstock* (Warner Bros., 1970).

213 **"most electrifying":** Al Aronowitz in the *New York Post*, quoted in Charles R. Cross,
Room Full of Mirrors: A Biography of Jimi Hendrix (New York: Hyperion, 2005), 271.

214 **musical career:** Ibid., 93–94.

215 **last known anthem:** For an account of Hendrix's many anthem renditions, see
Mark Clague, "'This Is America': Jimi Hendrix's Star Spangled Journey as Psychedelic Citizenship," *Journal of the Society for American Music* 8, no. 4 (November
2014): 435–78.

215 **Record Plant:** It was later released as part of the posthumous compilation album
Rainbow Bridge, in connection with the 1971 film of the same title (Reprise no.
2040, 1971).

215 **"a song that we was all brainwashed":** "The L.A. Forum Concert" (disk 4), in *Life-lines: The Jimi Hendrix Story* (Reprise REP 9-26435-2, 1990).

216 **brooding tone poems:** *The Jimi Hendrix Experience: 3 Nights at Winterland* (Rec-lamation RECD1013, 2006).

216 **Boys Choir of Harlem:** *The Boys Choir of Harlem Sings America* (3G Entertain-ment, 2001); St. Louis Symphony conducted by Leonard Slatkin, *The American Album* (RCA Victor 60778, 1991); Charlie Daniels Band, *Redneck Fiddlin' Man* (Audium AUD-CD-8159, 2002); Mormon Tabernacle Choir, *God Bless Amer-ica: 23 Patriotic Favorites* (Sony Masterworks, MDK 48295, 1973, reissued 1992); Beyoncé, *Star Spangled Banner* (Sony Music, CSK 58360, promotional single, 2004); Link Davis, Jr., *The Star Spangled Cajun* (Home Cooking Records, COL-CD-5524, 1994); Carla Bley, *Looking for America* (Watt Works / ECM Records, 2003); Bela Fleck and the Flecktones, *Flight of the Cosmic Hippo* (Warner Bros. 9 26562-2, 1991); and *Star Spangled Banner: Power House Edition* (CL01, 2001).

217 **redundant and obsolete:** General Order no. 170, October 15, 1905, para. 383, in *General Orders and Circulars, War Department, 1905* (Washington, DC: Govern-ment Printing Office, 1906).

217 **"universal recognition":** "Adopt Code for Honoring U.S. Flag," *Lancaster New Era* (PA), January 4, 1919, 4; "National Flag Code Conference Adopts Rules for Display of Old Glory," *Olsburg Optic* (KS), August 1, 1923, 3.

217 **flag code:** "Pledge to the Flag," *Altoona Tribune* (PA), October 21, 1942, 4.

218 **"should face the flag":** US Code 2015, Title 36, Subtitle 1, pt. A, chap. 3, sec. 301(b) "National Anthem," adopted June 22, 1942, rev. Dec. 22, 1942, July 7, 1976, and again in 2008.

219 **Feliciano offered:** "Soul Anthem Disgrace," *Dayton Daily News* (OH), October 8, 1968, 5.

220 **"I had heard from people":** Barbara Stanton, "Storm Rages over Series Anthem," *Detroit Free Press*, October 8, 1968, A1–2.

220 **"They were worried about Marvin":** David Davis, "The Day Jose Changed the Anthem Forever," *Detroit Free Press*, October 14, 2003, 28 and 31.

220 **no one objected:** Gaye's more personal, sultry rendition for the NBA All-Star Game was still fifteen years in the future. One wonders if this more soulful 1983 version, using a transformed melody, owes a debt of inspiration to Feliciano's example or, at least, to the criticism of Gaye by comparison.

220 **front page of the *Detroit Free Press*:** Stanton, "Storm Rages."

220 **angry ex-servicemen:** Bob Lardine, "Pop Goes the Anthem," *Daily News* (NY), October 14, 1968, 40.

220 **"a couple thousand letters":** David Davis, "The Day Jose Changed the Anthem Forever," *Detroit Free Press*, October 14, 2003, 1D.

221 **"I feel a fellow has a right":** Stanton, "Storm Rages," A2.

221 **more stunned than angry**: "The Anthem Is Rendered Soul Style," Associated Press, October 7, 1968. The video of Franklin's performance was available on You-Tube at youtube.com/watch?v=A8jwsBg4H5c.

221 **"I was afraid"**: Stanton, "Storm Rages," A2.

221 **"I came to New York"**: Lardine, "Pop Goes the Anthem."

221 **He soon began**: Ritchie Yorke, "Jose Recalls that Banner Day," *Courier-News* (Bridgewater, NJ), January 30, 1969, 15; and Nancy Ball, "Our Anthem: Should It Be Replaced?," Newsweek Feature Service, in *Dayton Daily News*, March 10, 1969, 20.

221 **"a standard rendition"**: "Why All the Furor?" *Detroit Free Press*, October 9, 1968, 8.

221 **"I met José"**: Ray Fitzgerald, "Rock Anthem: Some Cards Liked It," *Boston Globe*, October 9, 1968, 59.

222 **Younger listeners flooded**: Lardine, "Pop Goes the Anthem," 40; Yorke, "Jose Recalls."

222 **commercial 45**: "Spotlight Singles," *Billboard Magazine*, October 26, 1968, 93.

222 **his native land**: José Feliciano, "The Star-Spangled Banner," RCA Victor 47-9665, released October 1968.

222 **"The song had practically"**: Ball, "Our Anthem," 18.

222 **did not sing another pregame anthem**: "Feliciano Tunes Out Controversy," *Chicago Tribune*, October 13, 2003, 8.

223 **Feliciano appeared again**: Bill Shaikin, "Freese, Beltran Power Cardinals Past Giants," *Baltimore Sun*, October 15, 2012, D8.

223 **"Congo version"**: H. K. Williams, Jr., "Three Choices in November," *San Antonio Express*, September 3, 1968, 19.

223 **"unusual" or "jazzed up"**: Ferris, *Star-Spangled Banner*, 213.

223 **Some newspaper accounts**: Percy Shain, "Aretha's Anthem Stirs Small Storm," *Boston Globe*, August 28, 1968, 20.

225 **"The main difficulty"**: Ibid.

225 **"All I know is I sing"**: Lardine, "Pop Goes the Anthem."

226 **"television mega-star"**: Chuck Darrow, "Boardwalk Beat," *Asbury Park Press* (NJ), May 20, 1990, sec. E, p. 7.

226 **People's Choice Awards**: "People in the News," *Hartford Courant* (CT), March 13, 1990, 2.

226 **"the hopeless underclass"**: Barbara Ehrenreich, "The Undainty Feminism of Roseanne Barr," *New Republic* 202, no. 14 (April 2, 1990): 28–31.

228 **"Get us out of here!"**: Roseanne Barr, *My Lives* (New York: Ballantine Books, 1994), 203; departure confirmed by *Times-Advocate* (Escondido, CA), July 26, 1990, A2.

228 **called for a boycott**: "Boycott Roseanne," *North County Times* (Oceanside, CA), August 1, 1990; Lisa Grace Lednicer, "Fed-up Fax Man Seeks Bar on Barr," *Tampa Bay Times*, August 2, 1990, 123.

228 **"I think I did great"**: "Barr Booed after Singing Anthem," *Vincennes Sun-Commercial* (IN), July 26, 1990, 3.

228 **"roll over and die"**: Barr, *My Lives*, 204.

228 **letters poured in**: "Barr Strikes Out Singing the Anthem," *Los Angeles Times*, August 4, 1990, 38; "Letters to the Editor," *South Florida Sun Sentinel*, August 9, 1990, 22; Linda Washburn and Joan Verdon, "Fat Lady Sings, to Fans Dismay," *Record* (Hackensack, NJ), July 27, 1990, 1; and Mary Corey, "Barr Issues an Apology," *Baltimore Sun*, July 27, 1990, 1.

228 **"This woman, who"**: "Roseanne: Comedian Does Job on Anthem," *Times-Advocate* (Escondido, CA), July 26, 1990, A1, A2, A7.

229 **"in public for about"**: Geoff Edgers, "Roseanne on the Day She Shrieked 'The Star-Spangled Banner,' Grabbed her Crotch and Earned a Rebuke from President Bush," *Washington Post*, July 23, 2015.

229 **recorded evidence**: Barr, *My Lives*, 201–202. Barr's performance is widely available on YouTube.

229 **"I proved to myself"**: "Star Spangled Banner," *Roseanne's Nuts*, Season 1, episode 3, Lifetime Network, aired July 20, 2011; dialogue beginning at 20:10.

231 **the legend offers**: Unless otherwise noted, quotations and factual details regarding Stravinsky's anthem are taken from H. Colin Slim, "Stravinsky's Four Star-Spangled Banners and His 1941 Christmas Card," *Musical Quarterly* 89, nos. 2–3 (Summer–Fall, 2006): 321–447.

231 **"STRAVINSKY REVISES"**: "Stravinsky Revises National Anthem," *Daily Boston Globe*, January 13, 1944, 12.

231 **"At the start, the audience"**: Associated Press story by Tom Chase, see "'Star Spangled Banner' of Stravinsky Startling," *Des Moines Register*, January 15, 1944, 10.

231 **"Whoever plays"**: As of 2022, this law remains on the Massachussets books in General Laws, Part IV: Crimes, Punishments, and Proceedings in Criminal Cases, Title I, Ch. 264, §9.

232 **"Mr. Stravinsky"**: "State Law Prohibits Playing New Version Star Spangled Banner," *Daily Boston Globe*, January 16, 1944, C1, C19.

232 **he was not arrested**: Richard Drake Saunders, "Reviewer Hits Boston Arrest of Stravinsky," *Hollywood Citizen-News*, March 11, 1944, 12.

232 **"Searching about for a vehicle"**: The manuscript was donated to the Library of Congress in 1942 (LOC ML 96.S44 Case, Vault). See Slim, "Stravinsky's . . . Banners," 334–35.

233 **"noble American national chorale"**: The Stravinsky version fails musically at a faster tempo, as the alternation of the dotted motto and even quarters creates an unpalatable "sing-song" effect, making its symmetry tedious.

234 **A recording of Stravinsky**: *Stravinsky Conducts Stravinsky: Choral Music*, Columbia Masterworks, M 31124, 1972.

235 **"my version of the national anthem"**: René Marie, "A Statement from Rene Marie—July 2008," Renemarie.com/q-and-a.

235 **"the American Negro"**: James Weldon Johnson, *Along This Way: The Autobiography of James Weldon Johnson* (New York: Viking Press, 1933), 154–55. See also

Shana Redmond, *Anthem: Social Movements and the Sound of Solidarity in the African Diaspora* (New York University Press, 2014), 63–98.

235 **Marie's performance:** For a full explication of the performance, see Shana Redmond, "Indivisible: The Nation and Its Anthem in Black Musical Performance," *Black Music Research Journal* 35, no. 1 (Spring 2015): 97–118.

235 **"distress that may":** Marie, "A Statement from Rene Marie—July 2008."

236 **"It seemed apparent to me":** Ibid.

236 **"Let us march on":** René Marie, *Voice of My Beautiful Country*, Motéma Music, 2011, Audio CD MTM-59.

237 **developing into a setting:** *Anthem (Parts 1 & 2): A Community MusicWorks Story*, posted to YouTube on June 16, 2009, along with a complete recording of the work titled *Anthem in DC*, posted December 24, 2010.

237 **"personally conflicted":** "Jessie Montgomery—Banner," Facebook video posted by Cincinnati Symphony Orchestra, September 23, 2020.

237 **Quotations include:** Email from Jessie Montgomery to author, December 2020.

237 **"The Star Spangled Banner is":** Jessie Montgomery, artist statements on the websites of the Oakland Symphony and the Saint Paul Chamber Orchestra, 2017.

238 **"It's a tonal allegory":** "Jon Batiste—National Anthem (NBA Kick Off Performance)," July 30, 2020, YouTube. The quotes are from Batiste interview by Terry Gross, *Fresh Air*, March 11, 2021.

238 **Released in 2013:** Jon Batiste and Stay Human, *Social Music*, Razor & Tie Records, 7930183498-2, 2013.

239 **"those who have been":** "'Deconstructed Anthems' by Ekene Ijeoma —Betty Carter's Jazz Ahead Alumni Trio," April 18, 2018, YouTube; Ekene Ijeoma, "Deconstructed Anthems at Day for Night Festival," January 29, 2019, Vimeo; interviews by author, June and August 2021.

240 **Hewitt knew:** *The Star Spangled Banner* (New York: J. Hewitt Musical Repository, n.d.). See also Muller, *Star Spangled Banner*, 35; Filby and Howard, *Star-Spangled Books*, 133; and Clague and Kuster, *Star Spangled Songbook*, no. 31, pp. 110–12. Hewitt was a performing member of the Columbian Anacreontic Society and thus knew first-hand about the origins of *The Anacreontic Song*.

240 **"singable" variations:** *Our Star Spangled Banner* (John Henry Blake, 1910); *The Star-Spangled Banner: New Music Version* (Cleveland: Francis P. Kilfoyle, 1918), both at Library of Congress (LOC ML1630.3.S69 1814 [non-case]). See also "Singable Star Spangled Banner Wins Approval," *Tular Advance-Register* (CA), April 15, 1939, 5; and "Man Pushes Singable Star Spangled Banner," *Cedar Rapids Gazette* (IA), July 3, 1977, 23.

240 **Lou Reed:** Lou Reed, *Between Thought and Expression*, RCA PD90621-3, 1992.

240 **"a feedback strewn desecration":** Anni Banani, "Red House Painters: Anni Banani Meets Mr. Right," monsterbit.com/stammer/anuary/story2.htm, and http://www.carbonuk.com/turntable12.html, both accessed in 2003.

240 **Edmund Holbrook:** *Boston Globe*, July 4, 1897, 25. For other texts, see *Detroit News*, May 1, 1898, 19, and *New Verse Edition: The Star-Spangled Banner* (Phila-

delphia: George M. Vickers, 1907), in Library of Congress, no. ML1630.3.S69 1814 (non-case).

240 **sought to interweave:** *The Star-Spangled Banner: Words by Abraham Lincoln, Francis Scott Key, John Mokrejs* (New York: Odowan, 1927), in Library of Congress (LOC ML1630.3.S69 1814 [non-case]).

Postlude: Composing Nation

242 **"if a nation's songs":** "At a Political Meeting," in *Poems of the Late Francis Scott Key, Esq.*, ed. Rev. Henry V. D. Johns (New York: Robert Carter & Brothers, 1857), 195–203, punctuation adjusted, quoted here as realized by Delaplaine, *Life and Times*, 380–81.

243 **"the" or "our":** *Weekly Raleigh Register* (NC), July 31, 1837, 2; *Pittsburgh Daily Post*, May 10, 1845, 2; *Times-Picayune* (LA), July 20, 1847, 2.

243 **"it is regarded":** *Lebanon Daily News* (PA), May 23, 1900, 2.

244 **Words and Music:** Kitty Cheatham, *Words and Music of The Star-Spangled Banner Oppose the Spirit of Democracy which the Declaration of Independence Embodies* (New York: Kitty Cheatham, 1918). Its opening essay appeared on March 2, 1918, in *The New York Times* (excerpts) and in *Musical America* (entire) on the same date.

245 **1893 poem:** Katharine Lee Bates, "America," *Congregationalist* (Boston), July 4, 1895, 17; then as "O Beautiful, My Country" *Congregationalist*, 1905; then as *America the Beautiful* in 1908.

245 **Unknown until 1938:** For more, see Sheryl Kaskowitz, *God Bless America: The Surprising History of an Iconic Song* (New York: Oxford University Press, 2013).

246 **appropriate today:** In 1955 Virginia representative Joel T. Broyhill introduced a bill to create an official version of the anthem (text and music). Controversy ensued, and ultimately Broyhill was accused of attempting to "change" the anthem, and the resolution was rejected. See John C. Schmidt, "Our Anthem—What Is It?" *Baltimore Sun*, September 9, 1962, 45.

246 **shock and mourning:** Kaskowitz, *God Bless America*, 101.

246 **"All we say to America":** Martin Luther King, Jr., "I've Been to the Mountaintop" (speech), Mason Temple, Memphis, TN, April 3, 1968.

247 **refused to take the field:** Nancy Armour and Tom Schad, "Sports Team Owners Listen to Players, but Support Republicans," *USA Today*, October 2, 2020.

247 **"If we could just":** @RealJayWilliams, tweet, September 10, 2020, embedded in Joe Schad, "Miami Dolphins Criticize NFL, Plan to Stay in Locker Room During National Anthems," *USA Today*, September 10, 2020.

247 **social and political backdrop:** *The Star-Spangled Banner* imagines the community experience of unity, or "unisonance" in Benedict Anderson's parlance, against the backdrop of the individual's perceptions of the social world—that is, the "habitus" of Aristotle and Pierre Bourdieu.

Illustration Credits

85   **Band of the battleship *Oregon*, 1898**
     Harper's Magazine, author's collection.

95   *Das Star-Spangled Banner*, **song sheet, c. 1862–63**
     Library of Congress, Rare Book and Special Collections, American Song Sheets,
     series 1, vol. 8.

99   **Civil War recruiting poster, 1863**
     Courtesy William L. Clements Library, University of Michigan.

111 *The Star-Spangled Banner*, **March 1917**
     Author's collection.

112 *The Star-Spangled Banner*, **service version, later 1917**
     Author's collection.

120 *Boston Globe* **illustration, 1903**
     Author's collection.

122 **Patriotic pregame drill, 1917**
     Bettmann Archive via Getty Images.

123 **Woodrow Wilson first pitch, 1916**
     Library of Congress, no. LC-USZ62-9981.

132 **Harry Truman, Elmer Layden, and George Marshall, 1945**
     Associated Press Images.

135 **Whitney Houston singing at Super Bowl XXV, 1991**
     Getty Images / Michael Zagaris.

148 **U.S. Navy flogging, illustration, 1879**
     Edward Shippen, *Thirty Years at Sea: The Story of a Sailor's Life*. Philadelphia: J. B.
     Lippincott & Co., 1879.

153 **Enslaved man, *American Anti-Slavery Almanac*, back cover, 1843**
     Clifton Waller Barrett Library of American Literature, Albert and Shirley Small
     Special Collections Library, University of Virginia.

163 *Nuestro Himno* **recording artists at Ellis Island, 2006**
     Associated Press Photo / Jason DeCrow.

170 **World War I–era sheet music cover collage**
     Library of Congress, no. ML1630.3.S69 1814 (non-case) (left), and author's collection
     (right).

174 **Anthem performance at the Democratic National Convention, 2004**
     Associated Press Photo / Ron Edmonds.

183 **Men's 200-meter Mexico City Olympics medal ceremony, 1968**
     Associated Press Photo.

185 **Mahmoud Abdul-Rauf Praying before an NBA game, 1996**
     Associated Press Photo / Michael Spencer Green.

188 *Slave Market of America*, **broadside illustrations, 1836**
     Library of Congress, Rare Book and Special Collections Division, no.
     LC-USZ62–40900.

211 **Francis Scott Key Memorial, Golden Gate Park, San Francisco, 2021**
Author photo, used with permission of sculptor Dana King / *Monumental Reckoning.*

219 **José Feliciano singing at World Series, 1968**
Detroit Free Press via ZUMA Wire.

224 **Aretha Franklin singing at Democratic National Convention, 1968**
Bettmann Archive via Getty Images.

226 **Roseanne Barr singing at San Diego Padres game, 1990**
John W. McDonough / *Sports Illustrated* via Getty Images.

230 **Igor Stravinsky's U.S. visa photo, 1940**
Courtesy Paul Sacher Foundation, Basel, Igor Stravinsky Collection.

Index

Page numbers in *italics* refer to illustrations.

O SAY CAN
YOU HEAR?

Mark Clague

O SAY CAN YOU HEAR?

Mark Clague

DISCUSSION QUESTIONS

O Say Can You Hear? by Mark Clague is a fantastic selection for book clubs. Conversation flows easily as anyone living in the United States has a personal relationship to the song. These personal experiences resonate with the book and can inspire an engaging conversation. You'll undoubtedly have your own ideas for questions, but here are a few from the author to get you started.

INTRODUCTORY QUESTIONS

1. How do you feel personally about *The Star-Spangled Banner?*

2. What does *The Star-Spangled Banner* mean to you?

3. What did you learn from *O Say Can You Hear?* Did something surprise you or contradict something you had previously thought to be true? Did it impact the meaning of the song for you?

MORE DISCUSSION QUESTIONS

1. Which chapter was the most interesting for you and why?

2. Compare the original 1814 arrangement of the song to what you are used to hearing today. How is it different? How does the emotional impact of the song change for you? *See note about discussing music on the last page of this reading group guide.

3. Do you agree or disagree with the Mark Clague's argument that protest is an important part of Francis Scott Key's song? Is it wrong to use the anthem ritual as a platform for protest? Why?

4. What is your sense of Francis Scott Key as a person? Does his biography matter to the meaning of the song today?

5. Given that the lyric was written during a time when slavery was legal in the United States, does the use of *The Star-Spangled Banner* as a rallying cry in the Civil War redeem the song or change its meaning?

6. Do you think that the *The Star-Spangled Banner* should be performed at every sporting event?

7. For you, is the nation's anthem performed today too frequently, too infrequently, or just the right amount?

WRAP-UP QUESTIONS

1. What does patriotism mean to you? Does patriotism strengthen or weaken the nation?

2. Is *The Star-Spangled Banner* an effective national anthem for the United States?

3. What other songs might be considered as the U.S. national anthem? Why might they be better?

4. What do you think should be done, if anything, about the nation's anthem going forward?

LISTENING

Listening to music can also be a great way to jumpstart your conversation. Consider playing some of the famous anthem renditions discussed in the book and inviting everyone to share an observation or two. Be sure you have a playback system that is loud enough for the group to hear clearly.

Search on YouTube or Spotify for recordings of notable renditions by José Feliciano, Jimi Hendrix, Roseanne Barr, Whitney Houston, Jon Batiste, and the U.S. Army Chorus. Mark Clague has created a playlist of some of his favorites on YouTube at https://www.youtube.com/playlist?list=PLVy2jd QD7GRw8dr9NkoFaF7ny8McBuyHO.

SUGGESTIONS FOR DISCUSSING MUSIC

People can sometimes feel intimidated when discussing music because they are afraid to get things wrong or to not sound sophisticated enough. Encourage your group to share obvious and simple commentaries: Is it loud or soft, fast or slow, happy or sad? What words come to mind as you hear the performance? What in the sound of the music generates that idea? If the discussion leader can affirm these comments, it can help people feel much more willing to share their observations. Even if you don't feel the same way, saying "that's interesting" or "that's a helpful observation" can encourage others to share their thoughts. There is no right or wrong answer, especially when it comes to art and music. There is a unique, almost chemical, reaction between sound and listener that produces feelings. Following are a few questions that can help start the conversation.

1. How did the performance make you feel?

2. Did the performer enhance the meaning of the song in some way? How?

3. Did this artist inspire you to feel more connected to the song and its patriotic message? Did it instead take away from that message? Why or why not?

4. Are you familiar with this performer's other music? Does their anthem rendition express their overall style or musical approach? What makes you think so?

SELECTED NORTON BOOKS WITH
READING GROUP GUIDES AVAILABLE

For a complete list of Norton's works with reading group guides, please go to wwnorton.com/reading-guides.

Diana Abu-Jaber	*Life Without a Recipe*
Diane Ackerman	*The Zookeeper's Wife*
Michelle Adelman	*Piece of Mind*
Molly Antopol	*The UnAmericans*
Bonnie Jo Campbell	*Mothers, Tell Your Daughters*
Jared Diamond	*Guns, Germs, and Steel*
Andre Dubus III	*Townie*
Donna M. Lucey	*Sargent's Women**
Anne Enright	*The Green Road*
Amanda Filipacchi	*The Unfortunate Importance of Beauty*
Maureen Gibbon	*Paris Red*
Stephen Greenblatt	*The Swerve**
Lawrence Hill	*The Illegal*
Ann Hood	*The Book That Matters Most*
Dara Horn	*A Guide for the Perplexed*
Blair Hurley	*The Devoted**
Nicole Krauss	*The History of Love*
Maaza Mengiste	*Beneath the Lion's Gaze*
Claire Messud	*The Burning Girl*
Daniyal Mueenuddin	*In Other Rooms, Other Wonders*
Neel Mukherjee	*The Lives of Others; A State of Freedom**
Richard Powers	*Orfeo*
Kirstin Valdez Quade	*Night at the Fiestas*
Jean Rhys	*Wide Sargasso Sea*
Mary Roach	*Packing for Mars*
Akhil Sharma	*Family Life*
Manil Suri	*The City of Devi*
Madeleine Thien	*Do Not Say We Have Nothing*
Vu Tran	*Dragonfish*
Rose Tremain	*The Gustav Sonata*
Brad Watson	*Miss Jane*
Constance Fenimore Woolson	*Miss Grief and Other Stories**